Ukraine and the Empire of Capital

Ukraine and the Empire of Capital

From Marketisation to Armed Conflict

Yuliya Yurchenko

First published 2018 by Pluto Press
345 Archway Road, London N6 5AA

www.plutobooks.com

British Library Cataloguing in Publication Data
A catalogue record for this book is available from the British Library

ISBN   978 0 7453 3738 8   Hardback
ISBN   978 0 7453 3737 1   Paperback
ISBN   978 1 7868 0181 4   PDF eBook
ISBN   978 1 7868 0183 8   Kindle eBook
ISBN   978 1 7868 0182 1   EPUB eBook

Typeset by Stanford DTP Services, Northampton, England

Printed and bound by CPI Group (UK) Ltd, Croydon, CR0 4YY

To the victims of capital

Contents

Figures and Tables

FIGURES

TABLES

Abbreviations

ACC	American Chamber of Commerce
CIS	Commonwealth of Independent States
CPSU	Communist Party of the Soviet Union
CSTO	Collective Security Treaty Organization
CUSUR	Centre for US–Ukraine Relations
DCFTA	Deep and Comprehensive Free Trade Areas
EBA	European Business Association
EBRD	European Bank for Reconstruction and Development
ERT	European Round Table of Industrialists
ETG	Eural Trans Gas
FDI	Foreign direct investment
FIGs	Financial industrial groups
ICC	International Chamber of Commerce
IFIs	international financial institutions
IMF	International Monetary Fund
ISD	Industrial Union of Donbass (Індустріальний союз Донбасу)
JSCs	Joint Stock Companies
KIIS	Kyiv International Institute of Sociology
Maidan	Maidan Nezalezhnosti (Independence Square), the main square of Kiev
maidan	social movements associated with the Orange Revolution and the Bloody winter
NDP	(Narodno-Democratychna Party) People's Democratic Party
NRU	(Narodnyy Rukh Ukrayiny) People's Movement of Ukraine
PDAs	Priority Development Areas
PIIGS	Portugal, Italy, Ireland, Greece and Spain
SALs	Structural adjustment loans
SAPs	Structural adjustment programmes
SCM	System Capital Management
SDPU(U)	Social-Democratic Party (United)
SEZs	Special Economic Zones
SOEs	State-owned enterprises

SSR	Soviet Socialist Republic
UAH	Ukrainian Hryvnia – the currency of Ukraine
URPP	Ukrainian Union of Industrialist and Entrepreneurs
USUBC	US–Ukraine Business Council
WB	World Bank
WIDER	The World Institute for Development Economic Research
WTO	World Trade Organization
YeESU	United Energy Systems of Ukraine (Yedyni Energetychni Systemy Ukrayiny)
YES	Yalta European Strategy

Acknowledgements

All those who helped or hindered in getting this book done over the years – you know who you are and what role you played in the process. If I have not thanked you yet in person, it is only because there has not yet been an opportunity to do so. Thank you to those who helped for your support, I am eternally grateful and humbled for having you in my life and for knowing you exist. And those who hindered, thank you too; without you I would not know the stretch of the limits of my own possible.

I want to thank the production team at Pluto and particularly my editor, David Shulman, for his continuous support and encouragement to tell the story I wanted to tell yet which was at first hidden behind the formalised structures I thought I had to follow yet always disliked. I am thankful to the reviewers of the book proposal and the text sample whose comments gave me ideas about improving the narrative. All the shortcomings of the final result are solely mine.

Preface

In 2004 I came to Sussex, UK, as an aspiring interpreter, willing to work in the sphere of politics to assist understanding between the leaders of the world, obviously full of naiveté and boundless ambition. It seemed to me then that I could use my love of languages as contribution to address the unfairness and injustice in the world, and there was no shortage of those. I was politically apathetic, defeated, in a state of self-imposed intellectual coma that I felt was necessary to survive the lawlessness and civic impotence I'd experienced growing up in Kuchma's Ukraine. I saw miners on hunger strike in tents in central Kyiv being fenced off so a Christmas tree could be put up and their discomforting sight would not bring down the spirit of the festive crowd. I heard a university lecturer reply to my complaining about this with her approval of the city administration's actions. My uni friends and I were taken out of classes on a few occasions to take part in pro-president demonstrations by orders 'from above', our lecturers being asked to oversee us go. We didn't go, we 'got lost' en route to the demos, then we got into trouble with our department and that was also later reflected in our grades. All state institutions were subject to such pressure and demands to show 'loyalty' or else . . .

In 2004, the year of the Orange Revolution, I came to Sussex where an introduction to the inspiring faculty and IR scholarship motivated me to dig deeper, seek more, demand empirics. The Orange Revolution that started and pathetically failed soon after left me full of frustrations but also hope that things can change; people can rise, en masse. I had thoughts I needed to express in my own words, not in words translated by me; I needed to find a language, a framework that would help explain what precisely is going so wrong. Political economy gave me that language and the necessary analytical tools.

Some ten years after the start of that journey to piece together the jigsaw of Ukraine's metamorphosis, the book has finally been shaped. The deep recession in which I envisaged the country would stagnate now also is tarnished by a hybrid civil armed conflict with a foreign element. Few expected this to happen in twenty-first-century Europe; mainly because too many forgot that the most resilient empire in modern history has not fallen with the fading of the European empires but has grown stronger – the empire of (transnationalising) capital. And where empires spread, blood is shed. Blood has been shed continuously across the globe in the name of struggles for further accumulation of capital. Until only recently it soaked the fringes, sprinkled the frontiers of empire; hidden away from the eyes of the gentrified Europeans in the piazzas lit by now solar-powered, sustainable lights. Frontiers however have a historically documented quality – they shift and shrink as empires expand. And as they do, they absorb the remaining commons and first Thomas More's sheep and by now private capital/TNCs/legal persons eat physical persons. By privatising state- and municipality-owned assets, by privatising public services, by polluting the global environmental commons, by making the taxpayer accountable for corporate losses via austerity and international settlement mechanisms . . . the masters enclose. The dispossessed are left in that process to scrabble for crumbs and to hate those who scrabble next to them because the machine of capital that pauperised them is both too big to comprehend and to challenge; too invisible as a whole for its size.

The empire of capital still works through – and around – the state. It needs the state to operate. That is why the state is the ultimate platform where the class struggle occurs, where it is most visible still and thus can be challenged.

This book is inevitably and purposefully an interdisciplinary project that follows transnational historical materialist methodology with the adoption of contemporary tools for studying social forces and networks. Its scope of time and theme are rather wide so will inevitably leave some readers, particularly the more specialist, wanting more detail. They will have to look for it elsewhere, in specialist literature on area studies. The aim of this project is to provide a comprehensive politico-economic analysis of Ukraine's post-Soviet transformation through the class, means of production and social reproduction analysis. And it is exactly that.

While many themes occur and recur in the text, and terminology from various caveats of scholarship is utilised where deemed necessary to the analysis while not all of it is problematized. In some cases, it is so simply because I can find no argument with the cited definitions in the context of my analysis, i.e. I agree with definitions of social phenomena and categories as formulated by the authors I cite in concrete cases. This is not to say that debates about, say, religious communities and self-identification of the populace based on the criterion of religion are not socially important – to the contrary, in fact. Rather, I merely focus on different aspects of such important identification factors, in the main: I study their function in social conflict, not their genealogy, for example. The latter is to be left to those who specialise in such studies. I do not spend as much time as I might have on the events that marked the start of the Bloody Winter in Ukraine. I do not do that for two reasons. First, they are not essential for the story I am telling in the book and due to the vast scope and timeline I had to be very selective with inclusion criteria. The second reason is the abundance of contradictory evidence that requires a full scope investigation by an expert in such studies who I cannot claim to be.

I hope this book will help shed some light on the dynamics of pillage by capital that have been eroding the fabric of Ukraine's society for over two decades.

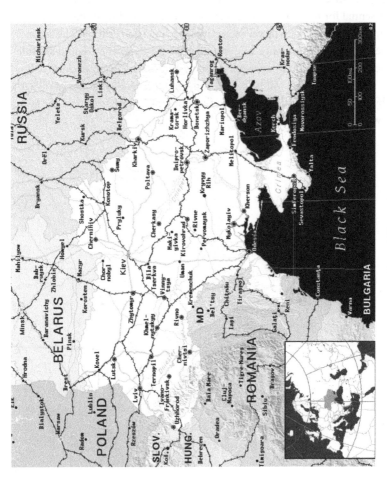

Map of Ukraine

1

Per aspera ad nebulae or to market through a hybrid civil war: survival myths of systemic failure

Three years into its deepest crisis since the demise of the USSR, Ukraine is on a brink of yet another Maidan. Weakened by civil armed conflict, corrupt state administration apparatus and paralysed by the excesses of the debt burden, Ukraine's economy is showing few signs of recovery while it continues to accumulate loans with increasingly draconian structural adjustment requirements. Simultaneously, the living standard, poverty and inequality are at their worst to date. The combination of ill-prescribed market transition reforms, loaned funds mismanagement and misappropriation by the kleptocratic ruling bloc have resulted in a toxic debt dependency that has become a tool for manipulation in the renewed geopolitical confrontation between Russia and the USA/EU. Debt geopolitics in the context of the Deep and Comprehensive Free Trade Areas (DCFTA) negotiations have cost Ukraine its residual de facto sovereignty and at the same time continue to undermine possibilities for stabilisation of the geopolitical order.

Ukraine is stuck in a vice of authoritarian neoliberal kleptocracy with fascicisation tendencies. Further implementation of DCFTA means more austerity, more inequality, more privatisation, and fewer support mechanisms for everyday social reproduction via access to health care, childcare, education, affordable utilities and food. The privatisation of land and re-privatisation of fracking fields also means an ecological catastrophe. The liberalisation on exports of timber to the EU already spells the destruction of Carpathian centuries-old forests for short-term economic gain. Debt has become a geopolitical tool in Ukraine's foreign relations to be used sparingly by its lenders. Exploration of the post-2013/2014 extremes of foreign debt dependency show that the latter, in the context of the kleptocratic neoliberal regime, has led to an effective erosion of Ukraine's sovereignty that by now barely hinges upon the dangerous rhetoric of 'patriotism', that is, the infusion of right-wing sentiment as a defensive mechanism against any criticism of the shaky oligarchic kingdom.

Crimea is not likely to be returned peacefully soon; nor is the Donbas conflict likely to be reconciled in the immediate future. What is certain is that authoritarian fascicising neoliberal kleptocracy is increasingly dispossessing and alienating the country's labour beyond the limits of the possible that are necessary for everyday social reproduction. As even the so-called 'right-wing patriots' are being disposed of as the enemies of the system in Poroshenko's address to the parliament this September, social discontent is brewing stronger. This dispossessed labour force is awake; it is aching from the freshly inflicted wounds and covered in the blood of its children; it is armed; and it is desperate. It is pregnant with the next Maidan.

In early 2014, when Ukraine became the frontline story of global media, few understood how pro-European Union association demonstrations had turned into armed clashes. The unprecedented violence that shook the country was alarming in that the extreme destabilisation of the increasingly dispossessed society brought to centre stage the geopolitical contestations that many thought had been left behind in the pre-1989 era. Speculations of a new Cold War, imperialistic clashes, and even looming Third World War flooded the discourse space of mass media, politics and academicians,[1] which more often than not contributed to the misunderstanding of the crisis.[2]

The conflict did not start with the first bullets fired in Kyiv in the winter of 2014. Putin's ambitions, Nuland's leaked cables, Biden's visits, McCain's and Tymoshenko's inopportune NATO comments, and the like have had little power to automatically translate into an armed conflict. The conditions had to be right. The bullets and the rest burst the floodgates of discontent that have been brewing for some 25 years and that were stirred by a set of dangerous myths in and of the post-Soviet space. The myths were a product of minds that were unwilling and often incapable of engaging with the social or economic reality of those whose future they dangerously had the most power to shape. In this book, I show that the story of Ukraine's degeneration into a hybrid civil and armed conflict is the story of ill-conceived myths used as foundations for real life politico-economic transformation and the dangers that that process entails. All myths are social constructs, which are created by people and exist for their specific purpose.[3] *The underlying purpose and effects of the myths that have been shaping Ukraine's transformation since 1991 are the securing of expansion of the empire of transnationalising capital. It is precisely the social effects of that complex process that have produced conditions where the civil confrontation and the armed conflict became possible and it is the investigation of that process that is the task of this book.*

The function of myths in a changing political and economic reality is to produce social cohesion, support, or – in the words of Gramsci[4] – to a specific mode of governance, production and social reproduction. The mode that since the 1970s has underpinned the global political economy is that of neoliberalism or financialised capitalism, which since the financial crisis of 2007–2008 and the ensuing recession has only become further entrenched,[5] and has been assuming overtly authoritarian features.[6] The most prominent aspect of the latter are the ongoing financialisation and enclosures,[7] that is, the privatisation of publicly owned assets and the assaults on social welfare provision. Market-based constitutionalism is the new world order[8] where we see the socialisation of corporate losses[9] combined with extreme disciplining in the workplace[10] and systemic social exclusion of labour[11] with added extortion by indebtedness,[12] in-work poverty[13] and austerity policies. All of the above are popular and successful exports from the core of the capitalist system to its semi-/peripheries to which Ukraine is no exception, as I will show in this book.

The expansion of the global capitalist system to the post-Soviet space since the early 1990s has created a pronounced intensification of transnational class struggles and East–West geopolitical tensions – primarily between the USA and Russia. Weakened by the demise of the USSR and later economically strengthened by the industrialised world's dependence on oil and gas, Russia became a state-run oligarchy that entered into a new competition with the USA, this time without a proper ideological component. Since the late 1990s, the Kremlin's aim has been to beat the USA at their own game, the capitalist competition/world dominance game; that has included, among other aspects, economic, political and military control over the post-Soviet states, which were slipping away from Moscow's gravitational pull one after another. The Commonwealth of Independent States (CIS; founded in 1991), the Collective Security Treaty Organization (CSTO; founded 1992, reformed in 2002), and the more recent formation of the Eurasian Customs Union in 2008 are some of the examples of Russia's attempts to re-establish and maintain dominance over the space it often used to control directly, even before the formation of the USSR. The USA's push to spread NATO to Eastern Europe and Russia's military involvement in Transnistria and Abkhazia are also part of the Washington–Moscow geopolitical game. The effective manufacturing of frozen conflicts in Moldova and Georgia led some to interpret Putin's annexation of Crimea and the military incursion into Eastern Ukraine as a reaction to fears over the expansion of NATO too.[14] What advocates of Russia's right to defend its interests[15] fail to acknowledge is that Ukraine is a sovereign state and that Russia's disagreement with its foreign and trade policy choices does not grant the Kremlin rights to violate Ukraine's borders. Nor does it justify the trans-formation of Russia's mainstream political discourse that, since the early 2000s, has been based on a bizarre mix of the resurrected and glorified imperial past and reinforced pride over monopolised credit for the Soviet Second World War victory. The use of the imperial history of 'ownership' of Crimea combined with the need to protect ethnic Russians as a pretext for military incursion into Ukraine speaks of the Kremlin's imperialist ambitions: the rhetoric of geopolitical self-defence is hard to sustain in the light of such 'diplomacy'. And indeed, the imperialist clashes of the West and East extend beyond the post-Soviet states and into the interna-tional military and economic arena. The confrontations between Russia and the West/USA over Libya and Syria in the UN are just some of the many illustrations of those clashes and their recent intensification.

The long and complex historical relationship with Russian Empire and the then Soviet Russia secured Ukraine a special place in the renewed geopolitical confrontation. Internally, the state-building process was complicated by the legacy of centuries of being divided between east and west, empires and forms of social organisation intermeshed with brief periods of sovereign statehood.[16] Unified in its current borders by the Soviets in mid-twentieth century, the multi-ethnic, multi-religious, multilingual nation needed a strong cosmopolitan foundation myth to bring it into a sovereign existence.[17] The pivotal principles of the country's Constitution, adopted in 1996, contained all the required ingredients for that. However, marketisation and geopolitical games in the post-Soviet space were in contradiction with the potential construction of a cosmopolitan, egalitarian society and thus, different, divisive myths were used to shape public imagination. A regime of neoliberal kleptocracy, where typical neoliberal features are exacerbated by omnipresent corruption and institutionalised state asset embezzlement, emerged.[18]

The country found itself placed into a vice of neoliberal kleptocracy and intensified geopolitical tensions. The effective dispossession of the masses and the manipulative divisive political myths used to manufacture consent to the regime of dispossession have continuously eroded social cohesion since the early 1990s.

Complex and far-reaching historical processes do not simply happen. There are social forces and people with names who drive them in specific directions. It is through the identification of those forces and the identification of their main interests that we can understand the reasons behind their strategic choices, however questionable those may appear – as at first it may seem to be in the case of Ukraine. One must look into the relationships between the systemic transformation of Ukraine as a part of the changing global capitalist system, associated geopolitical shifts and the class formation process, for example, the emergence of oligarchy, on the level of ideology and the changing individual material positioning towards the means of production in the process of privatisation, that is, accumulation by dispossession.[19]

In this book, I show how the problematic integration of Ukraine into the global capitalist system has fertilised internal political destabilisation, while simultaneously fuelling geopolitical tensions in the region, thus making the civil and armed conflict possible. The abstract separation of civil and armed conflicts is crucial here as political divisions are currently as rife in the country as are their armed expressions, while civil–political conflicts exist on and extend beyond the frontline of Eastern Ukraine.

THE EMPIRE OF CAPITAL, SOCIAL FORCES AND METHODS OF INQUIRY

The end of the Golden Era of capitalism in the late 1960s–early 1970s opened the door for the laissez-faire economy once more. 'The revenge of the rentier',[20] earlier 'euthanised' by the economic theories of John Maynard Keynes,[21] was imposed to overcome the limits of the possibility that the mass production/mass consumption based post-Second World War regime of 'embedded liberalism'[22] had by then been reached. Declining profitability, stagflation and the increased labour militancy[23] of the late 1960s–1970s in the USA and Great Britain was met with monetarism, business re-regulation[24] and neoliberalism, more generally speaking. Founded on the economic theories of Friedrich von Hayek (1899–1992) and Ludwig von Mises (1881–1973) and an update to nineteenth-century liberalism, neoliberalism was 'a consequence of incorporation of marginalist economic thought ... with critiques of equilibrium theory'.[25] The outcome rested on two tenets drawn from von Mises and Hayek respectively: (1) that 'egoism is the basic law of society'[26] and (2) that 'free markets lead to "spontaneous order" that solves the problem of economic calculation'.[27] It became a 'theory of political economic practices that proposes that human well-being can be best advanced by liberating individual entrepreneurial freedoms and skill within an institutional framework characterised by strong private property rights, free markets, and free trade'.[28] Crucially, neoliberalism was conceived as an ideological theory-project aimed to counter 'the inherent totalitarianism of collectivist and state planning of the economy drawing on economic theories which, in turn, posited the impossibility of economic planning in the first place'.[29] The irony here is that neoliberal distaste for planning is but declaratory and often selective as austerity politics, the redesigning of the international trade architecture and the demands for Structural Adjustment in low- and middle-income countries loudly testify. Both nationally, and globally, neoliberalism roots itself through the institution of the state as the main legislative authority capable to legitimately perform such rooting. Thus, the state is assigned a role 'to create and preserve an institutional framework appropriate [for neoliberal] practices'.[30] This transformation gave rise to what Robinson calls the 'transnational state'[31] – a key change of the recent decades that involves the extension of existing and the creation of new mechanisms for lessening state control on capital, while tightening control on labour in terms of regulations and taxation. The state itself is a terrain of class struggle, where the dominant classes and their fractions tend to determine its strategic direction;[32] in a transnational state, the transnationally orientated fractions are dominant. Structural adjustment programmes and loans (SAPs and SALs) exported the neoliberal trans-nationalisation model to the low-income countries after the 1980s Latin American Debt Crisis and, since the 1990s, to the post-Soviet states, including Russia and Ukraine.[33]

In a world shaped by increasingly transnationalising processes, societies and institutions, we need analytical tools that allow us to cut across the outdated categories and respective terminologies. Transnational historical materialism – or the Neo-Gramscian method – permits precisely that, as it is 'the application of the historical materialist method to the study of transnational social relations'.[34] It is a dialectical scientific method of Gramsci,[35] further articulated by Robert W. Cox,[36] Stephen Gill et al.,[37] and Andreas Bieler and Adam Morton[38] – among the more notable – that allows one to trace the formation of social forces in themselves and for themselves along the lines of the relations of production and through the processes of accumulation of capital, passive revolution and *trasformismo*. In the study of Ukraine, such an approach is highly useful in explaining how, through the process of privatisation (i.e. primitive accumulation of capital), oligarchic groups and financial industrial groups (FIGs) were formed (i.e. concentration of capital); how from the body of employees of the same state-owned enterprises (SOEs) few turned into oligarchs and the rest into workers/unemployed/ dispossessed (i.e. capitalist and working class-in-itself formation); how and why new political parties and movements emerged which were representative of or in alliance with concrete oligarchs (i.e. class-for-itself formation), and in support of different directions of foreign policy, for example, the global West versus East. The method allows us analyse how public consciousness transformed to consensually accept a concrete new regime, reforms and people in charge by bringing in the concept of *passive revolution*, that is, the gradual and consensual transformation of social order without meaningful inclusion of the interests of the subject or affected social groups; that is achieved partly by the process of *trasformismo*, where political forces strategically align despite their differences until the differences are submerged in the initially dominant group's framework.[39] Westernisation in all its forms – marketisation, cultural assimilation and so forth – is precisely the process of passive revolution and *trasformismo*.

Social forces are central to our analysis, so particular care is required when delineating the categories of analysis. Readers of scholarship on Eastern Europe are only too familiar with terms such as 'clans' and 'elites' (which I will delve into more detail in later chapters). Here, I propose to set them aside. Their assumed, essential homogeneity obscures the contradictions and frictions within which they are bundled as social groupings. They also fail to explain situations when those groupings cooperate, thus impeding potential clarity and compromising the validity of the final analytical results. How do we explain why members of different 'clans' cooperate and members of the same eliminate each other? Why do people from different social strata and classes protest together for months in freezing cold in the Kyiv's Maidan Square? Fluid categories are needed to achieve any precision in analysing fluid social contingencies such as societies undergoing major transformations, that is, Ukraine under scrutiny. Transnational historical materialism here too comes to rescue. We start with a situation as a unit of analysis, that is, Ukraine's civil and armed conflict, and identify who and why is interested and who is not in concrete outcomes of concrete scenarios of its making. Next, we identify their belonging to specific class fractions, classes and historic blocs depending on positioning in class alliances, the system of ownership of the means of production and ideological/ ideational consciousness – if very short-lived, such as during the Maidans of 2004–2005 and 2013–2014. The latter form is what Gramsci called 'historic blocs' – a 'unity of opposites and distincts',[40] 'complex, contradictory and discordant *ensemble* of the superstructure [that is] the reflection of the *ensemble* of the social relations of production.'[41] The contradictions and reactionary nature of the Maidan protest bodies, as historic blocs, are thus a direct reflection of the fact that Ukraine's (political) economy is an *ensemble* that is complex, contradictory and discordant. The ongoing nature of protests in the country that I address in the book also means that internal contradictions in that historic bloc have still not been reconciled – and that for a new, stable, hegemonic historic bloc/social consensus to be formed 'an appropriate political initiative is … necessary' to 'change direction' of forces that need to be absorbed.[42]

The empire of global capital spreads through transforming societies and their institutions by passive revolution and *trasformismo*, where the ruling bloc are often willing and responsible implementers and beneficiaries of marketisation reforms. Market fetishisation, that is, treating marketisation as the only viable reform option, is the myth on which the neoliberal comprehensive concept of control[43] rests. The latter is an ideological foundation that underpins the preferred dominant mode of accumulation in global economy as a temporary compromise between class fractions linked to different circuit of capital – commodity, productive and money,[44] – which under neoliberalism are more often interconnected via ubiquitous financialisation. In other words, a concept of control is a combination of an 'accumulation strategy' with a 'hegemonic project'.[45] Crystallised in economic models, the concept of control then is channelled indirectly via international institutions (International Monetary Fund [IMF], European Bank for Reconstruction and Development [EBRD], World Trade Organization [WTO],

the EU/EC and alike) and directly, via interest and lc
which in Ukraine, there are four: – American Chambei
(ACC), Centre for US–Ukraine Relations (CUSUR)
Business Council (USUBC) and European Business Asso
I discuss them all in detail later in the book. The concepts of control are
articulated in reform prescriptions to 'transition economies'/Ukraine,
among others via structural adjustment loans (SALs), where the myths
of growth though neoliberal marketisation aim to secure consent to the
reform implementation at any cost.

The demise of the USSR was a unique historic opportunity for transnationalising capital and the capitalist system as a whole. While Western
political leaders celebrated the 'end of history', business lobbies celebrated
the discovery of 'a new South-East Asia on [the EU's] doorstep' (a quote
from the former Secretary-General of the European Round Table of
Industrialists [ERT], Keith Richardson in an interview with the CEO).[46]
In the post-Soviet republics, people were also excited about the new
'market opportunities'. They were the liberal intelligentsia, fractions of
the nomenklatura who sought personal enrichment and the shadow
economic element who now could operate legally, if they chose to do so.
The latter two formed the criminal–political nexus[47] that would become
the backbone of the regime of neoliberal kleptocracy by exploiting
the accumulation mechanisms already present in the capitalist system
rushed on them by international financial institutions (IFIs). Transnationalisation of Ukraine's state was also part of the welcome package.
Where old economic ties were being broken, new were being forged by
old directors/new owners of privatising SOEs, paving the way for the
oligarchic conglomerates of today. Rivalries between Western, Eastern
and domestic forces in the process of capital accumulation and its
geopolitical expressions will shape the future of Ukraine and the rest of
the post-Soviet states for the years to come. Some got rich by dispossessing others while leading them into a desperate head-to-head clash
over the few remaining and mostly non-material treasures: language,
ethnicity, religion, and memory. Even with the breakout of the armed
conflict, the oligarchs have remained in power while the dispossessed
masses earned the privilege of shooting each other near border trenches
of the country's industrial east.

The economic results of Ukraine's marketisation are also shocking.
By May 2015, Ukraine's economy was one of the worst performing in

..e world, with nominal year on year GDP in US dollars down by 28.1 per cent and per capita 23.9 per cent between 2013 and 2014; in UAH (Ukrainian Hryvnia – the currency of Ukraine), the respective indices are up by 7.7 per cent and 13.9 per cent. In addition, Ukraine's economy is heavily dollarised, while being burdened with US$58.1 billion of debt at US$130.9 billion nominal GDP, with the US dollar exchange rate going up from 8 UAH on 1 January 2014 to some 21 UAH on 1 May 2015. Such abysmal performance can only partly be blamed on the 'anti-terrorist operation', the annexation of the Crimea and the loss of revenue from industries based in the territories controlled by separatists. It is rather a testimony of the expansion of transnational capitalist imperialism to which Ukraine is merely one of the many, compliant victims. It is a result of socially destabilising, economically expropriatory and rigged reform instrumentally adapted from ill-conceived transition modelling heavily prescribed to the country by the IMF, the World Bank and EBRD – the harbingers of now authoritarian neoliberalism. The modus operandi and survival of the latter are also based on the myth of the necessity of an ever-expanding market run by private capital as a solution to all social, economic and political problems; and thus, the myth of the need to transition to market is its direct extension.

In Ukraine itself, I identify four main myths that underlie its post-Soviet reality and sustain the shaky consent for the regime of neoliberal kleptocracy, allowing it to remain dominant and survive: (1) the myth of transition, (2) the myth of democracy, (3) the myth of two Ukraines, and (4) the myth of 'the Other'. Each of the four is complementary to the rest and is amorphous, that is, their definitions and perceptions are not clearly demarcated and have proven to change over time via situational instrumental adaptations by the ruling bloc and power shifts within it. It is important to stress here that despite the Orange Revolution and the insurrection of 2013–2014, the regime was not challenged – only some of its agents were dislodged and thus we do not talk of the dominance of concrete agents of the ruling class/bloc but of the materialisations of the class-for-itself, the Modern Prince,[48] the abstract party of the dominant regime. The reshuffling of concrete agents then becomes less important, even though still relevant. The resilience and reification of the four myths lies in their designed and contingent, while mutually reinforcing, nature. The myths together are the pillars on which the comprehensive concept of control of ongoing neoliberal financialisation rests.

THE MYTH OF TRANSITION

The myth of transition is a myth that cuts across the logic of capitalist empire expansion generally speaking. The relationship of the (post-)Soviet states and the IMF, World Bank, EBRD, and later the WTO, has produced not only damaging policy prescriptions but also a hegemonic discourse of what those policies can and cannot be. Prescriptions based on marketisation set the parameters of right and wrong necessitated by the underlying hegemonic belief of neoliberal economists that there is a need to help the newly independent countries to the 'correct path' of social evolution based on the free market model. One of the most (in)famous and influential manifestations of that sense of a historic necessity was Francis Fukuyama's *The End of History*.[49] Fukuyama's article, followed by the book, became a self-fulfilling prophesy for the new states that emerged not only at:

> the end of the Cold War, or the passing of a particular period of postwar history, but the end of history as such: that is, the end point of mankind's ideological evolution and the universalization of Western liberal democracy as the final form of human government.[50]

Such vision left little room for alternative scenarios in the face of 'liberal democracy' as the form of statehood, neoliberal capitalist market as the economic system, and the culture-ideology of consumerism[51] as the model of a societal consciousness.

The article by Jeffrey Sachs of Harvard University in *The Economist* on 13 January 1990, titled 'What Is to Be Done?', according to Peter Gowan, became a watershed moment in the above discourse.[52] The 'burden' that Sachs put on the shoulders of a 'white man' to accomplish, Gowan explains, boiled down to 'creating an international environment in which the domestic aspect of [Sachs' neoliberal] policy [advocated in the above-mentioned article] would become the only rational course for any government to pursue'.[53] Sachs promoted his suggestions in a series of lectures for what later became 'The Economic Theory of the Transition' module at the London School of Economics. The subsequent publication of the lectures by Massachusetts Institute of Technology (MIT) was quickly supported by policy makers in both the USA and Great Britain and these were soon exported to the post-Soviet space, where the authority of both Harvard and the MIT was rarely, if at all, doubted.[54]

The economic upheaval that followed the 'shock therapy' (i.e. one of the names that Sachs' approach obtained in the post-Soviet states) inspired by the above is widely documented elsewhere.[55] The upsurge of Sachs's ideas is a demonstrative example of how dangers inherent in theoretical abstractions fuelled by the mythological fetishisations of markets can materialise through careless application. Sachs, Gowan explains, is:

> Strongly committed to a vision of a globalized, unified capitalist world which he believes would benefit the whole of humanity and he evidently saw an opportunity for bringing that vision closer by becoming involved in formulating a policy for the transformation of the East European region. Like all rigorous policy, his contains a more or less explicit model of the behaviour of the relevant actors and of the ways in which they will interact in given contexts, faced with given constraints and incentives.[56]

Primarily due to its prescriptive nature, the straightforwardness of such an approach is misleading despite the acknowledgement of existence of 'constraints and incentives'. First of all, politico-economic reality is much more complex than the model presupposes as, apart from the (socio-)economic factors, there also are their political forms, for example, institutional, ideological and cultural. This means that, by default, the implementation process will have multiple negative consequences. Second, the model is premised upon an assumption that there must be a transition to neoliberal market capitalism in the first place and that it is the only alternative for the post-Soviet states; it is not clear at all why the above is treated as an axiom. Third, the process of 'transition' towards a certain mode of production and social reproduction – capitalist or otherwise – is steeped in teleology of itself. Thus, as any social prescription, it does not account for, if at all acknowledge, the social dialectic of its target locale. Moreover, teleology of transition to market fetishises a fictitious object, that is, a free market, which neither in theory, nor in practice was shown to either exist, or perform efficiently. Instead of acknowledging the many inadequacies and limitations of policy pre-scriptions, the transition approach arrogantly assumes both a possibility and a necessity of the prescribed 'transition' and attempts to predict its future as if that were possible. Such arrogance pronounced in Sachs's position (which is also the position of the IFIs that advocate neoliberal marketisation – the IMF and the World Bank) is addressed in the criticism of the economic theory of transition, or transitology, articulated by Ralf Dahrendorf in 1990 already. The latter correctly argued that: (1) the newly emerged states did not reject communism for capitalism (and thus did not need assistance in the construction of it); and (2) the existing social institutions in the post-Soviet space were to be respected and the institutionalisation of the new ones should have occurred through openness, debate, and compromise. To that Sachs's response stipulated an impossibility of successful reform without Western planning[57] – a process that ironically goes against the foundational tenets of the free market ideology and 'impossibility to plan' the market discussed earlier.

In April 1991, the European Bank for Reconstruction and Development (EBRD) was founded to aid the 'transition' in the post-Soviet space under the auspices of the European Union.[58] In the view of the founders of the Bank, 'the sudden and total collapse of the Soviet Union [was a signal] of the urgency to provide support to a region emerging from decades of political and economic dictatorship.'[59] Neoliberal marketisation as an economic strategy was chosen from the outset too, as for EBRD functionaries, it was clear 'that boosting the role of the private sector as the linchpin for free and open market economies was crucial in the democratic transition process.'[60] Being the only 'transition bank' in the world, the work of the institution began with 'establishing contacts with all interested parties, conducting preparatory missions to central and eastern Europe agreeing on procedures, and forging a strategy for the institution.'[61] EBRD transition support focus was set on '[fostering] transition through project financing, primarily in the private sector' and focuses on 'building the institutions necessary for underpinning the market economy, and demonstrating and promoting market-oriented skills and sound business practices.'[62] Serving different but complementing purposes, the three IFIs have since been the main vehicles of marketisation policy delivery. The subsequent avalanche of economic problems and political crises in Ukraine failed to translate into a shift away from 'the transition to market' dogma. Instead, as I document in this book, neoliberalism is being pushed onto the impoverished society with reinvigorated zeal. Transition is not limited to economic reform but also includes the installation of a democratic rule, which is yet another myth.

THE MYTH OF DEMOCRACY

The myth of democracy goes hand in hand with the myth of transition as, according to neoliberal orthodoxy, where there are markets, there is democracy and freedom of enterprise and individuals. The feasibility of democratic rule in a polity where private interests come before public ones is one of the more insidious yet resilient myths that allows for authoritarian neoliberalism to survive and spread. The political institutions that emerge as a result of transition are essentially undemocratic as not only is their shape imposed on societies externally but also that shape, that is, the transnational state, itself presupposes the loss of democratic control over its functioning. In such conditions, talking of democracy even hypothetically can be equalled to fictitious speculation. Instead, what can be witnessed in Ukraine is the institutionalisation of a regime of neoliberal kleptocracy,[63] where the political disempowerment of the voter became combined with their economic disempowerment[64] and the ideological hollowing out of political discourse.[65]

Little qualitative change on the level of cadre occurred in 1991. The old apparatchiks remained in power. It will be they and the criminals-turned-oligarchs, that is, the fractioned ruling bloc and their power contestations at any cost that will both maintain the façade of democracy and make the political order unstable to the point of insurrection and now armed conflict. Political disempowerment in Ukraine is manifest in the crisis of representation that stems from the declarative nature of Ukraine's party programmes and politics, which led to a general lack of trust in politicians and voter apathy.[66] The latter is being 'resolved' through voter bribing that, in conditions of economic deprivation, is relatively cheap and easily achievable. Additionally, potential voters' support became customarily won through 'information warfare' that became the determining factor of the election outcomes, as I argue elsewhere.[67] The amount of information in circulation was limited and an information vacuum was created.[68] In such manner, 'serious political and economic content which contradicted pro-establishment views was removed from the diverse, Western-looking and glossy landscape, creating a virtual reality, the aim of which was to disempower society and blur its consciousness. Many in Ukraine called this "zombuvannya lyudej" – making people into zombies.'[69] Gaining and maintaining political power was achieved via 'manipulative techniques inherited from the Soviet era', which failed to mature into 'contested politics'. The rulers' power 'was based on informal networks and 'corridor politics' (politics away both from the public eye and from a paper trail produced in offices)' customary till the present day.[70] The arsenal of manipulation methods, which Wilson describes as 'contracted out KGB services' included: 'agents everywhere, alongside agents provocateurs, divide and rule, kompromat ("compromising materials"), bribery and control'.[71] All this was modernised and made more convincing by the excessive use and manipulation of 'information technologies, creating dramas that were literally virtual because they mainly existed on TV; or later nudging, deflecting or reshaping the narrative of social media' in a form of Orwellian doublespeak.[72]

In order to service their accumulating ambitions, fractions of the competing ruling and eventually capitalist class of the newly emerged kleptocratic regime designed political shell parties,[73] whose survival rested on virtual politics and on breeding the next two myths – of the two Ukraines and of 'the Other'. While the fractioning of the ruling and capitalist bloc is real, the political differences between them are arbitrary and that contributes to the myth of democracy; that means that one gets marketisation with each electoral choice. Such a reality is due to the existence of a few rival ruling and capitalist bloc fractions who have dominated Ukraine's political scene since the early 1990s and who can be grouped by their industrial regions of origin: Dnipropetrovsk and Donetsk. The shifts of power between those blocs have shaped Ukraine's post-Soviet history in the following order.

The first post-independence period of 1991–1998/1999 was characterised by a clear dominance of the Dnipropetrovsk bloc led by presidents Kravchuk (1991–1994) and Kuchma (since July 1994), and Prime Minister Lazarenko, and was composed of the neo-nomenklatura and the capitalists in-the-making, who came from the milieu of the criminal–political nexus and Komsomol. During that period, the first oligarchic capitalists emerged in the spheres of gas, oil, lubricants and the fuel trade with Lazarenko, Tymoshenko and Pinchuk in the lead (KUB and later YeESU companies). Simultaneously and often through brutal criminal activity, a rival capitalist class fraction was in formation in the Donetsk oblast. In 1996, the Constitution of Ukraine was adopted, making it a Presidential Republic and thus maintaining centralised control in the hands of the presidential administration, that is, Kuchma and his cronies from Dnipropetrovsk.

In the second period of 1998/1999–2004, the growing leverage of the Donetsk bloc in both the economic and political spheres of Ukraine became noticeable. It included a number of top state administration appointments, for example, Prime Ministers Azarov and later Yanukovych. Capitalist class fractions formed through primitive accumulation of the SOEs and concentration of capital in the FIGs with pronounced dominance of the Donetsk forces. By the late 1990s, those forces emerged as class-fractions-for-themselves and formed the Party of Regions – and many others respectively – to pursue their interests through direct participation in the country's political decision-making. The gradual shift of power from the Dnipropetrovsk neo-nomenklatura to the Donetsk fraction commenced with the Lazarenko's money laundering scandal, Tymoshenko's and YeESU's loss of control over the gas market, and Kuchma's and Pinchuk's class fraction compromise with the Donetsk forces. In late 2004, prior to the presidential election, the Constitutional reform was adopted that shifted the power over to the Parliament in order to guarantee the Party of Regions/Donetsk leverage on the decision-making process in case of Yanukovych's potential defeat in the election.

The third period was a short interregnum of 2004–2007. In late 2004, the power struggle of the rival capitalist fractions in the presidential election resulted in a two-month long civil protest that became known as the Orange Revolution. It was led by the presidential candidate Yushchenko and his backer Tymoshenko, who were supported by fractions of Donetsk (ISD of Taruta and Mkrtchan) and Dnipropetrovsk (Privat Group of Kolomoyskyy and Boholyubov) capital and Ukraine's Western partners, the USA and the EU. The protest was a reaction to the electoral fraud by the Donetsk bloc's Yanukovych, whose candidacy was supported by the outgoing president Kuchma, SCM/Akhmetov, Interpipe Group/Pinchuk and Russia. Subsequently, the rival forces were unable to reach a political compromise. Conflict between the parliament dominated by the Party of Regions, opposition parties, their associated rival capitalist class fractions, and the inability of president Yushchenko to maintain allegiance with his previous backers led to: (1) Tymoshenko's loss of office; and (2) the subsequent appointment of Yanukovych as the new prime minister. Parties associated with Yushchenko and Tymoshenko were rapidly losing support and in the parliamentary election of 2007, the Party of Regions won the majority of seats, thus marking the beginning of the formal power centralisation by the Donetsk bloc.

During the period 2007–2013/2014, the Donetsk bloc usurped power in the country. Following the parliamentary election of 2007 and the formation of a coalition with Yushchenko's party Our Ukraine, Tymoshenko once again was appointed the prime minister. As the Global

Credit Crunch effects hit Ukraine's economy, Tymoshenko's rivalry with Firtash over the gas markets turned into the so-called 'gas wars' with Russia, which cost her popular support as the prime minister. The latter helped Yanukovych secure victory in the presidential election in 2010 that, in combination with the Party of Regions' parliamentary majority, now gave the Donetsk bloc control over the executive and the legislative branches of power. The centralisation of power now accelerated and among other aspects, included: (1) the vertical concentration of power in the hands of the president through the reversal of the Constitutional reform of 2004; and (2) extension of control to the judiciary by the adoption of *The Law on the Judiciary and the Courts from July 2010*[74] that: 'represented at one and the same time both an instrument for gaining and imposing power over the judiciary [by the president] and an attempt to improve the administration of justice.'[75]

Last but not least is the period that started in late 2013–early 2014 with the insurrection, the annexation of Crimea, the intensification of civil unrest and the breakout of the armed conflict. The latter was the direct result of the 'two Ukraines' and more recently 'the Other' manufacturing, without which Russian-supported separatism would not have been possible. The dislodging of the top figures of the Donetsk bloc and the Party of Regions not only beheaded their centralised state power pyramid but also effectively intensified the rivalry among the remaining capitalist fractions. In conditions of intensified rivalry and a lack of democratic mandate, the precarious ruling bloc relies increasingly on the compartmentalisation of society, the myths of 'two Ukraines' and each of them being the other's 'Other'. Such an intensely polarised society in a state of civil conflict can only be dominated by increased coercion, which paradoxically is legitimised by the very conflict that needs resolving. However, underneath the polarising rhetoric, the socio-economic struggle of the everyday is what unifies the many Ukraines and the conscious acknowledgement of that fact is the biggest fear of the precarious rulers whose political longevity now directly depends on the longevity of the conflict that they allowed to unfold.

THE MYTH OF TWO UKRAINES

First of all, the 'two Ukraines' division is fabricated;[76] it is a myth. Rather there are 'many' that overlap as it is a multi-ethnic, multi-cultural and multi-religious country.[77] Ukraine is diverse and non-homogenous, just like any other country and its 'heterogeneity is a historical norm, not the historical exception'.[78] Thus, the (co)existence of the many Ukraines does not become confrontational accidentally or spontaneously. The divisions within society have been manufactured into a conflict through the careless manipulations of discourse by political technologists, who worked to secure electoral support and/or the defamation of rival oligarchic groups and their political representations. Such manipulations had started in the 1990s already, when the striking miners of Donbas were pitched against the Kyiv government by their 'masters' to broker a market access deal with the Dnipropetrovsk neo-nomenklatura that was the government.[79] By the early 2000s, 'two Ukraines' were manufactured with virtuoso mastery by the above-mentioned political technologists from Russia and the dispossessed were systematically used in staged protests and electoral fraud, as I discuss in Chapters 4 and 6. The Yanukovych versus Yushchenko electoral campaign became the main defining moment, where the boundary between the two was demarcated making Riabchuk's 1992 declaration a materialised prophesy.

The ongoing conflicts in Ukraine that may appear ideological, ethnic or linguistic are often ideational/political, effective and manipulated rather than causal, and can be interpreted as structural ruptures necessitated by shifts in the balance of power within and between social blocs, classes and their fractions, which I have documented in the previous section. The true conflicts are class formation and accumulation struggles between foreign and domestic capital, that is, oligarchs, the EU, the USA and Russian business and their indirect engagement in Ukraine's policy making via various forms of advisory and financial 'support' organisations. The Maidan protests, also, were not ideological but counter-ideological, reactionary movements. According to a survey conducted by Bekeshkina and Khmelko from Democratic Initiatives Foundation and Kyiv International Institute of Sociology, on 7–8 December, of the 1,037 randomly selected Maidan participants, 92 per cent of them did not belong to any parties or NGOs. The three most commonly named reasons for joining the protest were: (1) police repressions, especially the beating of protesters on the night of 30 November (70 per cent of respondents); (2) the president's refusal to sign the Ukraine–EU association agreement (53.5 per cent); and (3) a desire to change life in Ukraine (50 per cent). Only 5 per cent said they joined the protest in response to political opposition leaders' call to do so. There was no class in itself in the historical materialist meaning of the term.

However, there was and still is a historic bloc. It is still amorphous but it's growing stronger, as I show in Chapters 7 and 8. The right-wing elements traceable at Maidan will either become marginalised (what Svoboda already feels)[80] or become a sacrificial animal for the accumulation needs of the oligarchs who led people to protest in the first place. That sacrifice is now manifest in the disposable attitude of the current rulers to the volunteer battalions in Eastern Ukraine, who are often underpaid and lack formal registration as participants of a military campaign, and whose families struggle to get so much as a state-funded funeral for the killed, let alone financial support for the surviving family members.[81]

THE MYTH OF THE OTHER

The regime of neoliberal kleptocracy survived the insurrection of 2013–2014, paradoxically due to the Russian intervention in Crimea and the 'Russian Spring' in the east of the country. The Russian gambit twisted the arm of the discontented citizenry into voting for Poroshenko as president and many of the usual suspects back into the parliament to withstand the Kremlin's attacks on the legitimacy of the government in Kyiv. The weakest electoral victory on record for the president and parliament alike,[82] however, is not itself sufficient to allow the ruling bloc to forget that Maidan did not accept their leadership. Multiple protests that preceded and followed the insurrection,[83] also serve as a pertinent reminder to the oligarchs that they are on borrowed time. In such conditions, reliance on coercion to preserve the dominant position becomes a matter of survival for the ruling bloc. The conflict in the east now has become both their biggest curse and their biggest blessing, as it serves as a convenient excuse for the lack of socially orientated reform, the deterioration of socio-economic conditions, the ongoing macroeconomic crisis, justification for a further push with privatisations, and the failures to address corruption. Most importantly, the armed conflict allows other social groups to compartmentalise society and make dissent impotent.

The many Ukraines guaranteed and stipulated in the Constitution of 1996 are now being transformed by their Othering. Where socio-economic deprivation has failed to breed large-scale xenophobia, the systematic manufacturing of the discourse of the 'two Ukraines' has succeeded, with a helping hand from Russia and later the USA/ West and their lapdogs in Ukraine. Discursive methods are intricate as, instead of blanket propaganda in the twenty-first century, 'it makes more sense to allow a contested media space, so that the local population feels its own narrative, even though the narrative has been manipulated for it.'[84] In Russia (where much of Ukraine's news content originates) – and to a lesser degree in Ukraine – it is done by 'an army of interferers, whose techniques are much more post-modern: party managers and financiers, official scriptwriters, Kremlin bloggers, trolls and so called web-brigady.'[85] For the main figures of Russian political technology, Sergey Markov and Gleb Pavlovsky, our 'postmodern' reality is such where the 'distinction between myth and reality [does] not exist'.[86] However, even if the distinction between myth and reality does not exist in the virtual discourse created by the likes of Surkov, Markov and Pavlovsky, reality is shaped by their virtual and irresponsible manipulations. These techniques were used by the Kremlin propaganda machine in manufacturing the myth of the oppressed Russian minority and 'the junta' too, as I show in Chapters 7 and 8. Ukrainian rulers borrowed both technologies and technologists from Russia to help them in manufacturing the two Ukraine electorates in the 2004 presidential campaign for the first time. Since then, Russian political drama directors have become a regular feature of the Ukrainian political scene. The annexation of Crimea, the war in Eastern Ukraine and the bifurcating dynamics of Othering are the direct effects of such myth-making.

The Ukrainian nation as an imagined community was weak when the country became independent and remained as such until the insurrection of 2013–2014. In fact, its amorphous and disjointed nature was one of the key factors that allowed for the protests to turn into armed clashes. It became popular to view the annexation of Crimea by Russia and the latter's active support for separatist forces as factors that forced the birth of the Ukrainian nation that had been in the making since the early 1990s.[87] Such a perception is valid but such nation-birthing is not unproblematic. The nation is 'imagined as limited because even the largest of them ... has finite, if elastic, boundaries, beyond which lie other nations,'[88] and it is important that an understanding of where those limits lie is shared by the imagined community's members and that the limits cut around, and not across, the community. It is always 'imagined as sovereign' and 'as a community, because regardless of the actual inequality and exploitation that may prevail in each, the nation is always conceived as a deep, horizontal comradeship.'[89] The systematic destruction of the latter by political technologists for over a decade has undermined that sense of comradeship.

The Ukrainian is now locked into defining themself in opposition to the Russian "Other" by the content of the infamous 'decommunisation laws'.[90] Moreover, the Russian Other is being chained to the communist/ Soviet, which now too is forced into being treated as 'the Other' by anti-propaganda and anti-communist legislation respectively. Such a shift of discourse and identity politics is paradoxical. First, what is meant by 'Russian' is not clearly defined and thus is subject to vast speculations and manipulations by nationalists first and foremost. Without categorical demarcation, it is not clear what is being rejected. Due to their shared history of polity, culture, religion and language and thus the mutual formative impact of their separations becomes extremely difficult, without becoming farcical. Second, 'the Russian' and 'the communist' are not the same thing – neither are present-day Russia and the USSR or the Soviet legacy. The conflation of those are just one more example of falling into the trap of defining 'the Ukrainian' and its future as 'anything-but-Russian'. The appropriation of the term 'the Soviet' as being equal to 'the Russian' is part of the Kremlin's imperialist rhetoric in their attempt to claim some supposed inherited rights to intervene in their little-brother nations' affairs and territories, as was the case for Georgia, Moldova and now Ukraine. The identification of 'the Russian' as 'the Soviet/communist' then is simply parroting the rhetoric as a failed attempt to reject it – as well as conveniently using the Soviet legacy as an excuse for present-day socio-economic degeneration, political, economic, security and civil catastrophe which I will detail in this book.

A national imagination which is based on dichotomising and juxtaposing identity to the Russian 'Other' is dangerous and constrictive. It links the formation and existence of Ukrainian national imagery to the transformation of the Russian by focusing on the negation of acceptability and the rejection as 'the Other' of 'the Russian'. There is one more, much deeper problem at play here and that is that Ukraine/Ukrainian and Russia/Russian have a shared history, culture and language. Defining Ukrainian as being 'anything but Russian' would then mean the partial amputation of what constitutes the Ukrainian identity presently and historically. So, the Othering occurs not only on the level of separation of society on separatist/Russia sympathisers and 'patriots' but also intrinsically, on an individual level through rejection of a part of one's cultural, historical, linguistic and religious identity. Thus, we are witnessing a process of fragmentation and forceful top-down reshaping of national identity and consciousness. Patriotism rhetoric and laws criminalising criticism of the ruling forces on either side of the frontline with Donetsk People's Republic (DNR) and Luhansk People's Republic (LNR) are doing precisely that, that is, making the new 'Others' within the geographical boundaries of yesterday's Ukraine. Social demarcations are reinforced by the dehumanisation of the Other which also, like the two Ukraines, were born out of the Yushchenko/Yanukovych electoral campaign. In 2014, already the image of 'Western Ukraine' was branded as banderite nationalists, full of 'not even humans but *kozly*',[91] while the 'Eastern Ukraine' was labelled as the land of drunks, drug addicts, simpletons and gangsters.[92] The divisions will remain until the artificial identification and Othering of 'the Russian', 'the banderite' and the 'Donetsk' are reviewed and ideally rejected – something that becomes less achievable with every passing day of the ongoing Ukraine–Russia diplomatic and armed confrontation and the manipulated political and media discourse.

The unification of the Ukrainian nation based on modernity and not on historical and/or cultural myths is needed, since the consolidation potential of the latter is very weak[93] and is having a destabilising effect as recent degenerations into ultra-nationalism and vassal separatism testify.

CONCLUSION

The armed conflict in east Ukraine has taken many by surprise, even after the shock of the Crimea annexation in April 2014 – and it should not have had. Empires do not implode overnight, nor do they spread without resistance. A paradoxical dichotomy that underlies the 'end of history' is that some believed the history could end while others were unwilling to accept that. Both were wrong – history does not end overnight but it is in a flux. The USSR was not an 'empire of evil' any more than any other in human history, no more than the USA has always been or than the state-run oligarchy of Putin and Co. is now. Russia, the EU and the USA, together with Ukraine's oligarchs are responsible for the fresh blood that has been shed in the name of markets and power.

Machiavellian/Gramscian consent is just one part of the foundation of power in a society. The second is coercion. The two complement each other and, in an ideal case, coercion is used as a last resort means of maintaining social order from violators of the social contract, that is, consensual mode of governance or mode of social reproduction. Such a state polity is a state where a ruling bloc, a party, a 'modern Prince' reigns hegemonically, where their dominance is accepted by popular consensus. Where the ruling bloc begins to lose legitimacy or popular consensus to their rule, mechanisms of coercion – symbolic and physical – need to be extended to repress the discontent and to guarantee the survival of the ruling bloc in question. In the process, the use of discursive manipulation or propaganda violations of previous social consensus and extensions of coercive apparati may appear to be justified to the public and thus become part of the changing consensus. When the changes are abrupt and extensive, they become more obvious and bear higher potential for the generation of first reactionary, in-itself and then coherent, for-itself counter-hegemonic historic bloc. The latter may later dissipate or be squashed. It can become co-opted into the hegemonic mode again via minor temporary concessions, which are still in the formative, reactionary phase. Alternatively, they can become transform-ative and even revolutionary for parts of the system or for the whole of it. Context, contingency and global scope in the latter cases may prove to be decisive factors.

The Ukraine's ruling bloc is running out of options as is testified by the agony of hiring foreigners to run its ministries. The larger destabilis-ing problem still is not that the rule of the leaders is questioned but that the ideological foundations of their regime and rule are not. The myths that have permeated public consciousness in Ukraine are not sufficiently challenged. However, there is already a reactionary counter bloc that, if mobilised, could present a serious challenge to the system; it is the bloc comprising the systematically dispossessed and alienated – that is its unifying condition, the condition of the exploited. Its weakness is in its compartmentalisation that also comes from the four myths and from the inability to see that they are just that – myths, and thus, need to be questioned and could be changed, rather than fetishised. If that is overcome, if the 'Othering' damage is undone, then we would see a serious challenge to the still hegemonic ideology of authoritarian neolib-eralism – and the ongoing social discontent is pregnant with that hope.

* * *

The rest of the book deals with the material and social reality that allowed the incorporation of Ukraine and Russia into the global capitalist system, accumulation rivalry and the associated socio-economic and political effects unravelling into an armed conflict. Chapter 2 looks into the beginning of the capitalist class and its fractioning formation during the

Perestroika years, the role and function of shadow economy and crime, and the forging of the criminal–political nexus. Chapter 3 follows the first post-independence years of transition to market, primitive accumulation, and the construction of kleptocracy facilitated by ill-conceived transition modelling. Chapter 4 looks into the class formation process and the effective emergence of the capitalist, ruling and dispossessed blocs. The concentration of capital in Financial-Industrial Groups and the role of fuel market rivalry are given particular focus. Chapter 5 addresses the institutionalisation of crime and the misconceptions that surround the role of foreign capital in Ukraine. I study the uneven performance of the US and EU business lobby groups that operate in the country, analyse the functioning of Priority Development Areas (PDAs) and Special Economic Zones (SEZs), foreign direct investment (FDI) and the recycling of capital through offshore. In Chapter 6, I focus on the virtualisation of politics, the manufacturing of the two Ukraines and the gas wars that characterise the Orange Revolution and its immediate aftermath. The rebalancing of the power within the ruling bloc towards Yanukovych/ Donetsk and within the CPN towards criminals-turned-oligarchs are examined. Chapter 7 concentrates on the ascent of Yanukovych's 'family', the socio-economic deterioration, the growing public discontent and the eventual insurrection in the aftermath of the DCFTA signing rejection. The social forces of the Maidans and the Anti-Maidans are examined as well as their historical instrumentality for the ruling bloc. To end, Chapter 8 analyses the aftermath of the revolt hijacked by the ruling bloc, shifts provoked within the latter and the mechanisms of its rein-statement as a ruling, dominant force. The annexation of Crimea, the Odesa Massacre and the unfolding of the conflict in Eastern Ukraine are investigated in the context of renewed geopolitical clashes between the USA/EU and Russia. Myths, realities and the utility of the far right in the survival of neoliberal kleptocracy are investigated and the chances of the newly strengthening left developing into a counter-force are evaluated.

2

Capitalist antecedents in the late USSR

The rivalry among the ruling and capitalist class fractions, foreign and domestic, that defined the course and the volatile nature of Ukraine's post-1991 transformation did not start in 1991. The fracturing and rivalry within the state class or nomenklatura that would finalise the demise of the USSR was palpable already in the 1980s. The volatility of the rupture process of the late 1980s–early 1990s found its formalised expression in a series of institutional reforms that systematically fragmented the increasingly dispossessed and disempowered labour.

Changes in the social relations around the means of production and the introduction of the institution of private property were the defining and the locomotive factors of the social rupture. From the transforming rival fractions, a new ruling bloc was also being forged, with its own internal contradictions. Capitalist class fractions emerged from the politico-economic contingency of the late 1980s; the state and other social institutions were transforming. This class formation process was the product of a long relationship between the ruling, managing and criminal social elements of the USSR that can be traced back to the early 1960s. After that point, a criminal–political nexus formed where gangsters serviced the shadow economy under the patronage of the Party officials, or nomenklatura, of various ranks. During Perestroika, the criminal–political nexus further crystallised as a semi-licit bloc of ruling and nascent capitalist forces. It extended to include Komsomol members and the so-called 'red/Soviet directors' to whom Gorbachev's reforms granted limited yet private entrepreneurial rights. Since 1991, that heterogeneous bloc of forces – that is, the (neo)nomenklatura, criminals, directors and Komsomol – have utilised political and economic marketisation reforms, as well as crime, to institutionalise themselves as the ruling and capitalist class of present-day Ukraine.

STATE OF ECONOMY, PERESTROIKA AND COOPERATIVES

In 1985, when Mikhail Gorbachev became the General Secretary of the Communist Party of the USSR, the need for economic and social restructuring was urgent.[1] Following the post-Second World War period, during 1950–1960 there was high economic growth of 7.2 per cent, and during 1960–1970, economic growth was at 4.25 per cent of GDP per capita; then, a slowdown began and growth measured at 3.2 per cent of GDP per capita during 1970–1975, before hitting a period of stagnation with a slump to 1 per cent during 1975–1980 and 0.6 per cent during 1980–1985.[2] While the numbers of the Soviet official statistics bureau, the TsSU, are at times up to many times higher – especially in the slowdown years – the socio-economic reality of the late USSR, the ongoing military engagement in Afghanistan and its effective growing costs, and the social unrest suggest that the Russian economist, Grigorii Khanin's calculations are indeed more accurate. The GDP growth was steady but slow and during 1980–1985, averaging at 1.9 per cent per annum, while the state budget deficit stood at less than 2 per cent of GDP by 1985.

After an array of futile attempts to restructure the USSR productive sector in 1957, 1965, 1973 and 1979, that since the time of Stalin had been over-centralised and focused on military industrial production, 'the basic operating features of the economy remained remarkably impervious to change'.[3] The system needed restructuring as the two prominent USSR economic sociologists Tatyana Zaslavskaya[4] and Abel Aganbegyan, among others,[5] have documented. The economy, however, was not the only concern. The system was over-bureaucratised, corrupt and inefficient, and by the mid-1980s, the USSR was ridden by a shadow economy that compensated for state consumer goods.[6] Gorbachev, together with a team of academics, had already begun to work on scenarios for the restructuring of the USSR economic and political systems while working as the Minister for Economic Policy under Andropov.[7] The USSR became, in all senses, a 'shortage economy'.[8] The economy was stagnating; it was the economy of shortage and it was such that,

> The administration of industry was inert. Industrial discipline was lacking; workers and employees lacked incentives. The industrial ministries acted as independent, autonomous bodies, becoming laws unto themselves. They were able to write their own plans, each ministry could act independently, and they would often deceive the central planners about their real economic resources. Plans would be fulfilled in a routine and bureaucratic fashion with little concern for quality.[9]

Gorbachev's administration set two goals for their reforms: (1) changes in economic mechanisms towards more autonomy of economic units – ministries, enterprises and so forth – from one another and the state; and (2) the democratisation of political control over the economy by granting larger powers to the organs of popular, local control, that is, Soviets.[10] The first, Lane summarises as follows:

- 'The growth and legitimation of market transactions;
- Increase in private and cooperative trade;
- Greater authority to productive units;
- Adoption of the accounting principle of *khozraschet* (which requires units to balance their income and expenditures)'.[11]

In June 1987, in an attempt to boost the economy through partial marketisation, a programme for economic reform was adopted by the Supreme Soviet of the USSR that was also followed by the abolition of the state monopoly on foreign trade. It revolved around three principles: independence, self-financing and the self-sufficiency of enterprises. The programme was aimed at breeding 'competition, market price regulation, and even bankruptcy now [became] an option'.[12] Domestically and abroad, an introduction of: (1) a market (socialist) system; (2) removal of centralised price creation mechanisms apart from those on key commodities; (3) new types of ownership and business forms (cooperatives, shareholding, lease-holdings) and an effective emergence of a stock market; (4) devolution in financing, wage and labour enterprise strategies; and (5) an 'active banking system' to service the new market actors.[13] Next, on the 1 January 1988, a law 'On State Enterprise (Venture)' came into force, which formalised a new concept of the 'state-imposed socialism'.[14] The law had a strong imprint of the Soviet central planning that was largely reduced by legislation on cooperatives adopted later that year. According to the latter, 'the new cooperatives would operate on a limited liability basis, would be allowed to employ non-cooperative labour, apparently with no upper limit, and with wages and working conditions subject to individual contract'.[15] In addition, the income distribution in cooperatives 'would be decided exclusively by the members of the cooperative, and cooperatives would have complete freedom as regards sales and purchases contracts', thus ensuring the gradual marketisation of economy. And last, cooperatives were allowed 'to raise capital by issuing shares, but only for sale to their own members and employees'.[16] The above was the reform that enabled the emergence of not only a strong managerial class and so-called 'red directors' but also of a propertied class as such.

The introduction of economic incentives through engagement in cooperatives became increasingly popular among Komsomol members and those who used Komsomol as a proxy. So,

> by mid-1988 cooperatives were employing between 100,000 and 200,000 people; by the first half of 1990 the figure had risen to 3.1 million (2.4 per cent of the work force) with cooperatives generating perhaps 3 per cent of Soviet GNP; [according to some Soviet economists] they could ultimately have accounted for as much as 10–12 per cent of national income.[17]

The problem with all of the above for the Centre was that the 'realisation of [those laws and the following, more liberalising, legislation] threw out of balance the whole system of economic management without guaranteeing production effectiveness growth'.[18] Instead, the above changes set into motion a process that, due to its controversial nature, is known as 'spontaneous privatisation' and must be considered, I argue, the first stage of privatisation of the state-owned enterprises connected to the post-1991 privatisation reform in the independent Ukraine. The above is often unacknowledged in publications on the emergence of private property in Ukraine[19] and in the post-Soviet space.[20] Spontaneous privatisation was a process of de facto devolution of authority to managers and directors of individual state-owned enterprises while retaining *de jure* state ownership of the enterprises in question.[21] Therefore, Johnson Kroll and Eder define 'spontaneous privatisation' as a process 'occurring when managers acquire, on their own initiative, residual rights of control over their firms'.[22] It is at this juncture, in the milieu of Komsomol, that the first traces of many members of both the ruling and capitalist class fractions of independent Ukraine become palpable. Tymoshenko (since 1988, Terminal cooperative; the KUB and YeESU), Tyhypko (PrivatBank, 1992), Kolomoysyy (Fianit cooperative since 1989; PrivatBank since 1992), Boholyubov (Fianit cooperative since 1989; PrivatBank since 1992), Pinchuk (Interpipe, 1990) and Firtash (NA; since the mid-1990s Itera, ETG, RosUkrEnergo, and finally Group DF) have all derived their political and economic capitalist agency from the structural institutional shifts that were embedded in the Perestroika reforms, as I will detail shortly.

First, the State Enterprise Law in 1987 that allowed limited yet marketisation through Komsomol and then the Law on Soviet Cooperatives
(which came into force on 26 May 1988) that allowed any persons aged
16 or above to form a cooperative, made private economic activity very
popular in Ukraine.[23] Thus, according to Goskomstat, out of a total of
77,548 cooperatives in the USSR, 13,534 were registered in Ukraine.
They employed 248,800 people and functioned in the spheres of natural
consumption (2,575 cooperatives), catering (852), retail (118), trading
(639), consumer consumption (4,252), intermediate goods (510) and
other spheres (4,588).[24] Many of the cooperatives were registered as
Joint Stock Companies (JSCs) with at least one foreign partner, and
they functioned primarily as importers/exporters of commodities.
In Ukraine at that time, as Pekhnyk (Пехник) argues, high deficits of
supply allowed the JSCs to overprice imported goods, thus making
imports profitable.[25] As for exports, they primarily involved being made
'temporarily competitive', due to artificially low production costs in
Ukraine subsidised by the government that, as an economic strategy,
was only deepening the crisis.[26] The characteristic feature of these joint
ventures of the late 1980s and the early 1990s was the attraction of
foreign capital though personal connections or family links.[27]

THE CRIMINAL–POLITICAL NEXUS

The Perestroika reforms set in motion the easing of private economic
activity and with that the inevitable restructuring of the Soviet societies,
structurally extending the agency of some groups. Komsomol, red
directors and Communist Party of the Soviet Union (CPSU) members
were the prime but not the only social forces whose agency Perestroika
extended. The legalisation of entrepreneurial activity, although with
limitations, made the decriminalisation of previously shadow economic
activities possible. Thus, the institutionalisation of the previously
criminal part of the criminal–political nexus was made possible also.
The nexus was forged as a result of numerous systemic restrictions and
the supply and demand problems in the USSR's planned economy and,
by the 1980s, became an inseparable component of Ukraine's state-
society complex. In the USSR, the law was primarily utilised to 'force
compliance with state objectives' and that meant that everything to do
with the CPSU official line of centralised authority – even in instances
of a breach of law – was not to be questioned.[28] The rule of law as an

instance of social and economic order in its own right was absent, and instead, the legal system was under constant pressure from the CPSU for the Plan targets to be met. Effectively, the legal and justice systems became tools of the state apparatus, that is, state class – nomenklatura, rather than being social institutions of relative autonomy in an approximation to their participatory democratic ideal type. In such conditions,

> legal officials had value not as objective enforcers of the law but only as persons who could achieve tangible results. Legal authority was personalised; a development that … [continued through the early 2000s; and continues until today]. The source [of justice] was not the law but the bureaucrat who held the position of responsibility.[29]

Moreover, since the Party was the highest authority in the USSR, where the legal system was subordinate to it, 'corrupt officials could justifiably feel that they were above the law'.[30]

Most of the industry in Eastern Ukraine serviced the military defence complex and, by the mid-1970s, included 60 per cent of all manufacturing and 80 per cent of machine construction plants. Consumer goods supply suffered as a result. After the Second World War, and especially in the 1960s, shadow economic growth accelerated to satisfy the increasing consumer demand in the USSR and Ukraine alike, where most of the production was geared towards the military.[31] Misallocation of resources with a focus on military production resulted in the systematic undersupply of consumer goods and services, the demand for which:

> [was] met only by the growth of an unofficial parallel market. Goods for this market came in the main from illegal production undertaken by managers of state enterprises, and this production involved such criminal offences as misappropriation of state assets, payment of bribes to superior officials, and, eventually, protection money to criminal elements. This was the core of the shadow economy, which grew to at least 15 per cent of the Soviet GDP by 1982.[32]

During the 1990s, the shadow 'service industry' also extended to include physical protection from racketeers, gangs, robbers and the like.[33]

The system of production and distribution in all branches of the economy was centralised and had a strong orientation towards the five-year plan fulfilment. Administrative punishment for the failure thereof and remuneration in *premias* (i.e. bonuses) for the over-fulfilment were standard. Combined with the inefficiency of the centralised system that often stood in the way of the plan fulfilment, provided that the rules/ law are followed, *blat* – or interpersonal networks – became customary and helped to compensate for the plan failures and beyond.[34] In her extensive study of informal networks in the post-Soviet Russian urban centres, Alena Ledeneva describes *blat* as 'an exchange of favours or access to public resources in conditions of shortages and state system of privileges'.[35] Neither a gift, nor a commodity, but an 'intermediary form of exchange', a transfer of 'alienable objects, … on the condition that social relationships already exist'.[36] All of the above contributed to the emergence of an extensive shadow economy, where some of the 'guardians of the law' and the Communist Party members were part of the network. They constituted the 'criminal–political nexus' as theorised by Roy Godson[37] and Louise Shelley[38] and confirmed by research of Todd Foglesong and Peter Solomon,[39] Ferdinand Feldbrugge[40] and Maria Łos.[41] The nexus had been in formation since the 1960s and functioned to service the consumer needs that the Soviet over-centralised economy failed to provide. The above dynamic will be documented in detail in Chapter 3, where I demonstrate that the criminal–political nexus became interwoven with Komsomol in the 1980s and especially during the years of Perestroika, when Komsomol members were allowed to engage in limited market activities. As an analytical category, the nexus provides a valuable insight into both the ruling and capitalist class formation in Ukraine. Conditioned by the constant under-supply of staple let alone consumer goods, combined with high-ranking Communist Party members being the only link in the supply and distribution channels, the criminal–political nexus became an integral part of the state–society complex of the USSR and, since 1991, of Ukraine. Most of Ukraine's ruling and capitalist class members originate from the above milieus, including two of Ukraine's presidents – Kuchma and Yanukovych, most of the prime ministers – Lazarenko, Zvyahilskyy, Masol, Kinakh, Yanukovych, Azarov and Tymoshenko – and the oligarchs. Once it became independent and was on the road to marketisation, Ukraine's economy became a space where the aforementioned social formations began to institutionalise as the propertied and capitalist class, and gradually, if only partially, both legalise their shadow economic activities and reform the country's legislation to serve their kleptocratic ambitions. It is not surprising, therefore, that the future capitalist class of Ukraine emerged from those networks of people who were linked legally and otherwise to the means of production and distribution, for example, the state apparatus functionaries, the State Property Fund, and so on. The above is confirmed by Kerstin Zimmer and Claudia Sabić[42] and Ichiro Iwasaki and Taku Suzuki[43] in their studies of corrupt practices in the post-Soviet states in the process of 'transition' through 'corporate exploitation' with continuities until the present. It must be stressed yet again that such practices of networked class formation are nothing historically unusual in the process of capitalist social construction, nor are strategic class alliances along concrete policy interests; rather, the use of social networks, both formal and informal, are quite standard. The work of Kees van der Pijl on the Atlantic ruling class formation,[44] Bastiaan van Apeldoorn on interest groups in the EU[45] and William Carroll's work on transnational capitalist class,[46] its organisations and networks highlight precisely that tendency. Extra-legal or 'corrupt' behaviour are also nothing new or unusual; the history of corporate functioning is littered with examples of wrong-doing, bribery, collusion, criminal tax avoidance and evasion, money laundering, and so on – where capital is to be appropriated, its appropriators tend to find the way.

Representatives of big industry played a role in the USSR as well. The dominance of representatives from Dnipropetrovsk and Donetsk oblasts – the two largest industrial regions of the country – is notable in both the ruling and the dominant capitalist forces of Ukraine. Dnipropetrovsk has enjoyed a strong presence in the nomenklatura of the USSR and Ukrainian SSR CPSS since the times of Nikita Khrushchev (1953–1964) and continued to be dominant until the Orange Revolution and the end of Kuchma's second presidency in late 2004. Donetsk oblast has for decades been a region of high economic importance, although its political party cadre in the Ukrainian SSR and in the republican ruling structures has been represented to a lesser extent than those from Dnipropetrovsk. When Ukraine became independent and the marketisation processes commenced, the Donetsk bloc eventually began to take over the leverage from the Dnipropetrovsk forces, economically and politically – with the exception of the oligarchic capitalist fraction of Pinchuk and his Interpipe Financial Industrial Group, and Boholyubov and Kolomoyskyy and their Privat Group – both in the legislative and executive branches of power and eventually in the judiciary also, as will be shown in Chapters 4 and 6. This resulted in what Zimmer and Sabić refer to as the 'captured state',[47] where economic and political backwardness became institutionalised and has, at the same time, cast doom on the economic rejuvenation of the economy. However, the dynamic at play was more complex than that implied in the concept of the 'captured state'. The state is an institutional crystallisation of multiple agencies and power hierarchies, which give it a partial autonomy from certain class fractions on the level of abstraction.[48] Due to those structurally embedded power hierarchies, the state is more autonomous from some class fractions than from others. Thus, to assume that there is a possibility of a state to be allegedly 'captured' is to deny the agencies that are counter to the ones that have 'captured' the state and in such fatalistic manner to then dismiss the possibility of a social change or a counter-movement. Instead, I argue that, in parallel with the stalled economic 'rejuvenation', the process of transnationalisation of the Ukrainian state was underway in order to facilitate the continuing and expanding primitive accumulation and concentration of capital by Ukraine's oligarchic capitalist class fractions. As with the concentration of capital, both the stalling of some and the rejuvenation of other parts of the economy will come into an eschewed, uneven fashion that the capitalist mode of production brings, for example, the construction of the new Interpipe Steel plant versus the degeneration of industry across the country.

As for the criminal–political nexus, Shelley documents four systemic conditions that facilitated its forging.[49] First, private property acquisition in the USSR was severely restricted. Second, state interests preceded those of an average citizen – with a partial exemption of the nomenklatura, who enjoyed the fruits of communal labour to a greater extent than average. Third, a commitment to legality by the state, that is, the nomenklatura, in the sphere of property rights protection was missing. And fourth, civil society was being systemically destroyed through direct (i.e. creation of groups and organisations run by the state) and indirect (i.e. ensuring the unavailability of amenities and resources) government control of social groups, their formation and agendas. Shelley adds factors such as 'absence of a free media, civilian watchdog organisations, or financially independent individuals who could afford to oppose the government.'[50] Also, some social forces had fewer opportunities to shape political life in the Union due to a limited political and social representation and thus the systemic social exclusion continued. So, ethnic Russians were historically a dominant and hegemonic social force in the Politburo between 1966 and 1991, at least, as Lane and Ross's analysis shows.[51] In conditions where ethnic minorities such as Caucasians, Jews, Tartars and

Central Asians were persistently 'excluded from positions of power in central government and circumscribed even at local level',[52] the shadow economy offered them opportunities for socio-economic activities as well as mobility which was denied them within the legal sphere. Indeed, many have taken that option, as is evidenced by a prominent presence of Caucasians, Jews and Tartars in the gang formations of the late 1980s.[53] Many also faced restrictions on employment mobility due to *propiska* rules, where citizens had to be registered with the police at a given postal address at all times, even if only temporarily during holidays or work-related travel. In practice, this meant that population mobility was controlled, so that no one would remain idle or left out for long as the police were also responsible for nudging people back into employment. Workers who wanted to relocate had to first prove to their home local authorities that they had a job and a place to live in the target location, which significantly limited their ability to relocate at especially long distances. This rule affected cross-republican migration the most and resulted in ethnic marginalisation and the criminalisation of migrant ethnic groups. Those unwilling to accept *propiska* restrictions worked in an informal economy or in crime for survival and subsistence. This contingency also conditioned the formation of ethnic gangs in Ukraine's Donbas – one of which was the gang of Akhat Bragin and his right-hand man of Rinat Akhmetov, whom I will discuss shortly.

FRACTURING OF RULING BLOC

The reinvigoration of Anglo-American imperialism in the twentieth century, van der Pijl argues, 'put the USSR on the defensive, paradoxically generating a passive revolution within "Socialism in One Country" that reproduced aspects of previous "Hobbesian" experiences ... but also allowed a progressive class to develop in the context of the planned economy.'[54] Until the late 1980s, the advance in a 'sense of a "progressive class" in the context of passive revolution remained surreptitious, based on molecular changes dependent on initiative "from above"' among the 'technocratic and democratic cadre class of managers, educators and specialists of all sorts' that emerged from a 'structural class compromise, a differentiation between class and society' in the USSR under Stalin.[55] By the 1980s, the progressive agenda was gaining popularity among the state class and party intellectuals, for example, Gorbachev, Zaslavskaya and Aganbegyan, and that meant that a structural change so long awaited and needed by the increasingly dissatisfied society was becoming possible. That change required significant reformatting of the USSR's institutions, first and foremost – the state.

The state as a unit of analysis is constituted of numerous forces and their agencies, that is, the society, which is not limited by but includes, as Nicos Poulantzas argued, the institution of the state.[56] The state and society are not separate but are deeply inter-penetrated entities that are nevertheless relatively autonomous. They constitute what Cox refers to as the 'state-society complex' which is what we in fact mean when we speak of 'the state' as it is not an empty 'bureaucratic entity' deprived of connection to civil society.[57] Transnational historical materialist methodology, first developed by Antonio Gramsci in his *Prison Notebooks*, then advanced by Robert W. Cox[58] and the Amsterdam School of political economy[59] helps us understand that 'relations among states are, as it were, embedded in a wider context of evolving transnational social relations'.[60] The restructuring of the state as an institution in the era of the Washington Consensus that Ukraine has been undergoing as part of its neoliberal marketisation is, essentially, an offensive on any other form of statehood.[61] It is a process of transnationalisation of the state as an institution and will be discussed in detail in Chapter 5. It is about granting the forces of capital a separate, not secondary, relational, but central place of its own in the state–society complex, turning it into a state–society–capital complex as is evidenced by the 'irremovable object' of 'free' market and private enterprise in the neoliberal discourse. While it can be argued[62] that the USSR and by extension the Soviet Ukraine acted as a capitalist entity in their foreign trade relations, inside the Union itself and in its state–society complex, there was no legal space for capital or a capitalist class due to the ban on private property and private economic activity. And while I stress in this book and elsewhere that the shadow economy was an endemic part of the Soviet everyday economy and became a launch pad for the future oligarchy, one cannot consider it as a part of the institutional make-up of the Union as there was no formal space for capital accumulation or production. The same applies to the lack of a capitalist class as a class is 'a real historical relationship ... [the existence for which rests on the social basis of the way] in which people are positioned in production processes', which creates potentiality for classes but 'does not *make* classes'.[63] The 'form of state has been found to be determining the influence on the development of modes of production relations, the orientation of classes toward the state, their channelling into political action, is a crucial historical question.'[64] This relationship between the modes of production, the classes and the state is pivotal for our understanding of the changes that occurred in the USSR under Perestroika and in post-Soviet Ukraine; it is crucial in any state–society(–capital) complex power dynamic, in fact. Thus, in the Soviet Ukraine, there was one mode of production – the socialist mode. Goods were produced collectively according to five-year plans and their legally binding targets. The goods were priced and distributed centrally, sold on global markets and the revenue was distributed by the state in society, as a form of foreign aid and so on. In the USSR, however, a potentiality was created for two classes to form: the nomenklatura and the workers. The first held by far the most power in what was the state/nomenklatura–society/workers complex. Thus, any systemic change short of revolution had to come from or through the nomenklatura as in a society where the labour is unionised, yet both the unions and the (civil) society organisations are an integral part of the state apparatus that runs the economy, and so the potential for political action via labour organisations is compromised.

The nomenklatura set out to change the country's course, but they too were not homogenous in their vision as to what had to be done due to the underlying dynamics of the class – in the case of the nomenklatura, state class – formation process. Due to the fact that a number of modes of social relations of production exist in parallel in any society, Cox argues, the class itself is affected by several factors:

1. not every group forms a class but sometimes remains 'a latent or potential class';
2. 'dominant or subordinate groups from two or more modes if social relations may combine to form a class';
3. various modes of production relations are linked in a manner of domination–subordination hierarchy that leverages class orientations of partaking agents; and
4. 'the classes formed around the dominant mode of social relations of production have a predominant influence over the formation and orientation of classes derived from subordinate modes, including the opportunity to form a hegemonic relationship with these other classes.'[65]

Scholars of the USSR break-up point out these centrifugal tendencies within the nomenklatura during Perestroika.[66] Thus, Kudryachenko

(Кудряченко) *et al.* argue that the fracturing of the Soviet power apparatus played a vital role in the dissolution of the system and that it had a direct impact on Gorbachev's reforms. According to them, by the late 1980s, there were four fractions in the nomenklatura: (1) the conservators of the old regime; (2) those who obtained their privileged position due to the new General Secretary personally; (3) those preparing for their future prospects of enrichment via Perestroika reforms; and (4) those making careers – political and economic alike – on more local levels, in separate republics of the USSR (an opportunity made possible by partial devolution). The second and third were not interested in preserving the system in any form and effectively undermined the support that Gorbachev needed to further his democratisation reforms into societies of member republics.[67] Lane and Ross also document that the 'political elite as a whole was fragmented and lacked moral cohesion.'[68] Moreover, the 'transformation of the regime ... was led [by those] ... closely allied to the leader, Gorbachev.'[69] It was they, the Gorbachev allied nomenklatura, who organised the *coup d'état* of August 1991 that led to the demise of the USSR. And it was they, who reorganised as pro-marketisation neo-nomenklatura in the newly independent post-Soviet states. The old regime conservators would mostly reorganise as *de jure* left-wing forces and would be supporting various forms of post-Soviet states economic reintegration, that is, the Commonwealth of Independent States since 1991 and the Eurasian Economic Community since 1996. The fourth category would experience the most structural political mobility in the early to mid-1990s, both upwards and downwards. In Ukraine, the ascent to power of the regional neo-nomenklatura from Donetsk, for example, Zvyahilksyy in 1993, and the ascent following the ousting of Lazarenko in 1995–1997 are examples of such mobility.

The nomenklatura and its fractions, however, were only some of the social formations that have emerged from the continuities of the Soviet contingencies and that have become institutionalised as the capitalist and ruling fractions after 1991. The rest emerged predominantly from two milieus. The first was the Komsomol and was constituted mostly of the young people for whom Perestroika reforms opened up private entrepreneurship opportunities that had been previously illegal in the USSR – as discussed earlier. The second was primarily the criminal element engaged in the shadow economy for whom marketisation reforms gave an opportunity to legalise their activity, if they chose to do so. The fractions did not exist in isolation from one another but rather functioned as a system based on favours and extra-legal exchange that filled the provision gaps where the Soviet state had failed; they were connected strongly by the networks of *blat* and locked in the criminal–political nexus. The workers, however, were increasingly marginalised by the shortages of the economy and the exclusivity of these substitute/complementarity structures.

LABOUR AND SOCIETY: THE BREWING DISCONTENT

In the 1980s, fragmentation and dissatisfaction were becoming common in the Soviet labour force. Decades of an imperial arms race competition with the USA had pushed the planned economy to disproportionately service the defence complex. Military expenditure combined with the foreign aid efforts kept stripping the country's finances. Production for social needs, thus, was relatively underfunded and aimed at needs, not wants as it would have been in a capitalist economic model. The needs, however, often went unmet and left gaps in demand. All decisions about what was to be produced and in what quantities were taken centrally by the ministries and the agencies of *Gosplan* (abbr. for 'state plan') and as such the system of supply had little flexibility or ability to respond to the unexpected shortages of goods due to miscalculated future demand. Shortages, queues and limited offers left many wanting more in the system, where money was sparse and where even its presence did not necessarily solve the problem of the unavailability of goods. Queues and 'hunting' for *deficit* goods were becoming a standard part of everyday life as was meeting the unsatisfied needs of the shadow economy, discussed earlier.

The problem of supply was only one of many. While there was full employment in the Union, perhaps the highest in human history,[70] figures often did not accurately represent the reality as they excluded frictional unemployment and rural underemployment. Such inaccuracies in the formal figures were due to a lack of comprehensive unemployment statistics. Ironically, the collection of unemployment data had been discontinued in the light of evident full employment since 1931.[71]

Labour mobility was limited due to the peculiarities and restrictions of the Soviet labour 'market'. Lane attributes that to six factors.[72] First, it was not until Gorbachev's leadership that wage differentials were used as an incentive to encourage labour mobility. There were exceptions, however, in the case of significant industrial projects, such as that of Donbas, where wages and social benefits were significantly higher, precisely in order to attract the required labour force. Usually, those projects also involved work in industries of high health risks, high mortality and low longevity, for example, chemical mining and refining, and deep underground mining. At the same time, such industries were a hot spot of worker solidarity and potential for coordinated action, that I will come back to shortly. Second, the labour 'market' did not operate according to market rules. There has been no national or Union level vacancy advertising, for example, and 'promotions have been arranged administratively within institutions'. Third, in the conditions of a 'shortage economy',[73] with a lack of a need to reduce the amount of labour force, 'enterprises hoarded' workers. Fourth, the turnover of labour was considered to have a negative effect on the production process, as the training and retraining of new employees would be disruptive. Fifth, the workers' *kollektiv* (collective) was designed by the state and the trade unions in a way that tied them together by providing the workers with 'housing, sports, leisure, holidays, food supplies, child care, medical facilities, and evening classes', thus holding everyone closely tied to their place of work. And last, the high rate of full-time female participation in the labour market made the husband and wife pair into a single sociological unit of that market; thus, doubly tying the two individual workers to their place of employment on a social level as well as on the level of having a means of subsistence. Such a bond is a strong deterrent against a geographic occupational move for both.

The shortage economy produced mixed effects on labour. Full employment and the lack of economic incentives in the workplace produced 'unintended consequences' such as 'poor motivation and poor quality of work' and reduced the economic ability to generate a surplus and growth.[74] Labour shortages lead to a loosening of labour discipline, absenteeism and low productivity that, in effect, leads to disruption of productive outputs 'and supply of commodities and services falls short of demand'.[75] The vicious circle locks onto unmet demand, queues and 'storming', further dissatisfying the unenthusiastic labour force. On the other hand, large quantities of workers concentrated in big enterprises and similar jobs creates the strong sense of community mentioned above, solidarity and shared experience, and thus creates possibilities for organised action against the perceived source of frustration; this leads to labour militancy. Full employment has its aggregate macroeconomic and social benefits, for example, 'it promotes social and political stability, [low standard of living is offset by certainty], and people are occupied in useful, or at least harmless, activities', while crime rates are kept very low.[76] However, if labour, organised on the level of solidarity and shared consciousness, loses some of the aspects mitigating a low standard of living, for example, security of employment or access to basic necessities such as food, political and social stability are also lost. The social discontent of the late 1980s is a colourful testimony of this.

The most significant and effective protests in the final days of the USSR took place in the most industrialised regions of the Union and Ukraine too. Mykhnenko documents that, by the late 1980s, the Donbas miners had 'all the basic components needed for collective contentious action'.[77] Most importantly, they 'perceived state socialism – "the system" – as their collective challenge and 'recognised the existence of exploitation as their shared belief and striving for "normal life" as their common purpose'. *This slogan, the call, the desperate scream for guaranteeing an ability to live a 'normal life' would reappear again, in this and a number of altered forms throughout all the protest action of independent Ukraine; the commonality that binds the dispossessed of the country across time and territory.* The workers shared a high sense of solidarity due to the 'oppressive working condition, high levels of occupational density as well as existing Soviet rituals of celebrating "the heroes of labour"'.[78] In the summer of 1989, the first wave of strikes occurred. Inspired by a single strike event in Mezhdurechensk of Kuzbass, Russia,[79] the strike in Donbas also started with just one mine, but quickly spread to 173 out of 226 collieries and over 500,000 miners were on strike.[80] Openly elected strike and mine committees were in charge of articulating and negotiating the demands of the strike, triggered by 'frustrated expectations, arbitrariness of authorities, lawlessness and anxiety that Perestroika was passing the miners by with no improvement in living standards'.[81]

As central authorities declined and Gorbachev's reforms were perceived as delegitimised, so the civic competence of the striking miners grew and the strike committees were transformed into standing institutions.[82] Yet the failures to form links with other industries and workers have weakened the movement over time. Friedgut and Siegelbaum noted in 1990 that that, combined with the need to 'further develop [the miners'] new-found sense of civic competence, [would lead to the movement being] outmanoeuvered by the forces of rationalization, and their victory will have been short-lived'.[83] Sadly, the authors were right. The miners' attempts to cooperate with the Ukrainian intelligentsia after the 1989 strike have failed. A clear lack of mutual understanding between the two groups was facilitated by the KPSS-controlled media's divide-and-rule tactics.[84] Miners showed a desperate urge for individual empowerment, social and political autonomy as is evidenced by their calls for educational programmes, lectures to help spread 'legal, economic and political knowledge',[85] which however bore no fruit due to the broken dialogue with the intelligentsia. Frustrations about the condition of life turned rallies into politicised, not merely industrial action events that now called for the Soviet government resignation. In July 1990, for example, a one-day strike was held by some 256 enterprises in the mining, steel and transport industries.[86] Colliers were withdrawing from KPSS in unprecedented numbers and formed the Independent Trade Union. While there was strength in the movement, solidarity with other industries and workers outside the heavy production complex of Donbas was weak. Burnosov shows that the image of the miners as 'over-privileged' and 'selfish', which was manufactured by the party-controlled mass media, was deeply entrenched in the public's imagination of the region, let alone beyond it.[87] *The image will survive the test of time and will keep resurfacing in the media coverage of Donbas unrest for decades.* The irony is that the social infrastructure the collieries had was – and still is in 2017 – significantly poorer than that of large industrial plants, for example, while the social grievances they endured were the highest.[88]

The demise of the USSR effectively brought the first wave of the miners' unrest to a conclusion. Towards the end, the movement was closely cooperating with pro-independence and anti-Communist groups as they all fought against one 'evil system'. One of the core failures of the movement was that the Soviet system was made number one enemy and enterprise autonomy was made number one priority. Once the USSR fell apart, there was no Soviet government left and the enterprise autonomy calls set the scene perfectly for the accumulation and concentration of capital, with its inevitable consequence of turning the workers into the dispossessed, as the rest of the book will show.

3

Social destruction and kleptocratic construction of the early 1990s

Nation-building was interrupted both as a process of construction of a national economy and as a process of construction of a nation as an imagined community. In the absence of an all-country independent movement built around conventional institutions of nationhood, that is, language, culture, ethos, religion and so forth,[1] some began to look for 'national ideas' from the past, pre-Soviet history of Ukraine. One of the problems with such excavations is that Ukraine has been independent of the multiple empires that have scavenged its territory for centuries, but only for limited intervals of time. The national identity imagery of those periods was often defined in a reactionary manner that reflected the realities and needs of the contemporary world and anti-imperialist necessities. The imperialism that Ukraine has had to overcome with the demise of the USSR was Russian cultural imperialism that the Russian Soviet republic carried over from the Russian empire into the architecture of the USSR cultural institutions, with a less dominating yet strong hegemonic presence. The Russian and Ukrainian cultures are distinct but are very difficult – if not unnecessary – to separate on the level of everyday life.

There is a danger in looking to the past in designing imagery of the future. Together with traditions, customs and replicated social institutions, there is an import of past inequalities, divisions, individual and community trauma. These imports are sowing seeds of enmity that will sprout once conditions are right. Historical identity searches tell us who our ancestors *were* but *cannot tell us who we are*. The 'who we are' is lived, negotiated, experienced, expressed, practised, understood, subconscious, conscious; it is *present*, even though it has historical roots. The past that shapes subjectivity in the most impactful way is its immediate past; for Ukraine, that was its Soviet past – over 70 years of it. *De jure* independence forced the necessity for the newly established nation to be defined as separate from other newly formed post-Soviet nations, most importantly as an entity separate from Russia. Centuries of Russian colonial imperialism complemented by multiple decades of Russian SSR's cultural imperialism conditioned the need to explore the past in order to define the imagined community whose boundaries and authenticity of identifiers were questioned. As Wilson documents, Ukraine was faced with a task more complex than other post-Soviet states, for example, Poland or Lithuania, because as well as building a new state, a new nation had to be built.[2] Due to its diverse history and ethno-cultural composition, ethno-nationalism would inevitably cause multiple divisions and conflict.

Galicia remained pivotal in Ukrainian patriotism and 'positive nationalism' due to its territory's late adjunction to the USSR and therefore belated Russification. Military intervention and suppression of local nationalist forces would be unthinkable within the 'house of friendly peoples' at the time when Galicia was annexed for a number of reasons and thus it was impossible to root out Ukrainianism fully. The latter, however, was not shared in the same form by the rest of the Ukrainians due to differences in cultural and political history and that fact would make Ukrainianism unsuitable as a unifying national idea. On the level of social forces, Ukrainian independence 'was the joint work of two elite groups' – the cultural intelligentsia and the national communists, that is, the apparatchiks. The initial phases of the movement 'involved a groundswell from below led by the local cultural intelligentsia'. But due to the idiosyncratic nature of the Soviet-type societies and also certain weaknesses in Ukrainian society in particular,

> the cultural intelligentsia was not strong enough to achieve power and universalise the national message alone. It was therefore the 'national communists' – those members of the nomenklatura who embraced Ukrainian nationalism at a relatively late stage – who finally made the decisive contribution by providing all important state resources.[3]

Two visions of community identification dominated the discourse of the late 1980s–early 1990s: a *monist nationalism* and a *pluralist nationalism*.[4] The first was 'driven by the idea that after several centuries of stunted statehood the Ukrainian nation has had to seize the opportunity' and finally become a nation state.[5] Centuries of divisions under foreign rule instilled fear of fragility into nationalising part of the ruling bloc. This, Sakwa argues, drove the insistence:

> on creating a unitary state ... [based on a monist model] of integrated nationalism, in which the state is a nationalizing one, drawing on tradition of Ukrainism to fill the existing borders with a content sharply distinguished from Russia ... monolingual, unitary and culturally specific.[6]

The model is riddled with contradictions as, while it acknowledges Ukraine's contested history, it fails to absorb that history's consequences, that is, it is a multi-ethnic country with Russian culture and language being the first and the second native to many. The construction of a unitary, unilingual state would inevitably marginalise a large part of the population and cause enmity and alienation. While it is important to decolonise Ukrainian culture and support its development, it should not come at the expense of marginalising any other cultures. The reality of cultural decolonisation, of course, is more difficult to approach on the level of policy when issues as sensitive as language are at stake. Here the second model is much more permitting. Sakwa calls it 'the *pluralist* to denote its appeal to broad principles of national inclusiveness'.[7] This model too is based on the construction of a common Ukrainian identity of the people living in the contemporary (1991–2013) boundaries of Ukraine, but the identity is a *civic* one. The model acknowledges the variegated histories of the different territories that make up contemporary Ukraine and that their historical experience is that of fragmented statehood. This model was supported by Vyacheslav Chornovil, the leader of Narodnyy Rukh movement and then the party. During the presidential race of 1999, the neoliberalising kleptocrats of Kuchma's apparatus arranged a suspicious car accident that took Chornovil's life before he could win the presidency and put his unifying plans into practice.

In order to move into a sovereign statehood, nation-building and cultural decolonisation had to occur in Ukraine; and while ethno-cultural nationalism bore in itself the seeds of future conflict, it was made inevitable by Russia's ongoing questioning, dismissal of the cultural distinctiveness of Ukraine, dismissal and unwillingness to accept it as an equal, as a separate entity, denying its right for an independent existence, failing to accept its sovereignty and sovereign rights over its territory, culture and policy making. The latter is evidenced in the multiple geopolitical games and manipulations in Russia–Ukraine relations, the so-called 'gas wars', the Crimea intervention and annexation, the breeding of separatism in Ukraine, and beyond. It is important to mention here that Russia's manipulation toolbox is not dissimilar to that of Ukraine's Western partners as both groups pursue their economic imperialist interests; yet the latter's selection contains a few pressure devices more sophisticated than those of the Russian, for example, delays in the IMF loan tranches, which can send the whole economy into a default. And indeed, no military intervention is needed if the road to capital is open. In the early 1990s, however, there was no need to choose between East or West but rather the concern was to move away from the Soviets.

The state was being transformed, merging with the capital-in-the-making, and with it the society was transformed – torn, disrupted, dispossessed of its previous property and state protection in a fast and tremulous rupture. Towards the end of the 1980s, demonstrations, strikes and protests became common in the USSR and in the Soviet Ukraine as well. The miners of the industrial east led the way for the growing popular unrest. Just as in the case with the miners,[8] where opposition to the civil restrictions and socio-economic problems mutated into protest against 'the system', the KPSS, the nomenklatura, the general tendency of protest went from calls to change the inefficient system to dismantling the USSR together via autonomy to local authorities and enterprises and independence to individual republics. Only the leap was too wide and went too far, mainly because it was not thought through sufficiently and lacked a solid ideological foundation. The changes in autonomy and essentially the self-governance of enterprise that workers demanded for their plants, factories and collieries could only benefit workers in cases where they would obtain and/or retain democratic control over those enterprises. The changes that would come with the dissolution of the Soviet state apparatus did not include such options. What followed was privatisation reforms in a poorly designed and sporadically executed manner, with ensuing primitive accumulation of capital and enterprises and their further concentration in the hands of a few – not the workers' collectives. The state would now become the guarantor of the interests of growing predatory capital, not the society overall, nor its labour. Instead,

> through emancipation of private property from the community, the state ... [becomes] an entity, beside and outside civil society; but it

is nothing more than the form of organisation that the bourgeois necessarily adopt both for internal and external purposes, for the mutual guarantee of their property and interests ... The state mediates in formation of all common institutions and the institutions receive a political form.[9]

In this somewhat reductionist view, Marx and Engels assign the state an instrumental role, portraying it as a tool manipulated by the bourgeoisie for their self-interest. That of course happens in concrete historical instances, however, the reality is more complex. Elsewhere in Marxist writing we see that the state is a terrain of struggle, the form of the state is the institutional mirror of the condition of that struggle; an evidence of expression and curtailment of the agencies of classes and their fractions that comprise the state in combinations of empowerment and disempowerment. There is no homogeneity of the state or the ruling and capitalist classes and fractions that supposedly manoeuvre the state; but there is a consensual, imposed, or a combined direction that the state takes. Labour too has agency in the process of state formation and functioning. The reality that Ukraine was entering was that of the increasingly transnationalising world economy, where state–capital relations were transcending the conventional boundaries of IR definitions of statehood or economy; national economies were becoming history, leaving an important function to the global labour while steadily shrinking its space-agency. Ukraine's nascent capital was also faced with a competition of proportions that it could not withstand. Yet it was luckier than the country's labour as the historic accident that positioned Ukraine as a geopolitical hinterland played to the budding oligarchs' advantage. They could grow strong while Russia was on its knees and its transnational contenders were occupied with absorbing the CEECs. In the (trans)formation of the Ukraine's state, this new, domestic capital with big ambitions played a key, intimate role, not unfamiliar to state–capital relations of the neoliberal era yet with its own idiosyncrasies. The neoliberal antecedents of that relationship were already spotted by Nikos Poulantzas in 1970s, who correctly noted that at the state–capital juncture the:

internationalization of capital neither [suppressed], nor [by-passed] the nation states... [I]nternationalization ... deeply affects the politics and institutional forms of [all] states by including them in a system of interconnections which is in no way confined to the play of external and mutual pressures between juxtaposed states and capitals.[10]

Similar to Gramsci's ideas of co-optation and passive revolution in the target locales of capital on its mission to expand globally, Poulantzas observed how '[peripheral] *states themselves take charge of the interest of the dominant imperialist capital in its development within the 'national' social formation,* i.e. in its complex relation of internalization to the domestic bourgeoisie that it dominates.'[11] And so the Ukrainian emerging state–capital nexus took on the task of neoliberalising the country's economy, transforming it and effectively rewriting the rules of social relations in a perverse image of a Thatcherite dystopia, a regime of neoliberal kleptocracy.

The form of a national capitalist state – and the form of a specific constellation of a state–society–capital complex – is a determining factor in 'the form in which the inherent contradictions of capital accumulation confront the state.'[12] Thus, the tensions between capital and labour can also be resolved, if temporarily, on a domestic level if there is an outward space – physical or virtual – into which capital can continue expanding, that is, having ongoing access to markets in new places and new products. All expansion has its limit and once that limit is reached, 'the barriers to accumulation reassert themselves and the contradiction comes to the surface.'[13] Global over-accumulation of capital, Clarke argues, presents itself to the state 'in the form of the barriers to the sustained accumulation of domestic productive capital'. And while the state:

cannot resolve contradictions inherent in capital accumulation, it can contain the political impact of those contradictions to the extent that it is able to secure the integration of the accumulation of domestic productive capital into the accumulation of capital on a world scale.[14]

That is the case if the state acts as a guarantor of domestic capital's interests on the world market. The state's ability to achieve the above domestically is:

partly set by the particular conditions of domestic accumulation and by the national form of the state, but are more fundamentally defined by the form of the international state system and the dynamics of global accumulation of which it is a part.[15]

One also needs to add to the state's ability, that is, agency exercise space, state's willingness and institutional potency that comes from the coherence of the ruling bloc and its possession of an effective, ideally hegemonic concept of control that has to align the interests of the given state–society–capital complex with the global comprehensive concept of control enshrined in the frameworks of the global policy platforms, that is, WEF, WBCSD, Trilateral Commission, ICC, and the Bilderberg group, and IFIs, that is, World Bank, IMF and EBRD. This is particularly important in the case of (semi)peripheral/post-Soviet states, where IFIs directly shape policy making on national and often even on local levels. In that vein, the transnationalisation of the Ukrainian state was and is determined by the inherent contradictions of the domestic capital accumulation process that relies on semi-licit mechanisms and neoliberal marketisation policy prescriptions from the IMF, World Bank and EBRD. Such a combination of options in a limited agency-space means limited choices for both states and their national capital within the global framework that favours large transnational capital of Western origin.[16]

With the default independence, a new modus operandi for the economy and society had to be manufactured, set in motion too, a capitalist mode – manufactured in a society where private property was practically non-existent. The main characteristic features of a capitalist economy are the presence of a market that serves as the main mediator of relations of economic exchange in a society built of classes of private owners of the means of production and the proletariat, that is, the army of (potential) workers who have to sell their labour force to the owners of the means of production in exchange for the means of survival, that is, wages. It is precisely this unevenness in terms of ownership and control over the means of production of goods and services that separates classes from one another and puts them into an endemically antagonistic position of class war dictated by their contradicting interests in that relationship. Thus, the owners will want to extract as much value out of workers as possible, while the workers aim to earn a higher wage and effectively have a higher share of the final surplus value generated in the process of production. This antagonism underlies what is known as the 'class war' and is typically mediated by the institution of the state via formalised rules, that is, laws, negotiated by and through trade unions, CSOs, lobbies and other forms of civil society organisations. The USSR, however, was a particular type of state, where organised civil society groups have not enjoyed the autonomy necessary for effective bargaining but instead were controlled by the state, as I discussed in Chapter 2. The means of production and all existing material and immaterial assets were state property or public via the state, not private property and that slowly began to change with the Perestroika reforms. The first waves of marketisation after 1991 thus were introducing a whole new system of social relations, that is, capitalist, with a whole new set of institutions that were previously missing in the post-Soviet societies to be operated by previously non-existent classes of people whose whole social positioning was transforming. Gil Eyal, Iván Szelényi and Eleanor Townsley described this as the 'capitalism without capitalists' approach or 'a distinctive new strategy of transition adopted by technocratic-intellectual elites in societies where no class of private owners existed prior to the introduction of market mechanisms.'[17] However, those particular forms of capitalism, they continue, do not exist *without a bourgeoisie*. On the contrary, there are two main *bourgeoisies* – that representing the possessors of the material property, and that consisting of possessors of culture or knowledge' – or possessors of property [and – potentially – the means of production – *author*] and the determiners of forms and directions of social reproduction. In such societies, they argue, 'post-communist capitalism is being promoted by a broadly defined intelligentsia which is committed to the cause of bourgeois society and capitalist economic institutions.'[18]

This, however, is not fully accurate. First of all, the split into two types of bourgeoisies is meaningful only on the level of abstraction as ontologically speaking one subject can easily be a property owner and a 'possessor of culture or knowledge' at the same time; neither does it mean that the combination rule applies to each subject. Next, markets – especially market/capitalist economies – do not emerge overnight. Similarly, the mere proclamation of market reform does not mean the *de facto* emergence of a market economy with functioning market institutions on all societal levels with necessary law obedience and mechanisms of law enforcement. It is through the evolution of social institutions that underpin capitalist ideology and through the emergence of substantial subjectivity supporting that ideology (i.e. emergence of a capitalist bloc) that market economies evolve and stay in place, that is, market economies operate effectively in societies where market ideology becomes hegemonic. A sizeable number of capitalists existed long before the demise of the USSR, even if in the shadow economy, which in essence denies the 'capitalism without capitalists' formulation, especially its 'possessor of culture or knowledge' or 'owners of property' component –

the disenfranchised were a party highly interested in marketisation too, even if they were not in the driving seat of the reforms that would steer in that direction. Through the Soviet times, especially Perestroika and then the 1990s, a capitalist class and bloc alike were formed that have eventually begun to channel their interests through political parties and/ or direct individual participation in the policy-making process.

DEFUNCT TRANSITION MODELLING

'The end of history' proclaimed by Francis Fukuyama[19] became the cornerstone upon which the myth of transition was being constructed. The belief in neoliberal market reform as the only path for a societal transformation for the post-USSR states, and the post-communist states generally, professed by neoclassical economists such as Jeffrey Sachs and political/economic scientists such as Fukuyama crystallised in a strategic orientation, or a concept of control, crystallised in the IMF and World Bank policies towards the newly independent states. Thus, the former World Bank economist William Easterly – who admits that he himself used to believe in the 'shock therapy and structural adjustment' – in *The White Man's Burden* rightly concludes that one 'can't plan a market' even by international institutions. He admits that the above 'planning' was in fact 'planned' with the best intentions in mind and that it has spectacularly failed.

> Markets everywhere emerge in an unplanned, spontaneous way, adapting to local traditions and circumstances, and not through reforms designed by outsiders. The free market depends on the bottom down emergence of complex institutions and social norms that are difficult for outsiders to understand, much less change. Paradoxically, the West tried to *plan* how to achieve a *market*. Even after evidence accumulated that these outsider-imposed free markets were not working.[20]

Easterly, however, like many other critics of the prescriptive nature of 'market planning' fails to mention that *the very assumption* that there must be a free market *is planning* in itself; that 'free market' is a teleological fixation that in reality is as unattainable as it is undesirable due to its socio-economically destabilising nature. Easterly explains that the 'shock therapy' approach was the materialisation of the IMF strategy called the 'structural adjustment', which came into being in 1979.[21] The latter was the 'brainchild of the World Bank president Robert McNamara and his deputy, Ernst Stern, who sketched out the idea on a flight the two took together to the World Bank/IMF Annual Meeting in Belgrade.'[22] Based on data collected by the IMF and the World Bank on 22 'transition' and 'developing' economies, Easterly shows that the belief that 'partial reform would not work unless all of the complementary reforms happened quickly and simultaneously' shattered in the process of policy implementation in the target countries.[23] This partly happened, he continues, because of what is called in economics, that 'the "unintended consequences" problem is greater with large-scale reform than with a smaller one'. So, out of the above-mentioned 22 economies, Ukraine having received ten IMF and World Bank adjustment loans, had the worst annual per capita growth rate from the date of the first loan 1993 to 1999 which equalled –8.4 per cent and the highest annual inflation rate from the first loan to 1999.[24] Unfortunately, despite both theoreticians', and practitioners' warnings about both the potential and actual repercussions embedded in the structural adjustment programmes, they are still in place and continue to shape policy making in Ukraine and elsewhere.

The institutional disciplining of transition economies is performed by organisations beyond the IFIs – some of those are custom-made. Thus, in April 1991, the European Bank for Reconstruction and Development (EBRD) was founded to aid the 'transition' in the post-Soviet space under the auspices of the EU. It was the materialisation of:

> an idea put forward by President François Mitterrand of France at the European Parliament in Strasbourg on October 25, 1989, came to fruition on May 29, 1990 with the signature of its agreement by 40 countries, the Commission of the European Communities and the European Investment Bank.[25]

In the view of the founders of the Bank, 'the sudden and total collapse of the Soviet Union [was a signalling] of the urgency to provide support to a region emerging from decades of political and economic dictatorship',[26] that was now ironically being planned to be replaced with a dictatorship of a different, capitalist kind. Neoliberal marketisation as an economic strategy was chosen from the outset too, as 'it became clear [to the founders of the Bank] that boosting the role of the private sector as the linchpin for free and open market economies was crucial in the democratic transition process.'[27] Being the only 'transition bank' in the world, the work of the institution began with 'establishing contacts with all interested parties, conducting preparatory missions to central and eastern Europe agreeing on procedures, and forging a strategy for the institution.'[28] A distinguishing feature of the EBRD as an international financial institution is that: '[it fosters] transition through project financing, primarily in the private sector' and focuses on 'building the institutions necessary for underpinning the market economy, and demonstrating and promoting market-oriented skills and sound business practices.'[29] In Gramsci's language, their main goal is to be an active facilitator of formation as well as of co-optation of the nascent capitalist and ruling classes and their fractions into the neoliberal market ideology, thus perpetuating the hegemony of transnational(-ising) capitalism and its empire.

Soon after its foundation, the EBRD launched an initiative aimed at finding theoretical and empirical solutions for the newly independent states in the form of a journal – *The Economics of Transition*. Planned as a subject platform, the journal was complemented by a more technical but no less prescribing Working Paper series. On the theoretical and policy-design level, one demonstrative exemplar of the economic prescription, based on what I argue is a reductionist and decontextualised analysis, is a publication by Rumen Dobrinsky of the United Nations Economic Commission for Europe, 'Capital Accumulation during the Transition from Plan to Market'.[30] In the article, he analyses the 'aggregate investment behaviour' in *all* transition economies of the Central Eastern European Countries and the CIS between 1995 and 2004, primarily focusing on 'the main determinants of business fixed investment in a transitional environment'. The speculative level of the arguments derived from the so-called 'scientific' economic models is as grandiose as their arguments are phantasmagorical. Dobrinsky, as many others whose example he follows, adopts microeconomic models upon the assumption that they 'describe the behaviour of representative firms in an economy' and that 'they also [can be and are] applied to the modelling of aggregate business environment at macro level'.[31] The above is materialised in an extensive analysis of the 'aggregate data' according to a neoclassical investment model 'derived from an *optimisation of the desired level of capital* over time by a firm that *faces no adjustment costs in a perfect market environment*'.[32] Such conditions, needless to say, do not exist, as the paper itself recognises. Yet, it is precisely this sort of 'research' that lies at the foundation of most transition modelling and that is the basis upon which most transition targets are set. Failure to meet those unrealistic targets then serves as a reason for the economically punitive actions of the policy prescribers towards the prescribed. In fact, the *Economics of Transition* is a publication full of similar contributions – both by academics and practitioners, such as Dobrinsky.[33] The application of those theories, let alone their materialisation, is problematic. However, those are the exact models that can be found in policy advice papers and action plans for reform sent in abundance to the 'transition economies' as benchmarks for economic reform and performance in general. Thus, Vedat Milor identifies two 'unmistakable elements' required by 'the reform package offered to Eastern European reformers'. Those two are 'coherence and optimal pace'.[34] Both elements can be clearly seen (among others) in the policy analysis first published in 1991 by The World Institute for Development Economic Research (WIDER) of the United Nations University in Finland. Authored by neoclassical economists – Olivier Blanchard, Rudiger Dornbusch, Paul Krugman, Richard Layard and Lawrence Summers – the book-report under the title *Reform in Eastern Europe* is a text strongly advocating the shock therapy approach to economic recovery in the region.

The initial enthusiasm of shock therapy advocates, however, was very quickly cooled by the aggravating economic conditions in the target economies.[35] Nevertheless, the latter were prescribed more reforms to fix the growing problems and now included comprehensive institutional restructuring in the true spirit of the Washington Consensus. In one such attempt to tackle the above-mentioned problems, Paul D'Anieri, Robert Kravchuk and Taras Kuzio argue against 'transitology' as an approach and the abundant 'transitology' literature of the 1990s, stating that it is problematic in three major areas.

> First, [it was assumed] that transition in the former USSR is identical to that of Central and Eastern Europe (and, by implication, the earlier transitions in Southern Europe and Latin America). Second, therefore as mirrors of the previous transitions, post-Soviet countries face only two transitions: one, from totalitarianism to democracy; and two, from a command-administrative to market economy. Finally, ... the former USSR did not differ to any great degree politically from its outer empire.[36]

The correction of the above 'two transitions' approach was seen to be made through adding more dimensions to the 'transition' process and making it 'triple' or even 'quadruple'.[37] Robert Bideleux and Ian Jeffries documented the need for the former in *A History of Eastern Europe: Crisis and Change*, where they carried out an extensive historical study of the whole geographical region and the tasks the latter had to accomplish in the process of 'transition' since 1989.[38] That task was the 'triple transition' and included transitions: 'from communist dictatorship to pluralistic democracy; from centrally administered to market economies; and from Soviet imperial hegemony to fully independent nation-statehood.'[39] They see the three processes to be achieved through 'liberal democratic and constitutional' standardisation.[40] As well as being achieved through the establishment of not only 'formal political and economic institutions [but also] … [sizeable, healthy and vital intermediary] layers, networks and associations, which stand and mediate between the state and individuals.'[41] All in all, the authors are concerned with the 'transition to market' and the difficulties of its implementation across Eastern Europe, rather than its usefulness or nature. They do turn to 'problems of transition' and evaluate the dangers and benefits of the 'big bang/shock therapy', 'gradualism' and 'circumvention and pragmatism', however, they do this merely to identify the potential pitfalls of the process and warn against the latter leading to a 'disillusionment with democracy and the market system'.[42] Thus, the whole intellectual exercise is essentially rooted in the advocacy of the 'return to Europe' through the marketisation move for the Central and Eastern European countries. Taras Kuzio goes further and advocates a quadruple transition that implies all of the elements of the triple transition, however treats the 'nation' and the 'state' as separate analytical categories thus even further reifies dichotomies and compartmentalises social reality.[43] The above approaches, therefore, echo the transitology of the early 1990s, where 'what is to be done' is the main analytical concern and which involves a complex restructuring of both the economic system and the governing institutions.

The call for restructuring in a fashion of the Washington Consensus resonated in academic discussions of the 1990s. For example, in a collection of essays edited by Mario Blejer and Marko Škreb, the authors present post-Soviet transformation as a 'transition from socialism', that is, a process 'centred around fundamental economic changes, transition is a multifaceted phenomenon that encompasses complex structural, institutional, and behavioural adjustments that go well beyond the realm of economics.'[44] Further, they applaud the commitment of the EBRD to assist the Central and Eastern European countries in that 'multifaceted' transition and they call for, and attempt in their volume to provide, a deep analysis of the conjuncture of the transition countries. On the one hand, their understanding of 'transition' may seem to address a broader set of issues and to be better suited as a recipe for the successful implementation of 'transition' policies. However, what is essentially implied by the process that Blejer and Škreb refer to as 'nation-building' is a fundamental ideological and institutional transformation of Ukraine's society into one that accepts a neoliberal market economy as a mode of production and social reproduction. The 'deep study' advocated by the contributors to the volume, however, is not aimed at understanding the needs of the studied societies. Instead, the aim behind it is to design the best fitted scenarios for the implementation of the transition medicine that is already prepared and is waiting to be administered. They go as far as to claim that 'because economists are dealing with a set of atypical problems does not mean that predictions and inferences cannot be made or that traditional analytical tools are not useful.'[45] However, macroeconomic stabilisation as a doctrine is based on a principle of making 'transition' palatable, not seeking a policy reform complex that a given society wants or needs. In other words, what is prescribed is a countrywide *trasformismo* and a *passive revolution.*[46] On a more practical note, the above-mentioned prescriptions and Western assistance through the International Financial Institutions (IMF, World Bank and EBRD), structural adjustment programmes (SAPs)/SALs, and an array of additional programmes such as USAID and TACIS, for example, that depend upon meeting the targets of 'marketisation', 'reform implementation' and 'democracy building' generally speaking, do not result into materialisation of those goals but rather breed a system of what Andrew Wilson describes as 'virtual politics'.[47] Thus, they contribute to what I call 'the myth of democracy' in Ukraine. The latter primarily involves imitations of reform implementation rather than their actualisation and serves as a façade to disguise omnipresent corruption and state asset embezzlement through continuous transnationalisation of Ukraine's state.[48]

THE QUESTION OF CLASS

Prescribed changes were at first implemented in their adaptations by the usual suspects of the late Soviet politics, as the *de jure* independence of 1991 did not bring significant changes to the composition of the country's ruling bloc. The former Secretary of the Communist Party of Ukrainian Soviet Republic, Leonid Kravchuk, now became the newly elected president upon which he 'simply re-appointed all heads of all of the Oblradas as representatives of the president of Ukraine in the regions without any system changes'.[49] Most of those neo-nomenklatura 'representatives' were from Dnipropetrovsk, a region of high economic significance and with strong political representation. The ascent of the Dnipropetrovsk bloc to national and all-Union level echelons of power began long before Ukraine's independence. In a selection of 54 biographies, presented in a study by Kononchuk and Pikhovshek, 'the skeleton of the ruling elite of Ukraine' or the decision-making core of the country as of 1996 is represented.[50] David Lane's research on the Soviet 'elites' also confirms both the significance of the Ukrainian nomenklatura role in the Soviet ruling apparatus and the Dnipropetrovsk cohort dominance in that group.[51] Thus, in 1990, a commission specially designated by Gorbachev in the Organisational Department of the Central Committee of KPSS conducted an investigation, which showed that 53 per cent of Ukrainian Communist Party executive cadre come from Dnipropetrovsk.[52] In fact, even before that, the Ukrainian Party 'elite' led the KPSS in Moscow twice, as well as dominated the Party structure within the Moscow metropolitan area, and ran the Party in Kazakhstan and Moldova. In addition, due to the high industrial and economic importance of the regions, party leaders from Donetsk, Dnipropetrovsk and Kharkiv had significant leverage in the decision-making processes of the USSR and in the Ukrainian SSR in particular.[53]

In 1991, Kravchuk followed the long-established tradition of the CPU and surrounded himself with people he could trust,[54] or the neo-nomenklatura. Kravchuk's Prime Minister, Leonid Kuchma was part of the Dnipropetrovsk fraction of the ruling bloc and gathered his own circle of 'his people' in the Cabinet who, due to Kuchma's long and successful career in the Soviet technology manufacturing sector, most recently in Dnipropetrovsk, were linked to industry as well. Kuchma's government was the first of the independent Ukraine and the first example of the ascendant capitalist and ruling-class fractions' attempt at institutionalisation of a class compromise. It included industrial directorates, regional 'elites', and the parliamentary democratic opposition coalition, Narodna Rada (*Eng.* 'People's Council'). Thus, representatives of the Donbas industry were part of Kuchma's Cabinet already and held positions strategic for their industries, that is, the Minister for Industry Holubchenko (Donetsk), the Minister for Energy and Fuel Complex Yoffe (Luhansk) and the Vice-Prime Minister for Industry and Construction Yevtukhov (Dnipropetrovsk). It is not until the mid- to late 1990s that Donetsk forces would begin to gradually take the lead in the ruling bloc of the country. Yoffe and Yevtukhov joined the Party of Regions in 2006, that was one of the many indicators of the centripetal dynamics within the ruling bloc of the county that will be addressed later.

Donetsk oblast and its representatives enjoyed both economic and political power during the USSR years due to 'the geographical concentration of the coal' and metallurgy industries in the area.[55] The economic importance of the oblast has helped its labour movement become historically strong as a class-for-itself. Such contingency has been systematically used by the local neo-nomenklatura, red directors, and, later, by oligarchs, as leverage in power bargaining with the ruling bloc in Kyiv, among other things – as I have already shown in Chapter 2. The labour intensive production of Donetsk oblast 'produced a powerful worker movement that since the 1970s was opposed equally to both Moscow, and Kyiv' – and any authority for that matter. That became manifest in the miners' unrest of 1989 where 'strikes were organised by ad hoc strike committees'.[56] The overall dissatisfaction with the authorities, the poor conditions of labour, low wages and the like undermined both their respect for and their willingness to cooperate with authorities; a general feeling of mistrust has taken over the mining community and the region as a whole. In the early 1990s, neo-nomenklatura from Donetsk,

> attempted to gain political autonomy for the region from Kyiv. Political mobilization remained high in the region owing to hyperinflation, the scarcity of goods and energy supplies and the proximity of the oblast to Russia where living standards were higher.[57]

Such a contingency resulted in a series of protests in 1993 that, according to Kovaleva,[58] were used by the neo-nomenklatura to demand autonomy for Donbas within an independent Ukraine. However, she continues, it was rather a bargaining manoeuvre used to gain expansion of political and economic power, space for exercise of agency of the nascent Donetsk capital and ruling forces, that is, neo-nomenklatura and red directors. The unrest produced a serious impact and contributed to both parliamentary and presidential elections being rescheduled to take place in 1994. Moreover, at this juncture the institutionalisation of Donetsk forces as the main fraction of the ruling bloc began with 'a "Donbas" government formation in Kyiv with Yukhym Zvyahilskyy, a red director, appointment as an acting prime minister from the position of director of Zasyadko coal mine'[59] on 22 September 1993. The latter was made possible because 'the Donetsk elite painted the unrest not as separatism, but as resistance to the early economic reforms of then-prime minister Kuchma.'[60] Thus, 'a Donbas government' of Zvyahilskyy was a trade-off where the separatist ambitions were dropped and 'Donetsk elites were allowed to continue dealing directly with Russia and to continue reaping benefits' from the delayed coal sector reforms.[61] This form of manipulation of labour's unrest by the 'masters of Donbas' would become systematic and eventually took on the ugly form of dehumanisation that made armed conflict possible.

The dispossessed labour was both a tool in political games and a convenient force in the accumulation games that often cost labour its members' lives.

PRIMITIVE ACCUMULATION, THE PRIMITIVE WAY

Many young people, who lacked alternatives in the early 1990s, joined gangs and were used as pawns in the process of accumulation by criminals, that I will detail shortly. Pyymachuk, the Head of Slovyansk (Donetsk) Militias testifies that by the mid-1990s,

> people disappeared by the dozen ... often in the process of the so-called 'cleansings' when [a group of youths were sent to murder someone and then all traces had to be removed]. ... Relatives would usually ask no questions ... and perhaps receive compensation.[62]

In times of overall corruption, unlawfulness and general state failure, many turned to 'barbaric' (as some later called them) means of an extra-economic nature to provide for themselves and later to expand their economic agency, that is, racketeering, blackmail, threats and even murder.[63] Those people later became known as 'clans'. They were, and still are, present throughout Ukraine, although those that are of foremost analytical interest due to their ruling position throughout Ukraine's post-Soviet history were formed in the industrial east of the country, mainly in Donetsk and Dnipropetrovsk oblasts. The richness of Donbas in resources, its abundant productive base, high unemployment and lawlessness in the early 1990s conditioned that development. There was also one more factor – the presence of a high number of 'redundant people', disenfranchised groups that were not uncommon in the rest of the country, nor were they of the highest rate in a cross-regional comparison, yet the high population density meant that there were high overall numbers of the redundant people ready to be utilised by the equally abundant aspiring capitalists and their cronies in the security forces. Anomie levels were growing across the country and some of its records were becoming a part of everyday negative stereotypes by cultural xenophobia that are typical for any society undergoing a period of economic hardship and fundamental transformation of its base institutions. A study by Mykola Riabchuk, for example, described Donbas as the area with the 'highest rates of crimes, drug addiction, alcoholism, abortions, divorces, and sexually transmitted diseases',[64] contrary to available statistics and also managed to link that 'record' to the Russian and Soviet legacy in the region.[65] Similarly, anti-Western authors drew caricatures of the Western Ukraine dwellers, customs and mores.[66] So, Ignatieff – a descendant of the Eastern Ukrainians critical of pro-independence nationalists saw them as those associated with 'images of peasant embroidered shirts, the nasal whine of ethnic instruments, phoney Cossacks in cloaks and boots, nasty anti-Semites'.[67] These negative stereotypes have been evolving for decades and turned into the archetypes of 'Othering' that would eventually make the armed conflict between the manufactured east and west possible.

During the 1980s–1990s, Ukraine's economy was becoming increasingly criminalised. In their study of the criminogenic situation in Ukraine and its change since 1977 (before that the crime levels throughout the USSR were unnaturally low), Peter Solomon and Todd Foglesong state[68] that 'between 1988 and 1997, Ukraine experienced a dramatic, two-and-a-half-fold surge in its overall rate of recorded crime'.[69] Inter-estingly, the change in this dynamic did not emanate in 'violent crimes (which experienced a small rise) but in property crimes (theft, robbery, swindling, and extortion) and in economic crimes (bribe taking, counter-feiting, and trading in narcotics)'.[70] This tendency was most pronounced among the socially excluded, as I mentioned earlier, and the youth who were hit hardest by the growing shortages, unemployment and general economic decline. Kudryachenko (Кудряченко) *et al.* document that between 1985 and 1988 the adolescent alcohol consumption rate grew by a third, the drug use and solvent abuse rate increased fivefold and that youths were responsible for 52.6 per cent of all documented crime in the country.[71]

In the 1990s, according to Serhiy Pryymachuk,[72] the process of centralisation of gangs commenced in Donbas. The records of oblast militia show 55 ordered murders in Donetsk in 1991 alone. The situation became even worse in 1992 with an average of five–six ordered killings in Donetsk per week. By comparison, in the western oblasts of Ukraine, the number was four–five ordered killings per year. Many petty criminals, butchers and professional gamblers joined mafia groups. The most brutal gang in Donetsk oblast was an ethnically Tartar organisation led by Alec the Greek, or Akhat Bragin, and his right-hand man, Rinat Akhmetov. Gang members did not shy away from murders that gave the gang a 'comparative advantage' in the process of accumulation by crime that eventually helped Akhmetov and Kolesnikov become the richest people in the post-Soviet space. By the late 1990s, those 'clans' or ascendant capital fractions concentrated their assets in FIGs – although some still rely on crime as a 'convincing' technique in that capital concentration process, as I will show in later chapters. In Table 3.1, I present the most notorious murder cases associated with capital accumulation in Donetsk oblast in the 1990s. Since 1995, a clear tendency towards centralisation is reflected in the high-profile murders and the consequential acquisition of the deceased person's capital assets by people associated with other gangs. This tendency contrasts with the dozens of murders of nameless cooperative owners and gangsters in the early 1990s.

Multiple journalistic investigations and conspiracy theories point to certain present-day oligarchs as culprits of the assassinations of the 1990s. It is beyond the scope of this book to investigate those murder cases. What I present here is the data on corporate ownership and the transfer of ownership rights previously held by the murdered entrepreneurs. It is safe to conclude that after the assassination of Akhat Bragin in 1996, the largest capital assets in Donetsk oblast were consolidated into business structures previously run by the deceased and now owned by his right-hand man Rinat Akhmetov and less so by Borys Kolesnikov. Around the same time, the two began cooperation with Viktor Yanukovych, who, by 1996, was the Governor of Donetsk oblast and soon after would become president of the country.

Table 3.1 Murder cases associated with economic activity in Donetsk in the 1990s

Name(s)	Business/ company name	Date of death	Beneficiary/-ies of business/current owners
55 ordered murders, names NA	NA, illicit	1 January–31 December 1991	NA
Yanosh Kranz	NA, illicit	10 November 1992, gang crossfire	NA
5–6 per week, NA	NA	1 January–31 December 1992	NA
Alec the Greek or Akhat Bragin	Lyuks	15 October 1995, VIP box explosion at a football match	Akhmetov with Vasylyev and Voloshchuk
Oleksandr Momot	Danko	16 May 1996, shot	Akhmetov (Danko is now part of SCM)
Oleksandr Shvedchenko	Itera	March 1996, shot	Kolesnikov (Roman's ex-partner; Akhmetov's right-hand man, now Minister for Economic Development of Ukraine; oligarch)
Serhiy Roman	Skandin-Yuh	Spring 1996, shot	See above
Yevhen Shcherban	DTEK, Aton	November 1996, shot at Donetsk airport	Akhmetov (now part of SCM)
Yuriy Pavlenko	Sarmat brewery	1998, tortured to death	Akhmetov
Volodymyr Hutsul	Budtekhnika Electronics retailer chain	1998, shot	Akhmetov
Vadym Hetman	Head of Ukrainian Interbank Currency Exchange	22 April 1998, shot	NA; since 2007, post held by Perezerzev; Donetsk bloc; 1995–2007 worked in SCM structures

Source: compiled by the author from data available in Vladimir Aryev, see Владимир Арьев, Донецкая мафия: Перезагрузка. Documentary/journalistic investigation (2007), Alexander Boyko, see Александр Бойко, Криминальная оккупация: История Партии Регионов (2007), Penchuk and Kyzin, see Борис Пенчук and Кузин Сергей, *Донецкая мафия*. Фонд 'Антикоррупция' (2006) and Elena Kovaleva, 'Regional Politics in Ukraine's Transition: The Donetsk Elite', in Adam Swain (ed.), *Re-Constructing the Post-Soviet Industrial Region: The Donbas in Transition* (London: Routledge, 2007).

During Soviet times, convicts from all over the USSR were sent to the areas of intensive industrialisation, where prisons were set up for the specific purpose of utilising convict labour in the production process. Ukraine was no exception; and neither was Donbas or any other industrial region. Out of 183 such institutions of the State Penitentiary Service in 25 oblasts of Ukraine, 19 are in Donetsk and 14 in Dnipropetrovsk oblasts with the imprisonment rate in Donetsk being an average of three–five times higher than elsewhere in Ukraine (e.g. out of 1,016 charges and 818 convictions, 244 and 195 respectively in the summer of 2010 were in Donetsk oblast).[73] This created a set of special circumstances that explain why, given the wealth of resources, crime could become such an important component of the accumulation process in Donbas and especially Donetsk. That alone, however, does not indicate that the region's population is inherently prone to crime or uncivilised.

The high crime rates signal the deep socio-economic problems that the state and local municipal government have systematically failed to resolve, not of the innate criminal nature of the region's dwellers. The vilification, criminalisation and victimisation of the economically deprived is nothing new in neoliberal discourse. What is particular about this in the context of manufacturing of the East–West divide, is the simultaneous treatment of the region's labour in general as social rejects, that is, 'alcoholics, drug addicts, criminals, layabouts', while the striking workers – and by extension all labour in the east – are depicted as greedy, overpaid and whiny. It is unclear how one can belong to both groups at the same time, to be both unemployed, drunk and overpaid, that is, employed; yet again, neoliberal victimisation and criminalisation narrative knows no logic in its compartmentalisation quest.

BUDDING REGIONAL POWER BLOCS

The Donetsk and Dnipropetrovsk blocs were taking a distinct shape, evidencing a lock with industry that would grow stronger over the years; the first one still weaker than the second but very ambitious. The 'Donbas government' that was established as a compromise with the Dnipropetrovsk bloc in Kyiv was not elected but appointed and had little chance to endure after the rescheduled elections. Such a contingency conditioned the forging of a ruling-capitalist class fraction compromised between the ascendant rival forces from Donetsk and the ruling fraction of Dnipropetrovsk neo-nomenklatura in Kyiv. Thus, Donetsk industry decided to support Kuchma's candidacy for president and also to guarantee their representation in the parliament as a force-for-itself. For that purpose, on 4 December 1993 (officially registered at the end of 1995), the Mizhrehionalnyy Blok Reform (Inter-Regional Bloc for Reforms) political party was formed. In that same year, Kuchma was elected as the President of the Ukrainian Union of Industrialist and Entrepreneurs (URPP), that was a clear indicator of his political leadership being chosen by the country's emerging capital. In an interview with his biographer, Kuchma himself claimed that the presidency was a move desired by the large industry owners and directors:

A few days after the [parliamentary – *author*] elections a whole delegation visited me in Dnipropetrovsk ... They were directors of the largest enterprises of Dnipropetrovsk, Kharkiv, Donetsk, my friends from Yuzhmash. The team was led by the Director General of Motor-Sich V. Bohuslayev. The conversation was turned to business straight away. '[The election result is good but could be better]. We mean "larger". We are confident that you shall ballot for presidency'. 'What?'. 'Presidency. Kravchuk does not have any real opponents ... We need a president capable of saving the industry. Once we save industry – we save the country' [...] At the end the decision was taken, not even mine, but rather collective. Decision to ballot for presidency represent and protect large industrial manufacturing and – in that sense – interests of the country.[74]

Such strong backing of the country's industry – and thus of the industrial, densely populated regions in the east and south of Ukraine – helped Kuchma win the 1994 Presidential election. Immediately upon assuming office, he began to forge the ruling bloc by appointing even more 'reliable' people from Dnipropetrovsk in his administration and Cabinet of Ministers.[75] According to the findings of Kononchuk and Pikhovshek, by the end of 1996, the overall number of Dnipropetrovsk representatives in

Kyiv's structures of power and other 'groups of influence' (executive, legislative, judiciary authorities, political parties, army, banks, church, mass media, youth, women, civil rights and veterans protection organisations, trade unions, state and privately owned business,

non-profit scientific and research institutes and foundations)
comprised 206 persons.[76]

The authors claim that the access to power by many who did not belong
to 'Dnipropetrovsk Family' was rather due to Kuchma's need to 'dilute
Dnipropetrovsk monopoly' on power).[77] In addition to the Donetsk
forces insertion into the ruling bloc of the country, the Dnipropetrovsk family itself was not a homogeneous force and, as Kononchuk and
Pikhovshek document, by the mid-1990s, there were two 'Dnipropetrovsk teams' and only one of them was supported by Kuchma's leadership.[78]
I hold that such correctly observed fractioning of Dnipropetrovsk ruling
bloc is better understood once the relations of Kuchma and Lazarenko
are positioned within the contemporary relations of production and
accumulation. By the mid-1990s, Kuchma represented Dnipropetrovsk's
ruling-class fraction that was in a class fraction compromising Donetsk
neo-nomenklatura and red directors. Lazarenko, and his partner
Tymoshenko, on the other hand, were in a position of rivalry over the
gas supply market in Donetsk with the forces allied with Kuchma, that is,
Gazprom related Itera and ISD, a firm newly established by an emergent
and partially decriminalising fraction of Donetsk capital.

By 1995, the power struggle was becoming even more acute in the
light of the new Constitution drafting. The main task for Kuchma and the
capitalist class fractions that supported him was to guarantee the highest
position for the institution of presidency in the new Supreme Law of
the country. As for the opposition forces, mainly the nationalist People's
Movement of Ukraine (Narodnyy Rukh Ukrayiny; NRU) and their leader
Vyacheslav Chornovil, options were poor. With less than two years left
before the parliamentary elections, popular support for the party was
insufficient to provide the majority in the Parliament or otherwise and
therefore, the NRU sought allies. The decision was made in favour of
the ruling forces led by Kuchma. The only other alliance option that
would allow considerable political leverage was the Communist Party
of Ukraine that, in the mid-1990s, still enjoyed more popular support
than any other party (24.65 per cent of votes in the 1998 parliamentary
election).[79] For the NRU, this was an ideologically unthinkable alliance.
The rest of the sizeable political parties were often mostly proxies to
gain access to state asset accumulation by embezzlement and administrative privileges. The Hromada Party (founded in 1993; 4.64 per cent
of votes in 1998),[80] led by Lazarenko (and Tymoshenko), mainly served

to guarantee his own business interests. The Narodno-Democratychna Party (People's Democratic Party or NDP; 5.01 per cent of votes)[81] was founded in Kyiv on 24 February 1996 as a result of a merge of seven other parties and social organisations[82] with Matviyenko as its leader (replaced by Pustovoitenko in 1999) and declared 'moral and political' interests of Ukraine's people as its political goal.[83] However, by 1997, the party's 'mission into power' had already transformed into a 'gateway to power' for officials on various levels, who began to join the party in large numbers to facilitate their own vertical career mobility.[84] One of the results of the latter essential alteration was the split of the party into two wings by the end of that year: (1) the democratic wing (Matviyenko, Stetskiv, Kolyushko, Filenko, Yemets and Syrota); and (2) the neo-nomenklatura wing (Pustovoitenko, Kinakh, Kushnaryov and Bezsmertnyy) as the appointment of Pustovoitenko became a source of disagreement between the two.[85] The rest of the parties that would make it into the Parliament in 1998 were the Socialist and the Peasant Parties' alliance (8.55 per cent of votes), the Progressive Socialist Party (4.04 per cent), the Green Party (5.43 per cent), and the Social-Democratic Party (United; 4.01 per cent). The first two were neo-nomenklatura with orientation towards status quo preservation in the county, the Green Party was the most ideologically cohesive and comprised mainly of environmental activists, and the last one was associated with the Kyiv fraction of the ascendant capitalist class.

The Kyiv fraction deserves a separate mention as, although it was small, it was politically very strong, especially in the first decade of Ukraine's independence.[86] Founded in 1990 as SDPU, and revamped in 1996 as SDPU (United), the party was a structure of the Kyiv ruling and emergent capitalist class fractions-for-itself. It included the first president of Ukraine, Kravchuk, Kyiv neo-nomenklatura and red directors among whom the most prominent became known as the 'Kyiv Seven'. The latter were in a ruling-capitalist class fraction compromise with the Dnipro-petrovsk 'family'.[87] The seven businessmen became acquainted through working in the Dynamo FC in the 1980s and by the early 1990s emerged as the largest business group in Kyiv. They were:[88] Victor Medvedchuk, Ihor and Hryhoriy Surkis, Valentyn Zhurskyy, Bohdan Hubskyy,[89] Yuriy Karpenko and Yuriy Lyakh.[90] The above ruling-capitalist class fraction compromise will last until the power usurpation by Donetsk bloc that will be addressed in Chapter 4.

Compromises with the ascendant ruling and capitalist fractions from Donetsk were being forged at the same time. Thus, a compromise between Kuchma/Dnipropetrovsk and V. Shcherban/Donetsk was reached, and the latter was appointed as the Governor of Donetsk Oblast by Edict 597/95 (July 1995). However, the above lasted only as long as the spheres of interest of the two regional class fractions did not overlap. As soon as V. Shcherban 'became involved in the energy sector and proposed in July 1996 that the management of the coal industry should be transferred to the oblast administration he was removed from office.'[91] V. Shcherban was de facto replaced by Viktor Yanukovych, when the latter was the Vice-Governor of Donetsk oblast (September 1996 to May 1997) and since 14 May 1997 *de jure*. Yanukovych's rapid ascent in the ruling structures at a regional and later at a country level began in the milieu of the criminal-political nexus discussed earlier. According to fellow inmates and militia officers interviewed by Aryev, while serving his two sentences in prison (1967 and 1970), the young Viktor Yanukovych collaborated with prison guards that helped him establish life-long connections with security service officials.[92] Starting in 1972, his career progressed from an electrician and then to a mechanic (1973), to multiple directing positions in enterprises dealing with the transportation of coal and by 1996, he became the director general of Ukrvuhlepromtrans, the enterprise in charge of all coal transportation networks.[93] Such a career trajectory meant that Yanukovych had direct access to the coal link in the commodity chains mentioned earlier. This explains his current and lasting relationship with Akhmetov, Kolesnikov and a number of other entrepreneurs, who emerged as capitalist class fractions-in-themselves by accumulation through those commodity chains. It is through the above personal and business connections, combined with Yanukovych becoming the Governor and next moving into the ruling structures in Kyiv, that institutionalisation of the Donetsk capital-for-itself as the ruling-class fraction began.

Meanwhile, the situation in Ukraine was becoming worse by the day and was described by some as hyper-stagflation with output shrinking by some 50 per cent and inflation reaching 10,000 per cent in 1993 alone while the decline in wages was more than 60 per cent in real terms.[94] By 1996 the state of affairs was at its worse in the whole history of independent Ukraine with GDP at $44.5 billion ($151 billion PPP adjusted) and the productive component of GDP being as low as 47.8 per cent of its volume in 1990.[95] In such conditions, the ruling bloc of neo-nomenklatura and red directors could not stall reforms any longer. That was mainly due to the fact that, in the light of growing popular discontent and falling profitability, the unreformed SOEs were no longer fit as cash cows. Conflict between the rival ruling and capitalist class fractions seeking to expand their political and economic agency escalated as the constitutional foundations of post-Soviet Ukraine were negotiated. The lack of consensus was further aggravated by two additional problems: (1) a mere absence of a comprehensive legislative framework[96] that accounted for the politico-economic transformations in Ukraine since 1990–1991; and (2) the effective complications of and obstructions for reforms on all levels in the country. An interim fractional compromise materialised in the Constitutional Agreement between the Parliament and the President 'On General Principles of Organisation and Functioning of State Authorities and Local Self-Governance in Ukraine until adoption of the New Constitution of Ukraine'.[97] The agreement further expanded the grip of the ruling bloc on decision-making in the country by granting President Kuchma unprecedented power. He could appoint the prime minister and members of the cabinet alone without any consultation (Article 22/1), the prime minister and the cabinet could function within limits designated by the President (Article 30), and effectively the president decided on the directions that every Ministry (i.e. area of society and economy) was to follow (Article 31). The State Property Fund was subject to his control now also (Article 24/1[7]) that was crucial for accumulation of SOEs by Kuchma's cronies.[98]

The adoption of the Constitution of Ukraine in 1996 became a watershed moment in the history of institutionalisation of the ascendant capitalist class fractions by proxy of links to Kuchma. The key issue was the division of powers between the judiciary (a range of courts with the Constitutional and the Supreme Court at the top of the hierarchy), legislative (the Parliament, oblast, and rayon councils), and executive (the president, the prime minister and the cabinet of ministers) branches stipulated in the supreme law of the country. The president, the prime minister and the cabinet now enjoyed much more administrative power while there was a notable loss of authority for the oblast and rayon councils. This indicated the centralisation of political power in Ukraine by the ruling bloc in Kyiv. Through the aforementioned strong links between the emerging oligarchic capitalist class fractions in the east of the country, reforms now could be put in place to aid further accumulation by the concentration of capital assets in FIGs.

4

Class formation and
social fragmentation

STATE, CAPITAL AND CRIME IN THE LATE 1990s

The 1990s marked a volatile period of social transformation in Ukraine where the unholy alliance of the state and capital-in-the-making merged into a regime of neoliberal kleptocracy. By the end of the 1990s, the foundations of appropriation and capital concentration strategy of the ruling bloc in the current composition and structure were precarious. At the time of the presidential election campaign, Ukraine's society was atomised as a result of economic hardship and instability as well as the lack of trust in political forces, which kept changing shape and direction. The country's politics were monopolised by Kuchma, his cronies from Dnipropetrovsk, and increasingly so from Donetsk as I discussed in Chapter 3. The two blocs of forces almost entirely usurped control over the Ukraine's economy and turned it inwards.[1] Unlike the Russian oligarchs, local capital in Ukraine preferred to attract new investment that they might get a share of but in a few years the direct equity investors were chased away due to Ukraine's 'ubiquitous chicanery, demand for bribes, taxes that often exceeded 100 per cent of profit, and ever-shifting law with arbitrary application.'[2] The practice of drawing companies into bankruptcy and manipulation of barter payments to maximise profits became rather common especially by gas companies[3] as I mentioned in Chapter 3 and will detail further in this chapter. By the end of the 1990s, the 'chronic schizophrenia' between the Western direction in foreign policy and 'domestic entropy' have soured Ukraine's relations with the EU[4] and jeopardised their political and economic rapprochement.

In the light of the continuous economic decline with GDP in 1999 reaching $31.58 billion at the current exchange rate, that is, the continuous fall from $81.456 billion in 1990,[5] Kuchma and the oligarchic capital associated with his administration realised the precarity of his bid for a second presidential term. In order to secure his victory, Kuchma and his supporters had to manufacture the popular consent. For that purpose, advisers and PR agents from Moscow, who had helped Yeltsin in his campaign and who employed the Russia-tested strategies in Ukraine, were hired.[6] The latter primarily meant smear campaigns and pressure on the independent press to present Kuchma in a favourable light. D'Anieri documented that: 'it was relatively easy either to force a newspaper to close or to use the threat measures [by the state executive apparatus] to persuade editors to modify their coverage.'[7] The above 'strategies' towards mass media remained throughout Kuchma's second presidency and were combined with direct ownership of mass media outlets by oligarchic capital as well as with physical and symbolic methods of coercion.

Administration of the old apparatchik Kuchma remained true to their criminal-political nexus ways too. In the run-up to the presidential election in 1999, two of the main candidates were killed. The first, Vadym Hetman, enjoyed high popular support due to the monetary reforms of 1994–1996 that he coordinated together with the then Head of the National Bank of Ukraine, Yushchenko. The reform stabilised the Ukrainian currency through devaluation and simultaneous introduction of a new currency, hryvnya. Since 1993 Hetman was the Head of the Ukrainian Interbank Currency Exchange and had high chances of winning the election if not shot dead by a Donetsk gangster in April 1998.[8] The second, Vyacheslav Chornovil, was the leader of the Narodnyy Rukh nationalist opposition party and died in a car crash on 25 March 1999. The accident was allegedly organised by Kravchenko, a proxy of Kuchma-allied forces who also financed the split of the Rukh party the same year.[9] With the main rival, Chornovil, removed, Kuchma's competition now were Symonenko (the Communist Party leader) and Moroz (the leader of the Socialist party). Moroz did not make it to the run-off. Symonenko had strong popular support especially due to the large proportion of the ageing population in Ukraine who in the light of deteriorating socio-economic conditions were nostalgic about Soviet times.[10] However, he still lost the election to Kuchma who received 36.5 and 53.6 per cent of the votes in the general election and the run-off respectively.[11] With Kuchma's victory, the oligarchic capitalist class fractions backing him won too. They were: Bakai and Medvedchuk from the Kyiv capitalist class fractions, Pinchuk from Dnipropetrovsk, and Akhmetov, Taruta and Mkrtchan from Donetsk. The latter, at this point, were still supporting Kuchma as their power proxy, however,

by the next presidential election, they had a candidate of their own –
Viktor Yanukovych.

This combination of kleptocracy, crime and manipulations of public
consciousness became the trademark of Kuchma's second term. This
too was the period when the power shift in the criminal–political nexus
occurred gradually as security forces and ex-apparatchiks were serving
the needs of Ukraine's own nascent criminal-turned-capitalist class. In the
parliament and elsewhere, oligarch-friendly politicians – often oligarchs
too – were adapting foreign advised neoliberal laws that subsidised their
FIGs at taxpayers' expense, gave them generous tax breaks, and allowed
offshore profits.

DOMINANT FRACTIONS AND THE FORGING OF FIGS

The oligarchic capital of Ukraine shaped through accumulation by dispossession and concentration in the industrial east of Ukraine primarily
revolved – and still does – around enterprises linked to three main
commodity chains: (1) coking coal–coke–leaf metal/pipes; (2) thermal
coal–power–metal; and (3) gas–metal–gas pipes visualised in Figure 4.1;
the last being the most profitable.[12] The gas-based commodity chain (3) is
built in the other two on nearly every step of the production process that
explains both the leverage of gas suppliers embedded in the specificity
of relations of production in Ukraine and the accumulation potential of
gas trade in the country.

The first Dnipropetrovsk oligarchs, Tymoshenko and Lazarenko, made
their fortune by accumulation through gas and lubricants supply along
those increasingly commodified chains. For the Donetsk capital that was
becoming increasingly concentrated in FIGs of industrial enterprises
heavy reliant on gas imports, control over gas supply and prices was
crucial. The latter was linked in the most profitable commodity chain (3)
'gas-metal-gas pipes' where 'gas was paid for with gas pipes but the terms
of the barter transactions overvalued the pipes relative to gas, permitting
companies trading gas pipes to accumulate significant profits through
arbitrage pricing of gas.'[13] The 'gas pipe' link of that commodity chain
was serviced by Interpipe owned by Pinchuk who was Tymoshenko's
business partner in 1994–1995. Together with Lazarenko, they co-owned
Sodruzhestvo corporation, a trader of Turkmenistan's gas in Ukraine.[14]
Lazarenko who at that point was the Governor of Dnipropetrovsk was
in charge of the business.[15] Donetsk industrial capital needed control

over the above commodity chain for two reasons. First, the expansion of that chain '[reduced] the liquidity in two other commodity chains'.[16] And second, as mentioned previously, Lazarenko, the YeESU, and Tymoshenko and the Russian intermediary Itera that was a part of Gazprom, controlled the gas chain in the mid-1990s. Tymoshenko's entry into the fuel market can be traced back to 1991 when together with her husband, Oleksandr Tymoshenko (and by proxy of Oleksandr Hravets), she founded the KUB (Korporatsiya Ukrayins'kyy Benzyn – Ukrainian Petrol Corporation).[17] KUB specialised in the purchase of fuel and lubricants from Russia and Turkmenistan, and sold those to

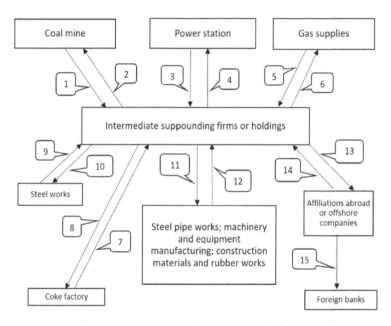

Flows/key: 1 – coke and thermal coal; 2 – steel, equipment and parts, conveyor belts, construction materials, power, mutual arrears, money for salaries; 3 – power; 4 – thermal coal, gas, mutual arrears clearing, money for salaries; 5 – gas; 6 – money; 7 – coke; 8 – power, gas, mutual arrears, clearing, money; 11 – steel, power, gas, mutual arrears, clearing, money; 12 – gas pipes, equipment and parts, conveyor belts, construction materials; 13 – steel, las pipes, equipment and parts; 14 – money, imported equipment and materials; 15 – cashed arbitrage profits.

Figure 4.1 The 'coking coal–coke–metal' and 'thermal coal–power–metal' commodity chains

Source: Adapted from Lyakh (2007: 87).

Ukrainian consumers especially in the agricultural sector in the early 1990s.[18] By 1995, Lazarenko had become a partner in the new enterprise founded together with the above three partners through re-registration[19] of KUB – Yedyni Energetychni Systemy Ukrayiny (YeESU – United Energy Systems of Ukraine).

By 1996, YeESU already had a monopoly in the energy market, and the Donetsk capitalist bloc with its heavily energy-dependent business sought control over energy resources. According to Lyakh, Donetsk business established Industrialny Soyuz Donbas (ISD) by proxy of the oblast's authorities for the purpose of competing against the Dnipropetrovsk-controlled YeESU.[20] Yevhen Shcherban, a Donetsk businessman whose ascent began in the criminal structures of Akhat Bragin and Rinat Akhmetov, was appointed as the head of ISD.[21] Scherban and Bragin were slaughtered in the late 1990s, and their business was transferred to Akhmetov who currently is one of the richest people in the post-Soviet space. 'The Donetsk Oblast Administration ensured that the largest iron and steel enterprises in the oblast purchased their gas from ISD' and soon after Lazarenko's resignation in 1997, they controlled some 80 per cent of Donetsk oblast gas market effectively removing YeESU from the market although not completely. Its corporate affiliates in gas transit schemes, after ousting Tymoshenko and Lazarenko, remained with the local ascending oligarchs, Pinchuk and Firtash.[22] The Russian gas supply intermediary, Itera, linked to Gazprom and the Moscow Solntsevo gang in 2002 was replaced by EuralTransGaz and then in 2005 by RosUkrEnergo.[23] Both EuralTransGaz and RosUkrEnergo are linked in Ukraine to Firtash and, less explicitly, to Pinchuk.[24]

By the end of the 1990s, the main oligarchic capital class fractions of the present-day Ukraine had been formed. They were: Akhmetov (SCM), Hayduk/Taruta/Mkrtchan (ISD), Pinchuk (Interpipe), Kolomoyskyy and Boholyubov (Privat Group) and Firtash (RosUkrEnergo and later Group DF). Emerging from this mêlée of neo-nomenklatura, red directors, Komsomol and gangs, and utilising the legal and extra-legal accumulation opportunities created by the market reforms, they all strove to gain control over the mechanisms of accumulation for their FIGs. The latter was achieved by the extension of transnationalisation opportunities for accumulation, which were already embedded in the joint venture legislation of 1987–1988. It involved the creation of Special Economic Zones and Priority Development Areas.

By the end of the 1990s, the oligarchic capital of Ukraine was already concentrated in vertically integrated FIGs that sought institutionalisation as a class-for-itself within the ruling bloc in Kyiv. By the end of the 1990s, the oligarchs of Ukraine were concentrating their capital in vertically integrated FIGs, using these as stepping stones to consolidate their power as a ruling bloc in Kyiv.

At the same time, the above FIGs comprise the unreformed enterprises that relied both on cheap energy supplies, and state subsidies. Building on the past industrial glory of the Donbas industrial region, Donetsk capital sought more political leverage as well as administrative devolution to make it easier to conceal profits and evade taxes.[25] However, the contribution of the Donetsk FIGs to Ukraine's economy was far less than that portrayed by the advocates of the regional industry. Lyakh points out a structural problem in the nominal indices of Donetsk industrial growth, that is, 'the economic power of the region is built on the hollow foundations of heavy industries' with doubtful prospects.[26] He goes on to explain that heavy industry was:

> less affected than final-product manufacturers by the break-up of technological ties among enterprises and the loss of energy resources, cheap raw materials, and sales markets after the disintegration of the USSR; ... while at the same time ... they appeared to be quite competitive in external markets mostly owing to low prices (as a result of [various] subsidies), low labour costs and ecological expenses.[27]

Lyakh explains that the hollow foundations of the seemingly rapid economic output indicator increase in 1999 and 2000 as compared to 1998 were attributed to five factors that also explain the drop in indices in the following years.[28] First, 'the high rates of economic growth are a statistical effect because they are compared to a very low base' and in fact in 1998 with a continuation well into 1999 'whole branches of regional industry (for example light industry, construction materials, glass industries and engineering) nearly disappeared or dramatically reduced in size'. Thus, indicators of output on the few still functioning enterprises leveraged the regional statistics although with a dramatic increase in the share of heavy industries. Until 2001,

> the share of ferrous metallurgy in the gross production of Ukraine reached about 27 per cent, whilst in the Donetsk region this share

exceeded half the regional output; thus even a small growth [in the sector] automatically reflected in the regional statistics as a growth of the whole economy.[29]

Metallurgy is a densely concentrated industry with some 20 large enterprises accountable for the oblast output as a whole and 'two huge metallurgical plants located in Mariupol' account for nearly half of the regional profit total and 36 per cent of the taxes collected from regional firms'. Second, an improvement of external market conditions for the basic goods (export of which account for some 70 per cent of the oblast total) in late 1999 and 2000 due to the growing demand in Russia, Belarus, and Western Europe have benefited Donetsk producers. Third, following the rouble crisis of 1998 and the subsequent depreciation of hryvnya, Ukrainian goods competitiveness increased both at home and abroad 'which led to a growth in the output of key exporters and the substitution of imports' (if partial). Fourth, the impact of monetary factors on the industrial growth of 1999 and 2000 was profound. So, 'settlement of budget arrears' and 'the sale of hryvnya for hard currency ... to service external debt resulted in an increase in the inflation rate from 19.2 per cent in 1999 to 25.8 per cent in 2000.'[30] However, such trends did not impact consumer demand thus increasing retail turnover. In 2001, the inflation rate decrease to 6.1 per cent, the resulting money supply decrease, and the appreciation of hryvnya 'meant that by the end of [the year] the impact of the increased money supply in generating economic growth was reduced by nearly a half.'[31] And the fifth, 'the non-payment of electricity and gas [bills] by heavy industrial enterprise increased their liquidity and encouraged industrial growth.'[32] In fact, what it meant was that 'one branch of Ukrainian industry – electricity generators and importers of gas from Russia and Turkmenistan – was a creditor to all other sectors of the economy.'[33] There is also a different interpretation of the effects of such schemes. Since all energy generation and distribution in Ukraine is at least partly owned and run by the state and is funded by the state budget, the big private industry was and still is subsidised by the state. Such practice of subsidising private enterprise at taxpayers' expense is standard in a neoliberal economy as it is in Ukraine. One more recent example is the law N3319-VI in May–July 2011 that wrote off UAH 14bn worth of utility bill fines and debts owed by oligarchic FIGs to the state-owned utility companies.[34] Such interpenetration of the oligarchic capital and the state became deeply institutionalised during the second term of Kuchma's presidency.

FUEL MARKET, POLITICS AND CRIME

One of the first decisions of Kuchma's second term was to propose Yushchenko's candidacy for prime minister that was approved on the 20 December 1999 by 296 of 246 required parliamentary votes.[35] Yushchenko's appointment can be interpreted as an attempt to save the declining popular support for Kuchma and his administration as the former was a popular reformer of the fiscal system together with the murdered Hetman. Tymoshenko was appointed Vice-Prime Minister for the Fuel and Energy Complex. The corrupt oligarchic connection was evident here too – she previously was the ex-Prime Minister Lazarenko's partner in YeESU (a company rival to Donetsk ISD and Russian Itera on Ukraine's energy market). In late 1998, Lazarenko's involvement in a money laundering scandal and the anti-monopoly legislation provided grounds to remove YeESU from the gas and energy markets and gave way to different monopolists, Firtash and Bakai, through Naftogaz Ukrayiny founded on 18 April 1998,[36] almost instantly after Lazarenko fled the country fearing international prosecution on corruption charges. Having assumed the vice-PM office, Tymoshenko continued the centralisation of Ukraine's energy sector assets, that is, the scheme that she commenced with Lazarenko as the co-owner of YeESU on the corporate level. The above implied removal of intermediaries and traders from the commodity chain and dealing with Gazprom directly through Naftogaz Ukrayiny.[37] Among those were Hryhoriy Surkis from 'the Kyiv Seven' and Konstantin Hrihorishin, a 'businessman' from Russia. In addition, Tymoshenko enforced collection of the outstanding debts of non-payment on Russian-supplied energy by oligarch-owned companies. Tymoshenko's seemingly anti-oligarchic behaviour is explained by two factors. First, she was spared in Lazarenko's descent and her competitors could now be disciplined by her ministerial hand. Second, the energy sector restructuring that she commenced was a continuation of accumulation strategy of YeESU only now via the state. By centralising the energy sector and introducing an international intermediary trader, a direct deal with Russia was struck where capital accumulation could continue via the state yet with minimal control, in a transnational fashion, a technically legal international state asset embezzlement scheme was launched.

The presence of the suspicious resale intermediaries did not improve but rather became worse when Putin became president of the Russian Federation in 2000 and began the consolidation of power and resources in the hands of his administration. The above was rooted in the Russian criminal-political nexus with its own idiosyncrasies where former KGB officials were in charge – Putin himself being a former agent,[38] however, with the strong criminal element still remaining. The latter was manifest in the case of Mogilevich, an international criminal who figures on the FBI most wanted list. He was released in 2010 after having been caught in Moscow in 2008 reportedly due to the 'absence of a crime in the act'.[39] Gazprom became Putin's pet project that he began with replacing Vyakhirev with Aleksey Miller, Putin's old KGB friend from St. Petersburg.[40] Such changes in Gazprom translated into the intensification of rivalry in Ukraine's energy market. Between August 2000 and January 2001, a series of criminal cases against Tymoshenko's husband's business and then her own YeESU were opened that served as grounds for her loss of office and thus control of the energy market via Naftogaz. The assets of the YeESU were reprivatised in 2001 by ISD and then in 2002–2003 transferred to Akhmetov's SCM. Tymoshenko effectively was removed from the energy market and her position of power. In Russia, Putin's next step was to replace Itera (by refusing to renew the contract that had expired in 2003) with EuralTransGaz (ETG); thus, instead of eradicating intermediaries, he inserted a new one into the scheme, only this time it was owned by Gazprom.[41] The exclusive role ascribed to ETG in the transportation of gas for both Gazprom of Russia and Naftogaz of Ukraine – state-owned, the countries' largest gas producers, importers/exporters and distributors – was suspicious. For example, in 2004, an internal memo from the OECD raised 'the possibility of connections between several of [the above] companies and associates of Semyon Mogilevich' and a few journalistic investigations have shown the same but were denied by Russian lawmen.[42] Moreover, such exclusive control over the gas supply market by ETG and thus Firtash explains Tymoshenko's rivalry with the latter that I will address later in this chapter. The carving up of YeESU assets by Donetsk oligarchs will later contextualise her so-called 'war on oligarchs' in the aftermath of the Orange Revolution.

ETG is one of the prime examples of shadow schemes the post-Soviet (and not only) markets are awash with since the 1990s. It was founded in December 2002 in Hungary in a small shop of the tiny village of Csabdi by four people: Louise Lukacs (an unemployed actress), two unnamed 'pioneers to the venture' – an IT worker and his partner (recruited by Lukacs), and Ze'ev Gordon – a Tel Aviv lawyer of Simeon Mogilevich, who was wanted by the FBI for racketeering, fraud and money laundering and who I mentioned above.[43] Gordon, in a personal interview with Misha Glenny claimed that he was 'merely asked to act as a shareholder for a Ukrainian businessman, [Dmytro] Firtash'.[44] The connection between Mogilevich and Firtash was later confirmed in one of the Wikileaks reports.[45] In the latter, the former ambassador of the USA to Ukraine, William Taylor, mentions that Firtash himself admitted connections to Mogilevich.[46] Meanwhile, ETG miraculously, in the first year, from a $12,000 business went to $2 billion turnover with pre-tax profit of $180 million.[47] Even more interestingly, Andras Knopp (then the CEO of ETG, former Hungarian Minister of Education and then the senior representative of Reemtsma tobacco in Moscow) said that: 'Strictly speaking, the shareholders remain three Romanian citizens and an Israeli, but the real parents are Gazprom and Naftogaz Ukrayiny.'[48] The above was done, he continues, in order for the two to qualify for the offshore status for the intermediary company after the gas conglomerates failed to obtain necessary papers for business registration in Hungary before 31st December 2002, 'the cut-off point for a new business' to register as off-shore to qualify for a 3 per cent company tax.[49] Before 2001, when Gazprom was chaired by Rem Vyakhirev, the intermediary company contracted to transport gas from Turkmenistan to Ukraine through Russia was Itera International Energy Corporation.[50] The latter company, allegedly, is controlled by the Solntsevo Brotherhood that is one of the most influential and internationally operating gangs from Moscow; the above-mentioned Mogilevich is part of the gang.[51] William Browler of Hermitage Investment (one of the US investors of Gazprom) conducted an investigation of the connection between Itera and Gazprom and discovered that large sums of money were transferred from the latter to the former for no obvious reason.[52] He discovered that payments totalling $120 million annually were made to Itera for merely transporting gas from Turkmenistan to Ukraine. Furthermore, Hermitage Investment's Vadim Klein wrote in the report 'How Should Gazprom Be Managed in Russia's National Interests and the Interests of Its Shareholders', that in 2004, Gazprom 'presented' ETG with $767 million for resale operations on Turkmenistan gas to Ukraine.[53] The nascent money laundering scandal with Gazprom was muffled by dropping ETG from the scheme and replacing it with RosUkrEnergo – yet another intermediary later confirmed to be owned by Gazprom and Firtash/Fursin.[54] In 2006, PricewaterhouseCoopers, auditor of RosUkrEnergo, identified Firtash in their report 'as 90 per cent owner and [Fursin – another Ukrainian businessman] as 10 per cent owner of Centragas Holding, an Austrian-registered company that owns the 50 per cent stake.'[55] Founded in 2005, RosUkrEnergo is an intermediary that in 2005 already received $478 million in revenue payment from Gazprom[56] and '[that by 2006 supplied] gas worth about $10bn (€8bn, £5.6bn) a year at current prices, with two-thirds going to Ukraine and the rest to the European Union.'[57] The gas market, however, was not the only sphere of the economy subject to semi-licit accumulation schemes. During Kuchma's second term as president, an overall institutionalisation of state–gangster connections in Ukraine occurred that sprouted from the criminal–political nexus of the USSR.

POLITICISATION OF THE OLIGARCHY

By 2002, the oligarchic fractions grew strong and their respective political parties were gaining weight. However, the parties' support alone was not strong enough to guarantee sufficient leverage in the new parliament that was necessary as a step in the formation of a class-for-itself. Therefore, the stakes on both the party lists and on the individual MP candidates in majoritarian constituencies were high. Moreover, as the 1999 presidential campaign showed, thorough strategising prior to elections (rather than ad hoc pulling of deputies into coalitions and oppositions more widespread previously) was essential. Also, due to the Kuchmagate crisis, the 2002 parliamentary election was the first in the history of independent Ukraine to be closely monitored by the EU, the USA and the country's financial partners, the IMF and World Bank, among others.[58] Close international attention largely limited the possibility for fabrication of election results, as was often a common practice.[59]

Political forces have divided into three main competing blocks as identified by the Norwegian Centre for Human Rights (with 21 parties and 12 blocks in general registered for elections): Our Ukraine, the Communist Party of Ukraine, and For a United Ukraine. The three 'gravitation poles' or 'electoral camps' began to form around those already in power, that is, members of the Cabinet of Ministers, Presidential

Administration and so forth.[60] In Table 4.1, I present the three largest blocks and the parties that comprised them. Such a concerted manoeuvre was strategic as it would ensure that the transition toward the new parliament and later, in 2004, presidency could be performed in the smoothest manner. Kuchma's influence within the ruling bloc as well as his popular support was fading and it was evident to his apparatus too. Simultaneously, the leverage of the Donetsk capitalist class was on the rise as well as the anti-Kuchma bloc was gaining momentum. One notable sign of that was the organised removal from office of the Vice-Speaker of the Parliament Medvedchuk by joint efforts of oppositional right and left-wing parties and fractions. The latter was the President's long-term ally and the leader of SDPU(U), the ruling bloc party. It was also the first time that national-democratic and left forces have acted together; the union that will take shape and become stronger by the 2004 presidential election. At this point, however, the parties went into the elections separately, that is, Our Ukraine of Yushchenko and BYuT of Tymoshenko.

Table 4.1   Three main blocks of forces competing in the parliamentary elections 2002

For a United Ukraine (4–5 parties)	Communist Party of Ukraine	Our Ukraine (10 parties)
Volodymyr Lytvyn People's Democratic Party (Pustovoitenko) Party of Regions (Semynozhenko) Labour Party (Tyhypko) Agrarian Party (Hladiy) The Union of Industrialists and Entrepreneurs	Symonenko Left	Leader: Viktor Yushchenko Rukh (Udovenko; right opposition) Rukh (Kostenko; right opposition) Reforms and Order (Pynzenyk; centre-right opposition)
Platform: Market economy Strong central authority 'To Europe with Russia' ('government/new oligarch' party)	Platform: Against privatisation of land Occasionally pro-establishment Pro-Russia and CIS Against NATO membership	Platform: Transparency in the economic sphere Balanced budget Market economy Western-oriented Pro-NATO cooperation Pro-EU

Source: compiled by the author on the basis of the Nordem Report (2009) and the Central Electoral Commission of Ukraine data (2002).

As result of the election, many of the so-called neo-nomenklatura and the Dnipropetrovsk family lost their seats in parliament and many other positions within the ruling bloc as I show in Figure 4.2. Instead, the new ruling bloc was beginning to include the capitalist class fractions.

With the new electoral legislation put in place just before the elections, the 450 seats of Verkhovna Rada were now to be distributed differently.

Under Ukraine's new election law, 225 of the Supreme Council's seats [were] allocated on a proportional basis to those parties that gain 4 per cent or more of the national electoral vote; the other 225 members [were] elected by popular vote in single-mandate constituencies.[61]

– all to serve a four-year term. The results were as shown in Figure 4.2.

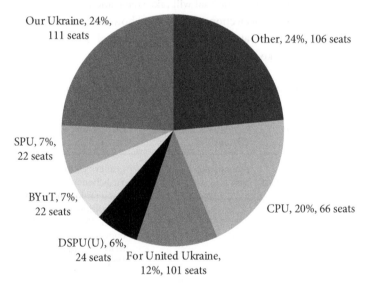

Figure 4.2   Results of the parliamentary elections of 2002: parties with percentage of votes and parliamentary seats allocation

Source: compiled by the author based on data from the Central Election Commission of Ukraine, 2002.

The support for the Communists (20 per cent) and the Socialists (7 per cent) was still strong, however, it was already weakening. The capitalist class fractions were clearly identified and gaining strength at this point. They were three: (1) Our Ukraine backed by Poroshenko

(Ukrprominvest), Taruta/Mkrtchan (IDS); (2) BYuT/Tymoshenko or the 'irremovable bloc of ex-oligarchs and ex-dissidents';[62] and (3) For United Ukraine/conservators of the Kuchma regime, Pinchuk (Interpipe) and Akhmetov (SCM). It is worth mentioning that Kolomoyskyy and Boholyubov (Privat Group) stayed out of direct political party support until the elections of 2004. Kovaleva shows that the Donetsk bloc 'has significantly influenced Kyiv's policies and has challenged the further development of market reform',[63] which is manifest in the individual political presence of the above in the ruling bloc of the country. My analysis of the *Korrespondent* Top-100 Most Influential People of Ukraine ratings also shows dramatic shifts in the ruling bloc of the country between 1990–1996 and 2003 that I will address shortly (see Figure 4.3 for details). However, some are noteworthy at this point. The career of the governor of Donetsk oblast, Viktor Yanukovych, who became the prime minister of Ukraine in November 2002, was the 'first example of a regional governor moving to a senior position in the executive power without having previously occupied an intermediate position in the central state administration',[64] – a number of Donetsk representatives' appointments followed soon after. The former head of the State Tax Administration, Mykola Azarov, became the first deputy prime minister and finance minister; Vitaliy Hayduk, a former director of ISD, became the deputy prime minister for the fuel and energy complex. Next, Serhiy Tulub 'was appointed minister for energy and later became the Director of Energoatom, the country's nuclear power company'.[65] Other representatives of the Donetsk elite included the former Finance Minister Ihor Sushko and Serhiy Lyovochkin, 'a senior aide to President Kuchma's top aide'.[66] Moreover, by the early 2000s, the Donetsk bloc exercised leverage in the parliament through the newly formed Party of Regions fraction and the Strong Ukraine fraction. In addition, Andriy Kliuev (PR) 'who was previously the deputy Head of the Board on Special Economic Zones in Donetsk oblast, became head of the Committee of Verkhovna Rada on the fuel and energy complex, nuclear policy and nuclear safety'[67] and thus guaranteed protection of the Donetsk bloc interest in the energy sector.

In the last days of his presidency, Kuchma and the forces he represented (Pinchuk and the Donetsk capital) had to guarantee their future access to decision-making in the country in the case of defeat in the forthcoming election. Thus, they had to make sure that the powers of the future President were to be restricted (that could always be reversed provided their candidate, Yanukovych, wins) and that the Parliament where their coalition now had 101 seats was granted more powers. The intention materialised in a draft law submitted by Kuchma on amending the Constitution of Ukraine. On 8 October 2004, the Decree N2222-IV was signed by President Kuchma where the Amendments to the Constitution of Ukraine described below were stipulated. The new Constitution was to enter into force on 1 September 2005 (provided it was adopted by the parliament prior to that date; 1 January 2006 otherwise). The powers of the president over the parliament in general were made stronger and mainly aimed at avoiding political stalemate through lack of Parliamentary majority for voting procedures in the future. Thus, according to the Amendments (Article 90), the President could dismiss the Parliament in three cases:

1. 'the Verkhovna Rada of Ukraine fails to form a coalition of deputy fractions in compliance with Article 83 of this Constitution within one month;
2. no new Cabinet of Ministers of Ukraine has been formed within sixty days after the resignation of the Cabinet of Ministers of Ukraine;
3. plenary sessions fail to commence within thirty days of a single regular session.'[68]

At the same time, the inability to dismiss the parliament elected at extraordinary elections after the early termination of powers of the parliament of previous convocation during the first year in the office was preserved. The Amendment of Article 93 removed the power to initiate legislation from the National Bank of Ukraine and that of Article 98 have granted the Chamber of Accounts the power to exercise control not only over the use but also over the revenue to the state budget. Next, in a case of early dismissal of the president, his duties were to be performed by the Chairman of the Verkhovna Rada (previously, it would have been the prime minister) apart from duties stipulated in the items 2, 6 to 8, 10 to 13, 22, 24, 25, 27 and 28 of Article 106 of the Constitution. Thus, as a result of the above reform, the president would be subject to parliamentary control and would not have the power that Kuchma enjoyed. The reform in such a manner allowed Kuchma's cronies from the Dnipropetrovsk bloc to continue exercise control over decision-making in the country through parliamentary representation provided the candidate they support did not become the next president in 2004.

CAPITAL IN ACTION: CONCENTRATION BY DISPOSSESSION

The capitalist class fractions associated with the ruling bloc ensured concentration of SOEs in their FIGs by dispossession,[69] that is, by launching a privatisation wave with Donetsk capital representative Chechetov in charge of the process. By the end of Kuchma's second term, most of the large industrial SOEs were concentrated in the hands of four industrial clusters/FIGs: SCM (Akhmetov, Donetsk), Interpipe (Dnipropetrovsk, Pinchuk/Kuchma), ISD (Taruta/Mkrtchan, Donetsk), and Privat Group (Kolomoyskyy/Boholyubov, Dnipropetrovsk). As his time in office was approaching its end, a wave of ambiguous privatisation cases or simply audacious expropriations of state property by oligarchs occurred. In 2003, Kuchma promoted Mykhaylo Chechetov from the First Deputy Head of the State Property Fund to the Head of the Fund; approved by the parliament (in a repeat vote as the first time they voted against) on 3 April. Now in charge of state-owned property, Chechetov launched a wide-scale privatisation of the latter (he would later be driven to suicide over investigation into these procedures). This practice of pre-election privatisation, will be repeated in 2012 and then from 2014–onwards wholesale privatisation will complete the process. Based on the data from the State Property Fund, a report by Paskhaver, Verkhovodova and Aheyeva (Пасхавер, Верховодова and Агеєва) of the Centre for Economic Development 'Privatisation and Reprivatisation in Ukraine after "the Orange Revolution"', and various newspaper publications; I have compiled a table of the enterprises privatised between 2003 and 2004, most of which were later called for re-privatisation and/or re-nationalisation (see Table 4.2). Figure 4.3 is the network visualisation of the same data.

As is shown in both Table 4.2 and Figure 4.2, the SOEs privatised in 2003 and 2004 were all acquired by the oligarchic FIGs (SCM, Interpipe, ISD, Privat, Smart Group, Saul) or by foreign businesses with criminal links (the rest of SOEs). The latter included FBI most wanted Mogilevich, who is linked to Firtash (and Pinchuk), and Alex Rovt, who is linked to Yanukovych through Alex Kiselev – the American PR agent of Yanukovych – who later spent some $1million in the USA on the salvation of Yanukovych's image in the presidential campaign of 2004. Interestingly enough, SOEs acquired by Privat Group of Boholyubov and Kolomoyskyy – who supported Tymoshenko and Yushchenko in the electoral campaign 2004 – were not listed for re-privatisation. Data

Table 4.2   The largest SEOs privatised in 2003–2004

Name of the enterprise	Share, per cent	Price, billion UAH	Buyer or final owner as of 2005
2003			
Krasnodonvuhillya JSC	60	770.3	SCM, Akhmetov
Komsomolets' Donbasu JSC	33.27	25.6	SCM
Alchevsk Metalworks plant JSC	23.86	5.5	ISD, Taruta and Mkrtchan
Petrovskyy Dniprovsk Metalworks plant JSC	42.26	65.8	ISD, later Privat – Boholyubov and Kolomoyskyy
Kominmet	59.49	10.81	Privat
Nikopol Ferroalloys plant JSC	50%+1 share	660.5	Interpipe, Pinchuk
Zaporizhzhya Aluminium plant JSC	25	38.92	Interpipe and Saul (Russia)
2004			
Kryvorizhstal	93.02	4260	SCM and Interpipe
Pavlohradvyhillya	92.11	1400	SCM
Ukrrudprom LLC, group of companies	50+1share	106	SCM
Tsentralnyy LLC, mining company	50+1share	207.6	SCM
Pivnichnyy LLC, mining company	n/a	n/a	Smart-Group, Novynskyy
Inhuletskyy LLC, mining company	37.57	162.9	Privat
Sukha Balka, mining company	25.78	60	Privat
Pivdennyy LLC, mining company	n/a	n/a	Privat
Kryvorizhskyy LLC, iron-mining integrated plant	n/a	n/a	SCM
Dokuchyevskyy flux-dolomite integrated plant, LLC	n/a	n/a	SCM
Kryvbasvybukhprom, LLC	n/a	n/a	SCM
Novotroyitsk LLC	89.48	346.7	Clearing House, Mogilevich
Crimean Soda plant			RSG Erste (Germany),
Tytan, SJC			Mogilevich
Rivneazot	53.86	48	Raiffeisen Investment (Austria), Mogilevich
Azot (Severodonetsk)	n/a	n/a	WorldWide Chemical LLC, Alex Rovt (USA, owned by Abu Dhabi Almansoori Specialized Engineering),
Chornomorskyy shipbuilding plant	90.25	119.35	Yanukovych
			Ihor and Oleh Churkin (Russia)
Dzerzhynskyy Dniprovsk Metalworks plant, LLC			ISD
Naddnipryanskyy oil refinery			Privat

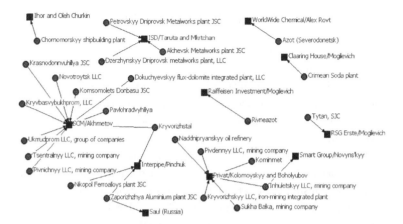

Figure 4.3 Network visualisation of SOEs privatised in 2003 and 2004 and companies/oligarchs who became their owners

Source: Compiled by the author from the data gathered in Table 4.1; due to software requirements apostrophes were removed from the names.

Key: dots indicate names of SOEs and squares indicate names of companies that acquired SOEs and the company owners.

on whether those SOEs were undervalued in the process of privatisation in 2003–2004 is unavailable. In addition to the rushed SOEs privatisation, control over gas supply had to be secured for the oligarchic FIGs linked to Donetsk capital fraction through Yanukovych, Akhmetov and Firtash.[70] That was done when the then Prime Minister Yanukovych signed a Government Regulation N1603 on 29 November 2004, during his last days as the prime minister, that sealed RosUkrEnergo's exclusive right to trade all imported gas on Ukraine's market.[71]

Kuchma's second term as president was characterised by the 'collapse of the national democrat–centrist alliance, the "Kuchmagate" crisis, the rise of a non-communist opposition in the 2002 elections and the election of Viktor Yushchenko in the 2004 elections following the protests that sparked the Orange Revolution.'[72] Meanwhile, in Ukraine, the electoral campaign of 2004 was in full sway. Kuzio argues that in 2004 'a new reconfiguration of Ukrainian politics emerged with the national democrats allied to the moderate left against the executive–centrist oligarchic alliance, culminating in the Orange Revolution,'[73] – the replacement of the previously dominant Dnipropetrovsk (and more recent Donetsk) bloc by the new people, as I will show in the following chapters.

The grip of the criminal–political nexus over Ukraine's economy was increasingly strengthening; the balance of power shifted towards the criminal-turned-oligarch class now and were serviced by the security officials, who had previously provided them with protection. The state was obtaining an increasingly transnational form, that is, one that allows for the processes of capital accumulation to circumvent the boundaries of the national regulations of various kinds – taxation, tariffs and duties – via schemes such as YeESU or ETG. Through both direct and indirect participation in the political process, the emergent capitalist class fractions of Ukraine ensured the continuous furthering of their economic agency by utilising the multiplicity of already available and constantly expanding mechanisms of accumulation in the global capitalist market system – legal and extra-legal. Conditioned by the permanent intra- and inter-fractional rivalry in the process of primitive accumulation, the amorphous ruling bloc of Ukraine was effectively steadily undermining the potential for a stabilisation of a new social order by ongoing dispossession of labour with little to no compensation.

THE MAKING AND THE UTILITY OF THE DISPOSSESSED

The labour side of privatisation

The making of the oligarchs came at the inevitable cost to the economy and the country's labour through excesses of uneven economic dislocation. Overall decline in GDP, hyperinflation and growing unemployment with little welfare compensation were taking their toll on the society. GDP fell by 57 per cent between 1989 and 1998.[74] Inflation went from 200 per cent in 1991 to hyperinflation following the removal of price controls on demand of the IMF and reached 2,730 per cent in 1992, and 10,155 per cent in 1993; this roller-coaster performance was followed by 'slowing down' to 401 per cent in 1994 and 182 per cent in 1995.[75] It did not begin to stabilise until 1996, when fiscal and monetary reforms were introduced dropping inflation to 40 per cent in 1996 and to 10 per cent and 19 per cent in 1997 and 1998 respectively.[76] After decades of full employment under Soviet rule, first 350,000 registered in 1997 and 1.2 million officially, up to 7 million unofficially were without jobs. Even before the figures soared many of those who were formally employed experienced economic hardship due to high inflation and ubiquitous wage arrears. The young were hit hardest with 30.5 of those

CLASS FORMATION AND SOCIAL FRAGMENTATION · 87

under 28 years of age being unemployed according to official figures, the real picture tends to be significantly worse.[77] Many of these disenfranchised young people will find alternative forms of 'employment' in criminal activity only to be used as pawns in accumulation games that will unravel within the criminal–political nexus. As the Minister for Interior of Ukraine at the time, General Kravchenko wrote:

> the ... unemployed are a considerable reserve for expanding and restoring the criminal potential ... and the curtailed social protection programs for poor layers of the society have made many people face the dilemma of choosing between legal and criminal ways of existence.[78]

The General too will fall victim to the same accumulation games a year after writing those words, the game will be of a higher calibre, the one of President Kuchma's involvement in the ordered killing of the journalist Georgiy Gongadze.

The industrial regions where most of the country's heavy and lucrative industry is concentrated, Donbas, the labour inadvertently was concentrated as well. This contributed to a stronger sense of workers' unity and shared worker identity that is so crucial for labour mobilisation. It is not by accident that Donbas would become the epicentre of the movement for Novorossiya and separatism but was a result of a series of connected and complex shifts in the socio-economic make-up of the region in the context of the growing inequality and disproportionality of wealth distribution and the accompanying shift in societal consciousness utilised by the 'masters of Donbas'. However, what had started as a social movement of over 500,000 coal miners in 1989 and served as one of the catalysts to the independence movement, as was discussed in two earlier chapters, was also systematically becoming disintegrated and disempowered through marketisation reforms and associated assaults on the worker's rights to organise, bargain and socially reproduce. This disintegration and disempowerment has had a strong and long-lasting effect on the utility that the dispossessed masses have for the regime of neoliberal kleptocracy as strikers, gangsters, protesters, corrupt or co-opted administrators and the like. Historically, however, the workers' movement in Donbas has been very strong. Drawing on the framework of Donatella della Porta and Mario Diani,[79] Vlad Mykhnenko shows the 'sequences of contention' in which the movement has been born historically via 'four characteristic aspects of the movement': (1) 'informal interaction networks', (2) 'shared beliefs and solidarity', (3) 'collective action focusing on conflicts', and (4) 'use of protest'.[80] First and foremost, he explains, 'the informal ties observed among the Donbas miners' are very similar to such ties in other miners' communities around the world where close networks and reliance on socialization result directly from working together in 'extremely dangerous conditions'.[81] By the 1980s, 254 mines and mining-related enterprises employed some 35 per cent of all the workforce of Donbas[82] thus providing a strong basis for a shared identity and network building. Moreover, the class structure of the overall workforce too was crucial; so in the Soviet census of 1989, '70 per cent of Donbas inhabitants were classified as working class (workers), a quarter ... as white-collar personnel (public service); and only 5 per cent were classified as peasants (collective farmers).'[83] People moved to Donbas in masses during the Soviet Industrial revolution that generated high demand for labour and during Stalin's Great Terror when the region became a harbour for fugitives.[84] This contributed to the region's population multi-ethnicity, with a high proportion of ethnic Russians, to the dominance of Russian language at the Soviet *lingua franca* in everyday use – over four-fifths of households, and to Russian cultural dominance due to the long period of structural powerlessness of the Ukrainian cultural tradition on the territory of Ukraine.[85]

Second, the workers had shared beliefs that resonated with the Marxist theory of value where the labour expended in the production process determined the real value of products;[86] they hold the materialist understanding of their work.[87] Surrounded by increasingly deteriorating conditions of life and work while risking life in outdated mines for steady production outputs, it is unsurprising that economic injustice and exploitation were clearly marked in the workers' consciousness. And indeed 80 per cent of coal mines, in 1988, were over 40 years old;[88] while it took 'four deaths and six serious injuries for every million ton of coal mined in the region.'[89] Such blatant injustice combined with the heroic image of miners in USSR popular imagery and, what Zimmer calls 'the trap of past glory' of the industrial region[90] might have added oil to the fire of the workers' discontent.

Multiple conflictual issues emerged as a result of systematic injustice embedded in the Soviet system that celebrated the miners on paper yet was unable to provide adequate compensation for hard work and deaths, Mykhnenko continues. Despite being the best-paid profession in post-war USSR with the highest pension from as early as 50, few could enjoy those benefits due to the high mortality and average life expectancy being *circa* 38 years.[91] The lack of appropriate housing and standard consumer goods shortages brought on by Perestroika only added to the grievances and thus conflictual issues.

The system was apparently failing Donbas workers so they turned to protest as a democratic means; the fourth characteristic aspect of the movement. Together with shortages of supply Gorbachev's Perestroika brought Glasnost and democratisation. The disenchanted miners used a variety of means to show their discontent: collective actions, 'refusals to work', hunger strikes, writing of telegrams, letters and petitions requesting independence of enterprise and wage increases.[92] At first, the workers targeted enterprise management and its form, that is, centralised and run from above, as the source of their problems. By the late 1980s, 'the system' of state socialism was perceived as their enemy as is evidenced by the demands for enterprise autonomy as I also discussed in Chapter 2. What was not clear at the time was that the enterprise autonomy via privatisation that the following reform would install, would bring a different form of centralisation through concentration of control and produced capital in the hands of oligarchs who were less socially accountable than the Soviet system. Instead of reallocation of authority and revenue, the workers were faced with wage arrears, even harsher shortages of goods, growing unemployment and a crisis of representation.

5

Neoliberal kleptocracy, FDI
and transnational capital

MULTI-VECTORAL POLICY OR A NEVER-ENDING
GAME OF PREFERANS

Kuchma's foreign policy was built on the *multi-vectoral* principle that meant trying to build good relationships with both western and eastern partners. Such choice was dictated by necessity – Ukraine was heavily dependent on IFIs' money, imports from east and west, and had large arrears from Russian gas import. A souring relationship with either of the partners could be catastrophic not only for the oligarchic energy-intensive production dependent on Russian gas but also for the borderline insolvent economy as a whole. The success of oligarchic state–capital 'enterprise' directly depended on access to foreign loans, on creation of legal avenues for transnationalisation of accumulation, for example, offshoring of revenue, and access to cheap energy imports to feed energy-intensive and ageing industry. Multi-vectoral foreign policy, however, was not without controversy. On the one hand, an effort to maintain a non-discriminatory good relationship with foreign partners was being made that is arguably still the best option for Ukraine. On the other, however, the devil is in the detail of the approach and in its consistency. While on paper it appeared as a solid policy option, in practice Kuchma's multi-vectoral engagements were often contradictory and incompatible. He was playing a risky game of international Preferans[1] diplomacy. The approach involved conflicting flirtations with multiple partners at the same time and included, among other, empty promises of policy reform to the IMF in exchange for loans, part-serious trade negotiations with CIS countries, the EU, the WTO and so on – sustaining the myth of transition.

One of the characteristic features of Kuchma's second term was institutionalisation of the mechanisms of semi-licit accumulation and accumulation by crime. The above was an entrenchment of economic practices that began to evolve long before the USSR disintegrated in the criminal-political nexus discussed in previous chapters. Basing his analysis on criminal activity and global mafia networks Misha Glenny concludes that during Kuchma's ten years as president of Ukraine, the latter 'presided over the total criminalisation of the Ukrainian government and civil service' and himself often covered up large-scale fraud and money laundering.[2] Arms trade, for example, was a popular means of making money even before Kuchma. Thus, Kravchuk established a commercial department at the Defence Ministry in 1991 'whose main aim was to turn the vast store of Soviet weapons inherited by Ukraine into cash'.[3] The subsequent arms trade scandals included the transportation of a ship filled with arms to Bosnian Serb forces by Global Technology Inc. against UN embargo[4] and a sale of '$100-million worth of high-technology anti-aircraft radar systems'[5] against UN sanctions to Iraq in 2002.[6] Glenny suggests that 'the Ukrainian experience was unprecedented' and even in Yeltsin's Russia some distance existed between the political and the economic.[7] In Ukraine, he continues, by the end of the 1990s, 'the oligarchs and government became one, fused together by the superglue of the SBU's, post-independence intelligence service'.[8] Glenny's findings are also confirmed by the infamous Melnychenko tapes released in 2000. The authenticity of the recording was tested and verified by the 'audiotape expert Bruce Koenig of Virginia-based BEK TEK'.[9]

In conditions of criminalisation of the state, the status quo of the ruling bloc that rested mainly on coercion and 'faking democracy',[10] any information leaks about Kuchma's administration had to be muffled at all costs. The apogee of lawlessness was the murder of Georgiy Gongadze in 2000. The latter was an investigative journalist, who founded an online newspaper, Українська правда (*Ukrayinska Pravda, Eng. Ukrainian Truth*), that produced anti-Kuchma publications.[11] The decapitated, heavily beaten body of the journalist was found months after his abduction. It was identified that he had died as a result of strangulation, and that the body was then covered in petrol and partly burned. His skull was only found nine years later.[12] The most recent investigation findings show that Medvedchuk, former head of presidential administration, Marchuk, former national security chief, and Derkach, former head of the Kyiv security agency, were all linked to the case.[13] Based on the Melnychenko tapes, it was discovered that Ukrainian Army General Pukach (as he admitted when interrogated) organised the abduction of Gongadze and personally strangled him following the order of General

Kravchenko.[14] Kravchenko was not able to confirm the above as he was killed the night before his testimony on 4 March 2005 – shot twice in the head; the police managed to log the case as a suicide.[15] At the time of writing, the Gongadze case is still open. His murder and the Melnychenko tapes resulted in 2000 in public unrest led by the anti-Kuchma fractions of the ruling bloc and became known in the Anglophone press as the 'Kuchmagate' crisis.[16] The political counter-movement 'Ukraine without Kuchma' was composed of 24 opposition parties and social movements some of which have been fighting against the rule of nomenklatura since the 1980s. The movement was led by Lutsenko (Socialist Party), Chemerys (social organisation Respublika Institute) and Shkil (leader of UNA-UNSO).[17] The protests were suppressed and the leaders and coordinators were prosecuted; some were also briefly incarcerated by the SBU.[18]

Such internal crisis of legitimacy and omnipresent lawlessness were damaging for foreign relations, political and trade. Western investors from the USA, the EU and particularly Germany (Ukraine's strongest EU-isation backers) became 'disenchanted with the country', however did not give up on it.[19] Instead, both US and EU capital have been making systematic strategic attempts to penetrate Ukraine's market. Indeed, the emergence of a huge market of approximately 150 million consumers and a vast availability of highly skilled and low-wage labourers were a great opportunity for capital expansion. In a personal interview with the Corporate Europe Observatory think-tank, the former Secretary General of ERT, Keith Richardson, said that the demise of the USSR was as if they 'have discovered a new South-East Asia on the [EU] doorstep'.[20] In 1999, EU businesses established the European Business Association in Ukraine that was aimed at lobbying their interests where the European Commission effort did not suffice. The EBA group has since functioned as a platform of co-optation of domestic corporate managerial cadre. The USA also has been actively extrapolating their geopolitical and economic interests, that is, the spread of the Washington Consensus by engaging with Ukrainian authorities via IFIs (World Bank and IMF) and state institutions directly; establishment of lobby and interest groups (American Chamber of Commerce, Council for US–Ukraine Relations, and US–Ukraine Business Council). However, their efforts had mixed results as mechanisms of influence institutionalised and effective in the EU and the USA were not yielding the same in Ukraine; here other mechanisms were at play. At the same time, Ukrainian capital in its

link with the state has succeeded in accumulation of assets across most
lucrative sectors.

FOUR STAGES OF FDI

Foreign capital presence was rather limited in the 1990s Ukraine.
Regulatory framework for investment was missing at first and thus risk
of market entry was too high. FDI occurred in four main stages.[21] The
first lasted from 1991 until adoption of the Decree 'On the Regime of
Foreign Investment'. It was described by Pekhnyk as a 'logic continuation
of the "cooperatives boom" of the last years of Soviet perestroika' with
legislation in many instances being still the same and most exchange
was based on personal or family links with investors. The second stage
began with the adoption of the Cabinet of Ministers Decree 'On Regime
of Foreign Investment' on 23 May 1993 (N28, Article 302) and lasted
until 1997.[22] The flow of foreign capital rapidly increased and many large
TNCs established their branches, representations and joint ventures
(e.g. Coca-Cola Amatil, Procter & Gamble, Philip Morris, R.J. Reynold's
Tobacco, Sony, Philips, Bosch, Daewoo (Electronics), Samsung and LG).
Despite the volume of investment being relatively insignificant (approximately $1.438 billion by 1 January 1997), it was a crucial stage in the
transnational(-ising) capital expansion into the Ukrainian market since
it is then that most foreign companies set roots in Ukraine. Those years
witnessed a large inflow of investors for a number of reasons. First, the
Law of Ukraine 'On Foreign Investment' (from 13 March 1992) provided
state guarantee to foreign investors on investment return and protection
from changes to investment and taxation legislation for ten years. Second,
the Decree 'On Regime of Foreign Investment' (from 20 May 1993)
relieved an array of TNCs from revenue tax for a period of five years
from the start of the qualifying investment/contract. Third, tax rates on
money transfer to parent companies were no higher than 15 per cent and
according to EEC standards the rates' maximum was lowered to 10 per
cent.[23] Lawlessness omnipresent in Ukraine at the time, combined with
a general lack of state control over TNCs' activities even in the key areas,
was risky yet potentially lucrative and thus attractive. Hardly anything
prevented foreign companies from market exploitation that is evidenced
by the large scale of financial speculations characteristic of that period.
It was estimated that $40–$50 billion was needed for normal functioning
of the Ukrainian economy in 1996. Since the government did not have

the money, foreign loans (discussed elsewhere in the book) and FDI had to be attracted at any cost. However, demand was much higher than supply. In the period from 1991 until 2001, the volume of FDI in Ukraine amounted to some $3.9 billion that corresponded to $79 per capita and is the second lowest after Belarus among the post-Soviet countries.[24]

The third stage of the foreign investor activity began in 1996 when the Decree 'On Regime of Foreign Investment' was abolished and many TNCs privileges were lost.[25] The result was a significant decline in investor activity until 1999, for example, R.J. Reynold's Tobacco closed one of their plants as did Coca-Cola Amatil; both in Lviv Oblast. The government's inconsistency of benefits abolition did not help investor trust either. Soon after the Decree was annulled, considerable privileges were granted to Nestlé (which acquired a controlling stake in JSC Svitoch) and Daewoo Motors. In the latter case, a pretext of Ukrainian automotive industry development was used that helped the plant achieve a near-monopoly on the Ukrainian market, not least due to considerable tax benefits. Once again, where domestic capital had the will, it found the way. Red directors-turned oligarchs needed to attract investment from abroad to inject needed capital into starved enterprises. Avtozaz, part of UkrAvto chaired by Tariel Vasadze did precisely that by forming a joint venture with the South Korean Daewoo Motors. After the latter went bankrupt in 2001, UkrAvto – a trustee of 82 per cent state-owned shares of Avtozaz-Daewoo – bought the enterprise in 2002 and merged it with ZAZ (UkrAvto).

The fourth stage partially overlaps with the previous three chronologically. It was marked by adoption of the law 'On the Changes to the Law of Ukraine "On the Budget of Ukraine for year 2005"' in March 2005. The latter annulled the Law of Ukraine 'On General Positions of Establishment and Functioning of Special (free) Economic Zones' (SEZs) from 13 October 1992 and an array of other laws and by-laws (see Table 5.1 for details) which theretofore regulated establishment and functioning of 12 SEZs and 72 PDA (Priority Development Areas). Economic freedoms granted to business in those areas, again, favoured domestic capital, as I will discuss later in the chapter.

FOREIGN CAPITAL IN UKRAINE: LOBBYING IN THE DARK

First neoliberalism and then authoritarian neoliberalism since 2007–2008, spread globally by the coordinated efforts of IFIs, global policy platforms (the WEF, the Trilateral Commission, the ICC, the Bilderberg Group, and the WBCSD), and a network of international, regional, and local lobby and interest groups. Global hegemony of capital must involve domination in the economic, political and social structures simultaneously.[26] Thus, it cannot be limited to mere market penetration by transnational corporations. Neither can transnationalisation of the state be reduced to perfunctory state membership in international organisations. The given state's legislation must be altered in accordance with the requirements set by the above organisations – for example, WTO, the IMF – and law enforcement must be guaranteed to provide smooth functioning of business and protection for investment. The state is to function and transform in accordance with the concept of control as it is envisaged by transnational(-ising) capital, that is, neoliberalism since the 1970s and authoritarian neoliberalism since 2007–2008. For that to be possible *trasformismo* of the ruling, capitalist and managerial classes must occur that will in turn eventually lead to a passive revolution in the rest of society as consent to the hegemonic concept of control is manufactured.[27] Failed or incomplete passive revolutions lead to popular unrest as they did in Ukraine. Joint class strategy or '*the articulation of capitalist interest requires sites beyond the boardrooms* [or] places where business leaders can come together to discuss issues of shared concern, to find common ground and to devise strategies for action.'[28] Co-optation and the subsequent *trasformismo* occur through *socialisation* – the adoption of certain codes of conduct, behaviour, dress and so on – on a state, corporate and individual level. There are multiple foreign groups that promote democratisation, EU-isation, and such in Ukraine; as for the corporate platforms of neoliberal socialisation in Ukraine – there are four, three US and one EU group: (1) the US–Ukraine Business Council (USUBC); (2) the American Chamber of Commerce (ACC); (3) the Centre for US-Ukraine Relations (CUSUR); and (4) the European Business Association (EBA). Starting as early as 1992, they began to set foot in Ukraine in an attempt to directly engage with the government and secure routes for its accumulation interests. Yet, just as IFIs and foreign governments, the lobbies found that their usual tools would need adaptations if they were to work in the Ukrainian context. By the end of the 1990s, when Ukraine's own primitive accumulation period began to translate into concentration of capital in FIGs, it too would begin to engage with the groups for personnel training, experience exchange, etc. and even set up its own platform for cooperation – Yalta European

Strategy (YES) launched by Pinchuk in 2004. Yet Ukrainian capital will continue to operate with its own idiosyncrasies and will continue to dominate the economy in the key sectors.

THE FOUR LOBBIES

Policy and lobby groups as organisations can be divided into two categories – those with individual/managerial (e.g. the European Roundtable of Industrialists, the Trilateral Commission, the Bilderberg Group) and company membership (e.g. the UNICE/BusinessEurope, the European Business Association, the Centre for US–Ukraine Relations, the American Chamber of Commerce, the US–Ukraine Business Centre). That is not to say that there is no individual interpersonal interaction within lobbies with company membership structure – on the contrary, individual representatives of companies and whole industries actively engage in both official meetings and forums and social events organised by the groups with company membership type. It does mean, however, that within those groups, there are different levels of interaction. The groups and forums with individual membership (e.g. the World Economic Forum) present much deeper integrated platforms for direct negotiating of interests and strategic plans of the transnational(-ising) capitalist class and politicians. Groups with corporate membership serve as platforms of co-optation and on the managerial level, implementing and socialising the concepts of control into business strategies. All those groups, local and global, are platforms where the 'comprehensive concepts of control [as] expressions of bourgeois hegemony reflecting a historically specific hierarchy of classes and class fractions' are generated.[29] Both individual and company membership groups regularly interact nationally and internationally with political and legal authorities and are often even established by the latter as it is the case with the EBA and the European Commission. Business interests are being discussed and further lobbied within and through a complex but very efficient network of groups and associations of entrepreneurs who are competitors and share the same strategic interests, that is, lower taxes, market and labour code liberalisation and so forth. Lobbying tactics include promoting or blocking certain laws and regulations that could affect specific economic activities. A crucial feature of such networks is engagement with politicians, corporations, and businesspeople in the target countries (i.e.

co-optation) through accepting them as members or honorary visitors/ speakers at meetings.

The most extensive empirical study of the policy groups, corporate interlocks and interlocking directorates to date is William Carroll's *The Making of a Transnational Capitalist Class: Corporate Power in the 21st Century* (2010). In the book, Carroll analyses five global policy groups – the World Economic Forum (WEF), the International Chamber of Commerce (ICC), the Bilderberg Group, the Trilateral Commission, and the World Business Council for Sustainable Development (WBCSD) – and shows their organisation internationally via both personal and company-member links.[30] There is a striking dominance of North Atlantic corporate-elite members in the five groups' leadership while the peripheral and semi-peripheral regions are more often represented on company-level with minimal personal representation of the transnational capitalist class in their interest groups on a regular basis.[31] The five groups are the 'commanding heights' of a global hierarchically structured network of lobby and interest groups that function to institutionalise the rule of transnational(-ising) capital. For example, the ICC has daughter organisations worldwide. The American Chamber of Commerce has its own global network and is the most developed branch of the ICC. The three US groups present in Ukraine – ACC, USUBC and CUSUR – essentially promote the same agenda, however, were established by different social forces. In Figure 5.1, I present a visualisation of interlocking company membership of the five global policy platforms and the four interest groups in Ukraine. Numbers indicate the number of interlocking member-companies in the organisations as of 2011, when Yanukovych's regime had fully usurped economic and political power in the country.

As shown in Figure 5.1, there are strong interlocks on a company level among the five global policy platforms and the four interest and lobby groups present in Ukraine. The data shows that there are multiple interlocks between the USA and the EU companies in their respective interest groups that confirms coordination in lobbying efforts of US and EU capital. It must be noted that full company membership and thus decision-making power in the lobbies are reserved only for companies of US and EU origin while all other companies are only associate members.

Transnational(-ising) capital permeates policy-making worldwide through both companies and hierarchically organised structure of policy and lobby groups where the agency of that capital is institutionalised on

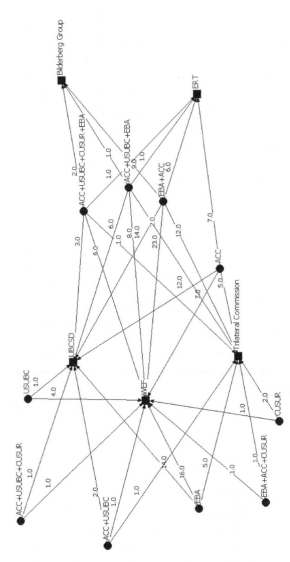

Figure 5.1 Interlocking company membership in the global policy groups and the foreign business lobby and interest groups' in Ukraine

Source: Compiled by the author based on data available on the websites of presented organisations (2011).

Key: squares indicate global policy groups; dots indicate lobby and interest groups in Ukraine; numbers show the numbers of company interlocks between the respective groups.

multiple levels, directly and indirectly. Transnational(-ising) capital is predominantly North Atlantic[32] with a noticeable shift towards German dominance in the network that started since 2000.[33] My analysis of the top 500 TNCs on both company (all 500) and directorates (top 100) level, shows that there are no interlocking directors between the top 100 TNCs and the Ukrainian corporations. However, there is significant company-level presence of the top 500 TNCs in the foreign policy groups in Ukraine where some companies are represented in more than one lobby simultaneously. In Figure 5.2, I present the visualisation of those findings.

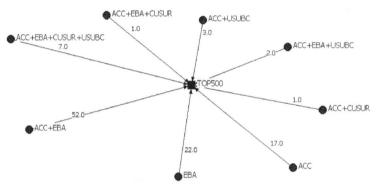

Figure 5.2   Top 500 corporations in the policy groups in Ukraine (the latter dataset was last updated by the author in December 2010

Source: Compiled by the author; Source: *FT* Top 500 TNCs and policy group websites, 2010.

Key: dots signify lobbies in Ukraine; numbers show the number of interlocking company members.

In Figure 5.2, there is a significant presence of the top 500 TNCs in the foreign interest and lobby groups in Ukraine. All in all, 105 of the top 500 TNCs were represented in the foreign interest and lobby groups in 2010. Also, a noticeably larger number of companies have interlocking membership with the top 500, the ACC, and the EBA – the trend is not surprising as there is a convergence in strategy or concept of control, EU and US capital despite companies being in a condition of competition with one another. One-fifth of the world's largest TNCs are present both on the Ukraine's market and in the lobbies.

The capitalist market must always grow and 'the need of a constantly expanding market for its products chases the bourgeoisie all over the whole surface of the globe. It must nestle everywhere, settle everywhere, establish connections everywhere.'[34] Thus, transnational(-ising) capitalist seeks expansion first by advocating institutionalisation of neoliberal market economy as a form of social reproduction and then by entering and taking over those market economies by its 'first-mover' advantage. Assistance of IFIs and the global hierarchically structured network of interest and lobby groups are crucial in this crusade. In the EU, the two major policy groups of the EU business in Brussels are the European Roundtable of Industrialists[35] and the Union of Industrial and Employers' Confederations of Europe (UNICE; since 2007 – BusinessEurope). Market expansion ambitions are manifest in the vigorous support of the two for 'expeditious integration of the newly market-oriented economies' to the east of the EU border into organisation's structure, that is, of the EU enlargement.[36] Apart from ERT's deep involvement with EU bodies in Brussels, especially the European Commission on the issue of Eastern Neighbourhood integration, most of the 49 members' companies are simultaneously members of the foreign interest and lobby groups representing their interests locally in Ukraine. In Figure 5.3, I present a visualisation of my analysis of the ERT company members' involvement in the EU and US interest groups in Ukraine.

Many companies are simultaneously members of two or more lobby and interest groups. Initially established to represent US and EU business in Ukraine, the lobbies eventually began to welcome Ukrainian companies as members, although not on the full basis. In Figure 5.4, I show my analysis of connections between the groups on the basis of interlocking company membership. Numbers indicate the number of interlocking companies.

As it is shown in Figure 5.4, there are strong interlocks among all four groups with a clear dominance of interlocking company membership between the ACC and the EBA with 228 (201 EBA/ACC + 22 ACC/EBA/ USUBC + 5 ACC/EBA/CUSUR) interlocking members. The ACC is also a group that has most interlocks with the EBA of the three US groups. The EBA has 17 interlocks with the CUSUR (5 EBA/CUSUR + 12 EBA/ CUSUR/ACC/USUBC) and 14 with USUBC (2 EBA/USUBC + 12 EBA/ CUSUR/ACC/USUBC). The three US groups are strongly interlocked. So, the ACC and the CUSUR had 12 interlocks (3 ACC/CUSUR + 4 ACC/CUSUR/USUBC + 5 ACC/CUSUR/EBA), the ACC and the USUBC 58 interlocks (20 ACC/USUBC + 4 ACC/USUBC/CUSUR + 12 ACC/USUBC/CUSUR/EBA + 22 ACC/USUBC/EBA), and USUBC and

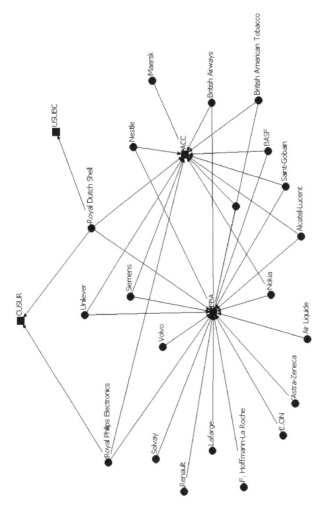

Figure 5.3 ERT members' companies representation in the EU and US lobby groups in Ukraine

Source: compiled by the author based on the data available on the groups' websites; last update January 2011.

Key: squares signify the lobby and interest groups; dots signify companies with identifies names; lines show interlocking membership of companies in lobby and interest groups.

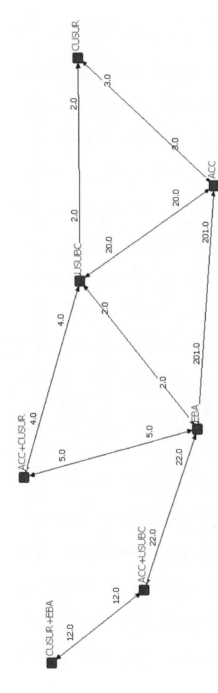

Figure 5.4 Company membership interlocks among four foreign policy groups in Ukraine

Source: Compiled by the author on the basis of data available at the lobbies' websites; last update: December 2011.

Key: squares indicate lobby and interest groups; lines indicate interlocks between the groups; numbers along the lines indicate the number of companies with interlocking membership.

CUSUR 18 interlocks (2 CUSUR/USUBC + 4 (ACC+CUSUR)/USUBC + 12 (CUSUR+EBA)/(ACC/USUBC). The above can be explained by similarities and differences in the goals and organisation of the groups. At the same time, the number of interlocking members between the groups is limited by the number of members in those groups. The EBA had 852 members in 2010, the ACC had 560, the USUBC had 203, and the CUSUR 182. The USUBC and the CUSUR had a significantly lower number of members than the EBA and the ACC. Thus, even though the interlocks between the EBA and the ACC are more numerous, their interlocks with the CUSUR and the USUBC are no less significant.

THE EUROPEAN BUSINESS ASSOCIATION (EBA)

The EBA was founded in 1999 as a forum for 'discussion and resolution of problems facing the private sector in Ukraine'. The initiative was launched by business people who 'saw advantages and benefits in the European business community acting together and was supported by the European Commission'. The EBA operates as an independent body that brings together 852 EU, Ukrainian and other international companies (as of 28 September 2011), is responsible to its members and has representing the interests of European and domestic investors in Ukraine as its core mission. The vision of the Association is defined as 'to enable and drive full establishment of the European business practices and values in Ukraine'.[37] The EBA is a non-profit association of legal entities and its 'mission' is claimed to be threefold: (1) '[Promotion of] ethical and lawful business practices and standards in Ukraine'; (2) '[Facilitation of] communication between the business and political communities'; and (3) '[Representation of the EBA] members' interests in political circles to improve the business environment using the EBA's expertise'.[38] All members are to adhere to the Code of Conduct and thus must:

1. 'Promote fair and transparent competition
2. Respect intellectual and other property rights
3. Promote and respect non-corruption practices
4. Encourage compliance with prevailing law at all times
5. Respect employees' rights, including health and safety, equal opportunities at work, and training
6. Seek to develop constructive relations with local and national government bodies to achieve a just and productive business climate

7. Respect local communities, and recognize the importance of environmental protection
8. Promote the application of these principles by those with whom [the EBA – and its members] do business.[39]

The Association offers a wide scope of services to its members in five main areas which are: (1) 'collective advocacy of members' interests'; (2) voicing the interests of business in the EU policy-making process; (3) provision of 'regular information support'; (4) maintaining networking opportunities and organising social events for the members; and (5) a range of other services, for example, a discount system for members on other member company services, etc. (EBA general). *De jure*, the EBA is a body that represents interests of both EU and domestic investors, however, *only EU companies* qualify for full membership and it is only full members that partake in decision-making of the lobby. Such procedure effectively funnels EU member companies' and their CEOs' outlook into the functioning of the EBA. The associate member companies' COEs, managers, and employees – the managerial class of Ukraine – are co-opted into those concepts of control via multiple forums, meetings, and programmes that result in emulation of corporate and individual professional behaviour, that is, *trasformismo* as I will show next.

The EBA holds annual General Membership Meetings that serve as a watershed in the organisation's activities. During the Annual Meetings, the President and the Executive Director update the members on the activities of the organisation in a given year and also brief them on the plans for the year to come. Governmental speakers are also invited to address the EBA members so as to provide them with 'first-hand information on prospects of Ukraine's investment climate development and discuss the most pending obstacles to investment in Ukraine.'[40] For example, in 2008, such honorary speakers were the Head of the Delegation of the European Commission to Ukraine HE Jose Manuel Pinto Teixeira, Vice-Prime-Minister of Ukraine on European Integration Mr Hryhoriy Nemyrya.[41] Aside the Annual Meeting, General Membership Meetings are conducted as necessary over the course of a year and serve as the main interaction platform for members' communication with both European and Ukrainian authorities (usually from the Cabinet of Ministers or deputies of the Verkhovna Rada of Ukraine). During such meetings, close dialogue is maintained with European authorities as for

EU–Ukraine relationship, investment climate prospects, Ukraine's rapprochement with the EU evolution, etc.

The EBA activities are monitored by 29 members of Executive Staff who consists of Lobbying department (the most numerous one – ten staff), Membership/events department, PR and Communication department, Administrative Support Department, Regional development department and are managed by the Executive Director.[42] The Executive Staff are supervised by the 16 Board Members who run the EBA, with the President at the top of the pyramid. The Board meets every month 'to approve acceptance of new EBA members and decide on other issues related to the EBA activity'.[43] It is a body of members elected every year for a two-year period at an Annual General Meeting. Every full member can nominate one candidate to the Elections and there cannot be 'more than three Board members from one industry and more than three representatives of one nationality'.[44] Elections to the Board as well as to the position of the President of the EBA are held in compliance with the Charter of the European Business Association and by the Internal Rules and Procedures of the Association.[45] Since it is *only full members* who can nominate candidates, participate in elections and therefore be directly involved in the decision-making process of the EBA, strategic orientation of the organisation effectively is pro-EU business and their interests. All the work of the organisation outside the General Annual Meeting is conducted by: (1) Regional Branches, (2) Committees, and (3) Working Groups. There are regional branches of the EBA in Donetsk, Dnipropetrovsk, Kharkiv, Odesa, Zhytomyr and Lviv. Unsurprisingly, the branches are located in the same oblasts that attract the highest flow of FDI in Ukraine as shown in Tables 5.2, 5.3 and 5.4 and that, until 2005, enjoyed tax breaks or lower taxes (SEZs and PDAs) and where most FIGs of Ukraine are concentrated. It is thus no coincidence that the interests of both foreign capital, presented through the EBA and its member companies, and the most domestic associate member companies – FIGs and otherwise – showed interest in deeper cooperation within the EBA platform in those particular locales. In addition, in October 2010, the EBA have opened a branch in Brussels defining its goals as 'to further promote the Association's mission of enabling the full establishment of the European business practices and values in Ukraine'.[46]

Special emphasis in the EBA is given to networking and for that purpose there are a few programmes run by and for the Association. One of the above is the 'EBA members' products and services' project which covers 14 various sectors, from Administration and Business Support to Transport and Tourism. Effectively and inevitably, a process of harmonisation of interests and strategies translates onto Associate members from the Full members though their leadership in the organisation, that is, the Europeanisation/EU-nisation of entrepreneurial sphere and business handling occurs. The EBA and its Associate membership scheme is a platform of re-moulding of Ukrainian businesses in a manner suitable to the EU standards – the latter ranges from the software used in companies' offices to bringing companies' statutes in accordance with EU legal standards to EuroDrinks parties introduced 'as a means of developing the idea of "Club spirit" and allowing businessmen working in Ukraine to gather regularly to socialise and exchange information and experience' (parties are held as a custom on the last Tuesday of each month either at Kyiv restaurants or various European Embassies).[47] There are many minor socialising events that the EBA holds for its members including film screenings in their own theatre at the Kyiv office as well as a few education programmes, such as English language courses for the member companies' employees and the EBA school project which provides various courses in smooth business communication, etc.

The EBA work complements the functioning of their mother organisation, the Delegation of the European Commission in Ukraine, in their cooperation with the Presidential Administration, the Cabinet of Ministers, and the Parliament of Ukraine on behalf of EU business. Also, because of the latter, the EBA works in cooperation with the Trade and Economic departments of the European Union Embassies in Kyiv. One of the cooperation and negotiation platforms between the EBA members and Ukrainian authorities is EuroDebates project, which is aimed at 'strengthening constructive dialogue of the business community with representatives of legislative and executive authorities.'[48] Debates are normally scheduled as the need arises and involve representatives of the companies interested and a representative(s) of a respective ministry or administration on Ukraine. For example, on the 28 August 2009 EuroDebates were held on the matter of pros and cons of the Amended Customs Legislation. The issues discussed involved: (1) the need of customs clearance simplification; (2) the influence of the amended customs legislation on the investment climate; and (3) possible changes the amended customs legislation would bring to the fiscal functions of Customs. The meeting was attended by some 50 members of the EBA, approximately 25 media representatives. The debate per se was held among eleven representatives of Customs Service and Ministry of Finance, representatives of diplomatic corps and experts in International Customs Law on the authorities side and two business representatives on EBA side – John Farfield (Head of European Association of Express Transporters) and Robert Peacock (Technical Consultant of International Criminal Investigative Assistance Programme).[49] Alongside the Committees, there are three Working Groups hosted by EBA – (1) the Euro-2012 Task Force, (2) the FTA Task Force, and (3) the Ad-Hoc Anti-Crisis group which deal with preparation to Euro-2012 Football championship, promotion of the Free Trade Area with the EU, and the issues related to the current global economic crisis and its impact on Ukraine respectively. Two of the six regional branches – Kharkiv and Lviv – host two additional regional Working Groups each, on Production Management, and on Export and Import.

There are six major tools that the EBA and its members use for lobbying. The first is the Investor's Council under the Cabinet of Ministers of Ukraine established in January 2007. The EBA was invited to become a participant of the Council. Ukrainian capital in the latter is represented by a Co-Chair who was elected in March 2008 – then of Swedbank Ukraine – Serhiy Tyhypko of the Donetsk bloc. The Investor's Council consists of 13 Working Groups: agricultural development; banking and finance; justice; corporate governance; fuel and energy; infrastructure; intellectual property rights; informational technologies; health care; land and real estate; tax and customs policy; technical regulation; macroeconomic development.[50] The Working Group of Justice is a body under the auspices of the Ministry of Justice and is co-chaired by EBA; so is 'the Working Group on Tax and Customs Policy under the Ministry of Finance [co-chaired by EBA – author] on behalf of the investors' community'.[51] The second is the Foreign Investment Advisory Council of Ukraine (FIAC); chaired by the President of Ukraine and is directly monitored by him/her. The EBA and some individual member companies were invited to join the FIAC in 2005; the opportunity was celebrated by the former since it is considered to be 'a highly efficient vehicle to contribute to elaboration and implementation of the state policy related to foreign investment into the national economy of Ukraine, acceleration of Ukraine's integration into global economic processes'.[52] Further, in Autumn 2005, a number of the Working Groups within the FIAC were formed to target specific issue areas of the economy, namely, 'market reform; fiscal and tax policy; banking and non-banking financial institutions and capital market;

comprehensive development of economy; information technologies; agriculture and food industry; image policy of Ukraine.'[53] Jointly with the Minister of Economy of Ukraine, Microsoft Ukraine and Western NIS Enterprise Fund (both companies being the EBA members), the EBA has also been invited to co-chair the FIAC Market Reform Working Group. Within the latter separate sub-groups were formed 'to deal with issues related to property, land use, elimination of administrative barriers, legal issues, special investment promotion regimes.'[54] The EBA is also actively involved in the functioning of FIAC Complex Economy Development Working Group.

Lobbying tool number three are the Governmental Committees (GCs) established by the Cabinet of Ministers of Ukraine on 18 July 2007 by Resolution 950 Cabinet of Ministers on 18 July 2007 to enforce the delivery of its authorities. The Committees' aims are defined as to '[ensure] efficient realization of Cabinet of Ministers authorities, [coordinate] of executive bodies' actions, preliminary consideration (examination) of draft legal acts, conceptions, strategies, major directions of state policy realization, other documents submitted for consideration of the Cabinet of Minister.'[55] Currently there are four working GCs: (1) Governmental Committee on the Issues of Economic Policy chaired by the First Vice-Prime Minister; (2) Governmental Committee on the Issues of Legal Policy, Defense and Enforcement Activity chaired by the First Vice-Prime Minister; (2) Governmental Committee on the Issues of Humanitarian and Social Policy chaired by the Vice-Prime Minister; and (4) Governmental Committee on European Integration and International Collaboration chaired by the Vice-Prime Minister.

Number four is the Public Councils that are established within Ministries and State Committees and serve as platforms for involvement and dialogue with the above for both business communities and wider public. The EBA has been enhancing its cooperation with the Public Councils since 2005 through partaking in Council meetings and otherwise.[56] The EBA holds an important place in the functioning of the Councils. Thus, it was invited to perform the role of the Deputy Head of the Public Collegium of the State Customs Service of Ukraine, it chairs the Sectorial Council on Budget that is part of the Public Collegium of the Ministry of Finance of Ukraine, and last but not least, it is 'a member of permanent commission on Consideration of Taxation Bills within the Public Collegium of the State Tax Administration of Ukraine'.[57] The fifth tools are the Working Groups in other than Ministerial Working Groups.

Thus, to mention a few, the EBA have actively promoted interests of its members in a Joint Working Group within the State Tax Administration (STA), the National Bank (NBU), the State Treasury and the Ministry of Finance of Ukraine on the issues of Value Added Tax legislation alterations; took part in a Working Group on Investment Promotion and Protection of the Ukraine–EU Subcommittee #1 on Trade and Investment under the Ministry of Economy of Ukraine; actively participated in the Expert Group under the National Bank of Ukraine On Development of Regulations On Export and Import of Capital, was part of the Steering Committee of the TACIS Bistro Project/2004/084-670 Combating Counterfeits Plant Protection Project, and many more.[58] Last, the EBA is a member of the Board at the Ukrainian Union of Small, Medium, and Privatised Enterprises and also the Supervisory Board of the Ukrainian Centre for Investment Promotion (UCFIP). The latter was founded by the Government of Ukraine in August 2005:

> to promote foreign direct investment in Ukraine through providing a range of services to existing and potential foreign investors: identify investment opportunities; offer information on site locations, vendors, service providers, local and regional resources; access to databases on investment proposals etc.[59]

The UCFIP is registered as 'an autonomous non-profit agency under the Ministry of Economy governed by a director and an external steering committee consisting of public and private sector representatives.'[60]

Indirect channels of interests' communication and general lobbying strategies of the EBA (i.e. networking, socialising and communication at multiple EBA events and beyond the latter) aside, *all* individual member companies can inquire for lobbying on their behalf. They fill forms online where they can state a problem they are having with certain legislation that restricts or otherwise hinders their business activities, list a Law or Legal Act that regulates a certain activity and also list other EBA-member companies affected by all the above. Companies are also given an opportunity to mention a specific authority they consider needed to be contacted (e.g. President, Cabinet of Ministers, etc.), address a competent EBA Committee or a Working Group that deals with a given class of issues as well as one of the regional branches of the EBA and suggest a preferred lobbying tool if they will to do so.[61] The Association via its Committees and Lobbying Tools in turn guarantees its full support and assistance in removal or lessening of the above-mentioned 'hindrances'. During the period between 19 January 2006 and 13 April 2011, there have been 34 cases of successful lobbying by the EBA and progress on further 15 cases has been achieved.[62] Interestingly, as my research shows all the above have occurred between 12 June 2009 and 13 April 2011,[63] that is, began during the second premiership of Tymoshenko under Yushchenko's presidency. Interestingly enough, since 2009, the number of lobbying successes has been growing and between April 2011 and March 2013 there have been 37 more such cases. All of the mentioned lobbying attempts were aimed at reduction of state control over economic activity and marketisation alike. The cases included simplification of import and export procedures (relaxed registration, simplified customs clearance, etc.), harmonisation of regulations with the EU in IT and electronics sector, revoking of medication advertising ban, creation of State Land Cadastre in preparation for land privatisation, simplification of market entry for pharmaceutical and insurance companies from the EU, and more. Prior to mid-2009, the Association's involvement with Ukrainian government was more indirect although rather active. The EBA representatives were invited to partake in conferences, presentations, and roundtables concerning both progress and future strategies of different sectors of economy. It was only in 2009, however, that the recommendations of the lobby were *directly* transformed into legislation that involves harmonisation of legislation with that of the EU in all the areas of the EBA Committees' work. Moreover, as my research shows, since 2009 until present there has been an acceleration in cooperation between the EBA and Ukraine's legislators as the growing number of lobbying successes show. However, those successes have been confined to the sectors of economy where import/export links already exist and need to be re-regulated or transnationalised, that is, insurance services, consumer goods and electronics specifically, pharmaceuticals. In the energy and heavy industrial sectors, however, both protectionism and preferential treatment of oligarchic FIGs still dominates.

THE US POLICY LOBBY AND INTEREST GROUPS IN UKRAINE

The US capital in Ukraine is represented by three lobby and interest groups – the American Chamber of Commerce (ACC, branch of the international ACC that in its turn is part of the International Chamber of Commerce discussed above), the US–Ukraine Business Council

(USUBC), and the Centre for US–Ukraine Relations (CUSUR). Although they all present interests of the US capital in Ukraine and are involved in lobbying business interests, and both corporate and individual co-optation, they were initiated by three sets of forces. The ACC entry of Ukrainian market was an extension of the global network of the Chamber's branches. The USUBC is a joint initiative of the US government and capital, and the CUSUR is an initiative of Ukrainian Americans diaspora – association such as the Ukrainian Congress Committee of America and their US Congress policy group, the Ukrainian Congressional Caucus. The three saw an increase in Ukrainian companies' membership since 1999 (especially 2004) and acceleration of cooperation with the President and the government since 2005. Then Yushchenko, the pro-Western president whose wife – among others – is a member of the US Ukrainian diaspora, and Tymoshenko assumed leadership in the two institutions respectively.

THE AMERICAN CHAMBER OF COMMERCE (ACC/AMCHAM)

American Chamber of Commerce is an influential corporate lobbying actor in both the EU, and Ukraine with its International Division that deals with ACC representations outside the USA accountable for 112 Chambers in over 100 countries.[64] The organisation has been 'fighting for your business' since 1912 and is currently the largest non-profit organisation in the world with '3 million businesses of all sizes, sectors, and regions, as well as state and local chambers and industry associations'.[65] In the USA, the Chamber is also deeply involved in shaping the legal sphere via two bodies: the Institute for Legal Reform and the National Chamber Litigations Centre (the latter is an in-house law firm). Activities of the above organisations are not limited to collaboration with businesses in USA and target countries and lobbying their interests both locally and internationally. The AmCham is a very active organisation in terms of strategies of co-optation into neoliberal marketisation aimed at ruling, capitalist, and managerial classes alike. Therefore, during 2010 alone it 'hosted more than 2,500 programs, meetings, seminars, and forums with various participants, including members of the Obama administration, members of Congress, and dozens of international leaders'.[66] The opposite side of the social spectrum is an important area of the Chamber's work as well and via a 'growing network of grassroots business activists, the Chamber makes a tremendous impact educating voters, turning out the business vote, and advancing legislation on Capitol Hill.'[67] Numerous social events are held for and by the members of the Chamber annually that are aimed at improving networking among its members by bringing businesses together and spreading the common system of ideals and values.

Moreover, the Centre for International Private Enterprise (CIPE) that functions under the auspices of the Chamber essentially serves as a bridge agency between the US Congress and Ukraine's authorities by proxy of ACC. The Centre is run by the Chamber but is in fact one of the four programs of the National Endowment for Democracy (NED) that is funded by the US Congress. NED in its turn is an institution 'dedicated to the growth and strengthening of democratic institutions around the world', that is, it is dedicated to institutionalisation of the Washington Consensus around the world.[68] Established in 1983, ever since the CIPE has been in close collaboration with 'business leaders, policy-makers, and journalists to build the civic institutions vital to a democratic society'; the above has been channelled through a variety of programs that include 'anti-corruption, advocacy, business associations, corporate governance, democratic governance, access to information, the informal sector and property rights, and women and youth.'[69]

The EU Committee of the American Chamber of Commerce was established in the EU capital in the early 1970s. In their extensive study of lobby groups in Brussels, the Corporate European Observatory think tank referred to AmCham's presence as being initially 'somewhat sleepy'. However, less than a decade after being established, the organisation underwent a major revival and became 'one of the first industry lobby groups to systematically monitor and influence European Commission policy making'.[70] The migration of AmCham to Western Europe, its initial 'sleepiness' and subsequent revival can be explained once located within a wider context of global political economy. The dissolution of the Bretton Woods' financial architecture, industrial revival of both Japan and Western Europe, oil crises of the 1970s – all contributed to the need for the US business to seek direct representation of business platforms around the world. Emergence of a vast market on the east of the EU border attracted the interest of ACC too. However, unlike the ERT and UNICE which worked their way into the Eastern and Central European markets by both lobbying the European Commission and working locally in the new market-orientated economies; despite being a part of the International Chamber of Commerce, ACC chooses to represent the

US capital worldwide directly. Although, they sustain close cooperation with their EU counterparts as will be shown shortly.

The Chamber began its operation in Ukraine in 1992 and is structurally a part of the Europe & Eurasia section of the International Division of the American mother organisation. The decision to establish a branch of the US Chamber of Commerce in Ukraine was made at the meeting called by the then Ambassador of the USA to Ukraine, Roman Popadyuk.[71] The latter himself has Ukrainian roots and can be referred to as one of the so-called 'Galician cousins'[72] who helped set up the first Joint Stock companies in Ukraine in the late 1980s–early 1990s.[73] The initial goal of ACC in Ukraine was defined as 'to gather the international business community and provide them with a networking and informational platform'[74] however, the range of goals and programs of the organisation has vastly grown since then.

The first Executive director was Mr Ihor Figlus and Mr Bohdan Kupych became the first President of the Chamber.[75] Both Figlus and Kupych are like Popadyuk of Ukrainian descent and before 1992 have already had successful careers in the corporate world of the USA as a financial analyst and an ITS General manager respectively.[76] By 1998, when Jorge Zukoski took over the leadership, ACC-UA had some 150 member-companies with chiefly American capital.[77] In the aftermath of the rouble crisis of 1998, a decision was taken to allow non-American companies to become members of the ACC-UA. Such change to the Chamber's membership criteria was an ambitious attempt to turn the latter into 'an umbrella organization representing the interests of the international business community operating in Ukraine while at the same time helping to establish a culture of western style lobbying.'[78] The Chamber's creed is that it is 'an apolitical organization [that] does not endorse or align with any single political party or personality but instead strives to work across party lines for the benefit of the internationally oriented business community and ultimately the Ukrainian economy.'[79] One particular feature of ACC-UA as a lobby group is that it does not limit its activity to advocating its members' interests to the government of Ukraine but 'also to all other governments, which are economic partners of Ukraine, on matters of trade, commerce, and economic reform.'[80] In the latter instance, the international connections and representations of the Chamber in over 50 countries around the globe make lobbying for members extremely beneficial and effective.

ACC-UA is 'an active and engaged Member' of a number of committees in Ukraine's government dedicated to investment and investors. Those are: the Investors Council under the Prime Minister of Ukraine (along with the EBA), the Foreign Investment Advisory Council under the President of Ukraine, and the Working Groups under both organisations. It also serves as 'a proactive Member' of a number of Public Councils, Expert Groups within the Ukrainian Ministries, the State Committees and Committees of the Ukrainian Parliament.[81] The Chamber keeps close ties both with the US government and its representatives in Ukraine and with EU authorities in Brussels and their mission in Kyiv. In June 2008, for example, they have proudly supported and hosted the first visit to the independent Ukraine of the US Secretary of Commerce, Carlos Guttierez. The latter met with both the Board of Directors and the Membership of the ACC-UA and have addressed the above 'highlighting the commitment of Washington DC to the business community operating in Ukraine',[82] a commitment to co-optation of Ukraine's ruling, capitalist, and managerial classes into the Washington Consensus. The Chamber coordinates strategies with their sister organisation in Brussels as well as with the 'relevant departments and individuals within the European Commission' to influence EU policy that impacts Ukraine.

The goal of the Chamber as a voice of its members is in channelling neoliberal marketisation and transnationalisation into Ukraine. Namely, the ACC aims 'to operate and conduct business in accordance with the law of the land and to accept certain guiding principles based on U.S. and Western business practices as a preferred code of conduct.'[83] The code consists of the following guidelines:

1. 'Members will make every effort to comply with the laws of Ukraine to which they are subject.
2. 'Members will avoid knowingly assisting any third party in violating any law of Ukraine.
3. 'Members will not knowingly pay or receive bribes or participate in any other unethical, fraudulent, or corrupt practice.
4. 'Members will endeavour to honour all business obligations and commitments that they undertake with professionalism and integrity.
5. 'Members will keep business records in a manner that properly reflects the true nature of their business transactions and activities.

6. 'Members will ensure that their management and supervisors are familiar with applicable labour laws and corporate policies and will take responsibility for preventing and detecting violations in the course of their business operations.

7. '[All member companies and their affiliates are encouraged] to adhere to the provisions of the Foreign Corrupt Practices Act of the United States'.[84]

Strict compliance with law and the codes of conduct is certainly to be advocated however it is the law and the codes that institutionalise trans-nationalisation of Ukraine's state and economy.

The mission of the organisation is manifold and includes bringing together the 'leading organisations of Ukraine', provision of an 'effective platform for networking, information sharing and achieving common goals', advocacy and support for 'a business environment governed by the fair and transparent application of the rule of law to enable private enterprises to flourish', and facilitation of 'access to information, resources, contacts and business support services to facilitate new investment'.[85] ACC-UA also seeks to establish itself as the 'leading voice of the internationally oriented business community in Ukraine', an interlocutor of the latter to the authorities of Ukraine and an irreplaceable partner to that community.[86] For that purpose, the ACC established a number of Committees and Working Groups. The former include Agricultural, Banking and Finance, Customs, Food and Beverage, Fuel and Energy, Health Care, Human Resources, ICT and Tax Committees. As for the Working Groups, by 2011 seven were established and functioned as a taskforce for ACC-UA. They are: Business Management and Education Training (BMET), Certification and Standards, Genetically Modified Organisms (GMOs; active since December 2009), Illegal Corporate Raidering (mid-2006), Joint Stock Companies (1 February 2007), Seeds (early 2008), and Waste Package Management (late 2006). In addition to the above, in 2011, the ACC-UA ran and promoted four Projects that were: (1) the Chamber Educational Project; (2) Euro-2012; (3) Coalition for Innovation, Employment and Development (CIED), and (4) the Coalition against Counterfeiting and Piracy (CACP). Both the Working Groups, the Projects and the Committees functions and goals are updated to correspond to the changing interest of its members as well as the changing economic and political dynamics in Ukraine and globally as is evidenced by the EURO-2012, Corporate Raiding, and Counterfeiting issues among others.

THE US–UKRAINE BUSINESS COUNCIL (USUBC)

The USUBC is an initiative supported by both the US government and business. By 2012, it had 203 member companies from the USA, the EU and Ukraine' membership growth has slowed down since and in 2017 constitutes 211.[87] The USUBC is 'a [501(c)6] private, non-profit trade association representing the interests of US businesses active in Ukraine'. The Council is registered in Washington, DC and focuses on promotion of 'US and Ukrainian commercial ties through regular interactions with US and Ukrainian business and government leaders, and through the analysis and advocacy of key policy issues impacting US businesses and the future of US–Ukrainian relations.'[88] Established in October 1995, 'to advance U.S. companies' trade and investment interests in Ukraine's significant emerging market, advocate for measures to improve conditions for bilateral trade and investment, and generally promote strong, friendly bilateral ties.'[89]

The legal status of the USUBC as an organisation allows a lot of flexibility in sourcing finances as well as in political, and economic activities thus making a body of low social accountability and state control. It is legally defined as an:

> association[s] of persons having a common business interest, whose purpose is to promote the common business interest and not to engage in a regular business of a kind ordinarily carried on for profit. Its activities are directed to the improvement of business conditions of one or more lines of business rather than the performance of particular services for individual persons.[90]

Qualifying associations' members must share a common 'business interest' where 'business' is used in a broad sense of the word and includes 'everything about which a person can be employed'.[91] Associations can be funded by essentially anyone without restrictions since they 'may receive a substantial portion or even the primary part of its income from non-member sources'.[92] Members must work to improve business climate for one or more 'lines of business' by which 'a trade or occupation, entry into which is not restricted by a patent, trademark, or other means that allow private parties to restrict the right to engage in the business' is meant.[93] They may engage in 'an unlimited amount of lobbying, provided that the lobbying is related to the organization's [tax] exempt purpose' and may 'make expenditures for political campaign activities'.[94]

According to the Bylaws of the Council, its Members 'shall comprise United States Companies, associations and other entities which endorse and support the mission of the Corporation which, broadly stated, is the promotion of strong United States investment and trade ties with Ukraine' (Article II, Section 2.01). Members are divided into three classes: (1) Regular, (2) Associate, and (3) Honorary (Article II, Section 2.02). In addition, qualifying associations 'may engage in political campaigns on behalf of or in opposition to candidates for public office provided that such intervention does not constitute the organization's primary activity'.[95] All Regular Members are represented on the Board of Directors – the highest policy-making body in the Council; the Board meets on an annual basis at minimum. In all other instances, the elected Executive Committee is responsible for the running of the Council where the CEO of the Council is the President who works jointly with the Secretary/Treasurer.[96]

The primary agenda of the USUBC includes eleven general 'key issues'. The main key issues identified are: Aerospace and Defence Industry, Agriculture/Agribusiness, Airline Safety, Customs, Economic data and analysis, Energy, Intellectual Property Right (IPR), the USA Presidential Administration, the IMF, the Pipeline Policy in Eurasia and general key issues.[97] The Council hosts and otherwise organises frequent events with agendas ranging from doing business in Ukraine and overcoming legal obstacles to investment to book launches for Ukrainian authors and exhibitions for Ukrainian artists both in Ukraine and the USA. In addition to the standing key issues and activities the USUBC organise ad hoc events to address political and economic issues as they emerge. So, in 2009, a conference to address the impact of the global financial crisis was organised in Kyiv under the title the 'First Annual International Forum on the Economic Development of Ukraine: The Impact of the Global Liquidity Crisis and the Road to Economic Recovery'.[98] The forum was held on 15 October 2009 in Washington, DC and included the ex-ambassador of the USA to Ukraine William B. Taylor, Jr. (Vice-President, Peace and Stability Operations, U.S. States Institute of Peace (USIP), US Support to Global Economic Recovery and to Ukraine), Bohdan Danylyshyn (Minister of Economy of Ukraine),

Hryhoriy Nemyria (Vice-Prime Minister of Ukraine), delegates from the Heritage Foundation, SigmaBlayzer, and many more. The event was planned as an annual occurrence however it has not taken place since October 2009.

In addition to various forums and conferences, the Council regularly publishes a newsletter called the Action Ukraine Report that between 2003 (start year) and 2010 has released over 950 issues. The report sums up the Council's aim as: 'Working to Secure & Enhance Ukraine's Independent, Strong, Democratic, and Prosperous Future', and the newsletter itself is 'a Free, Private, Not-For-Profit, Independent, Public Service Newsletter' where 'Articles are Distributed for Information, Research, Education, Academic, Discussion and Personal Purposes Only'.[99]

THE CENTRE FOR US–UKRAINE RELATIONS (CUSUR)

The Centre of US–Ukraine Relations was founded in 2005 however its formation was an ad hoc necessity that arose as a result of some six years of intensive cooperation among political bodies and social organisations of the countries. The history of the CUSUR commenced in December 1999 with a clear statement issued by the Presidential Administration of Kuchma and the Verkhovna Rada when both 'took clear steps to indicate a serious interest in pursuing a course of "eventual integration into the structures of the Euro-Atlantic world"'.[100] The latter was reciprocated by the Secretary of State at a time, Madeleine Albright in her speech given at Johns Hopkins University in January 2000 where she referred to Ukraine as 'one of the four key countries with whom the US had to deepen bilateral economic and security relations'.[101] The bilateral intention was confirmed on 14 April 2000 during an official visit of Albright to Kyiv. In a US–Ukraine Foreign Ministers Press Availability, Albright and Borys Tarasyuk (Minister for Foreign Affairs of Ukraine at a time) claimed that 'the United States will help Ukraine's reformers in every way' acknowledging the forthcoming difficulties of reform implementation and that 'the strategic partnership between Ukraine and the USA is confirmed' respectively. Tarasyuk also added that mutual understanding was achieved in all of the issues on the agenda of the series of meetings held that day with Albright, namely:

the issue of cooperation in the United Nations Security Council, the issue of the Chernobyl nuclear power plant, OSCE, the World Trade

Organization, Ukraine's cooperation with the European Union, reform of the energy sector, and, in this context, the Ukrainian route for Caspian oil.[102]

The above have signified a new page in USA–Ukraine relationships which was and still is marked by intensification of dialogue on various levels, increased volume of official and unofficial visits of politicians, emergence of, for example, roundtables, exchange programmes for professionals, students of various age, etc. The most prominent of the numbered were the visits and announcement of support for bilateral initiatives by US Presidents. First, Bill Clinton in a public address during his half-day visit to Kyiv on 5 June 2000 (the first time a US president had visited Ukraine since its independence) supported Ukraine's Western aspirations and pledged USA support in the course of reform. And then George W. Bush during his inaugural visit to Europe seconded his predecessor in the joint statement with Kwasniewski, saying that both 'Poland and the United States [reaffirmed] their support for future Ukrainian integration into Western institutions as a solid base for Ukrainian sovereignty, independence, free market economy and civil society.'[103]

The rapprochement described above was met with enthusiasm by the Ukrainian American community represented in the USA, that is, the 'Galician cousins' by numerous social and political organisations with the Ukrainian Congress Committee of America (UCCA) being the oldest, the most influential and embracing. The community's associations coalesced in April 2000 and agreed,

> to stage a conference that would bring together prominent represent-atives from academia and the governments of Ukraine and the United States to assess Ukraine's prospects for fuller ties to the Euro-Atlantic world in general and stronger bilateral relations with the US in particular.[104]

It was also decided to attract four sources of support and promotion to assist the project materialisation. First, the Ukrainian Congressional Caucus was called to generate political backing in the USA. Second, the Embassy of Ukraine to the USA was asked to 'garner political support in Ukraine'. Third, 'major American universities, think tanks, and NGOs were invited to serve as sponsors – to lend their good names and supply important contacts'. Last, some of largest 'commercial institutions were invited to serve as patrons – to provide the necessary financial wherewithal'.[105] The first success of the joint effort of the several from the above was the 'Ukraine's Quest for Mature Nation Statehood: A Roundtable' in Washington, DC. The attendees and sponsors list was impressive: Paul Wolfowitz, Borys Tarasyuk, Andres Åslund, Zbigniew Brzezinski, to mention a few.

Following the success of the Roundtable, round two was held in November 2000, where it was decided to make the meetings annual events. The RTs,

> [have] now reassembled ten times, to convene Roundtable II [Taking Measure of a US–Ukraine Strategic Partnership] in October 2001, Roundtable III [Ukraine and the Euro-Atlantic Community] in Oct. 2002, Roundtable IV [Ukraine's Transition to a Developed Market Economy] in Oct. 2003, Roundtable V [Ukraine's Transition to a Stable Democratic Polity] in September 2004, Roundtable VI [Ukraine's Transition to an Established National Identity] in Sept. 2005, Roundtable VII [Ukraine and NATO Membership] in Oct. 2006, Roundtable VIII [Ukraine–EU Relations] in Oct. 2007, Roundtable IX [Ukraine's Regional Commitments] in Oct. 2008, Roundtable X [Ukraine's Bilateral Relations/US–Ukraine and Canada–Ukraine] in Oct. 2009 and Roundtable XI [Ukraine's Bilateral Relations/Germany–Ukraine and Russia–Ukraine] in Oct. 2010.[106]

After the RT4, business-to-business networking conventions were included into the proceedings of the usual RTs. Later, they were formalised into the US–UA Business Network Forum and extended initiatives to establish 'the US–UA Security Dialogue Series, US–UA Energy Dialogue Series and the highly regarded UA Historical Encounters Series'.[107] By 2005, collaboration forums and projects became abundant however uncoordinated. In order to address the latter issue, the organisers agreed to form an 'entity capable of systematizing and, when deemed appropriate, expanding the Roundtable format', that is, the Centre for US–Ukraine Relations.[108] The Centre became an organisation that deals with a variety of issues through both occasional meetings and forums and special working groups and committees that function on a permanent basis and serve as linking mediums and preparatory platforms for RTs.

According to the CUSUR website the main objective of the Centre is:

to provide a set of 'informational platforms' or venues for senior-level representatives of the political, economic, security and diplomatic establishments of the United States and Ukraine to exchange views on a wide range of issues of mutual interest and to showcase what has been referred to as a 'burgeoning relationship of notable geopolitical import' between the two nations.[109]

By 2011, there were five of the above-mentioned platforms that convene on an annual basis on issues that include: the UA Quest Roundtable Series, the UA Historical Encounters Series, the US–UA Security Dialogue Series, the UA–US Business Networking Forum Series and the US–UA Energy Dialogue Series. The RTs are planned to address the highest number of areas and problems in both actual and potential collabora-tion processes. One more series of conferences is planned to be held in multiple EU and Ukraine locations, a series on Ukraine's Euro-Atlantic Future[110] and thus guarantee the US security interests protection in the EU–Russia buffer zone. The latter aims to supervise the wider EU and NATO accession ambitions of Ukraine or 'monitor the pace of Ukraine's NATO and EU accession process, though obviously in the context of the stated US-Ukrainian partnership'. The CUSUR also plan to publish the proceedings of the forums as well as establish the *Journal of Ukrainian Affairs* that would bi-annually bring together analyses about Ukraine.[111] The final ambition of the Centre is to establish a US–UA Working Group that would include 20 government and non-government experts from both the USA and Ukraine.

A separate mention must be made about the Ukrainian Central Information Service (UCIS) that functions as an 'administrative midwife' in the formation of the CUSUR and services numerous meetings and RTs.[112] The UCIS was founded by the Ukrainian American Freedom Foundation (one of the initiators of creation of the CUSUR) over 20 years ago and has since served as an active architect of various USA–Ukraine programmes that further deepen processes of neoliberal co-optation by extending education in the 'Western/democratic' values and vision beyond corporate activities and codes of behaviour. Some of the most successful of the latter include: (1) The Ukrainian Helsinki Group Informational Newsletter Project (1987–1989) that ensures promotion of the 'normalised' vision on human rights in Ukraine; (2) The Living History of Ukraine Project (1988–1992) that reflects the vision of Ukrainian American diaspora and their experiences both in Ukraine and their current domicile, the USA; (3) the NGOs of Ukraine Visitors' Program (1993–1996) that involve education of the NGO employees in Ukraine in the workings of the NGOs in the USA; and (4) The National Democratic Rada Deputies Visitors' Program (1994–2001) that deals with education of the people's deputies of Ukraine in performing parliamentary functions; and The Ukrainian Leadership Program Initiative (2001–2004).[113]

* * *

The wide range of activities and experience has helped US and EU business further their interests and co-optation strategies, yet it has not guaranteed the lobby members corresponding levels of success they are used to in Brussels or Washington. This is evidenced by domestic capital's high proportion of ownership of the largest and most high-yielding enterprises, success in privatisation tender auctions, and overall market presence. In 2014, Bernard Keysey, the then chief of Ukrainian ACC, and Leonid Kozachenko, head of the Entrepreneurs' Council of the Cabinet of Ministers, admitted that lobbies' functioning is restricted by a lack of a clear regulatory base on lobbying in Ukraine and lack of a clear line separating cooperation from corruption.[114] Informal ties that have developed over decades are too strong and effective and it is difficult to foresee those being abandoned soon. Those ties in combination with neoliberal reforms solidified in the state–society–capital complex of Ukraine as mechanisms of kleptocracy and embezzlement yet at the same time could be interpreted as a form of economic protectionism in the hostile domain of transnational capital and accumulation rivalries.

SPECIAL ECONOMIC ZONES (SEZs) AND PRIORITY DEVELOPMENT AREAS (PDAs)

Accumulation of capital by oligarchic FIGs was accelerated by offshoring of revenue, administrative devolution in SEZs and PDAs, and tax evasion. Creations of Special Economic Zones (SEZs) and Priority Development Areas (PDAs) helped the process and was one of the main examples of class fraction compromise between the Dnipropetrovsk 'leaders' in Kyiv and the ascending Donetsk capital. The latter had gained increasing political and economic leverage by the end of the 1990s due to the country's GDP heavily relying on Donetsk industry and Kuchma relying on Donetsk (the most densely populated oblast of Ukraine) electorate in the coming 1999 presidential election. In addition, by the late 1990s, the Donetsk capital was institutionalising as a class-for-itself, first, with Yanukovych becoming the governor of Donetsk oblast in 1997 and then with consolidation of their members in one political party, the Party of Regions, during the same year. Next, in 1999 Mykola Azarov of the Party of Regions was appointed the Head of the State Taxation Administration. That and increased parliamentary presence provided an opportunity for Donetsk capital to directly shape taxation legislation in the country and effective tax avoidance.

The areas were established with the adoption of the Law of Ukraine 'On general positions of establishment and functioning of Special (free) Economic Zones' (SEZs) between 1998 and early 2005 and an array of other laws and bylaws (see Table below for details) which theretofore regulated founding and functioning of 12 SEZs and 72 PDAs on 13 October 1992. In Ukraine, the territory of those areas comprised almost 10 per cent of the country. In addition, some zones were granted wider privileges than the other mainly 'Donetsk' and 'Azov' (both in Donetsk oblast, see Figure 5.4) were established for 60 years when the rest of the zones for 20–30 years. Investors in the special zones were given considerable tax breaks and other benefits presented in Table 5.1. According to Article 5, the Council of the above SEZ 'was formed as a management body for the two special economic zones: Donetsk and Azov (located in Mariupol) [port on the Azov Sea coast]. The power to appoint members of the Council was reserved by the Donetsk Oblrada (oblast council) and had multiple functions, among which were:

> [acting as] intermediary between investors, local authorities and central legislative and executive authorities and [supervising] the proper utilization of investment; ... [responsibility for] the development of appropriate measures to attract investment; ... [authorization to] control both regional businesses and investment flows into the region; ... [and functioning as a mediator] between the regional and central government interests.[115]

It was thus not surprising that those selected areas attracted the largest FDI inflow, most of which, however, was in fact recycled oligarchic capital.[116] The SEZs legislation in Donetsk oblast was of a rather selective nature and mainly benefitted large oligarchic FIGs than general improvement

Table 5.1 Major investor subsidies in Special Economic Zones in Ukraine; established 1998–2000

Subsidies / SEZ Name, City/Oblast, Law that regulated functioning	Special customs zone regime	Revenue tax relief	Investment tax relief	Custom duty and VAT relief	Compulsory sale of inflow in foreign currency relief	Land duty payment relief	Some budget funds tax relief
1	2	3	4	5	6	7	8
'Azov', 24 December 1998 N356 Mariupol/Donetsk	+	Rate – 20%	+	–	+	+ (plot assimilation period)	+
'Donetsk', Donetsk/Donetsk, 24 December 1998 N356	+	Rate – 20%	+	–	+	+ (plot assimilation period)	+
'Zakarpattya', Mukacheve and Uzhhorod/Zakarpattya 9 December 1998, N3039	+	Rate – 20%	–	–	+	–	
'Yavoriv', Yavoriv/Lviv, 15 January 1999 N402	–	+ (5 years), next years – 50%	–	+ (5 years)	–	+ (3 years), next – 50 % of active duty	+
'Avtoport "Krakovets"', Krakovets/Lviv	+	+ (5 years), next years – 50%	–	–	–	+ (3 years), next years – 50% of active duty	+
'Slavutych', Slavutych/Kyiv, 3 June 1999 N721	–	+ (3 years), 4–6th year – 50% of active tax rate	+	+ (5 years)	+	+ (3 years), 4–6th years – 50% of active duty	+

'Kurortopolis Truskavets', Truskavets/Lviv, 18 March 1999, N514	–	+ (3 years), 4–6th year – 50% of active tax rate	+	+	–	–
'Portofranko', Odesa/Odesa, 23 March 2000 N1607	+	+ (3 years), 4–6th year – 50% of active tax rate	+	+	–	–
'Reni', Reni/Odesa, 23 March 2000, N1605	+	Rate – 20%	+	+	–	+
'Port Krym', Kerch/Crimea, 27 June 1998 N740	+	Rate – 20%	+	+	+ (5 years)	+
'Irterport Kovel', Kovel/Volyn, 22 June 1999 N702	+	Rate – 20%	–	+	+ (5 years)	+
'Mykolayiv', Mykolayiv/Mykolayiv, 13 June 1999 N1909	+ (only ship-yard territory)	+ (3 years), 4–6th year – 50% of active tax rate, 4–10th year – reinvestment	+ (5 years)	+	+ (5 years)	–

Source: compiled by the author from data available at the Verkhovna Rada of Ukraine website and Paskhaver О.Й. Пасхавер, Л.Т. Верховодова and К.М. Агеева (2006) Приватизація та реприватизація в Україні після 'помаранчевої' революції. Центр економічного розвитку; 'Міленіум'.

of investment climate and regional development. So, 'ferrous metals, coal mining and electric power generation, [or industries associated with oligarchic FIGs, were] included in the list of priority sectors and industries in the law.'[117] As a result, the law's goal was far from:

> [encouraging] progressive structural change of the regional economy, which would create an alternative system of jobs and reduce region's dependency on volatile foreign markets for raw materials. Equally the law [encouraged] only large investments and [did] not support investment in small business, which can be active agents for effective restructuring.[118]

Moreover, as mentioned earlier, 'nearly half of the FDI in Donetsk oblast originated from offshore financial centres [e.g. British Virgin Islands – 42 per cent of FDI in the region, and Cyprus – 6 per cent respectively] that suggests that much of this investment consists of capital' that has left the country before returning to the region as FDI.[119] For example, SCM FIG of Rinat Akhmetov is legally registered in Cyprus.[120] The analysis of transition economies and investor behaviour in the CEECs by Carlin et al. confirms the tendency of foreign investors to 'avoid enterprises in branches requiring extensive restructuring, such as steel, coal mining, heavy machinery and basic chemicals'.[121] Based on Carlin's study, Lyakh too concludes that a high proportion of FDI flow in Donetsk oblast going towards heavy industry confirms the assumption of local capital recycling through offshore zones.[122] Lyakh's conclusion can be further substantiated by the fact that most industrial enterprises in the oblast are owned by Ukrainian FIGs rather than foreign companies. The situation in the late 1990s – early 2000s was further aggravated by low availability and high interest rates of credit, combined with low incomes that inhibited development of small and medium business. The trend was ongoing and, according to the data by the State Institute of Statistics, in the first six months of 2012, $5,810.1 million from Ukraine ended in offshore accounts of Cyprus alone.[123]

The declared goal for creation of SEZs and PDAs was to stimulate economic growth and attract FDI into the country. Instead, the zones became a contribution to transnationalisation of kleptocratic accumulation in Ukraine by legalising tax avoidance and facilitating transfer pricing, recycling, and offshoring of capital. It allowed the emergent oligarchic capital to funnel revenue out of the country by circumventing potential state capital controls. The latter, combined with increasing leverage in the ruling bloc of Ukraine, will eventually lead to the Donetsk capital becoming the most powerful in the country both economically and politically. After a short interval in the aftermath of the Orange Revolution, Donetsk forces with Yanukovych in charge will begin to swiftly remove competitive ruling and capitalist class fractions from key positions of power by administrative pressure, political persecution, and occasional yet habitual assassinations. The neoliberal transnationalisation reforms too will carry on although in a very particular, self-serving manner.

6

'Two Ukraines', One 'Family' and geopolitical crossroads

The second term of Kuchma's presidency was coming to an end and the reins of power had to be transferred to the candidate from Donetsk oligarchic bloc, Viktor Yanukovych. The latter enjoyed a speedy political career with assistance from friendly oligarchs and had good chances to win the elections. His main opponent was Yushchenko – the ex-Prime Minister and the ex-Head of the National Bank who also had oligarchic capital backing from both Donetsk and Central Ukraine. The chances for the latter were higher, especially in the western regions of Ukraine.[1] 'Most Ukrainians expected that Kuchma would end his 10 years in power by ensuring the succession of his hand-picked successor' – Yanukovych – who was also conveniently favoured by Moscow.[2] In the quest to manufacture electoral support, two Ukraines will be manufactured – east and west, pro-Russian and pro-Western – and the politics of alienation and dehumanisation will take their root.

The future of Ukraine's foreign relations depended on the outcome of the 2004 presidential elections. Yushchenko had a clear pro-Western leaning while Yanukovych and the industrial oligarchy of the eastern Ukraine supported close cooperation with Russia. For the USA and the EU, the result had to decide 'whether Ukraine would follow the path towards western liberal democracy or towards consolidated autocracy a la Putin's Russia.'[3] In other words, the future economic and political/security integration with the structures of transnational capital on the terms of the Washington Consensus and the EU/US/NATO respectively was at stake. The campaign of 2004 will bring two major changes – one in foreign, one in domestic partisan politics. The former will be reshuffling of the multi-vectoral foreign policy approach to include a preferred economic space integration vector, that is, the EU or the Eurasian Economic Union. The latter will manifest itself in transformation of partisan politics into virtual populist project. Political technologists from Russia designed their programmes to suit the wants of favourable constituencies and effectively split the country into two Ukraines, of Yushchenko and of Yanukovych.

THE ORANGE-BLUE CAMPAIGN, THE VIRTUAL POLITICS AND MANUFACTURING OF TWO UKRAINES

Political parties, actual and virtual,[4] had all split their preferences between the two candidates by the runoff. In Table 6.1, I show the general political preferences of political parties represented in the Verkhovna Rada in 2004.

Table 6.1   Political parties' preferences in 2003–2004

	Left	*Centre*	*Right*
Pro-Kuchma		For United Ukraine Social Democratic Party of Ukraine (United; Medvedchuk; Igor and Hryhoriy Surkis-Dynamo FC) Party of Regions (Akhmetov – SCM; Firtash – ETG; Pinchuk – Interpipe)	
Ambivalent	Communist Party		Our Ukraine (Taruta/Mkrtchan – ISD; Poroshenko – Ukrprominvest; Zhvaniy; Berezovskiy)
Anti-Kuchma	Socialist party	BYuT (Tymoshenko)	

Source: Compiled by the author from Wagstyl and Warner (21 December 2004) and van Zon (2007) and Volodarsky (2009).

The 'national democrats and moderate left'[5] mentioned above, many of whom were part of the movement for Ukraine's independence in 1989–1991 (Narodnyy Rukh Ukrayiny, for example), were not the only forces that supported Yushchenko and the Orange Revolution. Some had a genuine patriotic agenda, but both the oligarchs and some foreign actors, also were banking on the main candidates. The political parties were also split in the presidential candidate support that was traceable back to their behaviour throughout 2003–2004; oligarchs were often members of parties and provided them with financial support through their FIGs.[6]

In Figure 4.3, the preferences of the largest political parties in 2003–2004 are shown. Pro- and anti-Kuchma sentiments generally meant support or otherwise of the preservation of political and economic dominance of the Dnipropetrovsk capitalist class fraction, that is, Pinchuk/Interpipe and Donetsk, that is, Akhmetov/SCM.

The element of consent to the power of the ruling bloc continued to be based primarily on coercion, the element of consent had to be manufactured. That meant that potential voters' support had to be won through 'information warfare' that became the determining factor of the elections outcome as I argued elsewhere.[7] Kuchma's 'establishment' was limiting the amount of information in circulation and thus creating an *information vacuum*.[8] In such manner, 'serious political and economic content which contradicted pro-establishment views was removed from the diverse, Western-looking and glossy landscape, creating a virtual reality, the aim of which was to disempower society and blur its consciousness. Many in Ukraine called this "zombuvannya lyudej" – making people into zombies'.[9] However, it can be argued that by doing so a rather fertile soil was created for *any* new information to fill that vacuum – provided it was adequately and timely presented – which eventually happened once the information blockade was broken.

Most of the 2004 campaign and the subsequent Orange Revolution evolved along the lines of media wars. There are two types of media ownership in Ukraine – municipal or state and private (see Figure 4.3 for details); with the state unwilling to forfeit its dominance in the sphere of media control understanding the importance of it as a lever of influence on public opinion.[10] The main advantage of the online media was that it could not be subject to censure as there is less control over the content of publications. In the pre-run to presidential election 2004, 'alternative information and perspectives were available to Ukrainians through non-oligarch owned newspapers and [online media]'.[11] However, 'those media outlets were not considered highly influential since in 2004 only 12 per cent of Ukraine's population used the Internet on a regular basis, and polls show that fewer than 20 per cent of the population considered newspapers their main source of information'.[12] Both the ruling bloc and the counter-forces focused their media campaign effort primarily on television.[13] Scholarly analyses confirm the presence of media wars, smear campaigns and an information blockade enforced by Kuchma on a state level and the rival capitalist class fractions, who own most of the mass media outlets in Ukraine.[14] In Figure 6.1, I present a network visualisation of the media ownership by oligarchic capital in 2004.

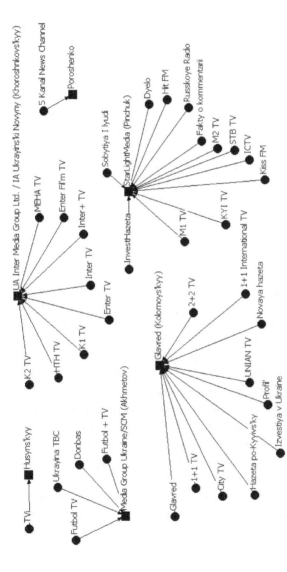

Figure 6.1 Largest mass media outlet (television channels, newspapers and radio stations) ownership in Ukraine by oligarchs and FIGs

Source: Compiled by the author using data available at *Teleprostir* (television and radio station information portal) for the list of media and individual websites of radio stations and television channels for company ownership.

Key: dots indicate the names of the media resources, squares indicate the owner company and the owner of the company.

As is shown in Figure 6.1, most of the media resources are owned by four oligarchs and their FIGs – Glavred of Kolomoyskyy, StarLightMedia of Pinchuk, UA Inter Media Group by Khoroshkovskyy and Media Group Ukraine/SCM by Akmetov. In the electoral campaign of 2004, the first did not demonstrate public support for any of the candidates, the other three supported Yanukovych. TVi and 5 Kanal of Husynskyy and Poroshenko respectively supported Yushchenko. In the conditions of an almost complete control of the media outlets by the capital backing Yanukovych combined with Kuchma's *temnyky* and administrative pressure, that is, elements of coercion, manufacturing of consent to the ruling bloc led by Yanukovych still proved problematic. The smear wars of 2004 did not go unnoticed by the Ukrainian public, so Poroshenko – the owner of 5 *Kanal* 24-hour news channel – claims, 'Before these elections, only 3 to 6 per cent of people were interested in political news. Today [on 21 December 2004] the figure is around 50 per cent.'[15] Numerous media monitoring projects were launched during the election campaign and they all report systematic bias, one-sided reporting of political events in favour of Yanukovych, and lack of equal access for all candidates.[16] The ruling bloc were involved in what Marta Dyczok termed the 'Stop Yushchenko' project through *temnyky* and overt censorship.[17] Moreover, attacks on mass media critical of Yanukovych and the members of the Party of Regions in general became customary during the 2004 electoral campaign – both administrative (i.e. harassment through unsubstantiated and unexpected State Taxation Administration checks and audit, searches of newspaper/television channel offices by SBU on fabricated pretexts) and physical (beating of journalists).[18]

In the poll of 31 October 2004, the first round of elections, the voter turnout was 79 per cent with Yushchenko and Yanukovych gaining 39.87 and 39.82 per cent of the votes respectively.[19] 'International observers and the opposition said the first round was a step backwards for democracy in the former Soviet republic of 48 million people, alleging widespread fraud and intimidation',[20] nevertheless, the run-off was scheduled for 21 November. The independent exit poll by the Ukrainian *Fond Democratychni Initsiatyvy* (Democratic Initiatives Foundation) data showed that Yushchenko was the winner by a margin of 43 to 54 per cent (Democratic Initiatives Foundation 27 November 2004) while a different poll by Ukraine's Social Monitoring Centre calculated Yushchenko was ahead by 49.5 to 45.9 per cent. The Central Electoral Commission unofficial poll to the contrary showed Yanukovych to be the winner by a margin of 49.5 to 46.6 per cent.[21] Very soon it became known that the election was a nationwide fraud 'planned since the spring and most of the other "technologies" also dependent on the complicity of the Central Electoral Commission and its equivalent local electoral commissions.'[22] The above facts confirm the continuous presence of the criminal-political nexus as an endemic component of the ruling bloc of the country both in Kyiv, and throughout the country. Clear falsification of election results brought some 10,000 people to the streets of Kyiv and other cities of Ukraine in late November–December 2004.[23] After the results of the second round of elections were finally annulled due to the public pressure and the abundant data that proved numerous violations of electoral procedures as well as votes' miscount,[24] the media situation began to change also.

FROM YUSHCHENKO TO YANUKOVYCH

As Wagstyl and Warner of *The Financial Times*, among many others, have predicted,[25] tensions emerged among Yushchenko's allies that included Moroz, the Socialist party leader, Kinakh, a former prime minister and an associate of Kuchma, and Tymoshenko. The above was furthermore complicated by the conflicting interests that the new ruling bloc represented, that is, Taruta, Mkrtchan, Poroshenko, and the central and Western Ukraine capitalist class fractions – and the Dnipro-petrovsk/Donetsk bloc (Akhmetov, Pinchuk, Firtash) that began to lose control over the policy-making. From the day the new government was appointed onwards, the velocity with which Ukraine is implementing reform necessary for the country's 'Europeanisation', or 'EU-nisation' was impressive. By January 2005, Yushchenko's administration adopted 19 decrees and five ordinances on the issue on EU integration and passed 27 decrees and 26 ordinances through the Parliament. The latter in its turn adopted 20 laws and ten decrees aimed at implementing the Action Plan for Ukraine that previously has been rather declaratory, than practical.[26] On the other hand, the political crisis caused by the elections and the Orange Revolution resulted in aggravation of the economic situation. The GDP of the country during the first two months of the Orange forces in power was three times as slow as the previous year and fell from 13.2 per cent to only 4 per cent in the first quarter of this year.[27]

Yushchenko began his presidency with ambitious claims to overcome corruption, build closer relations with the EU and deepen global capital markets integration through WTO membership, and rapprochement with NATO.[28] Reshuffling of the state administration apparatus and power structures in general – economic and political – was indeed impressive. A comparison of the ratings of the most influential persons in the country, which I compiled based on data from Kononchuk and Pikhovshek for 1990–1996 and *The Korrespondent* 'Top-100 Most Influential People of Ukraine' and present in Figure 6.2, show that by 2003–2005, only a few members of the Dnipropetrovsk 'family' remained in positions of influence. So, by 2003 only 15 out of the original 206 of Dnipropetrovsk neo-nomenklatura remained influential; by 2004, there were ten, and in 2005, in the aftermath of the Orange Revolution, only five: Kravchuk, Lytvyn, Moroz, Matviyenko and Yushchenko. The other 95 were the newcomers, primarily of various capitalist class fractions and who now comprised the new ruling bloc of Ukraine.

The Orange coalition of forces replaced the Dnipropetrovsk bloc, however, only temporarily and by 2008–2009 was replaced by other newcomers, from Donetsk.

In January 2005, as agreed before the elections, Yushchenko made Tymoshenko the prime minister. The latter immediately after appointment as prime minister launched a so-called 'war on oligarchs' that itself was a clear continuation of class fraction rivalry, was rather selective, and contained elements of favouritism towards the Privat Group of Kolomoyskyy and Boholyubov, who had helped Tymoshenko finance her electoral campaign. The 'war', in fact, primarily concerned those oligarchs who were in a continuous confrontation with her, that is, Pinchuk and Akhmetov and included: (1) mass re-privatisation through pricing re-estimation and resale of recently privatised SOEs; and (2) investigations into tax evasion by large FIGs including the abolition of SEZs. In the first six months of her being in office, 1,700 investigations into privatisation cases were registered by the Ministry of the Interior. The process, however, was complicated by the lack of adequate legislation, necessary resources and corruption, and effectively, many of the cases were quickly dropped. The case of Kryvorizhstal steelworks re-privatisation is worth particular attention.

In Ukraine in 2004, [the plant was] sold to a consortium headed by Rinat Akhmetov [Donetsk fraction] and Viktor Pinchuk [Dnipropetrovsk fraction] for $800 million (4.26 billion hryvnyas), despite US Steel and India's LNM Group offering $1.5 billion … To narrow

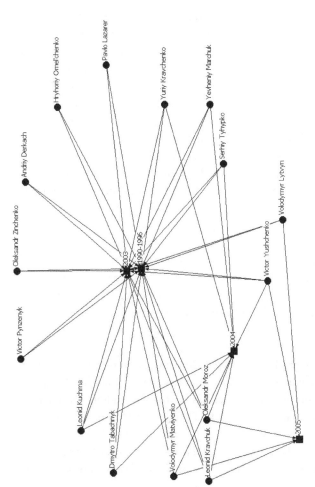

Figure 6.2 The most influential political, economic and public persons interlocks of 1990–1996, 2003, 2004 and 2005

Source: Compiled by the author from date available in Kononchuk and Pikhovshek (1997) and *Korrespondent* 'Top 100 most influential persons' annual rating 2003, 2004 and 2005.

Key: dots indicate the names; squares indicate the year of rating.

the field, the authorities insisted that bidders had to have produced 1 million tons of coke and 2 million tons of rolled steel in Ukraine for the last three years, with at least two of the years being in profit.[29]

In 2005, once in power, Tymoshenko's conflict with Pinchuk manifested itself in the privatisation re-evaluation that concerned his three enterprises – two fully owned, and one co-owned with Akhmetov. The three were: (1) Interpipe (two investigations launched in April 2005, both trials won by Pinchuk); (2) Nikopol Ferroalloys plant (bought in 2003 for $80 million when estimated price was some $1 billion, the dispute peaked in 2005 and won by Pinchuk when Kolomoyskyy – an oligarch who initially supported Tymoshenko in the dispute and generally is her ally – sided with Pinchuk and signed an agreement on co-ownership of the plant with Kolomoyskyy acquiring 26 per cent share in 2005, re-nationalised in 2005 by the state, the right to be relisted for future privatisation withheld in 2006); and (3) Kryvorizhstal steelworks (bought by Pinchuk in a dubious auction, re-nationalised and sold less than a year later to Mittal Steel for a staggering $4.8 billion).

Next, SEZs and PDAs were abolished by Tymoshenko in March 2005,[30] based on the evidence of substantial legislation misuse/violations and double-entry bookkeeping, tax and duty payment evasion, etc.[31] Despite the attempts to stop the abolition by a report released by the Donetsk branch of the National Institute of Strategic Research (adjunct to the Presidential administration) that contained warnings of possible negative consequences of such actions,[32] SEZs were removed, and some of the richest oligarchic FIGs from Donetsk had to pay taxes in full or hide their revenue offshore. Tymoshenko's 'war' did not last long. Her direct attacks on oligarchs as well as on the gas trading intermediary RosUkrEnergo that was linked to Firtash and Gazprom[33] made her inconvenient as the prime minister for the latter. In a Wikileaks report Firtash said to the then US ambassador in Ukraine, Taylor, that he stopped the formation of a coalition of BYuT and the PR last minute and did all possible to facilitate joining forces of the Party of Regions and Nasha Ukrayina/Yushchenko.[34] The Constitutional reform of 2004 that turned Ukraine into a Parliamentary Republic enabled Donetsk forces to forge a coalition in 2005 and force her resignation only seven months into her office. Tymoshenko was replaced by Yekhanurov who was a candidate better suited for oligarchic concentration of capital as she was against reprivatisation but pro 'talks, negotiations and ... [possible] settlements'.[35]

His appointment could be interpreted as a compromise between the rival forces of Dnipropetrovsk (i.e. Boholyubov and Kolomoyskyy among others) associated with Yekhanurov and the Donetsk capital behind the Party of Regions that approved the prime minister candidacy only in the second round of voting.

The schism between Yushchenko, Tymoshenko, and their respective parties was irreparable by the time of Parliamentary elections of March 2006. Now they were campaigning as two separate political forces with Yushchenko's popular support declining in the light of protracted rivalry within the Orange bloc and the schism with Tymoshenko. Such lack of homogeneity within the ruling bloc of the country facilitated an increase of support for the Party of Regions and Yanukovych as its leader. His ascent to power was a classic example of institutionalization of criminal elements in post-Soviet societies.[36] Combined with the strong connection with Donetsk mafia addressed in Chapter 3 his task now was to lead the latter into power.[37] The results of the elections of March 2006 visualised in Figure 6.3 show a clear strengthening of support for the Party of Regions with 32.14 per cent of votes and a loss of support for Our Ukraine with only 13.95 per cent of the votes. The elections also revealed that Tymoshenko now had enough support for her party to be considered a political force in its own right with 22.29 per cent of the votes cast for her BYuT. Tymoshenko's bloc now also included a few opposition parties.[38] By 2006, also a notable decline of support for the Socialist and Communist parties began to show for the first time since Ukraine's independence with them winning 5.69 per cent and 3.66 per cent of votes respectively. The number of their cadre in the influential positions within the ruling bloc of the country had significantly declined too and will continue to be minimal as I show in Figures 6.2, 6.3 and 6.4.

The schism between Yushchenko and Tymoshenko pushed the former's party Our Ukraine into a precarious coalition with the Party of Regions and a formation of the Government composed of ministers from the two parties. Yanukovych became the prime minister and soon after assuming office began restoration of the 'damage to oligarchs' caused by Tymoshenko's actions when in office in 2005. One notable example of such 'restoration' was the signing of a contract in the 'gas war' of 2006 on 6 January between Gazprom and Naftogaz that cancelled all direct supply of gas to Ukraine. Now RosUkrEnergo was the sole and exclusive company in control of supply/resale of all Central Asian and Russian gas to Ukraine.[39] As a result, money could now again be drained from

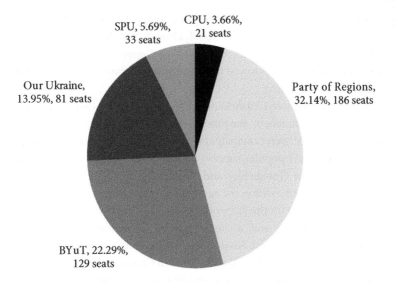

Figure 6.3   Parliamentary elections 2006 results and seat allocation

Source: compiled by the author from the data of the Central Election Commission of Ukraine (2006).

Gazprom, that is, Russia's state budget as well as from the Ukrainian state budget through artificially highly priced gas and redundant inter-mediaries. The unstable nature of Our Ukraine and the Party of Regions coalition combined with the strong opposition in the Parliament from BYuT and SPU resulted into a protracted political crisis that lasted from April to June 2007, a dismissal of the Parliament, and early Parliamentary elections that took place in September 2007.

UKRAINE'S FOREIGN DEBT AND THE POLITICS OF FINANCIAL CRISIS

Oligarchic tensions and the conditions in the country became further aggravated by the effects of the global financial crisis that reached Ukraine in 2008 and left it among those worst affected.

Ukraine had zero foreign debt when it became *de jure* independent in 1991, however, budgetary constraints and exponentially growing foreign debt have been its Achilles heel ever since. Foreign debt obligations were assumed by Russia who carried on the legal personality of the USSR and with that also it took on the history of relationships with foreign financial institutions as well as the remaining financial assets. There are two types of foreign debt in Ukraine: direct, that is, aggregate debt obligations for received and outstanding government loans, and guaranteed, that is, aggregate state-owned enterprises and other economic entities resident in Ukraine's debts of which are guaranteed by the state.[40] Both have a clear geopolitical dimension and foreign policy implications as the former primarily come from IFIs/Western capital while the latter is a mix with a strong component of arrears on Russian imports, primarily fuel (gas, oil and nuclear).

Ukraine's post-1991 foreign debt dependency formation can be split into four main periods.[41] In the first period between 1991 and 2000, Ukraine entered the market of international lending and introduced a system of state foreign debt management. During the second period that stretched between 1999 and 2007, the debt was restructured and a consolidated approach towards debt policy was adopted, however, marked by violations of terms of agreement by the Ukrainian party. The next period, the third, commenced with the onset of the 2008 financial and economic crisis in Ukraine, where the government was forced to seek funds with IFIs and accept stricter conditionality of borrowing. And last, the fourth period follows the outbreak of the civil armed conflict and oligarchic high-jacking of the achievements of the popular unrest by reinstating neoliberal kleptocracy and locking the country on the path of debt servitude for generations to come. Let's look into the first two in some detail in this chapter; the last two, I will cover in Chapter 7.

The first decade of borrowing history was characterised by 'borrowing by necessity' due to disintegrating economy that bore the fragmentation shocks of the Soviet economic system and thus disruption of supply chains and chronic budget deficit with necessitated accumulation of foreign loans. For example, it was not until 1995 that the governmental Decree #234 'On Priority Areas of Foreign Loans Spending' was adopted. The document limited the chaotic practice of granting state guarantee to enterprise borrowing and was the first serious step towards system-atisation of the country's relationship with foreign lenders, including development of instruments for a consolidated state borrowing approach. Domestic borrowing market was very limited and by 1995, the proportion of foreign debt in the state debt was 80 per cent. The network of economic relations was disrupted and reformatted and now made more intricate by an added dimension of debt relations, setting geopolitical leverages and vulnerabilities for years to come. Thus, by

1995, Ukraine owed $1.4 billion to Russia's Gazprom and $723 million to Turkmenistan.[42] Over the 1990s and beyond, the list of lenders expanded to include IFIs, USA, EU, and other Western partners, opening new economic and borrowing opportunities and creating more fragility in the system of foreign and financial policy balancing. The 'multi-vectoral' policy orientation designed by ex-president Kuchma in the 1990s, that is, foreign economic, financial, and security policy that engages with multiple partners/vectors, was proving increasingly difficult to manage yet is arguably the only option that may help stabilise the country and the geopolitics in the region as an effect.

In 1994, Ukraine and the IMF signed a 'Memorandum on Questions of Economic Policy and Strategy' that aimed to mobilise marketisation in the country and effectively limited Ukraine's government decision-making power. The main conditions of the memorandum were as follows: liberalisation of foreign trade, liberalisation of exchange rates and fiscal policy (including restrictions in prices regulation), cuts to state subsidies and introduction of individual welfare provision system, accelerated privatisation of SEOs, restructuring of natural monopolies and specified enterprises, reduction of state budget deficit, deregulation and administrative reforms.[43] The reforms created mutually reinforcing negative effect on the economy by opening up outdated industry for competition with foreign TNCs and by reducing financial state support for enterprises and citizenry thus making the latter poorer and the former even less competitive with expected negative aggregate consumption and potential revenue drop. Nascent domestic capital increased its 'competitiveness' by handing out state guarantees on loans to their own enterprises by proxy of the Currency and Credit Council of the Cabinet of Ministers.[44] The defaulted loans obligations were then simply shifted onto the state and amounted to $2.4 billion between 1992 and 1999.[45]

By the end of 1999, a new period of Ukraine's debt history commenced with the need to restructure the debt that reached some 60 per cent of GDP or $15.3 billion.[46] The period was characterised by systematisation of borrowing and debt policy. In 2000, the Central Bank was cut from the government oversight with the creation of the Council of the National Bank of Ukraine. This has gradually led to NBU's decision-making becoming a process controlled by the Council alone.[47] The latter chaired by the Head of the NBU appointed by the President of Ukraine is compiled of academics of neoliberal economic outlook and business representatives linked both directly and indirectly to the major oligarchic formations in the country. The decision-making process in both the Council and the Board of the NBU in their financial and fiscal policy response to global financial markets are conditioned by the IMF and the World Bank obligations and advice, which often complicated economic relations with Russia. This complex dynamic determines the nature of Ukraine's banking sector and the economy as a whole.

For the next five years, the Party of Regions comprised the majority in the Verkhovna Rada (see Figure 6.4). That secured more productive lobbying and adoption of legislation that favours that Party and its sponsors through holding 42 per cent of Parliamentary seats. The Party of Regions is currently one of the political parties with the largest number of members in Ukraine and has representative branches in all 17 administrative regions of the country with some 11,600 regional organisations.[48]

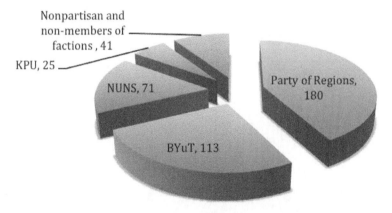

Figure 6.4   Parties and fractions in the Verkhovna Rada per number of allocated seats after elections of 2007

Source: compiled by the author using the data available at the Verkhovna Rada website.

In addition, in their annual analysis of the most influential people in the country, *Focus* magazine documented an unprecedented number (67 out of 200) of the same political party affiliates – the Party of Regions in 2011. The latter serves as one more proof of concentration of power of Donetsk bloc in the country as I show in Figure 6.5. As we can see, only five out of 2006 persons listed by Pikhovshek and Kononchuk that were present in power structures, have remained influential in 2010–2011.

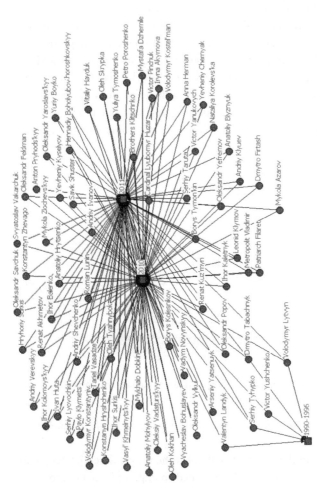

Figure 6.5   Interlocks of the most influential people of Ukraine 1990–1996, 2010 and 2011

Source: Compiled by the author based on Pikhovshek and Kononchuk (1998) and *Korrespodent* 2010 and 2011 top 100 most influential rating.

Key: circles indicate persons, squares indicate years of rating, connections between the two indicate presence of given persons in the ratings of given years.

Moreover, the dynamic of shifts of the interlocks among the ratings of the most influential people of Ukraine between 1990 and 2011 that I present in Figure 6.6 is a visualisation of the ruling and capitalist class fraction rivalry in the country since its independence. The first notable shift occurred between 1990–1996 and 2003 with the ascendancy of the new class fractions and the decreased leverage of old apparatchiks or neo-nomenklatura within the ruling bloc. The isolated dots linked to 1990–1996 squares signify the positions lost. The multiple interlocking as well as the multiple cases of isolated dots between 2003 and 2009 signify the intensity of the fractional rivalry within the ruling bloc year on year. The multiple interlocks mean that the core of the current ruling bloc as well as the counter-forces has been formed by and during that period. The simultaneous multiplicity of the isolated dots, or drop-outs means that the ruling class formation in the country has not yet finalised, that the political process is still predominantly shaped via fractional rivalry, and that there still are possibilities for the balance of forces to be changed despite the strong tendency towards power concentration by the ruling Donetsk bloc.

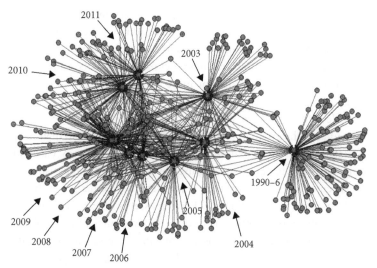

Figure 6.6   The dynamic of interlocks among the most influential people of Ukraine ratings, 1990–2011

Source: Compiled by the author based on Pikhovshek and Kononchuk (1998) and *Korrespodent* 2003–2011 top 100 most influential rating.

Key: Circles indicate persons, squares represent years of ratings, the lines connecting squares and circles indicate presence of persons in certain years' ratings.

By August 2012, according to the annual rating of *Korrespondent* magazine nine out of ten most influential people in the country are members of the Party of Regions, 37 out of 100 most influential people are also on in the top 100 richest oligarchs that includes the son of president Yanukovych, Oleksandr, who joined the rating soon after his father assumed office.[49] Rinat Akhmetov's documented revenue, for example, in 2011 alone – a year of economic crisis in the country – increased from $17.8 billion to $25.6 billion most of which still remains untaxed.[50]

CONCENTRATION OF CAPITAL IN OLIGARCHIC FIGS

By 2010, domestic capital dominated by Donetsk was in charge of the largest companies on Ukraine's market despite multiple ongoing and coordinated attempts by foreign capital to take the lead. This is confirmed by analysis of top 100 enterprises rating according to the *InvestGazeta* and information available at the individual companies' websites. The rating includes companies with annual revenue of UAH 10 million and over (level of indebtedness taken into account) in visible assets only. Additional facts taken into account are as follows: pricing of company shares owned by physical persons, real estate, and income (outflow) of capital from sale (purchase) of assets at the time of evaluation. In cases where property was (co-)owned by family members, cumulative assets estimate was calculated. In cases where two or more persons belonged to the same business group with a complex system of shared ownership, the estimate was calculated based on direct participation in the main company/ companies of the group in question. Open JS companies had their assets estimated based on capitalisation level as of 15 March 2010. Closed JS companies had their estimate measured by a method of comparison with similar companies that have their shares on stock exchanges of the CIS and Central and Eastern Europe. Foreign assets of the companies were included only in the cases where information was publicly accessible and reliable. Estimates of construction companies were based on the value of finished construction objects in their ownership. Companies on a verge of bankruptcy were not considered. Personal wealth and savings as well as companies and property ownership of which was being disputed during the rating compilation too were omitted.

In Figure 6.7, I present visualisation of my analysis of the rating data grouped according to type of ownership and countries of companies' domicile. In Figure 6.7, the visualisation is organised by principle of individual companies' belonging to corporate clusters. As it can be seen in Figure 6.7, only 17 companies are of Western or Russian – 13 and 4 respectively – domicile. The Western companies are from India (1), Germany (2), USA (4), Japan (1), Netherlands (1), Switzerland (2), UK (1) and France (1). The Indian Arcelor Mittal is included in the 'Western' category for two reasons. First, Arcelor Mittal is subject to the same rules and procedures in Ukraine as all foreign TNCs are unless otherwise specified in the sale contract. Second, division of foreign companies on the Ukrainian market into 'Western' and 'Russian' is useful due to Ukraine being a zone of conflicting interests of US/EU and Russia's state-run oligarchy,[51] both neoliberal and transnationalising. The rest of the companies are Ukrainian with 45 belonging to Ukrainian business clusters, 13 being of joint foreign and Ukrainian ownership, two of joint state and private ownership, and 19 of (near-)full state ownership. Analysis of the companies registered offshore, that is, Cyprus, offers even more peculiar results. The four companies registered in Cyprus are: SCM, Privat Group, Interpipe, and ISD, that is, the largest corporate clusters in Ukraine as I show in Figure 6.8.

As I show in Figure 6.8, in 2010 out of 45 companies in the top 100 rating, 14 were owned by the SCM of Akhmetov, five by ISD of Taruta and Mkrtchan, two by Interpipe of Pinchuk, two by the Privat group of Kolomoyskyy and Boholyubov, and one co-owned by Interpipe and

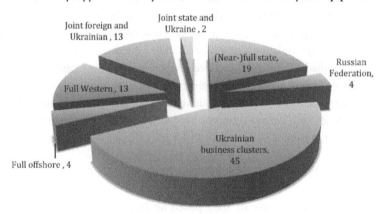

Figure 6.7   Top 100 companies in Ukraine's market (2010) as per type and country of ownership

Source: Compiled by the author based on the top-100 largest companies in Ukrainian market rating (version of *InvestGazeta,* 30 November 2009) and the information available at the individual enterprises' websites.

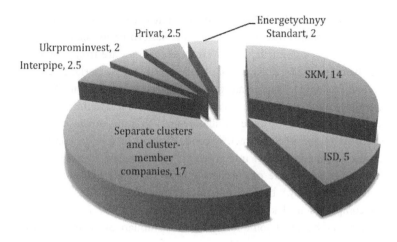

Figure 6.8 Ukrainian business groups' corporate clusters share in Top 100 by numbers (2010)

Source: Compiled by the author based on the Top-100 largest companies in Ukraine market rating (version of *InvestGazeta,* 3 November 2009) and the information available at the individual enterprises' websites.

Privat. Therefore, 24 companies – nearly a quarter of the 100 largest companies – are owned by four(!) FIGs all of which are registered offshore. That is to say that by 2010 the largest FIGs on Ukraine's market were owned by Ukrainians while registered offshore. Such corporate organisation guaranteed their access to transnational(-ing) mechanisms of capital accumulation and reduced state capital controls. Moreover, by 2010, the last obstacles to concentration of power and capital in the hands of Donetsk capitalist class were removed. With Yanukovych elected president and legislative and executive branches of power in control, the 'black holes' in Ukraine's economy used for oligarchic enrichment could be further expanded.[52]

USURPATION OF POWER BY DONETSK BLOC

Mykhnenko and Swain in 2007 posed an interesting question: 'Even though privatisation and macroeconomic stability had been achieved, how can economic growth be explained given the (alleged) absence of structural economic reform or despite the (alleged) presence of rampant rent-seeking "clans"?'[53] The answer, I argue, is that stabilisation has not been achieved but rather has been a temporary mirage based on hollow foundations of IMF loans, demand for Donbas steel fuelled by the real estate bubble, and cheap personal credit fuelled consumption in Ukraine.[54] The temporal sustainability of the latter was made possible by availability of cheap credit for Ukrainian banks from the EU as an extension of the Anglo-Saxon financialisation,[55] which they re-loaned in Ukraine at higher interest rates. By utilising the multiplicity of already available and constantly expanding mechanisms of accumulation, legal and extra-legal, fractions of the emergent capitalist class of Ukraine strive to ensure continuous furthering of their economic agency in the midst of permanent intra- and inter-fractional rivalry that undermines stabilisation of a new social order. Moreover, by concentration of capital in FIGs that engage in surplus creation through commodity, productive, and money circuits simultaneously combined with direct involvement in law and policy making, oligarchic capital of Ukraine strives to overcome the limits of the possible embedded in each of the circuits separately. It is achieved through domestic and foreign economic policies that involve selective liberalisation and protectionism that favours oligarchic capital and through creation of virtual spaces of accumulation for offshoring the revenue, or 'black holes' in the economy.[56] The latter is done mainly through four forms of state asset embezzlement: (1) privatisation – from primitive accumulation to concentration and centralisation of State Owned Enterprises in the hands of Financial Industrial Groups and essentially oligarchs; (2) FDI regulations, the chronology of their reform, and their uneven implications for accumulation by both domestic and foreign capital; (3) creation and functioning of Special Economic Zones and capital operation in those zones; and (4) tender and state purchasing legislation reform and procedure abuse. All four, I argue, are neoliberal mechanisms of accumulation that under the façade of free market democracy reform were utilised by oligarchic capital to create 'black holes' in Ukraine's economy and both entrench embezzlement in the fabric of law, and manipulate law for the sake of embezzlement.

When Yanukovych became president in 2010, the last obstacles to concentration of power and capital in the hands of Donetsk capital were removed. Now, with legislative and executive branches of power under control, the 'black holes' in Ukraine's economy used for oligarchic enrichment could be further expanded. Ukraine's economy was witnessing both political and economic inward orientated movement. In the first instance, political opposition leaders' prosecution most prominently manifest in the imprisonment of Tymoshenko and Lutsenko and the continuously deteriorating stalemate in negotiations with the EU, the IMF and USA resulted in an undeclared diplomatic isolation of the ruling forces of Ukraine, that is, the Party of Regions, Yanukovych and his administration. The second manifested itself in mass privatisation and restructuring of the energy sector. Privatisation auctions remained an imperative issue due to the lack of transparency, underpricing and preferential treatment for the Donetsk fraction of oligarchic capital. The most demonstrative example of the above is the recent privatisation of gas distribution SOEs where Gaztek and Finleks Ukraina associated with Firtash purchased 14 of 18 auctioned companies. Gaztek[57] earlier this year was given a loan by Nadra Bank – also owned by Firtash – of UAH 250 million to fund the above acquisitions.[58] The tactic of back door funding of their own companies' expansion is common in oligarchic FIGs and is an example of overcoming the limits of the possible in the process of capital accumulation. In Table 6.2, we listed the SOEs in question, percentage of shares per SOE auctioned, starting and sale prices, and the new owners based on information provided by SPFU. In addition, I include SOEs's market value prices calculated by Forbes.ua based on equivalent companies that trade shares on *Latvijas Gaze, Lietuvos Dujos, Hokkaido Gas, Southwest Gas* exchanges that show a difference of some $100 million of effective savings or potential state revenue embezzlement by the SOEs's new owner, Firtash.

In addition to the above, Ukraine's Parliament adopted a Draft Law N939 on 3 October 2012 that removes Naftogaz SOE monopoly on trade in imported gas in Ukraine. The Law N163 that eliminated intermediaries on the domestic gas market adopted by Tymoshenko's government on 5 March 2008[59] was effectively abolished. In the light of the recent wave of privatisation of gas supply and distribution SOEs where Firtash's companies took control over the sector, previously eliminated by Tymoshenko, intermediary monopoly of RosUkrEnergo is effectively restored.

The Ukraine economy's heavy reliance on Russian gas was an ongoing cause of both instability and increasing costs, on the consumer and state levels alike. However, instead of energy wastage reduction that according to OECD/IEA estimates can save from EUR 1–6 billion per year through residential consumption efficiency improvement alone, 10–30 per cent consumption reduction respectively,[60] Ukraine's government takes an environmentally damaging and unsustainable turn. The latter is beneficial for the oligarchic FIGs – SCM/DTEK and ISD, involved in coal mining

Table 6.2   Gas distribution SOEs privatised in August–October 2012

Name of gas company and percentage of shares auctioned	Starting price, million UAH	Selling price, million UAH	Investment obligation, million UAH	Share package estimate, Forbes.ua	Buyer
Mykolayivgaz, 25%	18.4	18.97		148	Gaztek
Chernivtsigas, 20.393%	6.7	8	2.3	63	Gaztek
Zhytomyrgaz, 15.864%	9.7	16	3.4	40.7	Gaztek
Tysmenytsiagaz, 26%	0.16	1	0.7	16	Gaztek
Sumygaz, 25.788%	15.6	16.9	4	64	Gaztek
Luhanskgaz, 26%	80.6	81.41	3.9	503.8	Gaztek
Zaporizhzhyagaz, 25%	14.1	16.8	3.9	327	Gaztek
Dnipropterovskgaz, 26%	58	58.65	5.2	350	Gaztek
Sevastopolgaz, 25%	4.2	4.45	0.6	6.8	Gaztek
Ivano-Frankivskgaz, 25%	32.6	33.35	4	69	Gaztek
Poltavagaz, 26%	20.1	20.305	3.7	350	Finleks-Invest (later resold to Vera Chetverikova)
Volyngaz, 23.4%	24.3	25.05	2.6	12	Gaztek
Lubnygaz, 26%	0.33	5.06	2.6	5	Finleks-Invest
Khersongaz, 20.82%	7	11.9	1.5	5.2	Sodruzhestvo
Gadyachgaz, 25.999%	3.1		0.3	n/a	Sodruzhestvo
Kremenchuhgaz, 26%	6.7	21.7	1	1.4	Sodruzhestvo
Vinnytsiagaz, 22.059%	1.5	3	3.3	305	Gaztek
Krymgaz, 23.989%	41.8	42.64	8	352	Gaztek

Source: SPFU of Ukraine and *Forbes.ua* (18 October 2012).

in the Donbas/Donetsk as it automatically creates a market for their increasing output of low quality coal.[61] Therefore, Yuriy Boyko, Minister for Fuel and Energy, announced the abolishment of the privatisation ban on 14 of 41 total TPSs and declared that there is an intention born of necessity to transfer all 41 from gas to coal as energy source that would allow reduction of gas consumption by 6 billion m^2 per year.[62] According to SPFU, privatisation of the TPSs was due to commence in November 2012 with the main pretenders for purchase yet again being companies linked to Firtash.[63] In addition to the above, the mass privatisation of 1196 of 1492 of SOEs that were previously protected from privatisation was planned to commence in 2013.[64] The SOEs in question include coal mines, alcohol refineries, broadcasting centres and publishing houses, elevators, oil and gas transportation SOEs, sport and leisure institutions, and more.[65]

The wave of tax reforms, the increasing neoliberalisation of the economy including talk of new SEZs creation,[66] a wave of the currently ongoing privatisation of energy generation and supply sector, as well as the restructuring of the latter so as to create market for oligarchic FIGs, for example, switchover of TPSs to domestically produced coal from imported gas as fuel,[67] all signal the increasing inward reorientation of economy as well as indicating a promise of a further aggravation of the socio-economic disparities. Nevertheless, the essential authoritarianism and usurpatory policies of Yanukovych and the Party of Regions already generate socio-political dissatisfaction in the country and the condemnation and sanctions threats from the USA and the EU. In the light of Ukraine's growing external debt, the increasing balance of payments deficit, and the heavy reliance of the oligarchic FIGs on state subsidies and procurement tenders make the country's economy as a whole dependent on IMF loans. Combined with the need of access to foreign markets for import and exports alike such dependency on foreign capital makes the current ruling bloc vulnerable to pressure from the West. The latter can generate shifts in the balance of power in Ukraine as is evidenced by the most recent Yanukovych pardoning of Lutsenko and five more political prisoners.[68]

By 1 January 2010, the ruling bloc of Ukraine became more homogeneous than ever before. It was expected that the neoliberal reform advised by the EBRD and the IMF as part of the TACIS/ENP programme and SALs respectively would permit easy market penetration for FDI and TNCs, as has previously been the case in Latin America and Sub-Saharan Africa.[69] Instead, TACIS/ENP and SALs, among others, were welcome by the international financial institutions, and created a discursive façade for the entrenchment of semi-licit mechanisms of accumulation in Ukraine as the ratings of the largest companies and richest persons and their formation confirm. Economic and political power usurpation by the ruling bloc dominated by Donetsk forces is characterised by continuous attacks on human rights and freedoms, freedom of expression and assembly,[70] and the carving of legislation to serve the interests of the oligarchic capital. On the level of class fraction rivalry, a gradual takeover of competing political and economic forces has been occurring by political prosecution and imprisonment of opposition leaders

(Tymoshenko and Lutsenko – to name a few), administrative pressure (Tyhypko), and murder. Simultaneously, occasional class fraction compromises have crystallised as is testified by the growing leverage of Priva tGroup of Kolomoyskyy and Boholyubov, Interpipe of Pinchuk and Group DF of Firtash. The authoritarian tendencies of Yanukovych's administration and the Cabinet are based on the principles of cronyism,[71] state asset embezzlement and the coercion of counter-movements. Such foundations of power of the ruling Donetsk bloc facilitate both the strengthening of the counter-movements and the increasing pressure from the West and Russia alike. The above was evidenced by the growing support for the right-wing parties in Ukraine, the stalemate in the EU Association Agreement negotiations and the threats of sanctions from the USA and the EU, and the Customs Union membership ultimatums respectively. Such a state of affairs has left the country's future and the future of the current ruling bloc largely uncertain, apart from one crucial aspect. Regardless of whether the current ruling bloc remains in power, or whether the counter/opposition movements take over, the course of the neoliberal transnationalisation of the state was most likely to remain intact. And that is precisely what will happen in the aftermath of the Bloody Winter events.

7

The Bloody Winter[1] and the 'Gates of Europe'[2]

INTRODUCTION

The multi-vectoral game of foreign policy Preferans was reaching its crescendo as the time to sign the trade agreement with the EU was approaching. Where lobbying efforts and IMF's SALs could not succeed, disciplining by debt and extensive enforcement mechanisms of DCFTA would finish the job and make entry and functioning of transnational – predominantly of EU origin – capital smoother; misbehaving oligarchy could be disciplined and pushed out of its controlling position as the case with Burisma Holdings and Privat will show. The agreement has been popularly sold as that which would bring Ukraine significant economic and social benefits, raise standards of living, wages, guarantee the rule of law, etc. In reality, the deal's objective was significant and predominantly one-sided liberalisation of trade with the EU. DCFTA would open up the last remaining public assets for privatisation and commercialisation while putting foreign capital in an advantageous position. The effects of the treaty on Ukraine's economy would be a further exacerbation of socio-economic inequalities and destruction of the remaining state social support system. Simultaneous flirtations with Russia about the Eurasian Union trade agreement were becoming unfruitful as Putin's administration grew frustrated with its exclusion from EU–Ukraine talks. In an attempt to stop this rapprochement between Ukraine and EU, Putin threatened to raise prices on gas and thus render Ukraine's energy intensive industry economically unsustainable. The industry in question makes up some 20 per cent of the country's GDP – that kind of loss no president would submit to suffer wilfully. The combination of heavy foreign debt dependency and the state budget on a permanent edge of default have put Yanukovych's administration before an impossible choice. Under pressure from the industry-owning oligarchy of Donbas, Yanukovych refused to sign the treaty at the Third EU Eastern

Partnership Summit in Vilnius in late November 2013. The long-term consequences of Ukraine's short-term approach to politics were about to spill into the deepest multi-level crisis the country has witnessed since the post-Second World War famines.

The Revolution of Dignity involved many undignifying facts and social forces that render the term a misnomer despite the indignation at lawlessness and injustice that brought people onto the streets. What the events of 2013–2014 became instead was, what I prefer to call the Bloody Winter, that lasts until today. The political winter that has been freezing Ukraine's move away from neoliberal kleptocracy since, solidified in the reality of the 'armed conflict', social fragmentation, and socio-economic destitution. Ukraine as the Gates of Europe, the nature of those as a boundary between Europe and Eurasia is being contested yet again.[3]

DCFTA: TIME TO GATHER STONES

The DCFTA entailed a series of reforms that went beyond deepening of trade relations. Ukraine already has a series of Free Trade Agreements with the EU, yet those were relatively limited in scope and were based on quota import–export model with selective tariff reductions. The new agreement was planned to take the relationship between the parties to a new, deeper level. It also included visa-free non-work travel for Ukrainian citizens – something Brussels felt was important to give to Kyiv since Ukraine's full EU membership aspirations were met with little enthusiasm by some of the Union's member states. DCFTA was aimed at 'facilitating convergence to the EU standards in various business-related regulations in the areas of food safety, technical standards, public procurement, competition policy, intellectual and property rights, etc. ('deep' and 'comprehensive' aspects).'[4]

DCFTA is the most far-reaching treaty that the EU has signed to date (except for membership treaties). In a recent analysis of its effects on the signatory countries, Amat Adarov and Peter Havlik conclude that in the long term, the economic effects are 'likely to be positive due to the ultimate convergence of the beneficiary economies to a more competitive state underpinned by better institutions, a more predictable and transparent legal setting, improved investment climate, as well as improvements along other dimensions,'[5] if implementation is successful. At the same time, they warn that 'the net benefits are highly asymmetric along the time dimension (high costs in the short and medium run –

benefits accruing mostly in the longer run)'[6] and divergence 'across regions and economic sectors' is high (less competitive sectors and regions will face particularly onerous adjustment costs). There are sizeable associated 'costs, challenges and risks' that:

> include, among others, fiscal costs of the legal approximation to the EU acquis, losses of traditional export markets, challenges of finding a market niche in the already highly competitive European markets, adjustment costs related to industrial restructuring leading to contraction of less efficient industries with potentially painful concurrent labour market repercussions, investment needs by the public and the private sector to finance the implementation of reforms and bridging the 'gaps' in infrastructure and productivity.[7]

Implementation success, however, would be hard to achieve without state support and subsidies to foster and strengthen local production in the face of intensified competition from EU business, big and small. Such support is not foreseen in the Treaty as it could be interpreted as 'state intervention in the market' that contradicts EU regulation on competition. What is offered instead is a possibility of the introduction of 'temporary state support in the form of access to information, advisory services, training, etc.'.[8] How training and advice will protect local farmers from the predatory corporate tactics of large EU TNCs remains unclear, as financial support and subsidies are not on offer. In agriculture, it is expected that '20 per cent more of agro-food products [will be exported once DCFTA is in force] with the main contribution by exports of tobacco, cereals, meat and miscellaneous edible products [and oil seeds]'.[9] With import duties dropped, an approximate 7 per cent growth in imports is expected, 'mostly due to increased shipments of beverages, vegetable oils and fats, meat, mineral or chemical fertilisers, animal oils and fats, and sugar'.[10] Such an exchange means that Ukraine will be exporting raw materials and semi-finished products to the EU and importing ready products with surplus value of which would be staying with the EU companies. Exports will allow the country to increase demand for its agricultural goods yet will not allow the generation of significant economic growth due to locking in the lowest segment of the production chain. A similar fate awaits heavy production where raw materials and semi-finished products will be shipped to the EU as components in supply chains, and then ready machinery and technological products will be exported back to Ukraine. That is not to suggest that the Ukrainian economy is placed at the bottom of production chains overall but to highlight the uneven nature on international organisation of production where North Atlantic capital comes out on top.[11] Following the period of primitive accumulation and then concentration of capital, Ukrainian FIGs – and many SMEs too – engage in all sectors of the economy with various surplus value.[12] Many FIGs already have extended to include enterprises in the EU, the USA and elsewhere, for example, SCM and DTEK.

In the light of high adjustment costs, the poor state of the country's economy, close yet uneven economic cooperation with the countries of both organisations, and conflicting oligarchic/industrial needs the choice between DCFTA and the Eurasian Union was a challenging decision to make. The signing of the DCFTA, at least on paper, would give Ukraine access to a market of 500 million of high purchasing power consumers and with an annual turnover of US$14 trillion. The Eurasian Union, on the other hand, offers a market of 170 million consumers with a comparatively lower purchasing capacity and with an annual turnover of US$1.5–2 trillion. Both options have their potential benefits. The DCFTA promises to bring potential economic mod-ernisation and growth. Eurasian Union membership offers lower gas prices that for energy-import dependent Ukraine is a highly attractive proposition yet it is dented by multiple memories of previous gas wars and trade ban manipulations. At the same time, many of the DCFTA and Eurasian Union constitutive frameworks and standards are mutually incompatible, making it impossible for Ukraine to hold membership in both. In addition, there is Russia's unwillingness to accept Eurasian Economic Union (EAEU) members' participation in the DCFTAs with the EU. The latter is confirmed by Putin's multiple declarations of such opposition and his 'unilateral withdrawal of preferences [for Moldova] under the CIS FTA safeguard clause' on 31 July 2014.[13] Moldova was effectively punished for signing the DCFTA with the EU and now trades with Russia and Belarus under the same MFN conditions as all other WTO members.[14]

Estimates of the potential benefits of economic integration with either partner gain more weight when measured against the real experience of other post-Soviet member states of the EU and not only best-case scenario economic modelling, whose vacuous nature I discussed in Chapter 3. Big companies, that is, large capital, tend to benefit from access to new markets while SMEs tend to largely suffer as competitive pressure rapidly increases. Even after a short period of trade liberalisation with the EU, we see precisely those effects being felt by business owners (see discussion below on the effects of the treaty) and the examples from CEECs signal of that as well.

Ukraine's big capital also had its reservations about the treaty. The opinions of the public and the oligarchs were divided, however, the latter seemed to be largely in favour of the DCFTA. This was confirmed at the Exporters Council of the Internal Ministry meeting in 2011 that included representatives of 13 of the largest FIGs.[15] In 2012, Kateryna Zarembo conducted a series of interviews with representatives of three out of seven of Ukraine's largest oligarchic corporate groups.[16] The author notes that, while Ukrainian oligarchs are infamous for their use of personal connection in conducting business, they were ready to welcome the DCFTA, conducted own independent assessments of the treaty's potential effects on their FIGs and economy as a whole, for example, SCM and Group DF, and were enthusiastic about the market opportunities.[17] The treaty, in fact, would not affect FIGs' day-to-day operation to any significant manner as their access to the EU markers was already guaranteed upon accession to the WTO in 2008. Economically crucial industries, that is, metal and mineral products that constitute some 50 per cent of exports, for example, have been enjoying tariff-free access to the EU market since then. On the one hand, the entry into a deep economic partnership with either the EU or of the customs union with Russia would restrict their freedom by tying them into more rules with demands for more transparency of corporate operation.

'On the other hand, there are (geo)political tensions that result from harmonisation of regulatory frameworks of Ukraine with that of the EU that comes with market access when the latter is at odds with Russian gas imports and affects the energy sector and the linked industries'.[18]

Matuszak shows that the 'oligarchs' attitude to economic integration initiatives [was largely] shaped by the nature of their businesses'.[19] For example, Firtash tends to favour closer relations with Russia as his chemical plants' profitability depends directly on gas prices. Akhmetov's heavy industrial plants too are energy-intensive yet, on the other hand, are export-oriented. This makes gas imports an important factor while it can be outweighed by prioritisation of target markets. In the latter regard 'third countries are much more significant (mainly from the Middle East and Asia) and – to a lesser degree – EU countries' than Russia while

'Russian companies are Ukraine's main rival' on third countries' markets in heavy industry and cereal exports too.[20] Thus, class fractions in ownership of energy-intensive FIGs were most susceptible to the Russian pressure. Yet, many oligarchs are against Ukraine's full 'membership in the customs union comprising Russia, Belarus and Kazakhstan (CU)' due to their 'fears that membership in the CU will in future lead to Russian business taking control over Ukrainian oligarchs' property.'[21] This is not unsurprising considering predatory behaviour of Russian oligarchy.

Moscow has repeatedly expressed its dissatisfaction with the EU–Ukraine rapprochement. Many in Russia still see Ukraine and other Soviet republics as part of one economic system and exhibit a pronounced sense of entitlement to interference in those republics' foreign policy as if it were their own. Putin referred to Ukraine's DCFTA ambitions – among others – as the EU attempt to 'choke' whole sectors of Russian economy that he would not accept.[22]

Complex geopolitical landscape, gas needs, and toxic debt dependency will play the decisive role in Yanukovych's DCFTA negotiation tactics, demanding money from the EU and Russia, and playing ultimatum games.

POLITICAL ECONOMY OF UKRAINE'S DEBT DEPENDENCY

Ukraine went from zero debt in 1991 to $70.97 billion and being the IMF's third largest borrower by December 2016.[23] In 2008, when the Global Financial Crisis rolled over to Ukraine, it caused a deep financial and political crisis in the country that was resolved via added lending from IFIs with more and stricter conditionality. While sporadic borrowing of the early 1990s was partly systematised, there was no decrease in borrowing. Poor banking and, specifically, lending regulations allowed for unsupported lending based on re-loaning combined with lending in foreign currencies (encouraged by lower interest rates than loans in UAH). Foreign debt and energy imports dependency in the context of the chronic budget deficit made the government vulnerable to geopolitical pressure that led Yanukovych to withdraw from signing the Deep Comprehensive Free Trade Agreement (DCFTA) with the EU. The effective unfolding of the Bloody Winter events in 2013–2014, the unrest, the fighting, the economic collapse and rescue through foreign lending, debt dependency and the loss of sovereignty have crowned the worst case of state failure the post-Soviet Ukraine has seen. Its economy's corpse is kept alive only by ongoing injections of more toxic loans. The IMF and the capital behind the IMF – being renowned dealers of prescription policy loans – design them in that way, the toxic way, (un)intentionally.[24] The loans are structured in a manner that makes them very difficult to be repaid,[25] while at the same time conditions are manufactured to continue collecting interest and serve as instruments of control over the borrower governments.

A toxic combination of debt dependency,[26] uneven financialisation, sectoral unevenness,[27] tax avoidance and evasion, and state asset and funds embezzlement, determines the nature of the political economy of Ukraine.[28] It is due to the above factors that Ukraine was among those hit hardest by the fallout of the Credit Crunch despite the country's integration in the global financial architectures being relatively limited and uneven as I will show in this section. In the literature on the effects of the financial crisis in Ukraine, there are three dominant factors that cumulatively lead to the economic collapse: first, the dive in prices on the international markets combined with slumping demand for steel; second, the endemic problems in the banking sector of Ukraine; and third, the cut of the gas supply by Russia in January 2009.[29] The price drop combined with a drop in demand for steel became crucial components in the worsening of the economic situation in Ukraine's industrial production that in 2008/2009 was cumulatively responsible for 27 per cent of the country's GDP and over 75 per cent of all exports[30] in the context of the overall long-term industrial output shrinkage that I address below. The incident with the gas supply from Russia that became a typical feature of seasonal geopolitics dealt an unusually heavy blow to the economy as it came in combination with the above-mentioned aggravating factors.

While analyses of crises involve references to physical territories, financial capital is often seen as that which is less constrained by spatiality. Indeed, some of its main characteristics are deemed to be its mobility, high liquidity, and flexibility of the terms of investment compared to industrial or commercial capital. Therefore, Nesvetailova and Palan argue, spatiality and geopolitics in particular are of a lesser importance in analyses of globalisation of finance.[31] The authors examine the link between geopolitics and financial economics and argue that such 'connection can be forged through an important, yet so far missing, aspect in the theoretical analyses of the nature of the [2007–2008] Financial Crisis'.[32] Financial economists who have focused their analyses on the supply side of liquidity, 'on the quality, provision and regulation of new financial instruments and the process of financial innovation as a whole' got it wrong.[33] Instead, what needs taking into account is the 'demand side' of financial instruments' circulation since the 'newly invented esoteric financial instruments do not find their customers by themselves [and] … even during the boom years, markets for these products needed to be created, and "liquidity" relied critically on demand being whipped up'. Incorporation of geopolitics makes the picture even more complex as the 'world that makes up the *demand* side for the products of financial innovation' is messy.[34] Although it is no doubt that 'the "subprime" mortgage was an American invention and the securitisation boom was crucially tied to developments in US housing finance', they continue, it is not only American banks or economy in general that have suffered from the fallout of the pyramid of fictitious capital. European banks have shared the blow from the Credit Crunch with their American 'colleagues' after they emulated American financial practices in the period of 2002–2007, which at the time yielded huge returns. Ukraine was a taker of financial practices set by the USA, the EU and the UK,[35] however the nature of its 'demand side' did have its own specific geopolitical stamp. Subprime borrowing was designed for the financially vulnerable[36] and domestic Ukrainian and EU daughter banks emulated the behaviour of rule-setters however particularities of Ukraine's banking regulations allowed for the demand to be moulded in a Ukrainian way. The country's demand context was characterised by loss of real economic base at a rate disproportionate to the growth required to maintain health of the economy or honour debts obligations, both state and private. Thus, as a result a double squeeze on the economy was produced due to the ongoing need for loaned capital (state, commercial, and consumer), complicated by inability to repay as the economy was further bled by heavy import dependency and weak currency.

Former Soviet Union (FSU) countries experienced rapid contraction of real economy sector in 1998; in Ukraine, the output comprised only 37 per cent of the 1989 level.[37] Between 1989 and 1998 'the real sector had accumulated a huge amount of outstanding debt and arrears and noncash payments had become a dominant feature of [FSU] economies'.[38] Thus, total payables to the enterprise sector dramatically exceeded receivables during the same period and noncash payment and barter transactions were on the rise. In commercial banking, the situation was rather different as the number of banks rose rapidly and many of those were owned by large firms. However, Huang, Marin and Hu et al. argue that despite 'the boom in the number of banks and their cross holdings in the real sector, banks failed to lend to firms, and banks' credit to the real sector declined substantially'.[39] Instead of lending to firms, banks concentrated on investment in treasury bills. In Ukraine, bank credit to the private sector in percentage of GDP comprised 5 per cent in 1994, 1 per cent in 1996, 2 per cent in 1997 and somewhat more optimistic 9 per cent in 1999.[40] Indeed,

> Russian and Ukrainian banks are among the worst performers in transition countries in terms of mobilising savings and allocating credit to the private sector, and they are a key factor underlying the surge of nonbank finance, including trade credit and barter trade, in these economies. The irony is that even bank owners in these economies chose nonbank financing for their manufacturing and trade, while letting banks absorb credit from these large firms and invest in government bonds.[41]

Crisis studies focused their macro-level analyses on 'persistent current account and savings imbalances' and micro 'on the flaws in the regulatory mechanisms, which enabled the explosion of risk-amplifying behaviour by borrowers and lenders alike'.[42] The 'strategic transformation of banking at the onset of the neoliberal era' being overlooked in the analyses of the crisis[43] is a problem that exists in analyses of Ukraine too, inevitably with its own nuances. While concrete behavioural changes of (mega)banks 'made at the onset of the neoliberal age in the 1980s enabled them, through lending, to generate financial risks without absorbing them', those same changes combined with a strong state–capital locking in Ukraine allowed for banks' avoidance of regulatory responsibility and functioning with further limited oversight (e.g. due to corruption and bribery of enforcement agencies). The state–capital locking that solidified in the 1990s has allowed for instrumentalisation of NBU and the Ministry of Finance functions and parliamentary law-making processes. The excesses of related party lending that recently became one of the reasons for nationalisation of PrivatBank are a long-established practice that has been allowed precisely via those mechanisms of instrumentalisation.

The savings that could be mobilised in Ukraine were limited. The country has fallen into the group of countries with a high level of popular financialisation, that is, high share of loans to physical persons such as mortgages and personal loans. Personal borrowing that the banks financed primarily through attraction of funds from abroad was popularised in the years prior to the crisis while there was a sizable gap between the volume of deposits and credits. This further restricted possibility for mobilisation of savings. The volume of individual credit kept increasing rapidly and by July 2008 its share in the total bank credit portfolio volume comprised 37.3 per cent. Across Eastern European countries, short-term surplus extraction oriented bank investment led to short-term credit and credit to non-productive sectors of the economy, that is, minimal crediting of private enterprise and real economy sector;[44] this too happened in Ukraine from the early 1990s till 1998[45] until the financial crisis dried up liquidity in the banking sector. When in 2008 the National Bank devalued the UAH by 40 per cent on demand of IMF, the fragile pyramid of Ponzi style consumer and mortgage lending collapsed. Consumer and banks' ability to repay loans taken out in foreign currency was dependent on relative stability of exchange rates as, apart from exceptional cases, consumers are salaried in UAH. Prior to the commencement of 'the financial crisis ... Ukrainian banks [of otherwise limited financial scope] could easily attract funds from abroad at 4–5 per cent interest rate and then sell them in Ukraine at 10–11 per cent' and often more.[46] Loans in UAH were offered as a higher interest rate due to the currency's weakness thus making US dollar and euro loans more appealing. The funds attracted by banks were through three- to five-year loans when the same banks loaned previously borrowed money for 10–20 years. The shortfall would usually be settled by re-financing existing loans with new loans obtained at the same low or even lower interest rates. As soon as 'the foreign banks have wrapped up their credit programs ... Ukrainian banks faced a liquidity crisis'.[47] Here their own accumulation scheme started to fire back as in order to service their foreign debt obligations, Ukrainian banks firstly 'had to refinance at much higher interest rates, and secondly, the newly-attracted funds from abroad became much more expensive too ... [and] as a result mortgage interest rates grew by 5–7 per cent'[48] while mortgage qualifying criteria were made stricter. In addition to the above, the National Bank of Ukraine has toughened requirements for credit operations in an attempt to contain the spread of a financial crisis in the country, which in its turn further added to interest rates on credit increase.

Just as financial integration of Central Europe 'failed to generate the promised optimisation of investment, let alone reduce macroeconomic risks',[49] financialisation of the Ukrainian economy and neoliberalisation of Ukraine's banking sector have failed to uplift the economy or at least stabilise it but left the country the second largest debtor of the IMF at the end of 2009, third in 2016. In his study of financialisation of Central Eastern European countries, Raviv argues against the conventional understanding of investment-led growth strategy promoted by IFIs and mainstream academia.[50] He suggests, instead of focusing on the needs of host economies (pull factors), to look into 'addressing the market pressures and structural contradictions faced by credit institutions in the already financialised economies of Western Europe' and elsewhere (mainly USA). Raviv argues that it is 'the latter rather than the former which shapes the actual motivations and strategies employed by western financial interests in their expansion in the peripheral economies'. In the months before the financial crisis hit the economy of Ukraine, it 'showed signs of overheating characterised by skyrocketing but volatile steel export prices, soaring wages and private consumption, strong capital inflows, a credit boom, high inflation (almost 30 per cent in mid-2008) and a widening current account deficit'.[51] In general terms, 'the increasing fragility of the country's external position as well as persistent political instability seem to have been the main reasons why Ukraine has been among the countries hit hardest by the crisis'.[52] Following the collapse of Lehman Brothers in September 2008, Ukraine saw severe disruption of the term of trade, 'capital flows reversed, Eurobond spreads and capital default swap (CDS) premiums rose by a far greater extent than those of other countries in the region, and the Ukrainian hryvnia depreciated sharply.' This led to 8 per cent year on year real GDP contraction in the last quarter of 2008 and 20.3 per cent and 18 per cent in the first and second quarters of 2009 respectively.[53]

Doroshenko suggests 'the consequences of the financial crisis could be much more serious provided the majority of large Ukrainian banks were not property of foreign banks'.[54] The international/foreign origin of the above banks allowed them to move funds from abroad and offer a better deal to their customers compared to other banks.[55] According to the data of Ukrainian National Mortgage Association, in 2008–2009, four out of five leaders of the mortgage market in Ukraine were daughter companies of foreign banks who held 56.6 per cent of the market. The banks in question were: Ukrsibbank (BNP Paribas) 17.7 per cent, Raiffeisen bank Aval (Raiffeisen Group) 12.2 per cent, Ukrsotsbank (Unicredit Group) 12.1 per cent and OTP Bank (OTP group) 8.0 per cent. There were 13 new private banks registered in Ukraine in 2007 alone or over twice as many as the previous years' average, while six were de-registered due to liquidation. At the same time, the number of banks with a share of foreign capital in them went from 19 in 2005 to 23 in 2006, 35 in 2007, 47 in 2008 and 53 in 2009.[56] Out of them with 100 per cent foreign capital were nine in 2006 to 13 in 2007 and 17 in 2008, while share of foreign capital in the banking system went from 11.3 per cent in 2003 to 19.5 per cent in 2006, 28 per cent in 2007, 35.2 per cent in 2008 and 41.14 per cent in 2009.[57] In 2008, the share of foreign capital in registered statutory capital of banks of Ukraine comprised 41.14 per cent, taking into account intermediate ownership through bank shareholders – 43.16 per cent, which is 7.96 per cent more that in 2007.[58] Over 2008 the volume of foreign capital in registered statutory bank capital of Ukraine increased by UAH 15.2 billion – or two times – and comprised UAH 30.3 billion. The ratio of foreign capital in registered statutory capital of functioning banks grew from 35 per cent to 36.7 per cent. Foreign banks' presence became more visible too as their assent in the sector rose from 49.4 per cent to 56.6 per cent, including credit operations – from 50.5 per cent to 57.6 per cent, liabilities – from 50.4 per cent to 57.8 per cent.[59] Unlike most countries in the EU (except Slovenia 29.5 per cent and Latvia 62.9 per cent) where in 2006 already the share of foreign banks in total banking assets was above 80 per cent,[60] the same ratio in Ukraine was only 28 per cent in 2006, that is, 8.5 per cent annual growth,[61] with further growth to 36.7 per cent by 1 January 2009.[62]

There are fundamental differences in the logic of financial accumulation as compared to commercial and manufacturing forms of capital.[63] The first is short-term oriented when success of the second rests on long-term investment and strategies; mobility versus immobility of assets of high and low liquidity respectively. The three forms of capital are intimately interconnected in each form of enterprise to various degrees[64] as oligarchic FIGs of Ukraine testify in overt manner, for example, Privat Group discussed above, SCM of Akhmetov with largest metallurgy, energy, and banking firms all of which in their own turn combine elements of the three forms of capital to various degree. Thus, problems with one circuit of capital lead to problems in the rest. So too financialisation 'is closely related to structural blockages in the productive sector and is very crisis prone' in general.[65] And structural blockages indeed were many even in the most industrialised part of the country, Donbas, with its concentration of value-making enterprises which suffered a heavy blow in the aftermath of USSR demise.[66] In the case of financialised accumulation founded on loans in foreign currency, 'the likelihood of crisis is even higher ... and the import of capital, a typical feature' in transition economies.[67] In the latter category of countries current accounts deficit is more common than not – and Ukraine is no exception. The problem with the current accounts deficit – apart from the obvious lack of funds in the country's budget – is that in the conditions of high inflow of FDI or other capital inflow into the economy the 'real and sometimes even nominal appreciation of the domestic currency' occurs. The latter in its turn 'further aggravates balance of payment deficits'.[68] The above dynamic bears dysergetic consequences for the whole economy. As soon as investors understand that exchange rate is unsustainable, Becker and Jäger argue,[69] 'capital flight sets in [which] puts further pressure on the exchange rate. If the currency is devalued the debtors having debts in foreign currency but income in domestic currency come under pressure.' Next, the 'currency crisis triggers a banking crisis' and leads to a financial and economic crisis in the economy, crisis along all three circuit of capital and its accumulation – that was the story of Ukraine in the post-Credit Crunch years.

TOXICITY OF DEBT DEPENDENCY, DCFTA AND GEOPOLITICS

The complex political economic and geopolitical reality situated on the crossroads of two decaying empires – US and Russian – has created conditions where multi-vectoral approach may not be only Kuchma's choice of foreign policy but a necessity in foreign and economic policy, a necessity for the sake of stability. However, the underlying paradox of multi-vectoral approach is that it is difficult to sustain in the long run as the simultaneous pull from the east and west force a uni-vectoral condition on Ukraine. As the crisis reached Ukraine in 2008, the NBU was forced to sell its gold and currency reserves and seek support of IFIs to fix the budget deficit and interest on loans.[70]

The crisis weakened Ukraine's economy in three main ways.[71] First, Ukraine has a huge current account deficit which is only likely to increase and will require external capital injection. Second, constantly increasing external debt, which over 2007 and 2008 was growing at 45 per cent annually and by the end of 2008 reached some $100 billion and where the largest fraction comprises the private sector debt. The latter equated to $85 billion at the beginning of 2009 already, $29 billion of which was short-term debt. Third, the banking sector of Ukraine was left rather weak

due to continuous shortage of liquidity in the sector. Financial vulnera-
bility with foreign borrowing as the only instrument available to prevent
the country from inevitable default set the scene for deep 'integration
without membership' with the EU[72] and disciplinary prescriptory policy
dispensing from the IMF. It is the latter that characterised the last two
stages of Ukraine's debt relations as described by Kravchuk[73] – (1)
restoration of active collaboration with IFIs in the context of financial and
economic crisis in 2008–2013; and (2) progression towards 'dictatorship'
of the IMF. This meant rapid accumulation of state debt that will not slow
down until 2015, as I show in Figure 7.1. Aggregate revenue has significantly increased primarily due to increase in tax revenue yet that revenue
is nearly identical to the current and aggregate expenditure while capital
expenditure and the balance of payments are extremely low (see Figure
7.2). Such state of economy makes any speculations about economic
recovery premature and unrealistic.

The signing of the DCFTA marked the completion of the biggest
step towards rapprochement with the EU/Western partners yet. The
agreement was to replace the earlier framework for collaboration, the
Partnership and Cooperation Agreement (PCA) and is unprecedented in
its scope and depth due to three particular features: 'comprehensiveness,
complexity, and conditionality'.[74] The results of the agreement can become

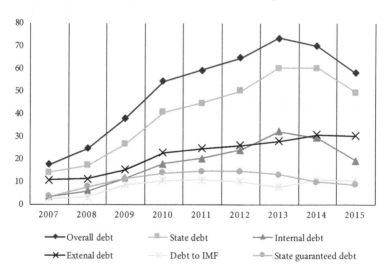

Figure 7.1   State debt accumulation dynamic, billion dollars

Source: Ministry of Finance (2016).

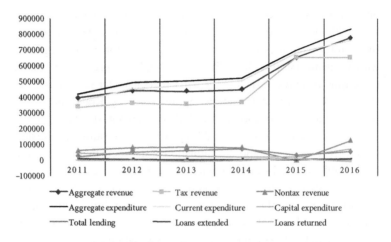

Figure 7.2   Consolidated budget indicators, 2011–2016, UAH million

Source: Ukrstat (2017).

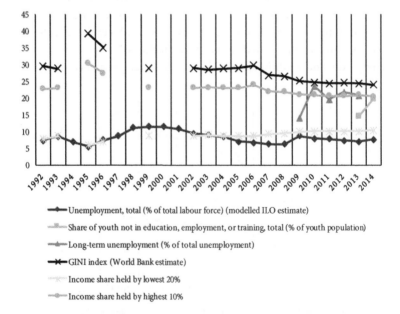

Figure 7.3   Gini, unemployment, and (hidden) income disproportionality, percentage; 1992–2015

Source: World Bank (2016).

catastrophic for the labour force of Ukraine who already bear higher distributional consequences of the financial crisis fallout than stronger economies.[75] The state of the economy is weakened by the consequences of the armed conflict and loss of industry in Eastern Ukraine at the estimated cost of $7–8 billion or some 6 per cent of GDP in late 2014 already.[76] As is shown in Figure 7.3, since the 1990s there has been a drop in the Gini co-efficient, the registered unemployment rate is at 7.7 per cent with 20.9 per cent being long-term; the real figures tend to be 2–3 times higher due to unregistered and hidden unemployment and labour emigration.[77] As for the youth – 19.98 per cent are disenfranchised, that is, neither employed, nor in education, nor training. The gap between the richest 10 per cent and the poorest 20 per cent is wide and currently stands at some 10 per cent that appears artificially low as the upper percentile includes disproportionalities of its own dictated by difference between the top and bottom of the category.[78] Despite their cumulative wealth shrinking by $23.8 billion or a third in 2015, the top 100 richest people of Ukraine, that is, the oligarchy,[79] still hold most of country's wealth.

HIJACKED REVOLT, SOCIAL FORCES, AND THEIR INSTRUMENTALITY: THE BLOODY WINTER

Since 1991, Ukrainian society has been divided in its opinion on multiple domestic and foreign policy issues – 'electoral support for major presidential candidates and political parties, status of the Russian language, Ukraine's membership in the European Union and NATO, and its relations with Russia.'[80] Such differences of views are common in any society yet it is not everywhere that they lead to armed conflicts. The regional character of those divisions is important and due to Ukraine's history of being under the rule of various empires simultaneously they run particularly deep in pre-border areas of the country's east and west. That is not to say that concrete regions are homogeneous in their support of concrete political forces or foreign policy options but to underline dominant political orientations.

Many analytics, including those on the political left, rushed to frame the Maidan protests and the Yanukovych ouster as a fascist coup[81] – it was not. Neither was it a coup orchestrated by the USA as some commentators tend to advocate.[82] While there are arguments to be made about Biden's personal economic interest in toppling of Yanukovych as his son's company, Burisma Holding, was eyeing shale gas resources then in possession of Yanukovych's son, to state that visits to Maidan of

Biden and Nuland somehow turned the historic course of events is a gross exaggeration. The protests were not ideological but reactionary, demographically and politically mixed, in Gramsci's words – there was a historic bloc at Maidan, not a political movement or class-for-itself; and while encouragement from the West served its discursive purpose, even the far-fetched analyses tend to avoid making direct links to the West.[83] Most analyses and government responses revolved around a false dichotomy of 'bandits versus Nazis'. So, the right-wing forces were tolerated in the fight against bandits in power while those fearing 'the brown plague' were willing to tolerate the bandits as a lesser evil.[84] In their study of protest dynamic in Ukraine since 2010, Ishchenko and researchers at the Centre for Social and Labour Research show strong presence of right-wing parties at Maidans and pre-Maidan demonstrations.[85] In a separate study of the right wing at Maidan and beyond, Ishchenko warns against discarding the significance of the right and suggests that it is not only the proportion but the role the right has been playing that shall be taken into account. And the latter was significant in 2013–2014.[86]

Right-wing forces were present at Maidans – and Anti-Maidans, for that matter, yet they were not proportionately dominant. They did not take power in the country in the immediate aftermath of Yanukovych fleeing, nor in the following elections where neither Svoboda, nor the Right Sector won the necessary minimum 5 per cent of votes required to sit in the parliament.[87] Socio-economic component, that is, class component, instead was pronounced in the protest, as I will discuss shortly. Ideological aspects do come to surface in the context of the 'patriotism games' played by the neoliberal kleptocracy regime that push towards fascicisation of the political mainstream.

One must remember how the Bloody Winter began and that it had much less to do with the EU as it was often presented in the mass media – both pro-Western and pro-Russian – if for different reasons. Euromaidan demonstrations in support of DCFTA signing were few and small and failed in comparison with some of the ongoing protests across the country that were on the rise since Yanukovych became president in 2010. Euromaidan protests proper began to magnify when Yanukovych refused to sign the treaty at the Third EU Eastern Partnership Summit in Vilnius in late November 2013. Yet the apogee was not reached until the beating of protesters in the middle of the night in late November. Euromaidans were not about the EU any longer but against the president and the omnipresent, long-seated lawlessness and corruption. Euromaidans in essence became Maidans, that is, they lost their EU association core and turned against the long-standing problems in Ukraine's polity. What made the protests noticeable was the exposure in mass media and particularly social media. Not unlike the situation during similar (post-)Arab Spring protests elsewhere, new media played an important role in making the Maidan/Anti-Maidan different from the media wars of the Orange Revolution period. Then, mass media discourse was manipulated via oligarch-owned and/or state controlled television and *temnyky* while internet use remained relatively low, especially in the countryside.[88] By 2013, the mass media and internet use demographic has noticeably changed; different tactics had to be used for manufacturing of opinions. Conventional media and television channels were still largely under oligarchic and state control but now it was the era of virtual social networks and Facebook, VKontakte, Twitter, and LifeJournal played a crucial role in mobilising and organising demonstrations.[89] Existing social networks and newly established web platforms, for example, YouTube and Hromadske TV,[90] have proven crucial in shaping public opinion, manufacturing it and dispelling manipulations too – they created a counterbalance in the information space.[91] Media space manipulations with sponsored use of 'bots' and 'trolls' by Russia became ubiquitous. In their study of Russian media space and disinformation campaign, Lucas and Pomeranzev document 'strategic tailoring' of narrative, relying on emotive language, manipulation of pre-existing stereotypes, complete fabrication of stories and video report, 'linking Ukrainian nationalism and German fascism in Russia and encouraging anti-US and anti-EU sentiment in Europe.'[92]

The old tricks of thugs in politics that were familiar from the days of crime and Kuchma were used yet again. People who poured onto the streets in late 2013 did not do so to prove their dignity to Europe as the name ascribed later to the revolt, that is, Revolution of Dignity, suggests. It was a sign of refusal to accept yet another lie, not of desperation to join the EU and its ephemeral 'European values'. Instead, as I briefly mentioned earlier, sociological data shows that it was the beating of the protesters that led to the escalation of the mass protests across the country and to counter protests – Anti-Maidans.[93] Both were accompanied by rather undignified accusation of virtual performative support for the West or the president and his party respectively.[94] According to a survey conducted by Bekeshkina and Khmelko from Democratic Initiatives Foundation and the Kyiv International Institute of Sociology on 7–8 December, of the 1,037 randomly selected Maidan participants, 92 per cent of them did not belong to any parties or NGOs. Three most commonly named reasons for joining the protest were: (1) police repressions, especially the beating of protesters on the night of 30 November (70 per cent of respondents); (2) the president's refusal to sign the Ukraine–EU association agreement (53.5 per cent); and (3) a desire to change life in Ukraine (50 per cent). Only 5 per cent said they joined the protest in response to political opposition leaders' call to do so[95] – Euromaidan was transformed into Maidan, the ongoing decades-long protest in its second national scale eruption. The protests against police brutality and refusal to sign the DCFTA with the EU, as is also confirmed by the data, were reactionary, counter-hegemonic movement without an ideological component or a single organising political force. Political parties' and politicians' presence in the Maidans was highest at the start of the protests (before 19 January 2014) at over 40 per cent while significantly dropped towards the end when violence escalated to 20 per cent between 10 and 23 February 2014.[96] The right-wing elements capitalised on that in the immediate aftermath of the police beatings and organised as a defence force at the Maidans in the absence of any other.[97] And indeed, the Maidans were many, diverse, and lasted from 21 November 2013 to 23 February 2014; out of 3,950 protests 3,235 were linked to Maidans and 365 Anti-Maidans. The latter were a series of protests in support of Yanukovych and his decision to decline the DCFTA signing. The rallies, it is widely believed and backed by unsystematised evidence that the rallies 'had a strong vertical component, i.e. many of the rallies and protest camps were organised from above and paid by the ruling Party of Regions.'[98] Divided into Maidan/pro-West and Anti-Maidan/pro-Yanukovych blocs with their multiple subgroups they clashed with each other and the security forces (mostly as a reaction to violence)[99] throughout the Bloody Winter on multiple occasions that included beatings and armed confrontations, while the police often were an inactive onlooker and/or an inciter of violence.[100]

There were two more peculiar social formations prominent at Maidans. The football fanclub-goers Ultras who acted as 'protectors' of Maidans from *titushki* and the police.[101] And the *titushki*, who first emerged during the 2010 electoral campaign.[102] They were 'notorious gangs of hired thugs', a new phenomenon of 'bands of militant hooligans. Their role was to instigate violence, act as a backup to the militia. The group 'membership' included:

people from a number of backgrounds like off-duty police officers and state security workers, members of more or less legal combat sports clubs, workers at industrial plants owned by pro-government forces, members of criminal gangs, and common convicts, and most likely also groups of football fans.[103]

The existence of such groups and their use would come as no surprise in the context of the PR past and present criminal links. Brigades of disenfranchised men have been used in accumulation games since the early 1990s (as I discussed in the earlier chapters) and now that criminals-turned-oligarchs were in politics proper, they had little intention of changing their customary mechanisms of maintaining control over assets, elections or public protest. The coercive apparati of the state, where crime is the state's integral component, will inevitably include thug brigades, especially under presidency of an ex-thug, that is Yanukovych, whose gang used such brigades to grow his 'Family's' capitalist pyramid, as discussed in earlier chapters. And the supply of 'volunteers' to join such brigades in exchange for a nominal fee and the perceived 'prestige' among other thugs was plentiful as the army of anomie-stricken youth keeps growing – thugs, *titushki*, ultras are all a product of the extreme and all-permeating dispossession.

DISINTEGRATION MOVEMENTS: THE CRIMEA, NOVORISSIYA AND THE BREAK-UP OF UKRAINE

Few expected that Ukraine would disintegrate, yet analyses warning of such a possibility exist. Dominique Arel, for example, documented a proclivity to break-up in his analysis of the Orange Revolution events already.[104] Ivan Katchanovski also conducted a detailed analysis and issued a warning of a disintegration scenario in his 'cleft countries' thesis.[105] Still, the possibility of disintegration was not treated seriously by politicians or by many scholars; after all, the existence of regional divergences do not always have to lead to a political split. However, even once the rebellion had started, the threat became very real; yet it was not treated with enough seriousness and local support for separatism was downplayed by the West and the interim government in Kyiv. Instead, all organising and leading responsibility was laid upon Russian army and separatism brigades. In Russian media and political discourse, support was instead exaggerated and portrayed as ubiquitous. Similar fictitious fiction was manufactured and disseminated with vengeance via Russian and separatist media about a 'fascist junta' that allegedly took power in Kyiv by force. The 'fascist *coup d'état*' – also known as Yanukovych's self-imposed exile – was then seen as a fascist threat and in that context 'separatists, including Russian volunteers, defended people of Donbas from Ukrainian "fascists"'.[106] Novorossiya project was fully launched and, according to Putin, included the territory of Kharkov, Lugansk, Donetsk, Kherson, Nikolayev and Odesa – oblasts that were not part of Ukraine prior to the Russian Revolution but 'granted' by the Soviets in 1920s.[107]

The Novorossiya project did not emerge overnight. Some believe that Russia had been planning it since the 1990s (Vitaliy Portnikov in Berezovets, for example) as part of its 'civilisational Slavic mission'. The main theoretical mind behind the new empire is Aleksandr Dugin, who is highly influential within Putin's administration.[108] According to Dugin, Russians have a 'great dream' of nationhood worth 'unthinkable sacrifice and destitution' and that dream's limit lies 'with an empire, at least'. This empire is seen as 'the only form of decent and natural existence of the Russian people and the only possibility to fulfil its historic and civilisational mission.'[109] The Novorissiya project was strategically manufactured as a 'politically coloured territorial "brand"' and advertised by 'pro-Kremlin intellectuals, activists of the Donbas rebellion, and internet users'.[110] In the construction of Novorossiya as a space, traditions had to be invented,[111] clipped together from disjointed historical experiences with new meanings and significance as 'usable pasts create usable spaces'.[112] Space was assigned geopolitical significance yet with little historical geopolitical or territorial accuracy; it was an ideological product that involved material, financial, and spatio-temporal planning.[113] Things, however, did not go as planned – if they were planned – since the avalanche of events started by the events of the Bloody Winter. Yet it is undeniable that the Novorossiya idea has been nursed in the south-east of Ukraine and the Crimea since the 1990s by funding publications in the local press and providing financial support for local organisations supporting the concept of Russkiy Mir. The latter's ambition spreads throughout the post-Soviet space generating frozen conflicts in its way. Yet what must be understood is that it is not the conflicts but their settlement that can be frozen;[114] conflicts can either continue or be reconciled. Similar conflicts occurred elsewhere on the fringes of disintegrating post-Soviet Russian empire or Eurasia 2.0;[115] they have occurred and have not yet been resolved – Transnistria, Abkhasia, Chechnya …

It is hard to imagine, however, that the Novorossiya project could take off with little to no local support. Indeed, Serhiy Kudelia suggests that the Donbas insurrection was 'primarily a homegrown phenomenon' where 'political factors – *state fragmentation, violent regime change, and the government's low coercive capacity* – combined with popular emotions specific to the region – *resentment and fear* – played a crucial role in launching the armed secessionist movement there.'[116] According to Kudelia, three factors contributed to feasibility of war in Donbas.[117] First, the emergence of regional self-governed enclaves in Western and Central Ukraine in late January 2014 that 'defied rule from Kyiv, created a sense of state fragmentation, and further accelerated in the final phase of the Euromaidan'; created a sense of a *fragmented state*. The interim authorities lost control over the country and failed to halt violence and the violent seizure of government buildings or 're-establish control over half of the country'. The dismantling of authority that could be recognised by the eastern and southern regions, the stronghold of the Party of Region, led to speedy alienation of local resident from the opposition's new rule in Kyiv. The Party of Regions too was disintegrating. Members were defecting en masse while those remaining partly aligned with the interim government (many have supported Yatsenyuk's premiership) while others refused to recognise it. Ukraine's disintegration was not helped by the agonising effort of some of the Party of Regions' representatives to hang onto power by means of igniting anti-Kyiv/'anti-junta' sentiments. For example, Hennadiy Kernes and Mikhail Dobkin, have actively contributed to the clashes between the Maidan and Anti-Maidan protesters in the east instead of attempting to diffuse tensions. One of the notorious cases was that of major of Slavyansk (a town in Donetsk oblast), Nelya Shtepa, who was actively supporting the separatist referendum and later was arrested on infringement of territorial integrity and sovereignty of Ukraine.[118] Oleh Tsarev of the PR went as far as to become the speaker for the DNR and LNR 'unity parliament confederation' and even represented the separatist entities during Minsk negotiations. This further destabilised the disintegrating country. The second was overall *low government legitimacy* that was particularly strong in Donbas. So,

in early April, approximately half of all respondents in the Donetsk and Luhansk regions expressed strong confidence in the illegality of the acting president and the new government, compared to about a third or fewer respondents in other southeastern regions with a similar view. Seventy percent of residents in the Donetsk region and sixty-one percent in the Luhansk region viewed the protest movement as a Western-sponsored armed coup. The average for the rest of southeast was almost half that number (37 percent).[119]

By the time new governors for Donetsk and Luhansk were appointed, neither they, not the Party of Region enjoyed local support. In fact, only 'four percent in each region wanted to see its members represented in the new government'.[120] A power vacuum emerged and previously marginalised politicians could take the lead. The third was the new government's *coercive failure*. Partly due to loyalty to the self-exiled Yanukovych, partly due to disregard of opposition's new authority, partly due to unwillingness to partake in violence against protesters, police and security forces, including the special force Berkut, remained reluctant to show violence towards people. The main signal of non-violent approach was the peaceful withdrawal of troops from the occupied Crimea. With Russia refusing to recognise the interim government as legitimate[121] and threatening invasion,[122] it was clear that Kyiv was unwilling to use force, at least not until an internationally recognised commander-in-chief, that is, the president, was elected.

The seeds of separatism indeed were sown in the 1990s, took root in the Blue-Orange campaign, and sprung out of Maidans and Anti-Maidans in 2013–2014. In the context of social divisions manufactured in accumulation rivalries for some two decades, Yanukovych and local Party of Regions leaders have paved the way for Girkin's army, the 'polite people', and Russian 'invisible' troops of Novorossiya project. Emotions of resentment and fear towards the new rulers in Kyiv[123] resulted from systematic portrayal of regional identity as separate from the rest of Ukraine.[124] Negative emotions were fuelled by lack of trust that was made worse by increasing dehumanisation of eastern dwellers in the mainstream political and mass media discourse. Terms such as 'Colorady' (that is 'Colorado bugs' slur) were used to mock the black and yellow stripes of the Ribbon of Saint George worn by separatists and their Russian instigators. Yet resentment and fear go both ways and were ignited in both Maidan and Anti-Maidan movements – again, regional aspect was important but not absolute, there were and still are supporters for either in the allegedly alien regions. Opposition in Kyiv did their dirty work in alienating the Maidans from Anti-Maidans too. Anti-*Sovok* and anti-Russian sentiment started there, again, first palpable in the Orange-Blue campaign as I documented in the earlier chapters.

The 'Maidan and Anti-Maidan movements were both highly complex phenomena where there was no clear position', no identifiable ideological component.[125] Both movements 'combined progressive and reactionary elements' to various extent[126] yet either of the final outcomes had little progressiveness in it. The Maidans were hijacked by the oligarchy, the Anti-Maidans by Russian separatists. Still it was the socio-economic component that led people to the streets, Euromaidans and Anti-Maidans (here we exclude paid protesters, who in their own way were also led to the streets in part by their socio-economic desperation and civil erosion, and the anomie that such entails). Indeed, research into the likelihood of rebel activity confirms that the 'pre-war employment mix is a more robust predictor of rebel activity than local ethnolinguistic composition' and that the areas that broke into high intensity violence were those most dependent for their employment on Russia.[127] The conflict is more complex than appearances may suggest. While there is an ethnic component and there are attempting puppeteers from Moscow, Brussels and Washington, in a stable socio-economic environment none of the above would have led to violence, let alone armed conflict. It is only the brink of despair that the working communities of the region have balanced on for decades that has made the conflict possible, the condition brought on by a strategically, if unwittingly, manufactured 'other' from Kyiv and Lviv; the other who has been 'leaching' off the hard labourers of the industrial east according to the Masters of Donbas.

THE BLOODY WINTER

On 17 December 2013, Putin and Yanukovych signed an 'Action Plan' that confirmed the withdrawal from the EU DCFTA option and rapprochement with Russia instead. The plan involved the revision of trade relations between the countries and a $15 billion loan to help Ukraine finance its foreign debt. The 'friendly' gas price of $410 per 1,000 cubic metres was to be lowered to $268.5 per 1,000 cubic metres – the price Germany has been paying all along. Yanukovych may have saved the economy from collapsing, in the short term at least, but the 'Plan' was not accepted by the people on the streets and the protests continued. In an attempt to disperse demonstrators and on advice of Putin,[128] in a grossly violated procedure, he pushed a package of laws repressing protest though the parliament.[129] The laws were almost verbatim copied from a similar package adopted earlier in Russia;[130] they were immediately condemned by Transparency International, OSCE, EU and US partners, among others. As a response to creeping authoritarianism, the protests radicalised. The first wave of violent stand-off with use of catapults, Molotov cocktails, cobblestones, etc. started on 19 January in Kyiv, on Hrushevskoho street after a rally of some 200,000 people and carried on for months since. On 22 January, two protestors were shot dead[131] that lead to a temporary retreat and a consecutive escalation – the kleptocratic oligarchy broke the social contract but its increased reliance on coercive apparati would not be accepted any longer. Following the protest ban, protesters and protest organisers were prosecuted, threatened, 'snatched from hospital beds', kidnapped, 'beaten and dumped in local forests'[132] – all tactics too familiar to the criminal capitalist fractions.[133] At the same time, the regime was cautious and reluctant to use direct force. In fact, compared to treatment of significantly less violent anti-austerity protests in the EU, for example, Ukrainian government showed excessive tolerance – in relative, not absolute, terms.

The USA and many other Western governments generally eschew the issue of civilian casualties, claimed lack of evidence to determine responsibility for the deadly attacks, or argued that the Ukrainian government forces showed restraint in using force. The same concerns the Odesa massacre of some 40 separatists and employees in a trade union building on 2 May 2014.[134] Yanukovych showed restraint in harnessing the protests. Even in the most violent moments, he refused to use 'live ammunition and military units to suppress the "Euromaidan"' as 'this would [have] likely resulted in a large numbers of casualties among the protesters, a full-fledged uprising in opposition stronghold in Western Ukraine, and probably a civil war'.[135]

The unknown snipers' simultaneous shooting of the protesters and security forces ignited most violent clashes of the Bloody Winter and took nearly a hundred lives, who would become known as the 'Heavenly Hundred'. Ivan Katchanovski conducted a detailed content analysis study based on:

> about 1,500 videos and recordings of live internet and TV broadcasts in mass media and social media in different countries (some 150 gigabytes), news reports and social media posts by more than 100

journalists covering the massacre from Kyiv, some 5,000 photos, and nearly 30 gigabytes of publicly available radio intercepts of snipers and commanders from the special Alfa unit of the Security Service of Ukraine and Internal Troops, and Maidan massacre trial recordings.[136]

In his detailed investigation, Katchnovski concludes that the shooting was a 'false flag operation' that was planned and carried out with an aim to overthrow the government and seize power. He points to 'an alliance of the far-right organizations, specifically the Right Sector and Svoboda, and oligarchic parties, such as Fatherland'. Some '20 Maidan-controlled buildings or areas' were confirmed to have had 'concealed shooters and spotters' in them during the sniper assault.

The manufactured 'banderites' from Lviv assuming dominance in the government was a gift to Putin. He now had a perfect excuse to annex Crimea under the pretext of 'protecting Russians and Russian speakers' from so-called masked militants 'running the streets of Kyiv'.[137] The perceived threat to Russians and Russian speakers was a fabrication spun out of Rada's revoking of the 2012 Law 'On the Principles of the State Language Policy' that granted Russian language – along with other minority languages – a right to serve as a second official language on a regional level. The opposition, that is, anti-Donetsk/Yanukovych bloc in the parliament, were against the law since its inception and protested its adoption in 2012.[138] As the parliamentary support base of the PR was eroding upon protesters' and armed forced deaths, the opposition blamed the instigation of events on Russian meddling in Ukraine's foreign and domestic affairs and called to revoke the law empowering the imperialist neighbour's culture. The motion was passed with 86 per cent support of the parliamentary vote. Putin's interpretation of such a move as a threat to Russians was a fabrication. All minority language rights were and are protected by Article 10 of Ukraine's Constitution. Thus, the motion was not a ban but a reduction in formal status. The timing of the revocation was poor yet the perceived need for it in the light of Russia's disregard for sovereignty of Ukraine's decision-making can be justified. It is precisely the geopolitics associated with language status that dictated the change and not the alleged attempts to instate Ukrainian superiority over Russian, it was an act of assertion of political and cultural sovereignty, act of near desperation. The assumption that all ethnic Russian supported separatism is too incorrect, even in the

Donetsk and Luhansk Region where they comprise nearly a half of the population – largest proportion in Ukraine after Crimea.

2014 KIIS Survey shows that ethnic Russians in Ukraine were split on the issue of separatism. Similar percentages of ethnic Russians, including people with mixed Russian and Ukrainian descent, supported preservation of the current unitary system (40 percent), mostly with expanded powers and different separatist options (44 percent), in particular, joining Russia (18 percent). In contrast, only 24 percent of Russian speakers, who include many ethnic Ukrainians, favored secession from Ukraine or regional autonomy in federal Ukraine.[139]

When so-called secession referenda were held in Donbas in March 2014, they showed overwhelming support for the move that was hard to believe as survey data contradicts those results.[140] According to a survey conducted by KIIS in 2014, '23 percent of the respondents in Donbas, favored autonomy as a part of federal Ukraine, compared to 8 percent supporting independence of their region and 23 percent favoring their region joining Russia.'[141] In comparison with other oblasts, there was very little support for 'preserving current status of their regions within a unitary Ukraine but with expanded powers' in Donetsk and Luhansk oblasts. At the same time, the survey showed that 'the views expressed by the Russian government and the media concerning widespread popular support for separatism in all Eastern and Southern Ukraine, referred to by President Putin and pro-Russian separatists as Novorossia, were unfounded.'[142]

In the Crimea, the situation was different from Donbas as the proportion of ethnically Russian population was higher. Many Russian military stationed with the Black Sea fleet retired and stayed here, never having to learn Ukrainian language or feeling the pressure to lose their attachment to Russian. Ethnic tensions do not arise when minorities of certain ethnic origin living in the host countries speak their original language as native but nonetheless belong to the host – in our case Ukrainian – nation 'understood as a political, territorial or civic nation of and for all its citizens, regardless of language and ethnicity, not as the nation of and for ethic Ukrainians'.[143] Given such thinking was typical of Russians in Ukraine, there would be no Russian, nor any other, 'national minority'[144] but one, Ukrainian nation.

A crucial role in alienating separatist regions from Kyiv was played by the Odesa massacre. The new old-new rulers failed to adequately control the conflicting groups and allowed for the tragedy to happen. As a result of demonstrators' clashes on the May Day 2014 (2 May) that again included thug brigades, two pro-Russian and two pro-Ukraine demonstrators died in gunfire and 42 pro-Russia demonstrators were burned alive in a blocked trade union building in central Odesa, as was mentioned earlier.[145] Resentment and fear in the southern and eastern oblasts was hard to stop beyond this point.

Despite growing dissatisfaction with Kyiv's rule, there was little cross-oblast coordination between the separatist groups and 'the spread of violent seizures of government buildings across the Donbas in April happened sporadically and in a decentralized manner'.[146] Moreover,

> the self-declared 'people's mayors' of different Donbas towns were local political opportunists who used the implosion of authority to claim power rather than members of a clandestine organization coordinated from a single center. Paramilitary commanders who propped them up were often in conflict regarding their respective spheres of influence. In addition, separatists in the Donetsk and Luhansk People's Republics followed different strategies that were adopted in an ad hoc manner – the former rushed to declare its independence in early April while the latter decided to announce its separation from Ukraine only after the referendum.[147]

A more centralised coordination of armed resistance in the Donetsk region appeared only in late May when Aleksandr Borodai's group and the Vostok battalion imposed their authority on disparate separatist groups in Donetsk.[148] After that Donbas was lost and armed conflict was unfolding instead. Politicians and oligarchs have failed to prevent but rather accelerated the development of this tragedy.

REINSTATEMENT OF OLIGARCHY

A brief hope for a chance of a systemic change in the country upon Yanukovych's escape was stolen from the fragmented dispossessed as the kleptocratic oligarchy capitalised on the effects of the Russian annexation of Crimea in March 2014. The dispossessed divided masses of what they were led to believe was two separate Ukraines now were led to a civil armed conflict with an element of foreign – that is, Russian – direct involvement in the fighting.

The oligarchs remained in power and the neoliberal kleptocracy survived as a regime. The power balance in the ruling bloc, however, shifted from east to west overnight. The interim government with Prime Minister Arseniy Yatsenyuk was composed primarily of Western Ukrainians. The east has lost its presidents, its ministers and its political dominance in the country, as with Yanukovych, many of his ministers had also fled the country. The 'junta' *coup d'état* myth had as much to do with the Right Sector and the like's role in the ouster of Yanukovych as it did with the 'banderites' taking ministerial seats. The 'two Ukraines' were now a reality and the one to the east felt robbed of the influence it was convinced was its right as the 'feeder' of the economy – influence that it already had stolen once before, in 2004, by the same 'alien formations', who 'do not understand Donbas'.[149] The new government, however technically legitimate, was a thorny issue as some,

> 60 percent of its top officials (ministers and above) come from the former Habsburg provinces [that were added to USSR after the Second World War and have historically been anti-Russian]. A third [or seven ministers were] from Lviv itself. Only two members of the new government (Interior Minister Arsen Avakov and Minister of Social Policy Lyudmila Denisova) hail from the country's south and east.[150]

Such national representation was unacceptable for the eastern oblasts as the ensuing separatist surge confirmed. Instead of a systemic change in the country following the vents of the Bloody Winter, a civil armed conflict broke out while oligarchy was largely intact. Fearing prosecution and the loss of assets and control over the state institutions, the oligarchs utilised the country's urgent need for legitimate representatives in power to push for a snap presidential and then parliamentary elections in the following months.[151] Putin's land grabbing behaviour helped oligarchs remain in power. The electoral campaign of the spring of 2014 was soaked in fears of a full-scale Russian invasion, cessation of the south-east and the creation of Novorossiya. The legitimacy of the interim government was being questioned by the Kremlin and Ukraine was in desperate and urgent need of a newly elected commander-in-chief to defend itself in military terms and to halt separatist movements' spread. Poroshenko won in the first round with 54.7 per cent of the 60 per cent voter turnout (minus Crimea and the separatist areas).[152]

The rule of oligarchy was once again restored with Poroshenko becoming president and key state administration positions being given to the cadre of oligarchy. The main change in the ruling bloc was not the displacement of the reign of capital as Maidan protests demanded but the erosion of the centralised control and influence that the Donetsk bloc had enjoyed in the country since 2007–2010.[153] The Party of Regions, the Donetsk capital party, 'saw massive defections from its ranks and the pro-Yanukovych majority collapsed in the Rada' in the winter of 2014[154] and the party did not take part in the snap election that followed. While their MPs made it into the new parliament through constituency votes and the newly formed pro-Russian Opposition Bloc party, their leverage in the parliament was weakened.[155] The regional composition of the state apparatus became more mixed,[156] marking renewed intensification of the oligarchic rivalry and who now however were much more susceptible to foreign/IFIs' pressure and had suffered financial losses.[157] The country's labour instead was impoverished, faced with IMF-forced market-adjusted utility bills that exceeded average wages and pensions, with the civil armed conflict on both sides of the frontline, and with destitution and slave labour in separatist republics in the east.[158]

The oligarchy fully realised the extent of the crisis of representation in the country and that they remained in power only due to the popular fears of power vacuum in the context of military campaign. In an attempt to instil trust in the newly elected parliament of predominantly corruption-stained representatives, three foreigners were hired to fill ministerial seats in an unprecedented move: US-born Natalie Jaresko as the finance minister, Lithuania's Aivaras Abromavicius as the economy and trade minister and Aleksandre Kvitashvili from Georgia as health minister.[159] However, a schism in the government and the team of foreigners hired to win, if temporarily, popular trust in the broken system they were asked to fix was growing as the change that oligarchs wanted was cosmetic. Instead of winning the trust of citizens, the kleptocrats lost the last residue of it, together with the small, newly found trust of IFIs, monitoring institutions and NGOs.

8

Geopolitics, the elusive 'Other' and the nebulous telos of Europe

THE CONFLICT AND ITS GEOPOLITICS

The act of the Crimean annexation was an act of imperial entitlement based on a total disregard of international law and the sovereignty of Ukraine. A fantasy legitimation based on vague and historically inaccurate connections between the Crimean town of Khersones, baptism of Prince Volodymyr of the Kievan Rus, and Russia's self-anointed right to carry on the Rus's legacy caused bemusement among historians of the region and tragedy to the people of Crimea and Ukraine.[1] Upon also fantastical results of an anti-constitutional referendum on secession, the Crimean autonomy and the city-port of Sevastopol were annexed to Russia by an equally illegal vote of the Russian Duma.[2] The irony of installing illegitimate rule in the peninsula to save an ethnic group from a phantom threat of another type of allegedly illegitimate rule (the one in Kyiv) was lost on the Kremlin.

There has been an international disagreement on how the conflict shall be handled. While EU leaders laboured to prevent escalation of violence and avoid a war on their doorstep, the USA was less cautious in their tactics. The leaked exchanges between Nuland and Pyatt confirm general disregard for the opinion of other negotiation parties[3] let alone civilians who would suffer from the military campaign and aggregate effects of Ukraine's destabilisation. For the USA, it was an opportunity to discipline Russia that could not be missed. The EU, on the other hand, with fresh memories of Yugoslavian wars, Chechnya, Georgia-Abkhazia and Transnistria conflicts showed restraint in supporting the military solution. However, credit must be given where it is due, and the role of domestic rivalrous class fractions in the crisis must be acknowledged. If domestic conditions did not favour 'an armed secessionist movement, external prodding would have failed to produce a sustained and large-scale insurgency'. Conditions were created where 'those who came to lead it [could merely capitalise] on public apprehension about the growing anarchy in Kyiv and resorted to long-established narratives to keep it in motion'.[4]

Foreign policy games and accumulating ambitions of Ukrainian oligarchy have dragged the country into an economic agreement that would destroy SMEs and downsize the economy, allow the last remaining state assets to be ripped by capital. One of the few things Yanukovych got right – by pressure and accident – was that the signing of DCFTA would have been irresponsible, criminal even. He was right in stating that the treaty would be damaging for the economy. That, however, cannot be used as justification for Russian capitalist imperialist ambitions to 'defend its interests' at any cost, be it military intervention or creation of frozen conflicts. On the crossroads of empires, the capitalist greed has brought the country into economic servitude, bred multiple Ukraines, and thrown national identities into transmutation. Many generations to come will have to struggle to disarm the seeds of enmity sown by the manufactured myth of the 'Other' within, in oneself, in one's past and memories sacrificed to the empire of capital.

THE FIGHTING AND RUSSIA'S INVOLVEMENT

Emboldened by the new legitimacy granted by the May 2014 election and backed by over-zealous volunteer battalions, Poroshenko-led oligarchy launched a military offensive on the self-proclaimed republics of DNR and LNR. The offensive was largely carried out by the volunteer battalions many without formal recognition; a large proportion of financing support also came from volunteers and donations.[5] Some of the battalions had formed at Maidans already. There were 37 of such battalions in total, with some 40,000 personnel.[6] It is at this juncture that Russian involvement in the conflict became decisive. Pro-Russian separatists had been on retreat 'from Sloviansk, Kramatorsk, and other areas of the Donetsk and Luhansk Regions to much more densely populated parts of Donbas, in particular, cities of Donetsk and Luhansk' since the beginning of July 2014.[7] Strengthened by Russia's military support, separatists were fighting back. Kyiv's forces, on the other hand, began to suffer defeat as large numbers 'of their members were encircled, killed, wounded, or captured, primarily near the town of Illovaisk, and they had to retreat from parts of the previously-held territories.'[8] High loss of human life and images of destruction by shelling were quickly undermining support for the military solution and forcing Poroshenko to review his strategy. At the same time, his refusal to recognise DNR and LNR leadership as legitimate negotiating parties was inhibiting the potential for a ceasefire, let alone a diplomatic solution. Nevertheless, the ceasefire was agreed with help and pressure from Western partners and Russia and with the inclusion of the separatist leaders in the Minsk negotiations on 5 September 2014. Russia was cautious of supporting the self-proclaimed republics whose leaders were Russian citizens and quickly replaced Strelkov and Borodai with local separatist leaders while the first two were returned to Russia.

Claims of Ukrainian and Western governments that 'Russian military and intelligence units or 'green men' were leading the separatist fight in Donbas since it started in spring 2014' are based on mixed evidence.[9] For example, Strelkov – also known as Igor Girkin – a retired officer of the Federal Security Service (FSB), his armed group, and its Russian members in Sloviansk and Kramatorsk were falsely accused of being part of Russian military intelligence (GRU) unit.[10] Still, while direct connections to Russian security forces is unconfirmed, it does not mean that there was no Russian hand in the operation of those units. It does, however, mean a lack of evidence confirming their formal status in the Russian security or intelligence structures. Kremlin dispensed similar tales of 'volunteers' rather than official servicemen engagement in the conflict even when currently conscribed soldiers were captured or killed in Donbas.[11]

Undeniable is Russia's trained military personnel and supply of weapons. Supplies included the BUK anti-missile system and the crew that shot down the Malaysian airlines plane in 2014. The tragedy occurred on 17 July in the morning, taking the lives of all 298 people on board. Separatists were well equipped by the time of the shooting, and during June–July over ten Ukrainian aircrafts were shot down including 'a transporter carrying forty paratroopers and nine crew on 13 July, two helicopters, and either one or two SU-25 fighters on 16 July', just before the MH17 tragedy.[12] Thinking they downed a military jet, the separatist commanders boasted about it on their website until the news of a civilian flight forced them to delete the record. Mounting evidence from intelligence units, eyewitnesses and the independent international investigation conducted by the Dutch Safety Board confirmed in 2015 the separatist link to the tragedy.

The accounts of the conflict and destruction that occurred in the months of intensified fighting are plentiful – Avdeevka, Shakhtarsk, Debaltseve, Donetsk Airport, Illovaysk, Kramatorsk, Marinka, Mariupol, Novoazovsk, Shyrokyne, Slovyansk, Luhansk, Svitlodarsk, Zelenopillya were the points of most brutal confrontation. Below I present the summary of the human cost of the ugly face the capitalist imperialist greed takes, where the dispossessed labour's children are gutted, demoralised, dehumanised, stripped of the civilisational superstructure, and whose selves are forever lost in accumulation manoeuvres. According to the Report on the human rights situation in Ukraine by the Office of the UN High Commissioner for Human Rights (OHCHR) launched on 8 December 2016, 'between mid-August and mid-November [2016], at least 32 civilians were killed in conflict-related incidents and another 132 injured'.[13] By the end of 2016, 'between mid-April 2014 and 1 December [2016], more than 2,000 civilians are estimated to have died', excluding the MH17 crash victims. To that date, 'conflict-related civilian injuries [were] estimated [to be] between 6,000 and 7,000'.[14] The overall number of casualties was nearing 10,000.[15] The total 'death toll from mid-April 2014 [to 1 December 2016 was] 9,758 with another 22,779 people injured'.[16] The United Nations Human Rights Monitoring Mission in Ukraine (UNHRMMU) reports that 'mortar, rocket, and artillery attacks between April 2014 and May 2016 killed over 9,000 people and injured more than 21,000 – including civilians and combatants on all sides – in Donetsk and Luhansk regions'.[17] The UNHRMMU also 'reported a 66 percent increase in civilian casualties from May to August compared to earlier in 2016, and documented 28 civilian deaths in the summer, many of which resulted from shelling and landmines'.[18]

The role of oligarchs in the fighting is still being studied, there are too many unknowns yet there are a few undeniable facts and also a few curious facts that make one question a lack of connection between the separatists and the local oligarchy. Rinat Akhmetov, for example, assumed a cautious stance from the start. He avoided making a public statement or making his position known during the Maidan/Anti-Maidan confrontations. Later, when the separatist movements started in Donbas, he appealed to his holding's workers, asking them to stand with the interim government in Kyiv. Neutrality of Akhmetov's position was questioned, however, by allegations of being a potential beneficiary of the fighting. Pavel Gubarev, one of the separatist leaders, claimed that the oligarch was financing the rebels yet Akhmetov denied the allegations.[19] The late Semenyuk-Samsonenko suggested in August 2014 that partial destruction would allow him cheap access to SOEs in the region. Later, in October 2014, reports emerged that a hangar where Akhmetov's private jet was kept was the only building remaining intact in Donetsk airport, that had been the site of some of the most violent fighting.[20] A few days later, the hangar was conveniently blown up; Akhmetov did not comment.[21] Kolomoyskyy, an MP, took a more proactive position. Being from Dnipropetrovsk and having his enterprise base in Eastern Ukraine, he feared the spread of separatism and thus loss of control in the oblast. In 2014, when the fighting started in the east of the country, he personally funded volunteer battalions who halted the spread of Novorossiya separatists to Dnipropetrovsk oblast. Kolomoyskyy was defending his own as it was his home district and the stronghold of the Privat Group. Due to the 'patriotic zeal', he was appointed the governor of the oblast for nearly a year before being scandalously dismissed for overstepping authority when he sent his armed men to 'protect' the state oil firm Ukrnafta's offices in Kyiv 'from illegal takeover'; he had a 42 per cent stake in the firm.[22] This behaviour will cost him the governor seat and later parts of business too. The 1990s criminal modus operandi of the economy was coming to an end for some but not all.

MINSK ACCORDS AND CEASEFIRE

Two milestones in the ceasefire negotiations were achieved by the Trilateral Contact Group on Ukraine. Minsk I was signed by OSCE, Ukraine, Russia and LND and DNR representatives on 5 September 2014.[23] Along with an immediate ceasefire, the Protocol was set to ensure decentralisation of power and adoption of the law 'On Temporary Order of Local Self-Governance in Particular Districts of Donetsk and Luhansk Oblasts' and a law that would protect persons involved in the events of Donetsk and Luhansk oblasts from prosecution and punishment.[24] The former would allow for a form of self-governance in separatist areas while the latter would spare separatists from responsibility for territorial disintegration.[25] This deal was a diplomatic failure. Bloody conflicts must involve punishment, however limited and targeted, yet a resolution, let alone reconciliation are impossible without it. Due to the hybrid nature of the conflict, Russia's unacknowledged involvement, and excesses of physical violence administered by both sides it was difficult to clearly demarcate what constituted a crime to be punished, especially if the ceasefire was to be achieved. Without potential punishment of leadership at least, the ceasefire was doomed to fail. Minsk II has not fixed the problems of the earlier Protocol or the problems the Protocols were aimed to fix. Kuzio laid out ten reasons why the agreement was a failure which included:[26] '12,000 Russian troops in Eastern Ukraine without signs of withdrawal', ongoing arrivals of Russian 'humanitarian' convoys without Kiev's official permission, Russian refusal to hand over control of Ukraine's border and Ukrainian nationalist battalions continued attacks on the separatists behind the frontline.[27] The Protocol did not address the problem of the Crimea occupation, and there are still illegally captured prisoners of war kept by Russia against international law, for example, the Ukrainian pilot Nadiya Savchenko, who was only released in May 2016.

The Minsk Agreements have not resolved the underlying issues that led to conflict in the first place. The realisation that 'merely suppressing the insurgency by force without addressing its deeper internal causes is unlikely to make the Donbas a less troublesome and volatile part of Ukraine'[28] must translate into the reconciliation effort or the conflict will not be resolved. Incentives to be friendly with separatists for vulnerable groups as that allows preferential access to humanitarian aid which is limited and hard to get – that is, the more Ukraine government cuts off support, the more likely local isolated populations are to support separatists even while there is no support for separatism.

As a response to escalating conflict and Kyiv's unwillingness – and now also inability – to forfeit the DCFTA and the EU membership aspirations, Russia added insult to injury by combining economic pressure with aiding the military assault. Overall, three levels of impact were employed: military, trade sanctioning and disciplining via gas price inflation. Following the Novorossiya operation and the annexation of Crimea, an array of trade restrictions was applied to Ukraine, which led to 'a threefold decline in Ukraine's exports to Russia'.[29] Next, as of January 2016, 'Russia unilaterally excluded Ukraine from the 2011 CIS FTA, something which, inevitably, further reduces Ukraine's trade with Russia, forcing a radical reorientation toward the EU and third markets'.[30] Now that Crimea was annexed and Russia no longer had to pay for the lease of its Sevastopol military base, the price of gas that hinged upon the fleet stationing agreement could be changed too. The agreement, known as the 'Kharkiv accord', included a gas price discount in exchange for Russia's access to the military base.

AUTHORITARIAN NEOLIBERAL KLEPTOCRACY

There was no fascist coup in the winter of 2014 Ukraine, yet at the time of writing the kleptocratic oligarchy has instrumentalised the right-wing rhetoric to the point of fascisisation of the mainstream politics with the inevitable parallel shift of the societal consciousness and political consensus to the right. Oligarchs of Ukraine have followed suit of their western and eastern teachers. In a trademark virtuoso performance, they combined authoritarian neoliberalism of the West with its austerity-driven dispossession and neoliberal authoritarian statism of Russia. The result was generously peppered with patriotic rhetoric and a hunt on the 'enemies of the people' – a group comprising anyone critical of Poroshenko's fiefdom. Some recent cases of such hunt include stripping MP Andriy Artemenko, Sasha Borovik and Mikheil Saakashvili of Ukrainian citizenship – all three were critical of the regime and made noise in the press about corruption in the government. Such punitive acts are a continuation of a long-standing tradition in Ukrainian politics that stand behind the competitive authoritarianism thesis that is to say – whoever is in power goes after whoever is not. The witch-hunt on the 'culprits' or *poperednyky* of Yanukovych's regime saw many flee the country to avoid prosecution while a number were dealt with in the manner standard since Kuchma's time – they were eliminated. As Yanukovych's power pyramid was dismantled upon his own and some ministers' self-imposed exile, fractional rivalry intensified. The interim government of Yatsenyuk was composed primarily of people from the Western and Central Ukraine, as I discussed in Chapter 7. Newly intensified competition between capitalist class fractions set in with now traditional parallel accumulation grab accompanied by a surge in crime. Two of the most notable cases were Lyudmyla Semenyuk-Samsonenko and Mykhaylo Chechetov. Both had previously held top positions in the State Property Fund of Ukraine and oversaw a series of privatisation grabs or simply 'knew too much'. Semenyuk-Samsonenko was outspoken about the corrupt privatisation schemes. In a series of television interviews, she exposed violations of procedures and essentially organised embezzlement since the 1990s.[31] In her last interview to the *Russia24* channel on 2 August 2014, she accused the oligarchs in using the war in their accumulation grab, depreciating SOEs in the area of fighting for cheaper privatisation auctions and strategic fighting around oligarchic enterprises.[32] On 28 August, she was found shot dead by a hunting rifle in her own home; the investigation is still open on suspected homicide, which was initially framed as a suicide.[33] Chechetov was under investigation on charges of abuse of power while in office since 20 January 2015.[34] He oversaw the concentration of assets by Donetsk oligarchs and Yanukovych's 'family' – among others – and was scheduled for an interrogation in this regard. Prior to giving evidence, he committed suicide by falling 17 floors down from his flat's window on 28 February 2015.[35] The case was treated as suspicious and investigations are technically still underway. If previous experience is anything to go by, the perpetrators will most likely never be found.

The International Monetary Fund and the European Union requested the setting up of an independent court that would handle the cases of high-profile corrupt officials as a condition of granting Ukraine further loans. Out of a $17.5 billion bailout for Ukraine, $13.6 billion had already been disbursed, and the latest IMF memorandum set a strict deadline of 14 June for the anti-corruption court bill to be approved by Ukraine's parliament. The call was supported by multiple domestic and international NGOs and politicians. By mid-2017, zero progress had been made in that regard. During the European Union–Ukraine summit in Kyiv on 13 July, Poroshenko managed to convince Jean-Claude Juncker that there was no need for such a court.[36] Instead, the Ukrainian president suggested forming an 'anti-corruption panel' within the Constitutional court which, according to Ukrainian civic activists and international watchdogs, would only bring 'cosmetic changes' to the corrupt system.[37] The evidence of that is mounting. For example, the work of the National Anti-Corruption Bureau of Ukraine – an independent agency created by the IMF in 2015 – on high-profile corruption cases has been systematically blocked by the regular courts.[38] Multiple accounts of 'outsiders' hired to fix the government confirm ongoing corruption and the obstruction of work across the ministries. Examples include the scandalous resignations of Aivaras Abramavicus, Minister for Economy and Trade since December 2014, and his whole team due to 'ingrained corruption'[39] in February 2016 and the National Bank Governor, Valeria Gontareva, in April 2017 upon receiving multiple death threats.[40] The newly elected MPs, Serhiy Leshchenko and Mustafa Nayem – journalists, heroes of the Maidan organisation and the fight against corruption – have also voiced multiple concerns and frustration and diminishing support for the government that is throughout corrupt.[41] The realisation that little has changed and that neoliberal kleptocracy has only got worse became ubiquitous as the centralised system of Yanukovych was decapitated, and oligarchic rivalry only intensified. Upon becoming president, Poroshenko has brought 'his people' into key positions of state administration. Such reshufflings of the governing apparatus are standard practice in most countries; the criminal–political connections behind these reshufflings, however, did have a peculiar Ukrainian stamp.

Military conflict in the country has dropped its investment attractiveness index and increased investment risk.[42] This has inevitably led to a rapid decrease in foreign investment flow from abroad – from $4.5 billion in 2013 to $410 million in 2014.[43] At the same time, the IMF and EU conditionality pressure to privatise the last remaining state-owned assets has been growing. This contingency meant two things. First, due to low interest and thus competition, state assets had to be sold cheaply to attract investment. And second, low completion, artificially low prices and the use of 'Dutch auctions' on multiple assets has made them easy to accumulate for domestic oligarchic capital. All but a handful of remaining SOEs are now prepared to be privatised; the dispossession of state assets is soon to be complete.[44]

DCFTA has been ratified and entered into force in July 2016, however, as Movchan documents, Ukraine 'received duty-free access to the EU market for most goods in April 2014' already.[45] Then '95 per cent of EU import duties on industrial goods and 84 per cent for agricultural products were cancelled' in alignment with still-to-be-ratified DCFTA, and thus in 2016 have granted no additional tariff reduction; the next phase is in 2017. In the first year after signing, the average duties on EU products decreased from 4.5 per cent to 1.7 per cent, while imports from the EU increased by 7.9 per cent in the first ten months of 2016.[46] Perceptions of domestic producers overall are less positive. A survey conducted at the end of 2016 shows stoic enthusiasm among Ukrainian businesses despite little positive evidence of the treaty's effects, particularly on small- and medium-sized business. One thousand respondents from across Ukraine were surveyed. Some 60 per cent had neutral views on the treaty effects, over 28 per cent of 'exporters and importers pointed to the positive effects of the Association Agreement, while only 6 per cent of respondents noted the negative impact'.[47] The most optimistic were the companies who 'conduct exports and imports, allowing them to participate in international production chains'; among those, 36 per cent have benefited from the implementation of the Agreement to date.[48]

According to the survey conducted as part of the 'Dialogue on Trade Facilitation,'[49] 23 per cent of small, 27 per cent of the medium, and 43 per cent of large enterprises highlighted the gain.[50] January 2016 marked the beginning of the 'countdown charts in commitments in the area of legislation harmonization', that is, 'technical regulations, food safety, customs services, trade in services, government procurement, intellectual property rights, competition policy, etc'. The proportion of change is immense, in a couple of years 'more than 14 thousand older standards were abolished' bringing the share of international European standards in Ukrainian standards system to 60 per cent.[51]

The import–export picture looks rather different in 2016 than it did in 2013. Exports to CIS countries fell to 16.6 per cent or by 77.3 per cent since 2015, imports from CIS countries also suffered a significant drop and now constitute 21.8 per cent or an 81.7 per cent decrease since 2015. Trade with the EU is growing yet is insignificant in comparison with the loss of the CIS markets – exports are up to 37 per cent or by 103.7 per cent since 2015, while imports stood at 47.3 per cent and 111.8 per cent of 2015.[52] Export and imports have significantly suffered since the Bloody Winter. Figures 8.1 and 8.2 and Tables 8.1 and 8.2 demonstrate a sharp decline in both between 2013 and 2016 with all three primary groups of export and import partners, that is, CIS other countries and the EU. Such a dynamic highlights the overall decline in trade and thus revenue that is not compensated for by the meagre 3.7 per cent year-on-year exports growth to the EU and an 11.8 per cent increase in imports from the EU

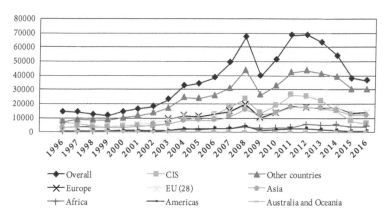

Figure 8.1   Geographic structure of exports (goods), 1996–2016

Source: Ukrstat (2016).

to Ukraine. Furthermore, 28.5 per cent year on year loss of cheap imports from the CIS countries has produced a double negative economic effect, as substitute products from the EU are significantly more expensive; not least due to the catastrophic depreciation of UAH since the conflict began. The loss of territories in the industrial east of the country has dealt a blow to the economy as is reflected by the figures. DNR, LNR, occupied Crimea, Sevastopol and parts of ATO territory that are under Ukraine's army control are not included in the data.

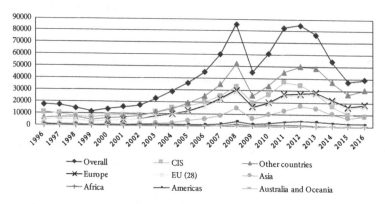

Figure 8.2   Geographic structure of imports (goods), 1996–2016

Source: Ukrstat (2016).

Over the years of its *de jure* independence, Ukraine cumulatively borrowed $44 billion and over 15.6 billion euros with the largest lenders being the IMF, the World Bank and the European Commission. As of 2014, the nature of debt management has also fundamentally changed. A credit rating drop, low investor confidence, an unstable and weak economy on the brink of foreign debt repayment default have contributed to Ukraine's inability to exercise sovereignty over its fiscal, banking and financial systems. A bigger role was being assigned to foreign consultants, IMF advisors were introduced to the ruling structures of NBU, foreign experts were included in the government, among others.[53] At the end of 2015, Ukraine's per capita GDP fell below $8,000 or was 113th in the world.[54] The country's share of global GDP has shrunk four times from 1.3 per cent to 0.3 per cent.[55] Ukraine yet again was about to default on its foreign loans payments and attracting more credit was the only option to avoid that scenario. Enter the IMF with more loans and more conditionality .... PrivatBank takeover was the final and largest in Gontareva's

Table 8.1 Geographic structure of exports (goods), 1996–2016

	Overall	CIS	Other countries	Europe	EU (28)	Asia	Africa	Americas	Australia and Oceania
1996	14400.8	7222.0	7178.8	3456.9	3321.2	2894.2	209.3	598.3	20.1
1997	14231.9	5536.3	8695.6	3675.3	3491.0	3878.6	472.4	652.5	16.8
1998	12637.4	4170.8	8438.6	3993.0	3873.0	3028.5	562.0	865.4	17.4
1999	11581.6	3210.1	8371.5	3790.2	3663.7	3225.9	617.1	692.4	45.1
2000	14572.5	4459.7	10112.8	4680.2	4576.3	3475.9	731.5	1217.5	7.0
2001	16264.7	4639.0	11625.7	5720.9	5536.1	4006.6	877.0	1011.9	7.4
2002	17957.1	4320.1	13637.0	6515.8	6384.0	5125.0	1055.2	936.9	4.1
2003	23066.8	5942.0	17124.8	9147.4	8705.9	5503.1	1250.3	1219.2	4.8
2004	32666.1	8409.4	24256.7	11764.3	11061.6	8178.3	1758.0	2544.2	11.7
2005	34228.4	10531.1	23697.3	10881.4	10293.3	8576.9	2393.9	1831.2	13.7
2006	38368.0	12351.1	26016.9	12625.5	12166.3	8446.2	2373.7	2550.9	17.9
2007	49296.1	18087.0	31209.1	14773.8	14021.3	10881.6	2792.0	2686.3	15.7
2008	66967.3	23166.3	43801.0	19732.8	18265.7	15887.0	3902.4	4144.0	64.0
2009	39695.7	13472.9	26222.8	10264.5	9514.3	12131.7	2627.8	1124.2	21.6
2010	51405.2	18740.6	32664.6	13829.6	13085.3	13715.4	3018.7	2000.0	28.4
2011	68394.2	26177.0	42217.2	18442.4	18021.5	17737.8	3344.2	2552.3	29.8
2012	68830.4	25318.6	43511.8	17424.0	17123.7	17681.1	5638.2	2607.7	50.9
2013	63320.7	22077.3	41243.4	17064.2	16758.6	16813.0	5094.7	2163.6	40.1
2014	53901.7	14882.3	39019.4	17122.1	17002.9	15350.9	5098.2	1372.2	23.5
2015	38127.1	7806.1	30321.0	13248.3	13015.2	12378.9	3803.3	785.6	13.6
2016	36361.7	6031.5	30330.2	13790.1	13496.3	11796.3	3865.1	735.2	18.3

Source: Ukrstat (2016).

clean-up that saw 87 'zombie-banks' shut down in the last year and one of the conditions of IMF loan tranche disbursement.[56] The last significant competitor to foreign banks was now nationalised and soon to be sold to those same competitors. While the sector is being cleaned up and banking activity is being streamlined, the current kleptocratic and the future governments alike are losing power to the dictatorship of the IMF in conditions of extreme debt dependency and socio-economic want. Reforming comes with high economic costs in the form of new loans and old/new debt servicing and with personal safety risks as the recently former NBU Head, Gontareva, who received threats from the oligarchs testified in an interview with *The Financial Times.*[57]

A large proportion of the economic growth of Ukraine's economy in the pre-crisis years was growth on paper, based on fictitious foundations

Table 8.2   Geographic structure of imports (goods), 1996–2016

	Overall	CIS	Other countries	Europe	EU (28)	Asia	Africa	Americas	Australia and Oceania
1996	17603.4	11172.1	6431.3	4655.6	4500.9	672.6	141.5	931.0	24.3
1997	17128.0	9871.7	7256.3	5451.6	5261.7	844.9	136.8	797.9	22.0
1998	14675.6	7889.2	6786.4	4998.5	4843.0	886.9	118.7	755.5	20.9
1999	11846.1	6737.2	5108.9	3547.4	3460.8	762.7	157.8	588.4	27.2
2000	13956.0	8029.6	5926.4	4311.5	4047.7	842.3	136.4	581.4	54.7
2001	15775.1	8821.0	6954.1	4981.7	4755.0	982.0	198.5	740.9	51.0
2002	16976.8	8952.4	8024.4	5751.1	5516.8	1187.4	177.3	856.7	51.5
2003	23020.1	11468.4	11551.7	8165.6	7883.2	2011.3	248.8	1072.2	53.4
2004	28996.8	15189.2	13807.6	9887.2	9564.8	2592.8	279.7	966.1	81.5
2005	36136.3	16988.3	19148.0	12666.4	12211.3	4685.5	426.2	1265.5	103.9
2006	45038.6	20112.3	24926.3	16804.2	16232.2	6143.7	413.0	1465.3	99.5
2007	60618.0	25469.3	35148.7	23048.9	22274.5	9042.2	673.1	2255.4	128.4
2008	85535.3	33377.8	52157.5	30477.0	28928.6	15497.7	1559.1	4190.6	431.7
2009	45433.1	19692.6	25740.5	16233.8	15438.5	6538.6	617.6	2197.9	149.4
2010	60742.2	26697.4	34044.8	20004.5	19151.4	10023.3	874.4	2879.4	261.4
2011	82608.2	37212.4	45395.8	27065.9	25805.8	13279.9	940.6	3913.9	194.0
2012	84717.6	34497.2	50220.4	27569.6	26237.2	17140.5	851.3	4446.7	195.7
2013	76986.8	27941.6	49045.2	28566.2	27046.5	15237.3	749.8	4339.9	93.7
2014	54428.7	17276.9	37151.8	22383.0	21069.1	10848.3	679.9	3021.5	182.2
2015	37516.4	10485.5	27030.9	16665.3	15330.2	7235.8	601.7	2336.6	169.6
2016	39249.8	8565.4	30684.4	18470.2	17140.8	8920.5	553.9	2594.8	120.6

Source: Ukrstat (2016).

of credit finance and mirage liquidity. Investment from abroad that flooded the country in the last few years, before the Lehman Brothers collapse, has been the last wave of Ponzi-type financialisation. Ukraine's banking sector growth since 2000 and especially during 2005–2008 was not a sign of the country's improving economic performance but rather a sign of growing dependency and integration with the global financial architecture. It was an expression of the last wave of financialisation that began in the USA and then spread over to Europe – first Western and later farther to the East. Since the goal of such credit injection was predominantly to fill the drying liquidity pool in the West with hard cash through attracting deposits and collection of interest payments on loans generously offered to the population (both in domestic and foreign currencies), the scheme rolled over to Ukrainian banking (increasingly)

in 2006 and onward with a sole aim to '[redress] the declining profitability of financial institutions operating in the already financialised
economies of [the USA and] Western Europe.'[58] The economic assistance
from IFIs comes with their standard agenda, that is, neo-liberalisation
therapy.[59] It means opening up the banking sector to oversight and
control of foreign/(Western) institutions and letting foreign banks onto
the market as will now be done in the case of Privatbank, for example.
Where Ukrainian oligarchs were uncooperative in previous decades,
they are being forced into cooperation through a looser regulatory
framework and harmonisation of standards that their FIGs find difficult
to embrace. Policy suggestions for streamlining the financial system and
removing barriers to market entry steadily squeeze out oligarchic capital,
making space for the usual TNC suspects.

DANGERS OF THE PATRIOTISM GAME,
NATION AND DECOMMUNISATION

Continuating the politics of blaming one's predecessors and faced with
a shortage of those left to blame, the rulers in Kyiv went after the ghost
of Communism. Decommunisation symbolically began on 8 December
2013, when the statue of Lenin was toppled in the centre of Kyiv.[60] That
event 'commenced the so-called Leninopad – the fervent process of disas-
sembling statues and other Communist symbols all over the country', the
embarrassing fight against statues that could be removed in a frustrated
misplaced anger against oligarchs who could not.[61] In 2014 alone, 504
statues of Lenin were taken down in grotesque celebration of neoliberal
anomie. Still 1,700 'out of 5500 which were in existence at the moment of
USSR collapse' remained.[62]

Decommunisation laws adopted in April 2015 banned promoting or
displaying Communist and Nazi symbols and made the act criminally
punishable with up to ten years of imprisonment.[63] The law was aimed
at: (1) condemning 'totalitarian regimes'; (2) halting the propaganda
of those regimes; (3) 'cleanse' the map of Ukraine of topographic signs
of communism; (4) fairly investigating the crimes of the totalitarian
regimes; and (5) honouring the memory of the victims with a national
remembrance day on 23 August – the day Molotov-Ribbentrop
non-aggression pact was signed. The latter event has contested historical
meaning as a neutrality pact that also designated the USSR and
Germany's 'spheres of interest' in Europe, discussed in Chapter 7. The

use of the term 'communist' is explicitly prohibited by this legislation, for example, that automatically rendered any political party or newspaper with the term in the name illegal – as was the case with many left-wing organisations prior to the local elections in autumn 2015. This 'reform', the effective ban of political parties from participation in the elections and their dissolution was condemned in their joint opinion by the Venice Commission[64] and the OSCE Office for Democratic Institutions and Human Rights (ODIHR).[65] The law #2558 'On Condemnation of Communist and National-Socialist (Nazi) Totalitarian Regimes in Ukraine and Ban of their Propaganda and Symbols'[66] became the banner of the 'patriotism game' that is utilised to shield the presidential administration and the government from potential criticism in two ways. First, since Russia is a 'descendant' of the USSR and Putin's model of authoritarianism is built on the resurrection of Stalin's might, Putin begins to equal Stalin and Russia equals decades of Stalinist repressions against Ukrainians. Defending communism then, in any form, is interpreted as a defence of Stalin's repressions (that, in essence, were a form of 'red' fascism, not communism) and of the aggressor – Moscow. Second, if criticism of Poroshenko and his cronies occurs, it is interpreted as treason and as a promotion of Russian propaganda, as 'helping the enemy'. The effects include arresting people for making 'communist' posts on Facebook[67] and wearing T-shirts displaying 'USSR' writing.[68] Perhaps the irony of using fascicisation rhetoric to condemn totalitarianism remains invisible to Ukraine's agonising oligarchs, but the effects are certainly convenient and palpable. There is a clear realisation that power can be held now only through criminalising criticism and protest, that is to say, through coercion. Such a position is unstable, and it is further dividing the broken nation. An even bigger danger lies in what the ban on communist rhetoric and symbols means politically. In addition to the physical and symbolic violence that the identifiable left endures, the alternatives to neoliberal kleptocracy are being criminalised.

A 'nation' is 'a named human population sharing a myth of common descent, historical memories and mass culture, and possessing a demarcated territory, common economy and common legal rights and duties.'[69] But *what is the 'Ukrainian nation'*? Does it need a revival or construction? If the latter, should it be from scratch or on the basis of some historical foundations? Kuzio and Wilson approach the process of the nation 'revival' of Ukraine by attempting to explicate the presence or absence of similarities between 'the great European and colonial revivals of the last two centuries' and the case of Ukrainian 'self-styled revival'.[70] What is nationalism then? It is 'an ideological movement for the attainment and maintenance of autonomy, cohesion and individuality for a social group deemed by some of its members to constitute an actual or potential nation'[71] and can contain ethnic or civic foundation. Ethnicity is a cultural phenomenon, but the state is a civic system and therefore 'the attempt by nationalists to combine the two is often problematic'[72] due to endemic incompatibility. More importantly, 'the nation and state are not codeterminous'; in the case of the Soviet Ukraine 'the conflict between the nation and the supranational state is of paramount importance'.[73] In the process of shaping the myth of the 'Other', a fraction of Ukraine's nationalists tried to 'advance the negative identity of Ukraine as a "non-Russia" *par excellence*' – a task impossible without significant 'rewriting of history in combination with geopolitical revisionism'.[74] In his recent book, *The Gates of Europe*, the historian Serhii Plokhy argues that the 'nation' is 'an important – although not dominant – category' in defining the narrative of his text, nor the history of Europe, nor the history of Ukraine.[75] The more important story is the one told by ethnographers and mapmakers of the late nineteenth and early twentieth centuries' which suggests that from the times of medieval Kievan Rus the rise of modern day nationalism frequently corresponded the borders of contemporary Ukraine.[76] Plokhy also shows how Ukrainians have been the largest demographic group and social force behind the creation of Ukraine as a state. The borders of Ukraine have changed 'faster than viewpoints and many within and outside Ukraine after 1991 still saw [the] country in terms of the Russian/Soviet or pre-war Polish grand narratives of national history'.[77]

The myth of nationalism is attractive; it has the power of 'transcending oblivion through posterity the restoration of collective dignity through an appeal to a golden age, the realisation of fraternity through symbols, rites and ceremonies.'[78] Then the individual's positioning within the notion of 'homeland' gives them 'a sense of worth to [their] identity'.[79] Kuzio succinctly notes that 'the official Soviet ideology and identity system's key failure was its inability to create and sustain the moral and cultural constructs by which a community can order its existence once *glasnost* was unleashed on peoples' historical myths and memories.'[80] Once the independent national identities had to be built, 'only nationalism could provide an alternative set of unifying myths, symbols, values and principles, a sense of identity (a "we")' where the Soviet unifying identity was lacking, and once it was unleashed it 'proved a powerful successor to the Soviet identity' that has never fully replaced the national in any case.[81]

Central to the post-Soviet phase and form of national idea formation is a particular relational configuration that determines what constitutes the nation and individuals' sense of belonging to the myth of that nation. It is a triangular relationship between national minorities, the newly nationalising states in which they live, and the external national 'homelands' to which they belong, or can be construed as belonging, by ethnocultural affinity, though not by legal citizenship.[82] Homelands are constructed, not given,[83] and it is important to unify the Ukrainian nation based on modernity and not on historical and/or cultural myths since their consolidation potential is very weak.[84] A new national myth must be created by taking positive aspects from history and by realising that Ukrainians are a multi-ethnic nation. The historical diversity of Ukrainian heritage must be recognised as of the main reason why one shall not look for Ukrainian national identity and consciousness to the past and the past only.[85] This new myth would be difficult to materialise, and consecutive rulers of the country failed to do so. The Ukrainian had to be envisaged as separate from the Soviet and the Russian, while complicated by alienation from the latter as the hostile due to the historical relationship of overlordship between Ukraine and Russia.[86] Ongoing mistrust in the relations between the countries highlights the viability of that history today, exposes the ghosts of past animosity and deep cross-cultural assimilation[87] if in conditions of cultural imperialism. This was evident to many[88] even before the civil armed conflict made national consolidation even more distant. Russian aggression has necessitated the identification of Ukraine's national idea to be framed by defensive narratives – when the country's right to exist, its sovereignty, separateness and individuality are brought into question, and its political sovereignty are being negated on the basis of that questioning, little room is left for cosmopolitan reckoning, yet it remains in the praxis of the everyday. And even at the frontline checkpoints, people speak both Russian and Ukrainian, crossing back and forth every day, welcome their friends and relatives in their lives as they did before, defying the radicalised minority's vision of animosity that has remained the minority's vision.

All these arguments about history are the work of small groups of nationalist intellectuals; ordinary people, whether Russian or Ukrainians, do not give a damn. History as such will not lead to serious trouble between Russia and Ukraine ... Ukraine is luckier than Russia ... precisely because it doesn't have this great load of history weighing on it. The more you think about your glorious past, the less you can cope with the modern world.[89]

Just as in the late 1980s–early 1990s, the state – rather than the cultural intelligentsia – is driving nationalism in Ukraine. More precisely, the neoliberal kleptocratic oligarchy, who have hijacked the revolt and appropriated its fruit, are appropriating the rhetoric of the nationalist groups too. The latter range from centre-patriotic to outright radical right wing and fascist. A sacrificial component in the nationalist narrative is instrumental in two complementing ways. First, due to Russia's military engagement in Ukraine, it is anti-Russian and goes well with the 'established western tradition of treating Russia as "Europe's other", a "barbarian at the Europe's gate", a constant historical "irregularity".[90] This provides oligarchs with an army of wilful servicemen and women needed to fight the ongoing battles in the east. Second, it feeds into the myth of the 'Other' which is necessary to sustain the survival of the kleptocracy, as I discussed earlier. Those who are not 'patriotic', are 'against the regime' and, as such, are treated as traitors. Such a mantra of fascicisation is becoming part and parcel of the neoliberal kleptocracy, and in Ukraine, it is visible more than elsewhere.

THE NEBULOUS TELOS OF EUROPE

What is Europe and why is it the EU who gets to decide what it is? Since its inception by the Treaty of Paris in 1951 as the Coal and Steel Economic Community and then deepening to the European Economic Community by the Treaty of Rome in 1957, the 1992 Maastricht Treaty has turned the organisation into the area of deepest international cooperation on the planet. It is not merely an economic but a far-reaching constitutional structure with shared principles and values, the hierarchy of which preserved some die-hard colonial sentiments as well as the primacy of some countries and cultures over the rest. The primacy of secularism and Christianity over Islam are some of the recently more noticeable imprints of the Western colonial past and cultural entitlement reflected in the European institutional and effectively legal architecture, including the monopoly which the EU claims over the term 'European'.

The EU is a controversial organisation with no less controversial interpretations of its nature and purpose. The debates include questions of whether it is, in fact, a successful union or otherwise, whether it is efficient, supranational or intergovernmental, democratic or lacking democracy, whether there is such a thing as 'European identity' or not?[91] The telos of Europe is thus nebulous as its geographical and terminological borders are not universally established nor accepted and that makes a 'move towards Europe' an equally vague, confusing adventure at best. How does one move towards the 'European' that has no clear definition, that, perhaps, does not need one? On the level of policy, things are clearer while they are also contested, as I will discuss below. Let's return to the question of proving one's Europeanness – as a rite of passage en route to the EU membership – and Ukraine's venture into that direction. How is one to attain what is not identifiable?! Ukraine's political and media discourses are flooded with the Europeanisation rhetoric. The nation is to prove its Europeanness – something that is perceived in contemporary Ukraine as the only qualifying civilisational measure for the polity. Most importantly, Ukraine must prove that it shares the 'European values' if it wants to be included in the EU club. What those are on paper and what they are in practice, however, are quite different forms of matter. In addition to the multiple endemic contradictions mentioned above, the EU is riddled with hypocrisy in regard to how they handle questions of democracy and human rights on paper versus in praxis, inside the Union and in their relations with the European Neighbourhood and beyond. Comparison of the Bloody Winter protests with the anti-austerity demonstrations across the EU is most illustrative in that regard – particularly so in the PIIGS group of countries. Images of beaten, tear-gassed, water-cannoned protesters in Spain, Greece, Portugal, UK, Belgium, France, etc. have flooded mass media in the post-Credit Crunch years. Such disciplining of the EU dispossessed done in the name of austerity, and transnational capital was performed under the watchful eye of the guarantors of rights and freedoms of EU citizens, who seemingly had no objections to the *anti-constitutional* cruelty of the security forces. When protests started in Ukraine in winter 2013–2014, where the army and the police alike at times tolerated the smoke of tyres and illegal – if *constitutionally* legitimate – downtown blockades for months, Yanukovych and his administration were labelled despots for not submitting to the demands of the demonstrators. There was a crucial difference, of course. EU interests coincided with the interests of the protesters in the latter case. The rule of law and civic order caution was thrown to the wind as they tend to be once the EU capital has its vested interests at stake.

In the meantime, Ukraine 'must prove' it is 'European' to be accepted as such. In the local context – and with geopolitical and nation-building consequences – the latter means something that excludes Russia[92] and thus all that is perceived as Russian, that is, anti-EU and the USA, steeped in Soviet nostalgia and thus backward, must be rejected by Ukraine in its quest for Europeanness. Only the latter is hard if not impossible to do. Transformation of social institution in the EU manner means carving those in the image of the old EU state-society-capital complexes that are a reflection of their own history of social struggle and social forces; history that is different from Ukraine's and thus is alien to its own institutional reflections of its own struggles and forces. Whether those need transforming or not is a separate discussion. What is crucial to understand here is that the underlying teleology of the transformation in question negates individuality and needs of one's transformation path, that is to say, that Ukraine is not being asked what it's social needs are but is being told what its society and institutions must become. That's the level of SSC. On the level of Europe as an imagined community in its ideal *de jure* condition we are witnessing a cosmopolitan super-institution – not a state – (as it does not hold monopoly on the use of violence against its citizens) where communities, cultures, religions, linguistic groups are intimately intertwined in an uneven fashion with various inequalities manifest to various extent across the EU territory. Thus speaking about Ukraine as a homogeneous unitary nation that is: (a) somehow more European than Russian (b) is or should be separate from Russian; and (c) should somehow transform itself into something it is currently not is a completely artificially manufactured political position that serves anti-Russian geopolitical rhetoric more than it does regional (geo) political consolidation and crisis resolution.

Bastiaan van Apeldoorn,[93] Laura Horn and Angela Wigger,[94] Magnus Ryner and Alan Cafruny[95] explain in detail the economic and class part of what constitutes the 'European'. In EU–Ukraine relations, the latter is a taker of an identity written by the big capital of the EU, the identity that is a veiled conformity to the rule of capital. The 'Ukrainian' would find it difficult to survive there with the current state of its economic affairs; its people's struggle, unwillingness, inability to accept the necessary sacrifice of dispossession is being seen as old-fashioned, outdated, unrealistic, utopian state-dependency of a 'lazy' homo sovieticus with their minds and actions still dictated by the ghosts of old Soviet 'masters'.

There is a level where Ukraine and the EU are similar – so is Russia – and that level is authoritarian neoliberal with elements of fascicisation. The latter is a heavily value-laden term and thus must be applied with care. What we are witnessing in the global political economy in the post-crisis years can hardly be called anything else. The right-wing shift is happening within the existing institution, it needs not new, nor new 'charismatic leaders' as the classic fascism theory would suggest would be needed. There is a crucial difference between fascism in the early to mid-twentieth century and fascism in the era of post-national, that is, transnational capitalism. The transnational class structure that underlies transnationalisation processes requires a very different set of institutions – if with very similar functions – to exercise its concept of control.[96] It has been termed recently as 'authoritarian neoliberalism',[97] 'new constitutionalism',[98] 'authoritarian constitutionalism',[99] or 'transnational fascism'[100] – all four are not identical in formulation nor signification. The consent element to the EU hegemony (from Gramsci's and Machiavelli's 'coercion and consent' hegemony model) must rest on a post-national framework to cement its 'imagined community'[101] and its hegemonic 'historic bloc'[102] as the latter combines too many nations with conventional, national imagined community attributes, that is, language, culture, ethnicity, religion, shared history – whatever that means – and '[their] our way of life – according to proclamations of some pseudo-left philosophers[103] and multiple EU politicians. The principles of '[the EU] way of life' are documented in the EU legal framework. Oberndorfer documents with detail how those include 'free' market capitalism as the cornerstone of constitutionalism and adherence to the latter means acceptance of 'our way of life'. It means adhering to the Copenhagen Criteria on EU entry:

> Membership requires that candidate country has achieved stability of institutions guaranteeing democracy, the rule of law, human rights, respect for and protection of minorities, the existence of a functioning market economy as well as the capacity to cope with competitive pressure and market forces within the Union. Membership presupposes the candidate's ability to take on the obligations of membership including adherence to the aims of political, economic and monetary union.[104]

With the last accession of the new members 'the way of life' – the Ukrainian 'aspiration' began to cover over 35 areas of national economies and 'life'.[105]

Through 'harmonisation' across the 35 plus areas, disciplining of the non-aligned with the agenda of transnational capital functioning occurs, including disciplining of governments and violations of their sovereign power as we can see in the infamous cases of post-Credit Crunch PIIGS.[106] The disciplining of Ukraine is occurring through DCFTA harmonisation. The EU member states as institutions on the national level then function to channel the authoritarian EU agenda aggravated by kleptocratic domestic adaptations. 'Our way of life' is also a way of the monied, better-paid EU dwellers that comes at the expense of those who are not, the exploited in the capital accumulation process in the variegated forms.

Since 2007–2008 this way of life, a capitalist way of life, is governed by a global regime of authoritarian neoliberalism and financialised accumulation that is now transmutating into a new phase, moving towards transnational fascism. This late fascism, as Alberto Toscano calls it,[107] is inevitably a transnational phenomenon as an intention and as an effect at the same time. Late fascism is transnational, for the reasons I outlined above, that is, where the structure of accumulation and capitalist class is transnational, fascicisation of its governance has to be transnational too to guarantee interests and reach of capital transnationally. It is so in all three intertwined circuits of capital circulation as articulated by Marx in *Grundrisse* and *Das Kapital*, in the structure of the capitalist class (and all its fractions), and, of course, in the form of institutions that make the global economy work for the two. 'Class, in contemporary attempts both to promote and to analyse fascistic fantasies and policies of "national rebirth", risks becoming in its turn a supplement (of both racism and nationalism), stuck in the echo chambers of serialising propaganda.'[108]

Propaganda is aimed at compartmentalising global labour via the inflammation of xenophobia; making labour powerless against the forces of capital – that is increasingly more mobile – by also restricting the mobility of labour, physical and otherwise. In order to resist the destructive infiltration by capitalist narrative we thus shall turn 'away from [the idea of class as a] totality [– that is false –], and [rethink] the *making* or *composition* of a class that could refuse becoming the bearer of a racial, or national predicate, as one of the antibodies to fascism'.[109] Then one can begin to think of class composition that could 'refuse becoming the bearer of a racial, or national predicate, as one of the antibodies to fascism', then authoritarian constitutionalism and neoliberalism could potentially be overcome. That same propaganda-bred xenophobia further cultivates and is cultivated by growing number and parliamentary representation of the right-wing parties across the EU propped up in their confidence by the rise of Donald Trump in the USA.[110] This growth is a symptom inflamed by neoliberal populist appeal to blaming the 'Other' for the destructive effects of the austerity dispensed to the poor in order to feed the ongoing accumulation by the rich. Precariousness in the workplace, mechanisation of labour and digitalisation of the economy, ongoing dispossession of the commons by the assault on public services and restructuring of trade further unbundle transnational capital from state–society control, further increase the autonomy of capital in the state–society–capital complexes of the EU and beyond. All of the above contribute to growing dispossession of labour and its targeted, strategic compartmentalisation; making it easier to manage. This is accompanied by also a strategic destruction of the institutional power of labour that is to say by erosion of organised labour's rights, restricting rights of trade unions and rights of people to unionise, rights to bargain in the workplace and on the streets.[111] Increasingly, militant labour sees[112] its reproductive capacity undermined as an effect of the accumulation of the last remaining commons, including public services. In Ukraine, the erosion of the reproductive base can be seen in the looming privatisation of land reforms[113] – the last state asset untouched by privatisation and banned from foreign ownership – and in the commercialisation of healthcare reform.[114] Recent healthcare reform aimed at commercialisation of healthcare is too an example of accumulation by dispossession of the commons. In fact, healthcare reform is a formalisation of an already informally commercialised sector, where patients have to shoulder the costs of even basic medications and surgery. The erosion of the reproductive base of labour is part and parcel of the neoliberal doctrine of financialised accumulation.

In his *Capital in the 21st Century*, Thomas Piketty documents how the post-Second World War 'golden age of capitalism' was a historical accident where due to the destruction of war and the growth in mass production-mass consumption complex labour–capital compromise and socio-economic mobility of labour could be achieved in the global north at the expense of the global south. Since the launch of the neoliberal era with uncoupling of the US dollar from gold by Nixon in 1971 and

Thatcher-Reaganomics of the 1980s, financialised accumulation that changed Fordism has reached its limits of the possible in the crescendo that was the Global Financial Crisis of 2007/2008. Instead of systemic change, authoritarian neoliberalism was brought in as the logic behind the SAPs and SALs that choked the 'third world' were adapted for application in their home, the global north.[115] The post-Second World War capital–labour class compromise was being broken. The limits of the possible of financialised accumulation were pushed to their artificial extension so that 'business as usual' could continue. The poor and the weak as a result had to 'suffer what they must' via excesses of austerity, stripping of the last survival mechanisms.[116]

Transnational fascism in its late form emerges as an accompanying phenomenon, part of the authoritarian neoliberalism agenda; it is a legitimation mechanism for increasing repression in the state/supra-state institutional apparati that Oberndorfer discusses.[117] The economic fascism[118] and authoritarianism of EU institutions is backed by the dynamics of transnational fascism that combines the elements of class, ethnicity, religion and culture in an unholy combination that is the cornerstone of the war on terror and the ensuing extreme surveillance rhetoric – surveillance of the other to the neoliberal authoritarian orthodoxy, of the non-compliant. In Ukraine, that other is the critic of Poroshenko's authoritarian neoliberal kleptocracy that too is churning fascicisation rhetoric with increasing speed. The state as an institution rests now on the ideology of authoritarian neoliberalism that serves transnational capital at the expense of its own citizenry thus forfeiting its Weberian function. At the same time governments work internationally in coalitions against the global labour and the global poor – including own domestic labour and own poor in the late fascism manner that has any subject potentially 'threatening' the rule of capital and 'our way of life' as its 'other'; 'other' that must be deprived of privacy, surveilled, victimised, prosecuted, labelled as terrorist, imprisoned, deprived of human rights if necessary (as UK's Tory party widely advocates). War on terror and protection of 'our way of life' by any means necessary are instrumentalised as justifications for the unconstitutional transformation of EU institutions.

On the back of growing xenophobia, the EU and its member states – among other – are then dragged into military conflicts in various participatory forms, 'hard' and 'soft', as the classic IR theory would frame it. Either via NATO, arms sale, personnel supply, humanitarian action, institutional and NGO support – through grants or experts, these 'civilising' and 'pacifying' interventions are nothing short of cynical in the context of authoritarian neoliberal modus operandi, its discriminatory nature, and fascicisation discourse they can be perceived as a perverted insult.

THE DISCIPLINING OF OLIGARCHY OR TRANSNATIONAL CAPITAL TAKES ITS COURSE

The oligarchic capital of Ukraine is now becoming exposed to the pressures of competition from foreign TNCs it managed to withstand earlier via its own convoluted, often extra-legal mechanisms. The end of 2016 was marked by two important events in Ukraine's financial life: nationalisation of the country's biggest private lender, PrivatBank, and yet another debacle over disbursement of yet another $1billion tranche of the IMF $17.5 rescue Loan Programme. The first, according to the Central Bank's governor Valeria Gontareva, was a response to 'a $5.5 hole in the [Privat's] balance sheet' whose position was further 'undermined by widescale related-party lending to entities close to owners' and failure to recapitalise the institution.[119] The state took 100 per cent ownership of Privat's 'diversified portfolio of assets spanning oil production, ferroalloys, media and chemicals' and guaranteed security of all deposits accounting to some $6 billion or over a third of all private deposits in the country.[120] NBU plans to sell the bank to private investors within the next three years. The nationalisation was part of the 'clean-up' that came as one of the requirements of IMF loan programme necessary if an economic default is to be avoided.

PrivatBank nationalisation can be seen as overdue and indeed controversial; in nature and the symbolism of power rebalance and misbalance in Kyiv. It was a clear signal of both partial loss of sovereignty in the country's financial decision making and of oligarchs' ability to dodge IMF disciplining being compromised. Ukraine's oligarchs are infamous for overstepping boundaries, violating terms of agreement with IFIs, being selectively cooperative[121] and corrupt.[122] PrivatBank was owned by Kolomoyskyy, Boholyubov and Martynov, some of the oldest oligarchs on the scene since the 1990s who were a standard fixture of the country's political life. The bank was part of a FIG Privat that was founded also in the early 1990s. The group comprises some 100 enterprises across banking, media outlets, energy, petrochemicals, aviation and mining; many of which are part of Privat's investment portfolio. The vertically integrated group with a diverse sectoral portfolio was a typical arrangement of early 1990s oligarchs, who set up their own banks to secure cheaper credit and thus finance their capital-intensive manufacturing enterprises; accumulation via consumer lending being an important yet additional component. The bank now was lost. The rest of Privat Group was left intact yet vulnerable as its enterprises lost their related party status with their main source of credit, for now, state-owned Privatbank. Soon after Privat Group has suffered another blow as its near-monopoly on budget air travel to the EU was put under threat by the arrival of Ryanair onto the Ukrainian market.

Dmytro Firtash has been under international prosecution on multiple corruption and fraud charges ever since he failed to guarantee the signing of the DCFTA and calm the protests in 2013–2004 Kyiv. He since has been hiding from extradition to the USA in Austria – the two countries have no extradition agreement. After losing his political currency, he as such became useless for the interests of Western capital in Ukraine and thus can be removed and his extensive business subsequently can be taken over in a manner similar to that of Privatbank. Tymoshenko is being spared as she is instrumental in pushing the DCFTA and NATO agenda, however detrimental to the economy and security in the region those are, particularly the latter.

THE DISPOSSESSED AND THEIR MANY UKRAINES

Human death and economic destruction are not the change Ukrainians were hoping for in their EU aspiration, nor in its rejection, Anti-Maidans and separatism. Ukraine is still the most corrupt country in Europe.[123] The unleashing of disintegration rhetoric and movements, the Crimea annexation, the clashes and deaths in Odesa, the insurrections and separation of DNR and LNR have split parts of the country on the map and divided public perception of what constitutes Ukraine as an idea, produced multiple Ukraines – the east, the west, the discontented South, the separatist Donbas … Neither of those have clearly defined boundaries on the maps; nor as concepts. They are not territorial but ideological, constructed, yet the lack of clarity of definition makes them no less real in praxis. They do serve as distinctive social labels that demarcate and separate one social bloc from another, split identities of their carriers, remind their adherents to distrust each other and that they are each other's 'Other'. This 'Other' is fabricated and only a short while ago did not exist or were present in a non-enemy state; yet the other's novelty does not make them any less real, any less of a potential perceived threat.

The fragmented dispossessed are left with their many Ukraines split apart by territorial lines and the lines of social consciousness. Divided by the greed of their rulers and geopolitical ambitions of global neighbours, driven by socio-economic destitution they were left to fight over their last remaining seemingly inalienable properties, that is, identity, language, right to exist. Now they are asked to give up those last ones too. Language politics signify of perceived 'threatened identities', Ukrainians have perceived theirs as such in their post-Soviet reality – a threat from the language[124] and from Russia.[125] The fears are not unfounded as once given equal rights, hegemonic cultures and languages take over as is evidenced by the post-Soviet countries' experience.[126] Now both Ukrainian and Russian are threatened; the first by Russia's multi-level aggression, the second by becoming the bearer of aggression and the target of defensive politics.

The country's fragmented dispossessed have their use value for the regime of neoliberal kleptocracy as workers, soldiers, protesters, voters and gangs, while being systematically disenfranchised. By 2017, the armed conflict in the east claimed more than 10,000 lives, displaced over 1 million people, and further deepened overall socio-economic crisis in the country. In the areas of conflict or former conflict, hundreds of thousands of civilians 'have limited access to basic sustenance and services' leading to food insecurity in the regional 'breadbasket' for the first time in decades that for the first quarter of 2016 'was the only European country to require and receive assistance from the World Food Programme'.[127] Overall, '1.5 million people in eastern Ukraine are food insecure, including 290,000 severely so and in need of immediate food assistance'.[128] The situation is further complicated by the government stopping support to public services in some areas, which 'includes funding to schools and hospitals, as well as the payment of social benefits and pensions'.[129] In a nation where population declined from 52 million in 1991 to 44 million people, in 2014, some '2.6 million Ukrainians have fled the war in the east initiated by Russian-backed separatists' by the end of 2015.[130] The IDMC estimate that of them 1,476,226 are internally displaced persons who are in turn 'a composite of two figures: IDPs in Ukrainian government-controlled areas and IDPs within Crimea'.[131] As of 28 August 2015, the Ministry of Social Policy had registered 1,459,226 IDPs in areas under government control.[132] The majority fled Eastern

Ukraine, while around 20,000 had fled Crimea by 2014, according to the Crimea State Emergency Service.[133] The NGO Crimean Diaspora, however, estimates that by August 2015, between 50,000 to 60,000 people have fled Crimea, though not all have been registered.[134] According to the United Nations refugee agency in October 2015 they were able to 'raise only 56 percent of the $41.5 million it says is needed to serve Ukraine's 1.5 million internally displaced people.'[135] The crisis extends beyond the IDPs and overall '5 million people [needed] $316 million of humanitarian aid [in 2015], and only 45 percent of that has been funded or pledged'.[136] State support is meagre and internally too those in need primarily rely on the support from volunteers for manpower and donations for food, clothes, medicines, funds, etc. The neglected are relying on the dispossessed and burdened by mounting socio-economic problems – prohibiting utility bills, unemployment, low wages and wage arrears, cuts to social services and demands of sacrifice of life.

The ongoing conflicts in Ukraine that appear ideological, ethnic, or linguistic are often ideational/political, effective and manipulated rather than causal, and can be interpreted as structural ruptures necessitated by the relocation of agency within and between social blocs, classes, and their fractions and fuelled by the political discourses that accompany those. The underlying conflicts are the class formation and accumulation struggles between foreign and domestic capital, that is, oligarchs, the EU, the USA, and Russian business and their indirect engagement in Ukraine's policy making via various forms of advisory and financial 'support'. Looking into the power and accumulation struggles helps one see the reasons behind instigation of violence on the basis of social diversity. Maidan protests too were not ideological but counter-ideological movements. There was no class in-itself or for-itself in a historical materialist meaning of the term. However, there was and still is a historic bloc. It is still amorphous, but it's growing stronger. The right-wing elements traceable and influential at Maidans[137] and celebrated as 'patriots' are becoming a sacrificial animal for the accumulation needs of oligarchs, which led people to protest in the first place. That sacrifice is now manifest in the disposable attitude of the current rulers to the volunteer battalions who they struggle to control.

Maidan of 2013–2014 was against the injustice brought on by the neoliberal kleptocracy, corruption of the judiciary, predatory militia, and widespread state asset embezzlement in the midst of deteriorating conditions of life. It was a culmination of a discontent that brewed for over 20 years and both in east and west of the country it had the grass-roots origin and included organised labour, miners too. The discontent over rising prices for food (58 per cent) and communal housing fees (54 per cent), loss of work (34 per cent) and wage and pension arrears (32 per cent), corruption (27 per cent) and crime (20 per cent) – that is what unifies Ukraine's people. Neither the EU, nor NATO; despite their growing popularity as a response to the current crisis. Ukraine–EU association agreement is a carrot that now does not match the stick anymore.

The combination of neoliberal marketisation and politically empowered kleptocratic and the internally heterogeneous ruling(/capitalist) bloc of Ukraine have created the combustive atmosphere in the country that has not gone away with Yanukovych's escape. Instead, the rule of neoliberal kleptocrats entrenched even deeper. The war in the east of the country now serves as a sanction for further anti-social austerity reforms that will further untie the hands of the oligarchs while they will keep the IMF and the EU satisfied. All this comes at the expense of further state dependence on foreign debt and effectively makes Ukraine's government more susceptible to external meddling in domestic policy-making in addition to making the economy increasingly vulnerable. The above developments are underlined by growing public disapproval of the official Kyiv manifest in the ongoing and growing number of protests in the country as the Centre for Social and Labour Research surveys show.[138] The second Maidan has not brought the change that many have already died for, yet it was only the beginning, not the end of the dispossessed fighting back. Ukraine is pregnant with the next, more violent Maidan.

Notes

1. *PER ASPERA AD NEBULAE* OR TO MARKET THROUGH A HYBRID CIVIL WAR: SURVIVAL MYTHS OF SYSTEMIC FAILURE

1. Among others, see Edward Lucas, *The New Cold War: Putin's Threat to Russia and the West* (New York: St. Martin's Press, 2014).
2. John Pilger, 'Nato's Action Plan in Ukraine is Right out of Dr Strangelove', *The Guardian*, 17 April 2014, at: www.theguardian.com/commentisfree/2014/apr/17/nato-ukraine-dr-strangelove-china-us; and John Pilger, 'Why the Rise of Fascism is Again the Issue', *JohnPilger.com*, 26 February 2015, at: http://johnpilger.com/articles/why-the-rise-of-fascism-is-again-the-issue; Chris Kaspar de Ploeg, *Ukraine in the Crossfire* (Atlanta, GA: Clarity Press, 2017).
3. Just like all theory is, as Robert W. Cox famously noted, see R.W. Cox, 'Social Forces, States, and World Orders: Beyond IR Theory', *Millennium: Journal of International Studies* 10(2) (1981): 126–155.
4. A. Gramsci, *Selections from the Prison Notebooks of Antonio Gramsci* (New York: International Publishers, 1971).
5. Kees van der Pijl and Y. Yurchenko, 'Neoliberal Entrenchment of North Atlantic Capital: From Corporate Self-Regulation to State Capture', *New Political Economy* 20(4) (2015): 495–517.
6. For a discussion of authoritarian shift in neoliberalism, see Ian Bruff, 'Authoritarian Neoliberalism, the Occupy Movements, and IPE', *Journal of Critical Globalisation Studies* 1(5) (2012): 114–116; and Ian Bruff, 'The Rise of Authoritarian Neoliberalism', *Rethinking Marxism: A Journal of Economics, Culture & Society* 26(1) (2014): 113–129.
7. David Harvey, *The New Imperialism* (Oxford: Oxford University Press, 2003).
8. S. Gill, *Critical Perspectives on the Crisis of Global Governance: Reimagining the Future* (London: Palgrave, 2015); C.A. Cutler, 'New Constitutionalism, Democracy and the Future of Global Governance', in S. Gill (ed.), *Critical Perspectives on the Crisis of Global Governance: Reimagining the Future* (London: Palgrave, 2015), 89–109.
9. Martijn Konings (ed.), *The Great Credit Crash* (London: Verso, 2010).
10. Phoebe Moore and Andrew Robinson, 'The Quantified Self: What Counts in the Neoliberal Workplace', *New Media & Society* 18(11) (2016): 2774–2792; Phoebe V. Moore, *The Quantified Self in Precarity: Work, Technology and What Counts* (Abingdon: Routledge, 2018).
11. Saskia Sassen, *Expulsions: Brutality and Complexity in the Global Economy* (Cambridge, MA: Harvard University Press, 2014).
12. A. Roberts and S. Soederberg, 'Politicizing Debt and Denaturalizing the "New Normal"', *Critical Sociology* 40(5) (2014): 657–668.
13. L. Pradella, 'The Working Poor in Western Europe: Labour, Poverty and Global Capitalism', *Comparative European Politics* 13(5) (2015): 596–613.
14. For example, see Richard Sakwa, *Frontline Ukraine: Crisis in the Borderlands* (London: I.B. Tauris, 2015).

15. Ibid., see also David Lane, 'Is the Russian Federation a Threat to the International Order?' (2016), at: http://valdaiclub.com/a/highlights/is_the_russian_federation_a_threat_to_the_international_order/?sphrase_id=173665; and David Lane, 'The International Context: Russia, Ukraine and the Drift to East-West Confrontation', *International Critical Thought* 6 (2016): 623–644; Pilger, 'Why the Rise of Fascism is Again the Issue'.

16. Serhii Plokhy, *The Gates of Europe* (London: Penguin, 2015).

17. Sakwa, *Frontline Ukraine.*

18. Yuliya Yurchenko, 'Black Holes in the Political Economy of Ukraine: The Neoliberalisation of Europe's "Wild East"', *Debatte* (April 2013).

19. Harvey, *The New Imperialism.*

20. J. Morris, 'The Revenge of the Rentier or the Interest Rate Crisis in the United States', *Monthly Review* 33(8) (1982): 28–33.

21. J.M. Keynes, *The General Theory of Employment, Interest and Money* (London: Palgrave Macmillan, 1970 [1936]).

22. J.G. Ruggie, 'International Regimes, Transactions, and Change: Embedded Liberalism in the Postwar Economic Order', *International Organisation* 36(2) (2000): 379–415.

23. On the problematic of the crisis of Fordism, see Giovanni Arrighi, 'The Social and Political Economy of Global Turbulence', *New Left Review* (March–April 2003), 20; Robert Brenner, 'The Economics of Global Turbulence', Special Issue, *New Left Review* (1998); Robert Brenner, *The Economics of Global Turbulence* (London: Verso, 2006); Robert W. Cox, *Production, Power and World Order: Social Forces in the Making of History* (New York: Columbia University Press, 1987), 273–354; Andrew Glyn, 'Productivity and the Crisis of Fordism', *International Review of Applied Economics* 4(1) (1990): 28–44.

24. Ph. Cerny, 'The Limits of Deregulation: Transnational Interpenetration and Policy Change', *European Journal of Political Research* 19(2–3) (1991): 173–196.

25. K. Birch and V. Mykhnenko, *The Rise and Fall of Neoliberalism: The Collapse of an Economic Order?* (London: Zed Books, 2010), 3.

26. Quoted in Richard Peet, *Geography of Power: The Making of Global Economic Policy* (London: Zed Books, 2007), 73.

27. Ibid.

28. David Harvey, *The New Imperialism*, 2.

29. Birch and Mykhnenko, *The Rise and Fall of Neoliberalism*, 3.

30. Harvey, *The New Imperialism*, 2.

31. William I. Robinson, 'Global Capitalism and Nation-State Centric Thinking: What We Don't See When We Do See Nation-States. Response to Arrighi, Mann, Moore, van der Pijl, and Went', *Science & Society* 65(4) (2002): 500–508, 'Social Theory and Globalization: The Rise of a Transnational State', *Theory and Society* 30(2) (2001): 157–200, *Theory of Global Capitalism: Production, Class and State in a Transnational World* (Baltimore, MD: Johns Hopkins University Press, 2004), and 'Global Capitalism: The New Transnationalism and the Folly of Conventional Thinking', *Science & Society* 69(3) (2005): 316–328.

32. Nicos Poulantzas, *State, Power, Socialism* (London: Verso, 2014 [1978]).

33. Harvey, *The New Imperialism*; David Harvey, *A Brief History of Neoliberalism* (Oxford: Oxford University Press, 2005); William Easterly, *The White Man's Burden: Why the West's Efforts to Aid the Rest Have Done so Much Ill and so Little Good* (New York: Penguin Press, 2006).

34. Henk Overbeek, 'Transnational Historical Materialism: Theories of Transnational Class Formation and World Order', in Mark Rupert (ed.), *Historical Materialism and Globalization* (London: Routledge, 2002), 168; A study which consists of:

> [1] a materialist philosophy of history ... which leads to the ontological primacy of 'social relations of production', (2) a rejection of separation between subject and object... and adoption of a dialectic understanding of reality as dynamic totality and as a unity of opposites [...], and (3) the method of abstraction as outlined by Marx in the Introduction to the Grundrisse.

35. Gramsci, *Selections from the Prison Notebooks*.
36. Robert W. Cox, 'Social Forces, States, and World Orders: Beyond IR Theory', *Millennium: Journal of International Studies* 10(2) (1981): 126–155; and Cox, *Production, Power and World Order*.
37. Stephen Gill, *Gramsci, Historical Materialism and International Relations* (Cambridge: Cambridge University Press, 1993).
38. Andreas Bieler and Adam Morton, *Images of Gramsci: Connections and Contentions in Political Theory and International Relations* (New York: Routledge, 2006).
39. Gramsci, *Selections from the Prison Notebooks*, 57–59.
40. Ibid., 137.
41. Ibid., 366.
42. Ibid., 168.
43. Ries Bode, 'De Nederlandse Bourgeoisie Tussen de twee Wereldoorlogen', *Cahiers voor de Politieke en Sociale Wetenschappen* 2 (1979): 9–50; Henk Overbeek (ed.), *Restructuring Hegemony in the Global Political Economy: The Rise of Transnational Neo-Liberalism in the 1980s* (London: Routledge, 1993); Otto Holman, 'Transnational Class Strategy and the New Europe', *International Journal of Political Economy* 22(1) (1992): 3–22, and *Integrating Southern Europe: EC Expansion and the Transnationalisation of Spain* (London: Routledge, 1996); and Kees van de Pijl, *Transnational Classes and International Relations* (London: Routledge, 1998); Kees van de Pijl, 'Two Faces of the Transnational Cadre Under Neo-Liberalism', *Journal of International Relations and Development*, suppl. Special Issue: *Transnational Historical Materialism* 7(2) (2004): 177–207; Kees van de Pijl, *Global Rivalries: From the Cold War to Iraq* (Pluto Press: London 2006).
44. Karl Marx, *Capital*, vol. 1 (London: Penguin, 1992), 109–199.
45. B. Jessop 'Accumulation Strategies, State Forms, and Hegemonic Projects', in *Kapitalistate* 10 (1983): 89–111; also see B. Jessop, 'The Capitalist State and the Rule of Capital: Problems in the Analysis of Business Associations', *West European Politics* 6(2) (1983): 139–162, and *State Theory: Putting the Capitalist State in Its Place* (University Park, PA: Pennsylvania State University Press, 1990).
46. In B. Balanya et al., *Europe Inc.: Regional and Global Restructuring and the Rise of Corporate Power* (London: Pluto Press, 2003), 29.
47. Louise Shelley, 'Russia and Ukraine: Transition or Tragedy?', in Roy Godson (ed.), *Menace To Society: Political-Criminal Collaboration around the World* (New Brunswick, NJ: Transaction Publishers, 2003).
48. Gramsci, *Selections from the Prison Notebooks*, 123–205.

49. Francis Fukuyama, 'The End of History?', *The National Interest* (Summer, 1989); and Francis Fukuyama, *The End of History and the Last Man* (New York: Free Press, 1992).

50. Fukuyama, 'The End of History?', 3.

51. For a discussion of culture-ideology of consumerism, see Leslie Sklair, *The Transnational Capitalist Class* (Oxford: Wiley-Blackwell, 2001).

52. Peter Gowan, 'Neoliberal Theory and Practice for Eastern Europe', *New Left Review* I(213) (1995): 3.

53. Ibid., 4.

54. Ibid.

55. For detailed analyses of the impact of the 'shock therapy' on the Central and Eastern European countries, see Alice Amsden, Jacek Kochanowicz and Lance Taylor, *The Market Meets its Match: Restructuring the Economies of Eastern Europe* (Cambridge, MA: Harvard University Press, 1998); P.J. Anderson, G. Wiessala and Ch. Williams *New Europe in Transition* (London: Continuum, 2000); Radhika Desai, 'Second-Hand Dealers in Ideas: Think-Tanks and Thatcherite Hegemony', *New Left Review* I(203) (1994); M. Ellman, E. Gaidar and G. Kolodko (eds), *Economic Transition in Eastern Europe* (Oxford: Blackwell, 1993); G. Kolodko, *From Shock to Therapy: The Political Economy of Postsocialist Transformation* (Oxford: Oxford University Press, 2000); D.S. Mason, *Revolution and Transition in East-Central Europe* (Boulder, CO: Westview Press, 1996); K. Poznanski, *Poland's Protracted Transition: Institutional Change and Economic Growth, 1970–1994* (Cambridge: Cambridge University Press, 1997); K. Poznanski, 'Building Capitalism with the Communist Tools: Defective Transition in Eastern Europe', *East European Politics and Societies* 15(2) (2001): 317–352, to mention a few.

56. Gowan, 'Neoliberal Theory and Practice for Eastern Europe', 4.

57. Ibid., 5–6.

58. It was the materialisation of,

> an idea put forward by President François Mitterrand of France at the European Parliament in Strasbourg on October 25, 1989, came to fruition on May 29, 1990 with the signing of its agreement by 40 countries, the Commission of the European Communities and the European Investment Bank.
>
> (EBRD 2010a)

59. Ibid.

60. Ibid.

61. Ibid.

62. Ibid.

63. On various theorisations of the regime, see Joel S. Hellman, 'Winners Take All: The Politics of Partial Reform in Post-Communist Transitions', *World Politics* 50(2) (1998): 203–234; Elena Kovaleva, 'Regional Politics in Ukraine's Transition: The Donetsk Elite', in Adam Swain (ed.), *Re-Constructing the Post-Soviet Industrial Region: The Donbas in Transition* (London: Routledge, 2007), 62–77; A. Åslund, 'Competitive Oligarchy: Russia, Ukraine and the United States', CASE Network Studies and Analyses (2005); Julia Kusznir and Heiko Pleines, 'Informal Networks in Ukraine's Privatization Auctions', in Julia Kusznir (ed.), *Informal Networks and Corruption in Post-Socialist Countries*, KICES Working Paper #6, (2006), 43, at: www.kices.org/downloads/KICES_WP_06.pdf; Taras Kuzio, 'Regime Type and Politics in Ukraine under Kuchma',

Communist and Post-Communist Studies 38 (2005): 167–190; Steven Levitsky and Lucan A. Way, 'Elections Without Democracy: The Rise of Competitive Authoritarianism', *Journal of Democracy* 13(2) (2002): 51–66, and *Competitive Authoritarianism: Hybrid Regimes after the Cold War* (Cambridge: Cambridge University Press, 2010).

64. Kyiv International Institute of Sociology (KIIS) (2000–2005), various reports, available at: www.kiis.com.ua/?lang=eng&cat=pub; Ukrstat (2000–2015), State Statistics Service of Ukraine. Reports on employment, migration, income and living conditions, available at: www.ukrstat.gov.ua/.

65. Andrew Wilson, *Virtual Politics: Faking Democracy in the Post-Soviet World*, 1st edn (New Haven, CT: Yale University Press, 2005); Andrew Wilson, *Ukraine Crisis: What the West Needs to Know* (London: Yale University Press, 2014); Marta Dyczok, 'Breaking Through the Information Blockade: Elections and Revolution in Ukraine 2004', *Canadian Slavonic Papers* 47(3–4) (2005): 241–264; Marta Dyczok, 'Was Kuchma's Censorship Effective? Mass Media in Ukraine Before 2004', *Europe-Asia Studies* 58(2) (2006): 215–238; Marta Dyczok, 'Do the Media Matter?: Focus on Ukraine', in M. Dyczok and O. Gaman-Golutvina (eds), *Media, Democracy and Freedom: The Post-Communist Experience* (Bern: Peter Lang, 2009), 17–42.

66. Andrew Wilson, *Ukraine's Orange Revolution* (New Haven, CT: Yale University Press, 2005); Wilson, *Virtual Politics*; Wilson, *Ukraine Crisis*; Taras Kuzio, *State and Institution Building in Ukraine* (New York: St. Martin's Press, 1999); Taras Kuzio, 'Regime Type and Politics in Ukraine under Kuchma', *Communist and Post-Communist Studies* 38 (2005): 167–190; Paul J. D'Anieri, *Understanding Ukrainian Politics: Power, Politics, and Institutional Design* (London: M.E. Sharpe, 2007) – to mention a few.

67. Yuliya Yurchenko, 'The Role and Locus of Mass Media in the Orange Revolution in Ukraine', Conference paper. Newcastle University EU Postgraduate Conference, 2008.

68. Dyczok, 'Breaking Through the Information Blockade', 245.

69. Ibid.

70. Wilson, *Ukraine Crisis*, 20.

71. Ibid., 21.

72. Ibid.

73. Wilson, *Virtual Politics*; D'Anieri, *Understanding Ukrainian Politics*; Sharon L. Wolchik and Jane L. Curry, *Central and East European Politics: From Communism to Democracy* (Lanham, MD: Rowman & Littlefield, 2011); Mikhail Myagkov, Peter C. Ordeshook and Dimitri Shakin, *The Forensics of Election Fraud: Russia and Ukraine* (Cambridge: Cambridge University Press, 2009).

74. For the full archive of the law amendments until present, see Verkhovna Rada, 'Law on the Judiciary and the Status of Judges'; the most current amendement is: #1402-VIII from 02.06.2016, #31, Article 545, at: http://zakon2.rada.gov.ua/laws/show/2453-17.

75. P. Solomon, 'Yanukovych's Judicial Reform: Power and Justice', *Ukraine Watch*, 2 March 2011, at: https://ukrainewatch.wordpress.com/2011/03/02/yanukovychs-judicial-reform-power-policy/.

76. M. Riabchuk, 'Two Ukraines?', *East European Reporter*, 5(4) (1992), and 'Ukraine: One State, Two Countries?', *Eurozine* (2002), at: http://shron.chtyvo.org.ua/Riabchuk/Ukraine_One_State_Two_Countries7__en.pdf.

77. For a variety of discussions on the topic, see S.M. Plokhy, 'The History of a "Non-Historical" Nation: Notes on the Nature and Current Problems of Ukrainian Historiography', *Slavic Review* 54(3) (Autumn 1995): 709–716; Plokhy, *The Gates of Europe*; Andrew Wilson, 'Elements of a Theory of Ukrainian Ethno-National Identities'. *Nations and Nationalism* 8(1) (2002a): 31–54; Andrew Wilson, *The Ukrainians: Unexpected Nation* (New Haven, CT: Yale Nota Bene, 2002b); S. Velychenko (ed.), (*Ukraine, The EU and Russia: History, Culture and International Relations* (Basingstoke: Palgrave Macmillan, 2007); Marko Bojcun 'Where is Ukraine?: Civilization and Ukraine's Identity', *Problems of Post-Communism* 48(5) (2001a): 42–51; Marko Bojcun, 'Russia, Ukraine and European Integration', EUI Working Paper HEC No. 2001(4), at: http://diana-n.iue.it:8080/bitstream/handle/1814/56/heco1-04. pdf?sequence=1&isAllowed=y; Marko Bojcun, M. 'Ukraine and Europe: A Difficult Reunion'. Dossier Series of the London European Research Centre (London: Kogan Page, 2001c); T. Zhurzhenko, *Borderlands into Bordered Lands: Geopolitics of Identity in Post-Soviet Ukraine* (Stuttgart: Ibidem, 2014); and Sakwa, *Frontline Ukraine*, 7–14, among others.

78. Rajan Menon and Eugene B. Rumer, *Conflict in Ukraine: The Unwinding of the Post-Cold War Order* (Boston, MA: MIT Press, 2015), 1 *et passim*.

79. Kovaleva, 'Regional Politics in Ukraine's Transition'.

80. B. Dreyfuss, 'Ukraine's Far Right Loses Big, but Europe's Russian-Backed Fascists Make Major Gains: The Crisis in Ukraine Winds Down in the Wake of Poroshenko's Chocolate-Covered Win'. *The Nation*, 30 May 2014, at: www. thenation.com/article/ukraines-far-right-loses-big-europes-russian-backed-fascists-make-major-gains/.

81. *DW*, 'Забуті державою: Родичів загиблих на Донбасі активно підтримують волонтери' ['Forgotten by Their Country: Relatives of Those who Perished in Donbas Get Support from Volunteers'], 12 February 2015; and Radio Svoboda 'Сім'ї загиблих в АТО мусять збирати три пакети документів' ['Families of the Fallen Made Prove Reation with Three Different Document Packages'], 21 April 2015, at: www.radiosvoboda.org/a/26969078.html.

82. V. Ishchenko, 'Ukraine's Fractures', *New Left Review* 87 (May–June 2014); and Olga Zelinksa, 'Ukrainian Euromaidan Protest: Dynamics, Causes, and Aftermath Authors', *Sociology Compass* 11(9) (2017).

83. V. Ishchenko, 'Far Right Participation in the Ukrainian Maidan Protests: An Attempt of Systematic Estimation', *European Politics and Society* 17(4) (2016): 453–472.

84. Wilson, *Ukraine Crisis*, 22.

85. Ibid.

86. Quoted from personal interviews in Wilson, *Ukraine Crisis*, 23.

87. 'Ukraine's Protests. The Birth of the Nation?', *The Economist*, 14 December 2014, at: www.economist.com/node/21591642.

88. Benedict Anderson, *Imagined Communities: Reflections on the Origin and Spread of Nationalism* (London: Verso, 2006), 7.

89. Ibid.

90. The Verkhovna Rada of Ukraine, Law #2558 'On Condemnation of Communist and National-Socialist (Nazi) Totalitarian Regimes in Ukraine and Ban of their Propaganda and Symbols', 9 April 2015, full text, at: http://w1.c1.rada.gov.ua/ pls/zweb2/webproc4_1?pf3511=54670.

91. V. Yanukovych, Voter Address, [video broadcast], 2004, at: https://youtu.be/
eelo-ZuFtoE; in a public meeting with the voters infamously referred to the
supporters of other candidates as '*kozly*', a slur that literally means 'goats', and
figuratively means 'low lives', 'those beneath you', 'untouchables'; the term
originates from prison slang and is used to identify one of the lowest ranks in
the gangster hierarchy. This excerpt is from the address: 'All those sceptics will
not succeed in obstructing our path. I believe that there are much more sane
people than those *kozly* who won't let us live [peacefully]'.
92. Wilson, *Ukraine's Orange Revolution*; and Wilson, *Virtual Politics*; Dyczok,
'Breaking Through the Information Blockade'.
93. V. Yevtukh, *Ethno-social Processes in Ukraine: Opportunities for Scientific
Interpretations* [author's translation] (Kyiv: Stylos Publishing House, 2004),
220.

2. CAPITALIST ANTECEDENTS IN THE LATE USSR

1. Tatyana Zaslavkaya, 'A Voice of Reform', *Studies in Comparative Communism*
25(1) (1992): 79.
2. Grigorii I. Khanin, 'The Soviet Economy: From Crisis to Catastrophe', Working
Paper 33 (Stockholm Institute of Soviet and East European Economics, 1991),
85; M. Harrison, 'Soviet Economic Growth since 1928: The Alternative
Statistics of G.I. Khanin', *Europe-Asia Studies* 45(1) (1993): 151.
3. Peter Rutland, *The Politics of Economic Stagnation in the Soviet Union: The Role
of Local Party Organs in Economic Management* (Cambridge: Cambridge
University Press, 1993), 10–11.
4. Zaslavskaya, 'A Voice of Reform', 79; Tatyana Zaslavskaya, *The Second Socialist
Revolution: An Alternative Soviet Strategy* (London: I.B. Tauris, 1990).
5. Abel Aganbegyan, *The Challenge: Economics of Perestroika* (London:
Hutchinson, 1988).
6. Leon Aron, 'Everything You Need to Know about the Collapse of the Soviet
Union is Wrong: And Why it Matters in an Age of Revolution', *Foreign Policy*,
20 June 2011; Louise Shelley, 'Russia and Ukraine: Transition or Tragedy?', in
Roy Godson (ed.), *Menace to Society: Political-Criminal Collaboration around
the World* (New Brunswick, NJ: Transaction Publishers, 2003).
7. David A. Dyker, *Restructuring the Soviet Economy* (London: Routledge, 1992),
79–80.
8. János Kornai, *Economics of Shortage* (Amsterdam: North-Holland, 1980), 233.
9. David S. Lane, *Soviet Society under Perestroika* (Boston, MA: Unwin Hyman,
1990); David S. Lane, *Soviet Society under Perestroika* (London: Routledge,
1992), 36.
10. Mikhail Gorbachev, *Perestroika New Thinking for Our Country and the World*
(New York: Harper and Row, 1987).
11. Lane, *Soviet Society under Perestroika*, 38.
12. M. Boguslavskii and P.S. Smirnov, *The Reorganization of Soviet Foreign Trade:
Legal Aspects* (Armonk, NY: M. E. Sharpe, 1989), 5–6; P.B. Stephen,
'Perestroyka and Property: The Law of Ownership in the Post-Socialist Soviet
Union', *The American Journal of Comparative Law* 39(1) (Winter, 1991): 35–65.
13. For more details, see Dyker, *Restructuring the Soviet Economy*, 94–95 *et passim*.
14. Andriy Kudryachenko, see Андрій Кудряченко, Політична історія України
XX століття [*Political History of Ukraine*] (Київ: МАУП, 2006), 371.

15. Ibid.
16. Dyker, *Restructuring the Soviet Economy*, 95.
17. Ibid.
18. Kudryachenko, Кудряченко, Політична історія України XX століття, 371.
19. See, for example, A. Åslund, *How Capitalism was Built: The Transformation of Central and Eastern Europe, Russia, and Central Asia* (New York: Cambridge University Press, 2007); Rumen Dobrinsky, 'Capital Accumulation during the Transition from Plan to Market', *The Economics of Transition* 15(4) (2007): 845–868; Gil Eyal, Iván Szelényi and Eleanor R. Townsley, *Making Capitalism without Capitalists: Class Formation and Elite Struggles in Post-Communist Central Europe* (London: Verso, 1998); Karoly Attila Soos, *Politics and Policies in Post-Communist Transition Primary and Secondary Privatisation in Central Europe and the Former Soviet Union* (New York: Central European University Press, 2010).
20. For some notable exceptions, see S. Johnson, H. Kroll and S. Eder, 'Strategy, Structure, and Spontaneous Privatisation in Russia and Ukraine', in V. Milor (ed.), *Changing Political Economies: Privatisation in Post-Communist and Reforming Communist States* (London: Lynne Rienner Publishers, 1994).
21. A question arises as to whether such devolution of authority and granting of relative autonomy of enterprises can be deemed as privatisation at all. It is my position that it can since 'spontaneous privatisation' in the case of the post-Soviet states was a part of the primitive capital accumulation by the emerging capitalist-minded historic bloc.
22. Johnson et al., 'Strategy, Structure, and Spontaneous Privatisation in Russia and Ukraine', 174. The authors use the term SOE 'to refer to a particular legal form, and firm to refer to a set of assets'.
23. D.M. Nuti, 'The Role of New Cooperatives in the Soviet Economy', in B. Dallago and G. Ajaniand B. Grancelli (eds), *Privatization and Entrepreneurship in Post-Socialist Countries: Economy, Law and Society* (New York: St. Martin's Press, 1992), 251–253.
24. Ibid., 251.
25. Andrij Pekhnyk, see Андрій Пехник, Іноземні інвестиції в економіку України: навчальний посібник (Київ: Знання, 2007), 42.
26. Ibid.
27. Ibid.; E. Pond, *The Rebirth of Europe* (Washington, DC: Brookings Institution Press, 2002), 146.
28. Shelley, 'Russia and Ukraine', 202.
29. Ibid.
30. Ibid.
31. Ferdinand J.M. Feldbrugge, 'Government and Shadow Economy in the Soviet Union', *Soviet Studies* 36(4) (1984), 207, and 'The Soviet Second Economy in a Political and Legal Perspective', in E.L. Feige (ed.), *The Underground Economy: Tax Evasion and Information Distortion* (Cambridge: Cambridge University Press, 1989), 297–338; Gregory Grossman, 'The "Second Economy" of the USSR', *Problems of Communism* 26(5) (1977): 25–40; Aron Katsenlinboigen, 'Coloured Markets in the Soviet Markets', *Soviet Studies* 29(1) (1977): 62–85.
32. Todd S. Foglesong and Peter H. Solomon, jnr, *Crime, Criminal Justice and Criminology in Post-Soviet Ukraine* (Washington, DC: U.S. Dept. of Justice Office of Justice Programs National Institute of Justice, 2001), 74.

33. Feldbrugge, 'Government and Shadow Economy in the Soviet Union'; and Feldbrugge, 'The Soviet Second Economy in a Political and Legal Perspective'.

34. L. Randall, *Reluctant Capitalists: Russia's Journey through Market Transition* (New York: Routledge, 2001), 54–63; Alena V. Ledeneva, *Russia's Economy of Favours: Blat, Networking, and Informal Exchange* (Cambridge: Cambridge University Press, 1998).

35. Ledeneva, *Russia's Economy of Favours*.

36. Ibid.

37. Roy Godson, *Menace to Society: Political-Criminal Collaboration around the World* (New Brunswick, NJ: Transaction Publishers, 2003).

38. Shelley, 'Russia and Ukraine: Transition or Tragedy?'.

39. Foglesong and Solomon, *Crime, Criminal Justice and Criminology in Post-Soviet Ukraine*.

40. Feldbrugge, 'Government and Shadow Economy in the Soviet Union'.

41. Maria Łos, 'From Underground to Legitimacy: The Normative Dilemmas of Post-Communist Marketization', in Bruno Dallago, Gianmaria Ajani and Bruno Grancelli (eds), *Privatization and Entrepreneurship in Post-Socialist Countries: Economy, Law, and Society* (New York: St. Martin's Press, 1992).

42. Kerstin Zimmer and Claudia Sabić, 'Ukraine: The Genesis of a Captured State', in Melanie Tatur (ed.), *The Making of Regions in Post-Socialist Europe: The Impact of Culture, Economic Structure and Institutions: Case Studies from Poland, Hungary, Romania and Ukraine*, 1st edn (Wiesbaden: VS Verlag für Sozialwissenschaften, 2004).

43. Ichiro Iwasaki and Taku Suzuki, 'Transition Strategy, Corporate Exploitation, and State Capture: An Empirical Analysis of the Former Soviet States', *Communist and Post-Communist Studies* 40(4) (2007): 393–422.

44. Kees van der Pijl, *The Making of an Atlantic Ruling Class* (London: Verso, 1984).

45. Bastiaan van Apeldoorn, *Transnational Capitalism and the Struggle over European Integration* (London: Routledge, 2003).

46. William K. Carroll, *The Making of a Transnational Capitalist Class: Corporate Power in the 21st Century* (London: Zed Books, 2010).

47. Zimmer and Sabić, 'Ukraine', 105–130.

48. Nicos Poulantzas, (1975) *Political Power and Social Classes* (London: New Left Books; Sheed and Ward, 1975).

49. Shelley, 'Russia and Ukraine', 201–202.

50. Ibid.

51. David Lane and Cameron Ross, *The Transition from Communism to Capitalism: Ruling Elites from Gorbachev to Yeltsin* (London: Palgrave Macmillan, 1999), 35–36.

52. Shelley, 'Russia and Ukraine', 203.

53. Louise I. Shelley, 'Transnational Organized Crime: The New Authoritarianism', in H.R. Friman and P. Andreas (eds), *The Illicit Global Economy and State Power* (New York: Rowan and Littlefield, 1999), 85.

54. Kees van der Pijl, 'Soviet Socialism and Passive Revolution', in Stephen Gill (ed.), *Gramsci, Historical Materialism and International Relations* (Cambridge: Cambridge University Press, 1993), 240.

55. Ibid., 248.

56. Nicos Poulantzas, *State, Power, Socialism* (London: New Left Books, 1978).

57. Robert W. Cox, 'Social Forces, States, and World Orders: Beyond IR Theory', *Millennium: Journal of International Studies* 10(2) (1981), 205.

58. Ibid.

59. On differentiation of the Amsterdam School from the cultural political economy, see B. and N.-L. Sum, 'Putting the "Amsterdam School" in its Rightful Place: A Reply to Juan Ignacio Staricco's Critique of Cultural Political Economy', *New Political Economy* 22(3) (2017): 342–354.

60. Henk Overbeek, 'Transnational Class Formation and Concepts of Control: Towards a Genealogy of the Amsterdam Project in International Political Economy', *Journal of International Relations and Development* 7(2) (2004): 113–141.

61. See Kees van der Pijl, *Transnational Classes and International Relations* (London: Routledge, 1998).

62. For example, T. Cliff, 'State Capitalism in Russia', (1974), at: www.marxists.org/archive/cliff/works/1955/statecap/index.htm.

63. Robert W. Cox, *Production, Power and World Order: Social Forces in the Making of History* (New York: Columbia University Press, 1987), 355.

64. Ibid.

65. Ibid., 356.

66. Andriy Kudryachenko, see Андрій Кудряченко, Політична історія України XX століття (Київ: МАУП, 2006); Lane and Ross, *The Transition from Communism to Capitalism*, 89–121.

67. Kudryachenko, see Кудряченко, Політична історія України XX століття, 375.

68. Lane and Ross, *The Transition from Communism to Capitalism*, 90.

69. Ibid.

70. David Lane, *Soviet Society under Perestroika* (London: Routledge, 1992), 32.

71. Ibid.

72. Lane, *Soviet Society under Perestroika*, 32–33.

73. János Kornai, 'Resource-Constrained Versus Demand-Constrained Systems', *Econometrica* 47(4) (1979): 801–819.

74. Lane, *Soviet Society under Perestroika*, 34.

75. Ibid.

76. Ibid.

77. Vlad Mykhnenko, 'State, Society and Protest Under Post-Communism: Ukrainian Miners and their Defeat', in C. Mudde and P. Kopecký (eds), *Uncivil Society?: Contentious Politics in Eastern Europe* (London: Routledge, 2003), 98.

78. Ibid.

79. Kuzbass (Kuznetskiy Basseyn – *Rus.*) – the Kuznetsk Basin in south-western Siberia is one of the largest coal mining areas in the world.

80. Anatolii Rusnachenko, *Probudzhennia: Robitnychyi rukh na Ukraiini v 1989–1993 rokakh* (Kyiv: KM Academia Publishing House, 1995).

81. Mykhnenko, 'State, Society and Protest Under Post-Communism', 98. See also Theodore Friedgut and Lewis Siegelbaum, 'Perestroika from Below: The Soviet Miners' Strike and Its Aftermath', *New Left Review* I(181) (1990): 5–32; V. Kostiukovskyy, *Kuzbass: zharkoe leto 89-go* (Moscow: Sovremennik, 1990); A.T. Gavrilov and N.I. Lavrov (eds), *Zabastovka: vynuzhdennaia mera zashchity zakonnykh prav, no tot li eto put'?* (Moscow: Profizdat, 1989).

82. Mykhnenko, 'State, Society and Protest Under Post-Communism', 99; Friedgut and Siegelbaum, 'Perestroika from Below', 32.

83. Friedgut and Siegelbaum, 'Perestroika from Below', 32.

84. Mykhnenko, 'State, Society and Protest Under Post-Communism', 99.

85. T. Kuzio and A. Wilson, *Ukraine: Perestroika to Independence* (Canadian Institute of Ukrainian Studies Press, 1994), 105–106.
86. Rusnachenko, *Probudzhennia*.
87. Ibid.
88. Mykhnenko, 'State, Society and Protest Under Post-Communism', 100.

3. SOCIAL DESTRUCTION AND KLEPTOCRATIC CONSTRUCTION OF THE EARLY 1990s

1. Benedict Anderson, *Imagined Communities: Reflections on the Origin and Spread of Nationalism* (London: Verso, 2006).
2. Andrew Wilson, *Ukrainian Nationalism in the 1990s: A Minority Faith* (Cambridge: Cambridge University Press, 1997), 1 *et passim*.
3. Taras Kuzio and Andrew Wilson, *Ukraine: Perestroika to Independence* (Basingstoke: Macmillan, 1994), 3.
4. Richard Sakwa, *Frontline Ukraine: Crisis in the Borderlands* (London: I.B. Tauris, 2015).
5. Ibid., 14.
6. Ibid., 14–15; also 16–25.
7. Ibid., 23.
8. Vlad Mykhnenko, 'State, Society and Protest Under Post-Communism: Ukrainian Miners and their Defeat', in C. Mudde and P. Kopecký (eds), *Uncivil Society?: Contentious Politics in Eastern Europe* (London: Routledge, 2003), *inter alia*.
9. Karl Marx and Friedrich Engels, *The German Ideology*, edited by C.J. Arthur (London: Lawrence and Wishart, 1970), 80.
10. Nicos Poulantzas, *Classes in Contemporary Capitalism* (London: New Left Books, 1975), 73.
11. Ibid.
12. Simon Clarke, 'Class Struggle and the Global Overaccumulaiton', in R. Albritton, M. Itoh, R. Westra and A. Zuege (eds), *Phases of Capitalist Development: Booms, Crises and Globalizations* (Basingstoke: Palgrave, 2002), 80.
13. Ibid.
14. Ibid.
15. Ibid.
16. The work of Kees van der Pijl, *Atlanticism & the European Ruling Class* (Pub By Ve, 1984a), *The Making of an Atlantic Ruling Class* (London: Verso, 1984b), and *Global Rivalries: From the Cold War to Iraq* (Pluto Press: London, 2006), *inter alia*; Bastiaan van Apeldoorn, *Transnational Capitalism and the Struggle over European Integration* (London: Routledge, 2003); William K. Carroll, *The Making of a Transnational Capitalist Class: Corporate Power in the 21st Century* (London: Zed Books, 2010); and Robert W. Cox, *Production, Power and World Order: Social Forces in the Making of History* (New York: Columbia University Press, 1987) confirms the dominance of Western capital in global business networks and institutions.
17. Gil Eyal, Iván Szelényi and Eleanor R. Townsley, *Making Capitalism without Capitalists: Class Formation and Elite Struggles in Post-Communist Central Europe* (London: Verso, 1998), 3–4.
18. Ibid., 1.

19. Francis Fukuyama, 'The End of History?', *The National Interest* (Summer, 1989); and Francis Fukuyama, *The End of History and the Last Man* (New York: Free Press, 1992).
20. William Easterly, *The White Man's Burden: Why the West's Efforts to Aid the Rest Have Done so Much Ill and so Little Good* (New York: Penguin Press, 2006), 53–54.
21. Ibid., 7–8.
22. Ibid.
23. Ibid., 58; 53–98.
24. Ibid., 59.
25. EBRD, 'Our History', 8 April 2010, at: www.ebrd.com/pages/about/history.shtml.
26. Ibid.
27. Ibid.
28. Ibid.
29. Ibid.
30. Rumen Dobrinsky, 'Capital Accumulation during the Transition from Plan to Market', *The Economics of Transition* 15(4) (2007): 845–868.
31. Ibid., 846.
32. Ibid.
33. For some examples, see Zoltan Acs and Felix FitzRoy, 'A Constitution for Privatizing Large Eastern Enterprises', *Economics of Transition* 2(1) (1994): 83–94; E.C. Perotti, 'A Taxonomy of Post-Socialist Financial Systems: Decentralized Enforcement and the Creation of Inside Money', in *Economic of Transition* 2(1) (1994): 71–81; G. Roland, 'The Role of Political Constraints in Transition Strategies', *Economic of Transition* 2(1) (1994): 27–41; J. Aizenman and P. Izard, 'Production Bottlenecks and Resource Allocation during the Transition to a Market Economy', *Economics of Transition* 3(3) (1995): 321–331.
34. Vedat Milor, *Changing Political Economies: Privatization in Post-Communist and Reforming Communist States* (Boulder, CO: Lynne Rienner Publishers, 1994), 1.
35. Ibid.
36. Paul D'Anieri, Robert S. Kravchuk and Taras Kuzio, *Politics and Society in Ukraine* (Boulder, CO: Westview Press, 1999), 2.
37. Ibid.
38. Robert Bideleux and Ian Jeffries, *A History of Eastern Europe: Crisis and Change* (London: Routledge, 1998).
39. Ibid., 590.
40. Ibid., 593.
41. Ibid.
42. Ibid., 608–619.
43. Taras Kuzio, *State and Institution Building in Ukraine* (New York: St. Martin's Press, 1999).
44. Mario I. Blejer and Marko Škreb, 'Stabilisation after Five Years of Reform: Issues and Experiences', in Mario I. Blejer and Marko Škreb (eds), *Macroeconomic Stabilization in Transition Economies* (New York: Cambridge University Press, 1997), 1–2.
45. Ibid., 2.
46. Antonio Gramsci, *Selections from the Prison Notebooks of Antonio Gramsci* (New York: International Publishers, 1971).

47. Andrew Wilson, *Virtual Politics: Faking Democracy in the Post-Soviet World*, 1st edn (New Haven, CT: Yale University Press, 2005).

48. Yuliya Yurchenko, 'Black Holes in the Political Economy of Ukraine: The Neoliberalisation of Europe's "Wild East"', *Debatte* (2013).

49. Elena Kovaleva, 'Regional Politics in Ukraine's Transition: The Donetsk Elite', in Adam Swain (ed.), *Re-Constructing the Post-Soviet Industrial Region: The Donbas in Transition* (London: Routledge, 2007), 67.

50. S. Kononchuk and V. Pikhovshek, *The Dnipropetrovsk Family-2*, 2nd edn (Kyiv: Ukrainian Center for Independent Political Research, 1997).

51. David S. Lane, *Elites and Classes in the Transformation of State Socialism* (London: Transaction Publishers, 2011).

52. Kononchuk and Pikhovshek, *The Dnipropetrovsk Family-2*.

53. Ibid., 8–9.

54. Alexander Boyko, see Александр Бойко, Криминальная оккупация: История Партии Регионов [*Criminal Occupation: History of the Party of Regions*]. Documentary/journalistic investigation (2007), at: http://video.i.ua/user/613823/8535/252016/.

55. Kovaleva, 'Regional Politics in Ukraine's Transition', 65.

56. Ibid.

57. Ibid., 67.

58. Ibid.

59. Ibid., 68.

60. G. Oosterbaan, 'Clan Based Politics in Ukraine and Implications for Democratisation', in J.S. Micgiel (ed.), *Perspectives on Political and Economic Transitions after Communism* (New York: Columbia University Press, 1997), at: www.cc.columbia.edu/sec/ciao/conf/eceo1/eceo100g.html, 2.

61. Ibid.

62. In an interview with Boyko, see Бойко, Криминальная оккупация [*Criminal Occupation*].

63. Vladimir Aryev, see Владимир Арьев, Донецкая мафия: Перезагрузка. Documentary/journalistic investigation (2007), at: http://video.i.ua/user/2689167/30891/164471/; and Boris Penchuk and Sergei Kyzin, see Борис Пенчук and Сергей Кузин Донецкая мафия. Фонд 'Антикоррупция' (2006), at: http://dony07.narod.ru/dm.html#a2; Los (1992); Louise Shelley, 'Russia and Ukraine: Transition or Tragedy?', in Roy Godson (ed.), *Menace to Society: Political-Criminal Collaboration around the World* (New Brunswick, NJ: Transaction Publishers, 2003).

64. Mykola Riabchuk, 'Дві України' ['Two Ukraines'], *Krytyka* (2001) 4.

65. Ivan Katchanovski, *Cleft Countries: Regional Political Divisions and Cultures in Post-Soviet Ukraine and Moldova* (Stuttgart: Ibidem-Verlag, 2006), 36.

66. Ibid., 36–37.

67. Ignatieff (1993: 79) quoted in Katchanovski, *Cleft Countries*, 37.

68. Peter H. Solomon, jnr and Todd S. Foglesong, 'The Two Faces of Crime in Post-Soviet Ukraine', *East European Constitutional Review* (2000), 72–76.

69. Data analysed in the report is drawn from A.G. Kulik and B.I. Bobyr, *Prestupnost v Ukraine: Biulleten zakonodavsta i iuridichnoi praktiki Ukraini 2* (1994), 5–37, and, 'Prilozhenie', 134–186; and also an unpublished sequel (1999), quoted in Solomon and Foglesong, 'The Two Faces of Crime in Post-Soviet Ukraine', 72.

70. Due to space limitations, I will only address the criminalisation of sectors relevant to main oligarchic groups' capital formation. For details on various crime rates, ratios and dynamics, see Solomon and Foglesong, 'The Two Faces of Crime in Post-Soviet Ukraine'.
71. Andriy Kudryachenko, see Андрій Кудряченко, Політична історія України XX століття (Київ: МАУП, 2006), 395.
72. Ibid.
73. State Penitentiary Service (2010).
74. Quoted in Bondarenko, see Константин Бондаренко, Леонид Кучма (Харьков: Фолио, 2009: 58–59).
75. Horbylin, Pustovoitenko, Yutsuba, Derkach, Kuznetsov, Borodych, Shmarov – to mention a few in the highest positions. For the full list, see Kononchuk and Pikhovshek, *The Dnipropetrovsk Family-2*, 15–16.
76. Kononchuk and Pikhovshek, *The Dnipropetrovsk Family-2*, 6.
77. One of the proofs of the above can be seen in the statement Kuchma made in an interview on 19 October 1995: 'I can sense I will be blamed for more people from Dnipropetrovsk being appointed to Kyiv' (in Kononchuk and Pikhovshek, *The Dnipropetrovsk Family-2*, 18). The appointees were: Osyka, Udovenko, Yekhanurov, Poltavets, Durdynets, Pynzenyk (Пинзеник), Kinakh, Kuras, Sabluk, Radchenko, Dankevych, and Svatkov (Kononchuk and Pikhovshek, *The Dnipropetrovsk Family-2*, 18). The second wave of appointments from 'the team' included: Ovcharenko (Minister for Social Citizens' Protection, appointed in 1996), Bochkarev (Minister for Energy and Electrification), Khorishko (Minister for Agriculture and Food), Kistrutska (Head of Main Archive Administration at the Cabinet of Ministers, appointed on 3 September 1996), and Minchenko (State Minister for Fuel and Energy Complex and Policy, appointed in September 1996 (Kononchuk and Pikhovshek, *The Dnipropetrovsk Family-2*, 16–17).
78. Kononchuk and Pikhovshek, *The Dnipropetrovsk Family-2*.
79. The Central Electoral Commission (1998), 'Parliamentary Elections Results, 1998', (1998), at: www.cvk.gov.ua/pls/vd2002/webprocov?kodvib=1&rejim=0.
80. Ibid.
81. Ibid.
82. Partiya Demokratychnoho Vidrodzhennya Ukrayiny (National Renaissance of Ukraine Party), Trudovyy Konhres Ukrayiny (Labour Congress of Ukraine), Soyuz Pidrrymky Respubliky Krym (Union for Crimea Republic Support), Soyuz Ukrayins'koho Studentstva (Ukraine's Students Union), 'Nova Khvylya' (New Wave), political clubs of 'Nova Ukrayina' (New Ukraine) and Asotsiatsiya Molodykh Ukrayins'kykh Politykiv ta Politolohiv (Association of Young Ukrainian Politicians and Political Scientists).
83. NDP, at: http://ndp.org.ua/index.php?pid=1287388855&id=17.
84. Bondarenko, see Бондаренко, Леонид Кучма, 102.
85. Ibid.
86. Slavomir Matuszak, 'The Oligarchic Democracy: The Influence of Business Groups on Ukrainian Politics', *OSW: Centre for Easter Studies* 42 (2012), 14 *et passim*.
87. Dimitry Popov and Ilya Milshtein, see Дмитрий Попов and Илья Мильштейн, Оранжевая принцесса: загадка Юлии Тимошенко (Издательство Ольги Морозовой, 2006); Victor Medvedchuk in an interview with *Investgazeta* (2003), among others.

88. 'Киевская семерка' ['The Kiev Seven'], Инвестгазета [*Investgazeta*], 10 March 2003, www.investgazeta.net/politika-i-ekonomika/kievskaja-semerka-144187/. Accessed on 23 March 2012.

89. Scientist (Physics and mathematics), in 1993 – advisor to the President on financial stabilisation; since 1998 – people's deputy in Verkhovna Rada (MP).

90. President of Ukraine's Credit Bank; previously, advisor to the prime minister in the late 1990s; he worked in Inkombank and the Delovaya Rossiya bank in Russia in 1991 and chaired the Currency Reserve department in Ukrayina bank in 1992 (Ukraine). He committed suicide in 2004; the incident is treated as suspicious.

91. Kovaleva, 'Regional Politics in Ukraine's Transition', 69.

92. In Aryev, see Арьев, Донецкая мафия.

93. KMU, Yanukovych Viktor Fedorovych [Bio note] (2011), at: www.kmu.gov.ua/kmu/control/en/publish/article?showHidden=1&art_id=85175689&cat_id=1290720&ctime=1184067660889.

94. Daniel Vaughan-Whitehead in Milica Uvalic and Daniel Vaughan-Whitehead (eds), *Privatization Surprises in Transition Economies Employee-Ownership in Central and Eastern Europe* (Cheltenham: Edward Elgar, 1997), 230, see full chapter for details, 230–265.

95. Ukrstat, 'Gross Domestic Product by Production Method and Gross Value Added by Type of Economic Activity', (2011), at: www.ukrstat.gov.ua/operativ/operativ2008/vvp/vvp_ric/vtr_e.htm.

96. From the moment of independence and until the 1995 Constitutional Agreement, the highest law of Ukraine was (later amended on multiple occasions) the Constitution of the Ukrainian SSR, which adopted as long ago as 1978.

97. For the full text of the Agreement, see http://zakon.nau.ua/doc/?uid=1069.1704.0. The code of the document in the Verkhovna Rada library catalogue is: N 1к/95-ВР, 08.06.1995.

98. Even though in 1995, for example, only 25 per cent of the targeted large industrial enterprises were privatised, the figure can be considered to be very impressive since the emerging capitalist class in Ukraine were not interested in enterprises that required vast investment at the time but rather focused on extraction industries. As for foreign investors, they were more interested in light industry. Additionally, the lack of stable legislative platforms for business operation topped with ineffective law enforcement and omnipresent corruption scared many potential foreign investors away; for details, see Andriy Pekhnyk, Андрій Пехник, Іноземні інвестиції в економіку України: навчальний посібник (Київ: Знання, 2007), 42–50.

4. CLASS FORMATION AND SOCIAL FRAGMENTATION

1. E. Pond, *The Rebirth of Europe* (Washington, DC: Brookings Institution Press, 2002), 145–147.

2. Ibid.

3. Andriy Pekhnyk, Андрій Пехник, Іноземні інвестиції в економіку України: навчальний посібник (Київ: Знання, 2007), 42–44.

4. Pond, *The Rebirth of Europe*, 147.

5. Ukrstat, 'Gross Domestic Product by Production Method and Gross Value Added by Type of Economic Activity', (2011), at: www.ukrstat.gov.ua/operativ/operativ2008/vvp/vvp_ric/vtr_e.htm.
6. Paul J. D'Anieri, *Understanding Ukrainian Politics: Power, Politics, and Institutional Design* (London: M.E. Sharpe, 2007), 86–87.
7. Ibid., 86.
8. Vladimir Aryev, see Владимир Арьев, Донецкая мафия: Перезагрузка. Documentary/journalistic investigation (2007), at: http://video.i.ua/user/2689167/30891/164471/; Alexander Boyko, see Александр Бойко, Криминальная оккупация: История Партии Регионов [*Criminal Occupation: History of the Party of Regions*]. Documentary/journalistic investigation (2007), at: http://video.i.ua/user/613823/8535/252016/.
9. Andrew Wilson, *Virtual Politics: Faking Democracy in the Post-Soviet World*, 1st edn (New Haven, CT: Yale University Press, 2005), 154–157.
10. Taras Kuzio, 'Civil Society, Youth and Societal Mobilization in Democratic Revolutions', *Communist and Post-Communist Studies* 39(3) (2006): 365–386.
11. Robert Kravchuk, *Ukrainian Political Economy: The First Ten Years*, 1st edn (New York: Palgrave Macmillan, 2002), 81.
12. A. Lyakh, 'The Evolution of the Industrial Structure in Donetsk Region', in Adam Swain (ed.), *Re-Constructing the Post-Soviet Industrial Region: The Donbas in Transition* (London: Routledge, 2007), 78–96.
13. Ibid., 88.
14. Sergii Leshchenko: Сергій Лещенко, 'Юлія Тимошенко зарила "сокиру війни" з Віктором Пінчуком', Українська правда, (2009), at: www.pravda.com.ua/articles/4b1aa85922e52/.
15. Ibid.
16. Ibid.
17. The three were part of the Komsomol enthusiasts, who made use of the relaxed legislation of the late 1980s and started their business in 1988 by opening one and later a chain of private video-screening salons (i.e. small cinema theatres that usually operated VHS recordings of foreign films in local youth clubs, etc. in charge of which was Komsomol). Information from Y. Tymoshenko's personal website, accessed at: www.tymoshenko.ua/uk/page/about.
18. Ibid.
19. Re-registration was chosen over registering a new firm in order to preserve the tax privileges that KUB enjoyed due to its partly foreign ownership, that is, KUB was co-founded with Somalli Ltd. registered in Cyprus (*Korrespondent*, 'Top 100 Most Influential People of Ukraine: 2010', at: http://files.korrespondent.net/projects/top100/2010).
20. Lyakh, 'The Evolution of the Industrial Structure in Donetsk Region'.
21. Elena Kovaleva, 'Regional Politics in Ukraine's Transition: The Donetsk Elite', in Adam Swain (ed.), *Re-Constructing the Post-Soviet Industrial Region: The Donbas in Transition* (London: Routledge, 2007).
22. M. Rachkevych, 'U.S. Official: Austrian Bank's Ties to RosUkrEnergo Suspicious', *Kyiv Post*, 3 December 2010.
23. Misha Glenny, *McMafia: Crime Without Frontiers* (London: Bodley Head, 2008), 94.
24. Ibid.
25. For details, see Pekhnyk, Пехник, Іноземні інвестиції в економіку України, 50–54.

26. Lyakh, 'The Evolution of the Industrial Structure in Donetsk Region', 78.
27. Ibid., 79.
28. Ibid., 79–82. For a detailed analysis of Donbas industrial structure and the restructuring and the regional economic divergence in Ukraine, see Vlad Mykhnenko, 'Ukraine's Diverging Space-Economy: The Orange Revolution, Post-Soviet Development Models and Regional Trajectories', *European Urban and Regional Studies* 17(2) (2010): 141–165; and Adam Swain and Vlad Mykhnenko, 'The Ukrainian Donbas in "Transition"', in Adam Swain (ed.), *Re-Constructing the Post-Soviet Industrial Region: The Donbas in Transition* (London: Routledge, 2007), 7–46.
29. B. Pynzenyk, see В. Пинзеник, 'Оцінка тенденцій економічної динаміки у 2002 році'. Економічні есе: Інститут реформ 1(12) (2002): 5–13.
30. Verkhovna Rada, 'Law N3319-VI on Certain Issues Regarding Gas and Electricity Arrears', (2011), at: http://zakon3.rada.gov.ua/laws/show/3319-17.
31. See also Pynzenyk, Пинзеник, 'Оцінка тенденцій економічної динаміки у 2002 році'.
32. 'US Embassy Cables: Gas Supplies Linked to Russian Mafia', *The Guardian*, 1 December 2010, at: www.theguardian.com/world/us-embassy-cables-documents/182121.
33. Ibid.
34. The Verkhovna Rada of Ukraine, Верховна Рада України, 'Закон України № 3319-VI. Про деякі питання заборгованості за спожитий природний газ та електричну енергію, Верховна Рада, (2011), at: http://zakon.rada.gov.ua/cgi-bin/laws/main.cgi?nreg=3319-17.
35. Kravchuk, *Ukrainian Political Economy*, 82.
36. Slavomir Matuszak, 'The Oligarchic Democracy: The Influence of Business Groups on Ukrainian Politics', *OSW: Centre for Easter Studies* 42 (2012).
37. Ibid.
38. D.P. Solomon, 'A Tsar is Born: The Consolidation of Power in Putin's Russia'. The Centre for Security Policy, August, 2006.
39. Ibid.
40. Glenny, *McMafia*, 96–97.
41. Adam Swain, 'Disputed Links to an Alleged Crime Boss', *Financial Times*, 14 July 2006.
42. Glenny, *McMafia*, 97.
43. Glenny, *McMafia*, 94. Mogilevich was 'a powerful man and close associate' of the Solntsevo mafia of Moscow and operated in Moscow and most of CIS, including Ukraine, Israel, the USA and England. The crimes involved arms trade, contraband cigarettes, the Heating Oil Scandal that hit Europe in the 1990s, money laundering and fraud in gas and oil trade, through ETG, among other scams, see Glenny, *McMafia*, 88–89.
44. Ibid.; Boris Nemtsov and Vladimir Milov, see Борис Немцов and Владимир Милов, Путин и Газпром (Москва, 2008).
45. Matuszak, 'The Oligarchic Democracy'.
46. Ibid.
47. Glenny, *McMafia*, 94.
48. Ibid., 94–95.
49. Ibid., 95.
50. Nemtsov and Milov, see Немцов and Милов, Путин и Газпром.
51. Glenny, *McMafia*, 112.

52. Ibid., 96.
53. Nemtsov and Milov, see Немцов and Милов, Путин и Газпром, 16.
54. Victor Chyvokunya, 'RosUkrEnergo – Matryoshka Firtash-Fursin', 27 April 2006, at: www.pravda.com.ua/articles/2006/04/27/3100046/; Tom Warner, 'RosUkrEnergo Hits at Critics by Naming Owners', *The Financial Times*, 27 April 2006, at: www.ft.com/cms/s/0/bc326650-d58a-11da-93bc-0000779e2340.html#axzz1YlE6Hpkx.
55. Warner, 'RosUkrEnergo Hits at Critics by Naming Owners'.
56. Nemtsov and Milov, see Немцов and Милов, Путин и Газпром, 17.
57. Warner, 'RosUkrEnergo Hits at Critics by Naming Owners'.
58. The participant organisations were: BSEC, CE, CEI, CIS, EAPC, EBRD, ECE, GUUAM, IAEA, IBRD, ICAO, ICC, ICCt (signatory), ICRM, IFC, IFRCS, IHO, ILO, IMF, IMO, Interpol, IOC, IOM, ISO, ITU, MONUC, NAM (observer), NSG, OAS (observer), OPCW, OSCE, PCA, PFP, UN, UNAMSIL, UNCTAD, UNESCO, UNIDO, UNIFIL, UNMEE, UNMIBH, UNMIK, UNMOP, UNMOT, UNMOVIC, UPU, WCL, WCO, WFTU, WHO, WIPO, WMO, WToO, WTrO (observer) and ZC; see CIA, 'The World Factbook', (2003), at: www.cia.gov/library/publications/resources/the-world-factbook/index.html/.
59. Wilson, *Virtual Politics*.
60. 'Ukraine, Parliamentary Elections', OECD: Final Report, 31 March 2002. The Norwegian Centre for Human Rights/NORDEM (2009) 'Ukraine: Parlimetary Elections', (2006), at: www.jus.uio.no/smr/english/about/programmes/nordem/publications/2006/1106.pdf.
61. CIA, 'The World Factbook'.
62. Bondarenko, see Константин Бондаренко, Леонид Кучма (Харьков: Фолио, 2009), 145.
63. Kovaleva, 'Regional Politics in Ukraine's Transition', 64–65.
64. D. Mendeleyev, 'Украина: Именем «РосУкрЭнерго»...' ['Ukraine: In the Name Of RosUkrEnergo ...'], 4 February 2011, at: https://zn.ua/POLITICS/ukraina_imenem_rosukrenergo.html.
65. Kovaleva, 'Regional Politics in Ukraine's Transition', 64–65.
66. Ibid.
67. Ibid.
68. A. Åslund, 'Problems with Economic Transformation in Ukraine'. Testimony at the Fifth Dubrovnik Conference on Transition Economies (1999), at: http://carnegieendowment.org/1999/06/23/problems-with-economic-transformation-in-ukraine-pub-60.
69. Harvey, *The New Imperialism*.
70. Glenny, *McMafia*, 92–94.
71. Mendeleev, see Дмитрий Менделеев, 'Украина: «Именем «РосУкрЭнерго»...», Зеркало недели (2011), at: http://zn.ua/articles/74825.
72. Taras Kuzio, Kuzio, 'The Opposition's Road to Success', *Journal of Democracy* 16(2) (2005): 117–130.
73. Ibid.
74. Ukrstat, 'Gross Domestic Product by Production Method and Gross Value Added by Type of Economic Activity'.
75. Åslund, 'Problems with Economic Transformation in Ukraine'.
76. Ibid.

77. O. Korniyevskyi, 'Unemployment in Ukraine: Estimates and Forecasts', *Ukrainian Center for Economic and Political Studies* (2000), at: www.uceps.com. ua/ eng/all/journal/2000_2/html/27.shtml.

78. Y.F. Kravchenko, 'People's Trust is the Highest Appraisal of the Work of Police', *Kiev Imenem Zakonu* (December 1997), 5.

79. Donatella della Porta and Mario Diani, *Social Movements: An Introduction* (Oxford: Blackwell Publishers, 1999).

80. Vlad Mykhnenko, 'State, Society and Protest Under Post-Communism: Ukrainian Miners and their Defeat', in C. Mudde and P. Kopecký (eds), *Uncivil Society?: Contentious Politics in Eastern Europe* (London: Routledge, 2003), 94–97.

81. Ibid., 95.

82. F.D. Zastavnyi, Географія України (Львів: Світ, 1990), 262.

83. Goskomstat SSSR (1993: 16), quoted in Mykhnenko, 'State, Society and Protest Under Post-Communism', 95.

84. H. Kuromiya, *Freedom and Terror in the Donbas* (Cambridge: Cambridge University Press, 1998).

85. G. Smith and A. Wilson, 'Rethinking Russia's Post-Soviet Diaspora: The Potential for Political Mobilisation in Eastern Ukraine and North-East Estonia', *Europe-Asia Studies* 49(5) (1997), 847.

86. Mykhnenko, 'State, Society and Protest Under Post-Communism', 95–96.

87. S. Crowley, 'Coal Miners and the Transformation of the USSR', *Post-Soviet Affairs* 13(2) (1997): 167–195; L.H. Siegelbaum, 'Freedom of Prices and the Price of Freedom: The Miners' Dilemma in the Soviet Union and Its Successor States', *Journal of Communist Studies* 13(4) (1997): 1–27.

88. T.B. Reshetilova, B.L. Raihel and S.V. Poliakov, угольная Промышленность в Развитии Производительных Сил Украины [*Coal Industry in Evolution of Productive Power of Ukraine*] (Moscow: Moscow State Mining University Press, 1997), 103.

89. Sarzhan (1998: 163) in Mykhnenko, 'State, Society and Protest Under Post-Communism', 96.

90. K. Zimmer, 'Trapped in Past Glory: Self-Identification and Self-Symbolisation in the Donbass', in Adam Swain (ed.), *Re-Constructing the Post-Soviet Industrial Region: The Donbas in Transition* (Abingdon: Routledge, 2007).

91. L.H. Siegelbaum and D.J. Walkowitz (eds), *Workers of the Donbass Speak: Survival and Identity in the New Ukraine, 1989–1992* (Albany, NY: State University of New York Press, 1995), 121–122.

92. Anatolii Rusnachenko, *Probudzhennia: Robitnychyi rukh na Ukraiini v 1989–1993 rokakh* (Kyiv: KM Academia Publishing House, 1995), 68.

5. NEOLIBERAL KLEPTOCRACY, FDI AND TRANSNATIONAL CAPITAL

1. Kuchma is famed for being an advanced cards player with Preferans (a popular Eastern European game similar to poker) being his favourite.

2. Misha Glenny, *McMafia: Crime Without Frontiers* (London: Bodley Head, 2008), 108.

3. Ibid., 108–109.

4. M. Bromley, *United Nations Arms Embargoes: Their Impact on Arms Flows and Target. Behaviour Case Study: Former Yugoslavia, 1991–96* (Stockholm International Peace Research Institute, 2007), 12.

5. iWatch News, 'Special Report: Kuchma Approved Sale of Weapons System to Iraq', The Centre for Public Integrity: *iWatch News*, 15 April 2002, at: www. iwatchnews.org/2002/04/15/3197/special-report-kuchma-approved-sale-weapons-system-iraq.

6. Jonathan Marcus, 'What Ukraine's Kolchuga Radar Does', *BBC World News*, 14 October 2002, at: http://news.bbc.co.uk/1/hi/world/europe/2326451.stm.

7. Glenny, *McMafia*, 100.

8. Ibid.

9. P. van Niekerk and A. Verlöy, *Kuchma Approved Sale of Weapons System to Iraq*. Washington, DC: Public Integrity Project, 15 April 2002, at: http://projects. publicintegrity.org/report.aspx?aid=209. Also, as a result of an investigation conducted by the FBI, the authenticity of other fragments of the tapes has been acknowledged by the US government and the sale of the high-technology anti-airplane radar system Kolchuga to Iraq in 2000 was confirmed (Taras Kuzio, '"Pro-Ukrainian" or "Pro-Kuchma"?: Ukraine's Foreign Policy in Crisis', *RFE/RL Newsline* 6[79], 26 April 2002). The lawmaker, Oleksandr Zhyr, reported that on 3 March 2002, Kuchma was informed that the parliamentary commission that led the investigation had undeniable evidence of his involvement in the Kolchuga sale (van Niekerk and Verlöy, *Kuchma Approved Sale of Weapons System to Iraq*). A mere three days later, Malev, the Chief of the State Arms Exporting agency, Ukrspetseksport, was killed in a car crash. Zhyr claims that the accident was premeditated and needs to be investigated in the light of the Kolchuga scandal (van Niekerk and Verlöy, *Kuchma Approved Sale of Weapons System to Iraq*). Moreover, he claims that it was suspiciously similar to the one that killed Chornovil a few years earlier. On 9 April 2002, *The New York Times* wrote that, since 1997, six people had been killed and two injured in car accidents in Ukraine, who all have 'threatened the established power structure' (van Niekerk and Verlöy, *Kuchma Approved Sale of Weapons System to Iraq*).

10. Wilson, *Virtual Politics*.

11. The newspaper was one of the few independent anti-Kuchma publications in Ukraine. One more example is *The Kyiv Post*, a Kyiv-based Anglophone newspaper. The latter also released many critical articles about Kuchma, however, their American expatriate owner, Jed Sunden, was dealt with differently. In 2000, after a series of 'harassing inspections' of *Kyiv Post* by the tax police, he was pronounced persona non-grata without explanation and would have had to leave Ukraine if not for, as he himself said, 'some diplomatic wrangling' (*Kyiv Post*, 19 October 2005). It appeared that Kuchma and his cronies could still be slapped on the hand, at least by US officials. Gongadze's case was different; he was a Georgia-born Ukrainian and could not secure the same diplomatic protection as Sunden.

12. BBC World News, 'Ukraine Finds "Reporter's Skull"', 28 July 2009, at: http:// news.bbc.co.uk/1/hi/world/europe/8173441.stm.

13. Roman Olearchuk, 'Ex-Leader Focus of Ukraine Scandal', *The Financial Times*, 1 April 2011.

14. BBC World News, 'Ukraine Finds "Reporter's Skull"'.

15. ForUm, 'Страшные подробности смерти Кравченко', 23 April 2007, at: http://for-ua.com/ukraine/2007/04/23/112635.html.

16. Taras Kuzio, 'Oligarchs, Tapes and Oranges: "Kuchmagate" to the Orange Revolution', *Journal of Communist Studies and Transition Politics* 23(1) (2007): 30–56.

17. The supporters built a protest camp on Maidan Nezalezhnosti on 15 December and later 'led a 5,000-strong pack of protesters from Maidan to the Verkhovna Rada, and then on to the Presidential Administration on December 19' (Kuzio, 'Oligarchs, Tapes and Oranges'). Under the pretext of street reconstruction works, the camp forced to leave on 27 December, however, it was rebuilt on 14 January 2001, only to be removed again, this time by force, on 1 March. The protests were supported by a newly created public committee, 'For Truth!', established on 19 December 2000 and led by former political activists of the early 1990s – in Lviv (led by Markiyan Ivanyshyn), in Kyiv (Oles' Doniy and Vyachslav Kyrylenko), in Kharkiv (Yevheniy Zolotaryov), in Rivne (Mykola Lyakhevych; Bondarenko, see Константин Бондаренко, Леонид Кучма [Харьков: Фолио, 2009], 128).

18. Istorychna Pravda, see Українська Правда, '9 березня 2001 року: спогади активіста', Історична правда, 3 March 2011, at: www.istpravda.com.ua/blogs/2011/03/9/30359/.

19. Pond, *The Rebirth of Europe*, 151.

20. B. Balanya et al., *Europe Inc.: Regional and Global Restructuring and the Rise of Corporate Power* (London: Pluto Press, 2003), 29.

21. Andriy Pekhnyk, see Андрій Пехник, Іноземні інвестиції в економіку України: навчальний посібник (Київ: Знання, 2007), 42–44.

22. Ibid., 43.

23. Ibid. 43–44.

24. Boris Lanovyk, see Борис Лановик, З. Матисякевич, *and* Роман Матейко. Економічна історія України і світу (Київ: Вікар, 2006), 462.

25. Pekhnyk, see Пехник, Іноземні інвестиції в економіку України, 44.

26. Robert W. Cox and Timothy J. Sinclair, *Approaches to World Order* (Cambridge: Cambridge University Press, 1996), 37.

27. Henk Overbeek and Kees van der Pijl, 'Restructuring Capital and Restructuring Hegemony: Neo-liberalism and the Unmaking of the Post-War Order', in Henk Overbeek (ed.), *Restructuring Hegemony in the Global Political Economy: The Rise of Transnational Neo-Liberalism in the 1980s* (London: Routledge, 1993), 1–28.

28. William K. Carroll, *The Making of a Transnational Capitalist Class: Corporate Power in the 21st Century* (London: Zed Books, 2010), 37.

29. Overbeek and van der Pijl, 'Restructuring Capital and Restructuring Hegemony', 3.

30. Carroll, *The Making of a Transnational Capitalist Class*, 38–56.

31. Ibid., 36–56.

32. Ibid., 50.

33. Kees van der Pijl, Otto Holman and Or Raviv, 'The Resurgence of German Capital in Europe: EU Integration and the Restructuring of Atlantic Networks of Interlocking Directorates after 1991', *Review of International Political Economy* 18(3) (2011): 384–408.

34. Karl Marx, *The Communist Manifesto: Principles of Communism* (New York: Monthly Review Press, 1964 [1848]).

35. For a detailed study of ERT's role in shaping EU policies, see Bastiaan van Apeldoorn, *Transnational Capitalism and the Struggle over European Integration* (London: Routledge, 2003), *inter alia*.

36. Balanya et al., *Europe Inc.*, 28–29; 65.
37. EBA General.
38. Ibid.
39. Ibid.
40. EBA AGM 2009.
41. Ibid.
42. EBA Staff 2010.
43. Ibid.
44. Ibid.
45. EBA Board 2009.
46. EBA Brussels 2010.
47. EBA Eurodrinks 2011.
48. EBA Eurodebates 2011.
49. Ibid.
50. EBA Investors Council 2008.
51. Ibid.
52. EBA FIAC 2010.
53. Ibid.
54. Ibid.
55. Cabinet of Ministers of Ukraine (2007; updated 2014) 'Проект постанови Кабінету Міністрів України "Про внесення змін у додатки 4 та 5 до постанови Кабінету Міністрів України від 25 грудня 2013 р. № 950"' ('Draft the Draft Resolution of the Cabinet of Ministers of Ukraine [hereinafter – the CMU] "On Amendments to Annexes 4 and 5 to the Resolution of the Cabinet of Ministers of Ukraine dated 25 December 2013 №950"'), at: www.me.gov.ua/Documents/Detail?title=ProektPostanoviKabinetuMinistrivUkrain iproVnesenniaZminUDodatki4-Ta5-DoPostanoviKabinetuMinistrivUkraini Vid25-Grudnia2013-R950-
56. EBA General.
57. Ibid.
58. EBA Services.
59. EBA Lobbying.
60. Ibid.
61. EBA Lobbying Club Form.
62. EBA Lobbying Successes.
63. Ibid.
64. ACC/AmCham.
65. Ibid.
66. Ibid.
67. Ibid.
68. National Endowment for Democracy, About.
69. CIPE, Mission and background.
70. Balanya et al., *Europe Inc.*, 45.
71. ACC History.
72. E. Pond, *The Rebirth of Europe* (Washington, DC: Brookings Institution Press, 2002), 146.
73. See Pekhnyk, Пехник, Іноземні інвестиції в економіку України, 42–44 and Chapter 6 of this book.
74. ACC History.
75. Ibid.

76. Ihor Figlus in 2012 and Bohdan Kupych in 2012. See 'American Chamber of Commerce in Ukraine's Jorge Zukoski will Leave at Year's End', *Kyiv Post*, 19 September 2013, at: www.kyivpost.com/article/content/ukraine-politics/ president-of-american-chamber-of-commerce-in-ukraine-jorge-zukoski-decides-to-resign-by-year-end-329518.html.

77. ACC History.

78. Ibid.

79. Ibid.

80. Ibid.

81. Ibid.

82. Ibid.

83. ACC Code of Conduct.

84. Ibid.

85. ACC Mission and Vision.

86. Ibid.

87. USUBC Membership.

88. USUBC, About (2011).

89. Ibid.

90. J.F. Reilly, C.C. Hull and B.A.B. Allen, 'IRC 501(c)(6) Organizations'. Exempt Organizations-Technical Instruction Program for FY 2003. Internal Revenue Service, USA, at: www.irs.gov/pub/irs-tege/eotopic03.pdf, 3.

91. Ibid., 8.

92. Ibid., 14.

93. Ibid., 23.

94. Ibid., 3.

95. USUBC By-Laws, 'US-Ukraine Business Council Articles and By-Laws', (2011), at: www.usubc.org/site/u-s-ukraine-business-council-usubc-articles-by-laws.

96. USUBC Mission, 'U.S.-Ukraine Business Council (USUBC) Mission', (2011), at: www.usubc.org/site/u-s-ukraine-business-council-usubc-mission.

97. USUBC Key Issues, 'Key Issues', (2011), at: www.usubc.org/site/key-issues/key-issues-archive/.

98. USUBC, 'The Impact of Global Liquidity Crisis in Ukraine and the Road to Economic Recovery', 1st Annual International Forum on the Economic Development of Ukraine Newseum, Washington, DC, Thursday, 15 October 2011. Minutes available at: www.usubc.org/site/economic-data-analysis/the-impact-of-the-global-liquidity-crisis-in-ukraine-and-the-road-to-economic-recovery-2.

99. See USUBC (2010–2011) Action Ukraine Reports (Archive), at: www.usubc.org/site/action-ukraine-report-aur.

100. CUSUR, 'History: How It All Started' (2017), at: http://usukrainianrelations.org/.

101. Ibid.

102. CUSUR (2000) 'US, Ukrainian Foreign Ministers Press Availability Transcript' (Economic Reform, Kharkiv Initiative, KFOR/Peacekeeping, Trafficking, START II, ABM Treaty, Chernobyl). Distributed by the Office of International Information Programs, US Department of State, at: http://usukrainianrelations.org/index.php?option=com_content&task=view&id=221.

103. CUSUR, 'History: How It All Started'.

104. Ibid. Also see UCCA, 'History', at: http://ucca.org/ucca/index.php?option=com_content&view=article&id=13&Itemid=10&lang=en.

105. CUSUR, 'History: How It All Started'.
106. USUBC Roundtables.
107. Ibid.
108. Ibid.
109. CUSUR Mission (2011) 2.
110. Ibid., 1
111. Ibid.
112. Ibid., 2.
113. Ibid.
114. A. Kovalchuk, 'Peculiarities of national lobbying', *Forbes*, 13 June 2014, at: http://forbes.net.ua/ua/magazine/forbes/1372294-osoblivosti-nacionalnogo-lobizmu.
115. Elena Kovaleva, 'Regional Politics in Ukraine's Transition: The Donetsk Elite', in Adam Swain (ed.), *Re-Constructing the Post-Soviet Industrial Region: The Donbas in Transition* (London: Routledge, 2007), 72–73.
116. Andriy Pekhnyk, see Андрій Пехник, Іноземні інвестиції в економіку України: навчальний посібник (Київ: Знання, 2007), 44.
117. Pekhnyk, see Пехник, Іноземні інвестиції в економіку України, 45.
118. Ibid.
119. Ibid.
120. Bloomberg, 'Company Overview of System Capital Management Limited', (2017), at: www.bloomberg.com/research/stocks/private/snapshot.asp?privcapid=49700742.
121. W. Carlin, S. Estrin and M. Schaffer, *Measuring Progress in Transition and Towards EU Accession: A Comparison of Manufacturing Firms in Poland, Romania, and Spain*. WP 40 (London: EBRD, 1999).
122. A. Lyakh, 'The Evolution of the Industrial Structure in Donetsk Region', in Adam Swain (ed.), *Re-Constructing the Post-Soviet Industrial Region: The Donbas in Transition* (London: Routledge, 2007), 78–96.
123. Institute of Strategic Studies [Інститут Стратегічних Досліджень], 'Кіпрський Офшор «По-Новому»' ['Cypriot Offshore "The New Way"'], 17 September 2012, at: http://ukrstrategy.com/uk/analitika/item/51-kipr-po-novomu.html.

6. 'TWO UKRAINES', ONE 'FAMILY' AND GEOPOLITICAL CROSSROADS

1. Taras Kuzio, 'The Opposition's Road to Success', *Journal of Democracy* 16(2) (2005): 117–130.
2. S. Wagstyl and T. Warner, 'Ukraine has been Transformed by the Political Turmoil of Recent Months', *The Financial Times*, 21 December 2004.
3. Kuzio, 'The Opposition's Road to Success'.
4. Andrew Wilson, *Ukraine's Orange Revolution* (New Haven, CT: Yale University Press, 2005).
5. Kuzio, 'The Opposition's Road to Success', 130.
6. In an interview with Marta Shokalo, 'Хто такі олігархи і чи слід їх боятися' ['Who Are Oligarchs and Would One Fear Them?'], BBC (2008), at: www.bbc.com/ukrainian/indepth/story/2008/03/080311_marta_chaynyk3_oh.shtml.

7. Yuliya Yurchenko, 'The Role and Locus of Mass Media in the Orange Revolution in Ukraine', Conference paper, Newcastle University EU Postgraduate Conference (2008).

8. Information vacuum was a phrase suggested by Iryna Pohorelova (a journalist from the Glasnost era, who never submitted to censorship; in 2004 – freelancer for a number of media including *Ukrayinska Pravda*) and Natalia Ligacheva (founder and editor of the Telekritika website) in a personal interviews conducted on 20 June and 22 July correspondingly in Kyiv.

9. Ibid.

10. V. Ivanov, *Kratkiy Obzor Ukrainskih Media*, (2004), at: www.aup.com.ua/upload/1100609203UeberMediensituationUA_ua.pdf, 20.

11. Marta Dyczok, 'Breaking Through the Information Blockade: Elections and Revolution in Ukraine 2004', *Canadian Slavonic Papers* 47(3–4) (2005), 241.

12. Ibid., 247. This account is based on 'Bigmir.net Estimated the Size of Ukraine's Internet Audience', *Sputnik Media*, 4 November 2004, at: http://sputnikmedia.net/news/330; and 'In December the Size of Internet Audience Grew by Six Percent and Reached 5.9 Million Ukrainians', *Sputnik Media*, 11 January 2005.

13. Ibid.

14. Dyczok, 'Breaking Through the Information Blockade', 245.

15. Wagstyl and Warner, 'Ukraine has been Transformed by the Political Turmoil of Recent Months'.

16. See Ukrainian Monitor, Media Monitoring Project, Final Report Summary, (2004), at: http://prostir-monitor.org/all_rez.php?arh_data=98; AUP and Institute of Sociology, Monitoring of Political News.

17. Dyczok, 'Breaking Through the Information Blockade', 248.

18. For more details, see D. Kolodiy, *The Orange Chronicles* (Maplewood, NJ: DK Productions, 2007).

19. Central Electoral Commission, 'Presidential Election Results, 2004', (2004), at: www.cvk.gov.ua/pls/vp2004/wp0011.

20. BBC World News, 'Poll Dispute Sparks Ukraine Rally', 22 November 2004, at: http://news.bbc.co.uk/1/hi/world/europe/4031127.stm.

21. A. Karatnyky, 'The Fall and Rise of Ukraine's Political Opposition: From Kuchmagate to the Orange Revolution', in Anders Åslund and Michael McFaul (eds), *Revolution in Orange: The Origins of Ukraine's Democratic Breakthrough*. Washington, DC: Carnegie Endowment for International Peace, 2006), 38–39.

22. Andrew Wilson, *Virtual Politics: Faking Democracy in the Post-Soviet World*, 1st edn (New Haven, CT: Yale University Press, 2005), 107. Some of the most staggering facts of electoral fraud documented in Wilson, *Virtual Politics*, 105–121 were:

> (1) Serhii Kivalov, head of Central Electoral Commission responsible for collection, count, and announcing of results of elections, 'supplied a secret Yanukovych team housed in the Zoriany cinema … with accessed passwords to the Commission's computer base' and thus Zoriany team, not the Commission, counted the votes. The conversations were recorded by SBU where both candidates had their supporters and the tapes made their way to Yushchenko's right-hand man, Ryabachuk almost immediately. As one of the Commission members Ruslan Kniazevych confirmed in his testimony to the Supreme Court on 2 December 2004, 'a million votes [1.1 million to be precise] were thrown in after 8 o'clock' – the time when the polls closed. Half of the above votes were supposedly cast in Donetsk oblast' – home of

Yanukovych. There 'turnout shot up from 83.7 to 96.6% ... or an extra 511,780 votes, of which 96.2% were ... [for] Yanukovych'.

(2) Blatant intimidation of voters, 'padding the turnout with "dead souls" [voters still on the list yet not alive anymore] ... and "cookies" (extra ballot paper)' ... and a "carousel technology" [where voters go to multiple polling stations with premarked fake ballots] ask for genuine ballots, deposit the fake, and move on'.

(3) Absentee voting fraud; provided for the invalids, in some places, for example, Mykolyiv reached 30 per cent that was far beyond a realistic number.

(4) An invention called 'electoral tourism'. The interior minister, Bilokon, issued a directive in May 2004 stipulating that in the forthcoming elections it was not necessary to register with authorities in order to cast vote in other than one's designated polling station. According to various estimates, some 1.5–2 million votes were cast by 'electoral tourists'. The then Minister of Transportation, Hryhorii Kirpa, provided 125 additional trains over the period of October–November 2004 paid for by the Party of Regions, Russian Orthodox associations, and various private enterprises. The trains were used to transport absentee ballots, 'electoral tourists', and support anti-Yushchenko propaganda campaign.

23. H. Fawkes, 'Battle Lines Drawn in Ukraine Vote', *BBC World News*, 20 November 2004, at: http://news.bbc.co.uk/1/hi/world/europe/4029347.stm.

24. International Elections Observatory Mission/OSCE, 21 November 2004, see details at: www.osce.org/odihr/elections/2004.

25. S. Wagstyl and T. Warner, 'Ukraine has been Transformed by the Political Turmoil of Recent Months', *The Financial Times*, 21 December 2004.

26. European Integration Committee/Verkhovna Rada (2004).

27. Ukrstat, 'Gross Domestic Product by Production Method and Gross Value Added by Type of Economic Activity', (2011), at: www.ukrstat.gov.ua/operativ/operativ2008/vvp/vvp_ric/vtr_e.htm.

28. KMU, 'Inaugural Address of the President of Ukraine Victor Yushchenko to the Ukrainian People on Independence Square', (2005), at: www.kmu.gov.ua/control/en/publish/article?art_id=11100895.

29. Wilson, *Virtual Politics*, 114.

30. Ukraine, Verkhovna Rada of Ukraine, Law 'Про загальні засади створення і функціонування спеціальних (вільних) економічних зон', 17 February 2006, at: http://zakon2.rada.gov.ua/laws/show/2673-12.

31. Andriy Pekhnyk, see Андрій Пехник, Іноземні інвестиції в економіку України: навчальний посібник (Київ: Знання, 2007). See also Ukraine, Verkhovna Rada of Ukraine, Law 'Закон України. Про внесення змін до Закону України "Про Державний бюджет України на 2005 рік" та деяких інших законодавчих актів України N2505-IV', 2005.

32. Makohon (NISS, Donetsk), '"Нові форми організації територій з особливим податковим режимом (СЕЗ і ТПР)". Аналітична записка', *National Institute of Strategic Studies*, 2005.

33. Victor Chyvokunya, 'RosUkrEnergo – Matryoshka Firtash-Fursin', 27 April 2006, at: www.pravda.com.ua/articles/2006/04/27/3100046/; Tom Warner, 'RosUkrEnergo Hits at Critics by Naming Owners', *The Financial Times*, 27 April 2006, at: www.ft.com/cms/s/0/bc326650-d58a-11da-93bc-0000779e2340.html#axzz1YlE6Hpkx. In 2006, PriceWaterHouseCoopers, auditor of

RosUkrEnergo, identified in their report Firtash 'as 90 per cent owner and [Fursin – another Ukrainian businessman] as 10 per cent owner of Centragas Holding, an Austrian-registered company that owns the 50 per cent stake'. Founded in 2005, RosUkrEnergo is an intermediary that in 2005 already received \$478 million in revenue payment from Gazprom and '[that by 2006 supplied] gas worth about \$10bn (€8bn, £5.6bn) a year at current prices, with two-thirds going to Ukraine and the rest to the European Union'.

34. 'US Embassy Cables: Gas Supplies Linked to Russian Mafia', *The Guardian*, 1 December 2010, leaked cables from 10 December 2008, at: www.theguardian.com/world/us-embassy-cables-documents/182121.

35. Quoted in 'Ukraine has a New PM – Yuriy Yekhanurov', CBC, 22 September 2005, at: www.cbc.ca/news/world/ukraine-has-a-new-pm-yuriy-yekhanurov-1.553729.

36. His path began in a troubled family, his young life was equally troubled (he was imprisoned twice), he married a woman from a family with party connections and after that his convictions were written off and his career had witnessed a spectacular flight.

37. Adam Swain, 'Yanukovich Hits the Campaign Trail Early Ukraine Election', *Financial Times*, 10 December 2004.

38. Fatherland Party (Tymoshenko/Turchynov), Ukrainian Republican Party 'Sobor' (Matviyenko/Omelchenko), Ukrainian Social Democratic Party (Lukyanenko). Source: BYuT, Fatherland Party (2006) Statute, at: http://ba.org.ua/.

39. Nemtsov and Milov: Немцов and Владимир Милов, Путин и Газпром, 17.

40. Minfin, 'State Debt', (2016), at: www.minfin.gov.ua/news/borg/derzhavnij-borg.

41. O. Kravchuk, 'History of Ukraine's Debt Dependency Formation', *Commons*, 30 April 2015, at: http://commons.com.ua/formuvannya-zalezhnosti/.

42. Ibid.

43. Ibid.

44. Ibid.

45. Ukraine State Treasury (2002).

46. Ministry of Finance.

47. The National Bank of Ukraine/NBU (2001–2017) 'Law of Ukraine on the National Bank of Ukraine'. Full evolution and amendements archive can be viewed at: https://bank.gov.ua/doccatalog/document?id=47478.

48. The Party of Regions (2011).

49. 'Top 100 Most Influential People of Ukraine. 2011'. *Korrespondent*, 31 August 2012, at: http://files.korrespondent.net/projects/top100/2011.

50. 'Золотая сотня: полный список самых богатых людей Украины' ['The Golden Hundred: Full list of the Richest People of Ukraine'], *Korrespondent*, 9 June 2011, at: http://korrespondent.net/business/1227140-zolotaya-sotnya-polnyj-spisok-samyh-bogatyh-lyudej-ukrainy.

51. M. Balmaceda, *On the Edge: Ukrainian – Central European – Russian Security Triangle* (Budapest: Akaprint, 2000), and *Energy Dependency, Politics and Corruption in the Former Soviet Union, Russia's Power, Oligarchs' Profits and Ukraine's Missing Energy Policy, 1995–2006* (London: Routledge, 2008).

52. Yuliya Yurchenko, 'Black Holes in the Political Economy of Ukraine: The Neoliberalisation of Europe's "Wild East"', *Debatte* April 2013.

53. Adam Swain and Vlad Mykhnenko, 'The Ukrainian Donbas in "Transition"', in Adam Swain (ed.), *Re-Constructing the Post-Soviet Industrial Region: The Donbas in Transition* (London: Routledge, 2007), 40.

54. Yurchenko, 'IMF, Ukraine and the Toxic Debt Dependency' *Third World Thematic* – Special Issue edited by Andreas Antoniades on 'Global Debt Dynamics: Crises, Lessons, Governance', forthcoming 2018.

55. Martijn Konings (ed.), *The Great Credit Crash* (London: Verso, 2010); A. Nesvetailova, *Financial Alchemy in Crisis: The Great Liquidity Illusion* (London: Pluto Press, 2010); Or Raviv, 'Chasing the Dragon East: Exploring the Frontiers of Western European Finance', *Contemporary Politics* 14(3) (2008): 297–314.

56. Yurchenko, 'Black Holes in the Political Economy of Ukraine'.

57. Gaztek is legally owned by the Cypriot companies Porala Venchers Limited, Pasler Enterprises Limited, Nesiba Venchers Limited and Krezer Holdings Limited that are linked to Firtash.

58. 'Фірташ прикупив собі 26% ще й Тисменицягазу' ['Firtash Added 26% of Tysmennytsiagaz to His Portfolio'], *UNIAN*, 13 September 2012, at: www.unian.ua/politics/693515-firtash-prikupiv-sobi-26-sche-y-tismenitsyagazu.html.

59. Verkhovna Rada, 'Ruling on Realisation of Imported Gas on the Territory of Ukraine #163' from 8 March 2008, last amended on 3 October 2012, at: http://zakon3.rada.gov.ua/laws/show/163-2008-%D0%BF.

60. M. van der Hoeven, 'Energy Policies beyond IEA Countries: Ukraine 2012, Review'. OECD Report (2012).

61. Euracoal, Annual Report (2012), at: https://euracoal2.org/download/Public-Archive/.../EURACOAL-Annual-Report-2012.pdf.

62. 'На инвесторов повеяло теплом: Украинские ТЭЦ отдадут в частные руки' ['Investors are Warming Up: Ukrainian Thermal Power Stations to Be Privatised'], *Kommersant*, 23 January 2012, at: www.kommersant.ru/doc/1856938.

63. 'Интересы в тепле: Государство начинает приватизацию ТЭЦ' ['Interests in Heating: State Commences Privatisation'], *Kommersant Ukrayina*, 8 October 2012, at: www.kommersant.ru/doc/2046882.

64. 'На инвесторов повеяло теплом: Украинские ТЭЦ отдадут в частные руки' ['Investors are Warming Up: Ukrainian Thermal Power Stations to Be Privatised'], *Kommersant Ukrayina*, 23 January 2012, at: www.kommersant.ru/doc/185693; 'Страну готовят к распродаже: Государство избавится от 1200 предприятий' ['The Country is Readied for a Sale: Government Will Get Rid of 12000 SOEs'], *Kommersant Ukrayina*, 26 September 2012, at: www.kommersant.ru/doc/2030491.

65. Ibid.

66. 'Депутати благословили вільні економічні зони' ['MPs Gave Their Blessing to Create New Free Economic Zones'], *ePravda*, 6 September 2012, at: www.epravda.com.ua/news/2012/09/6/334292/.

67. 'Интересы в тепле' ['Interests in Heating'], *Kommersant Ukrayina*.

68. Арьев: Янукович помиловал Луценко, поскольку не смог договориться с Россией' ['Aryev: Yanukovych pardoned Lutsenko as could not Reach Agreement with Russia'], *Censor.net*, 8 April 2013, at: https://censor.net.ua/news/238335/arev_yanukovich_pomiloval_lutsenko_poskolku_ne_smog_dogovoritsya_s_rossieyi.

69. W. Easterly, *The White Man's Burden: Why the West's Efforts to Aid the Rest Have Done so Much Ill and so Little Good* (New York: Penguin Press, 2006).
70. 'Press Freedom: Too Many Attacks go Unpunished'. Report. Transparency International (2012) at: www.transparency.org/news/feature/too_many_attacks_on_journalists_and_press_freedom_go_unpunished.
71. Die Frankfurter Allgemeine Zeitung, 'Das Prinzip Familie', 27 August 2012, at: www.faz.net/aktuell/politik/ausland/praesident-janukowitsch-das-prinzip-familie-11870003.html.

7. THE BLOODY WINTER AND THE 'GATES OF EUROPE'

1. I refer to the events known as 'the Revolution of Dignity' as 'the Bloody Winter'. The latter is my own term, suggested and preferred to the former, which I consider to be a misnomer. First, there was no revolution. Second, there certainly has not been a revolution of dignity. And last, the conduct of the involved actors in the events of the winter 2013–2014 needs to be scrutinised and investigated in the guise of many unresolved crimes (murder, beating, torture, kidnappings, etc.) the very existence of which puts into question appropriateness of 'the Revolution of Dignity' as a name.
2. Reference here is made to Serhii Plokhy, *The Gates of Europe* (London: Penguin, 2015).
3. Plokhy, *The Gates of Europe*.
4. Amat Adarov and Peter Havlik 'Benefits and Costs of DCFTA: Evaluation of the Impact on Georgia, Moldova and Ukraine', Wiener Institut für Internationale Wirtschaftsvergleiche (WIIW) working paper, 20 January 2017, at: https://wiiw.ac.at/benefits-and-costs-of-dcfta-evaluation-of-the-impact-on-georgia-moldova-and-ukraine-n-191.html.
5. Ibid.
6. Ibid.
7. Ibid.
8. Mykola Ryzhenkov, Svitlana Galko, Veronika Movchan and Jörg Radeke, 'The Impact of the EU-Ukraine DCFTA on Agricultural Trade', German–Ukrainian Agricultural Policy Dialogue (October, 2013).
9. Ibid.
10. Ibid., 3.
11. William K. Carroll, *The Making of a Transnational Capitalist Class: Corporate Power in the 21st Century* (London: Zed Books, 2010); William I. Robinson, 'Social Theory and Globalization: The Rise of a Transnational State', *Theory and Society* 30(2) (2001): 157–200, 'Global Capitalism and Nation-State Centric Thinking: What We Don't See when We Do See Nation-States. Response to Arrighi, Mann, Moore, van der Pijl, and Went', *Science & Society* 65(4) (2002): 500–508, and *A Theory of Global Capitalism: Production, Class and State in a Transnational World* (Baltimore, MD: Johns Hopkins University Press, 2004); Kees van der Pijl, Otto Holman and Or Raviv (2010); Kees van der Pijl and Yuliya Yurchenko, 'Neoliberal Entrenchment of North Atlantic Capital: From Corporate Self-Regulation to State Capture', *New Political Economy* 20(4) (2015): 495–517, among others.
12. Adam Swain and Vlad Mykhnenko (2007) 'The Ukrainian Donbas in "Transition"', in Adam Swain (ed.), *Re-Constructing the Post-Soviet Industrial*

Region: The Donbas in Transition (London: Routledge, 2007), 7–46, among others.

13. Pasquale de Micco, 'When Choosing Means Losing: The Eastern Partners, the EU and the Eurasian Economic Union'. European Parliament, Policy Department, Directorate-General for External Policies, March 2015, at: www.europarl.europa.eu/RegData/etudes/STUD/2015/549026/EXPO_STUD%282015%29549026_EN.pdf.

14. Ibid.

15. Олигархам необходима ЗСТ с Евросоюзом / «Укррудпром», 1 November 2011, at: http://ukrrudprom.ua/news/ Oligarham_neobhodima_ZST_s_Evrosoyuzom.html.

16. The author sent requests to seven (SCM/Akhmetov, Group DF/Firtash, Finance and Credit group/Zhevago, EastOne/Pinchuk, Privat/Kolomoyskyy and Boholyubov, ISD/Taruta, Ukrprominvest/Poroshenko); only three replied.

17. Ibid., 3.

18. Kataryna Wolczuk, 'Managing the Flows of Gas and Rules: Ukraine Between the EU and Russia', *Eurasian Geography and Economics* 57(1) (2016): 113–137.

19. S. Matuszak, 'How Ukrainian oligarchs view economic integration with the EU and Russia', Centre for Eastern Studies. *Eastweek* (2011), at: www.osw.waw.pl/en/publikacje/analyses/2011-09-14/how-ukrainian-oligarchs-view-economic-integration-eu-and-russia.

20. Ibid.

21. Ibid.

22. 'Ukraine-EU Trade Deal "Big Threat" to Russia's Economy', BBC, 26 November 2014, at: www.bbc.co.uk/news/world-europe-25108022.

23. For more on state debt data, see, Minfin, 'Statistical Materials on state and state guaranteed debt of Ukraine', 2 February 2017, at: www.minfin.gov.ua/news/view/statystychni-materialy-shchodo-derzhavnoho-ta-harantovanoho-derzhavoiu-borhu-ukrainy_2016?category=borg&subcategory=statistichna-informacija-schodo-borgu; and Figure 7.1.

24. W. Easterly, *The White Man's Burden: Why the West's Efforts to Aid the Rest Have Done so Much Ill and so Little Good* (New York: Penguin Press, 2006).

25. Ibid.

26. O. Kravchuk, 'History of Ukraine's Debt Dependency Formation', *Commons*, 30 April 2015, at: http://commons.com.ua/formuvannya-zalezhnosti/; and 'Changes in Ukrainian Economy after Maidan', *Commons* (Ukrainian; own translation), 29 June 2016, at: http://commons.com.ua/zmini-v-ukrayinskij-ekonomitsi-pislya-majdanu/.

27. K. Birch and V. Mykhnenko, 'Varieties of Neoliberalism?: Restructuring in Large Industrially Dependent Regions Across Western and Eastern Europe', *Journal of Economic Geography* 9(3) (2009): 355–380.

28. Andriy Pekhnyk, see Андрій Пехник, Іноземні інвестиції в економіку України: навчальний посібник (Київ: Знання, 2007); Yuliya Yurchenko, 'Black Holes in the Political Economy of Ukraine: The Neoliberalisation of Europe's "Wild East"', *Debatte* (April 2013).

29. I. Doroshenko, 'Global Financial Crisis and its Impact on Ukraine's Economic Development' (in Ukrainian). *Problems of a Systemic Approach to The Economy Enterprises* 3 (2008).

30. Ukrstat, 'Gross Domestic Product by Production Method and Gross Value Added by Type of Economic Activity', (2011), at: www.ukrstat.gov.ua/operativ/operativ2008/vvp/vvp_ric/vtr_e.htm.
31. A. Nesvetailova, and R. Palan, 'A Very North Atlantic Credit Crunch: Geopolitical Implications of the Global Liquidity Crisis', in M. Konings (ed.), *The Great Credit Crash* (London: Verso, 2010), 198–222.
32. Ibid., 199.
33. Ibid.
34. Ibid., 199.
35. Ibid., 200 *et passim*.
36. J. Montgomerie, 'Neoliberalism and the Making of Subprime Borrowers', in M. Koning (ed.), *The Great Credit Crash* (London: Verso, 2010), 103–119.
37. J. Becker and J. Jäger, 'Development Trajectories in the Crisis in Europe', *Debatte* 18(1) (2010).
38. H. Huang, D. Marin and C. Hu, 'Financial Crisis, Economic Recovery, and Banking Development in Russia, Ukraine, and Other FSU Countries', *IMF Working Paper* WP/04/105, 2004, at: www.ckgsb.edu.cn/uploads/professor/201607/15/Huang-Marin-Xu_Russia%20WP04_105.pdf, 3.
39. Ibid., 3–4.
40. Ibid., 5.
41. Ibid., 4–5.
42. Gary A. Dymski, 'From Financial Exploitation to Global Instability: Two Overlooked Roots of the Subprime Crisis', in Martijn Konings (ed.), *The Great Credit Crash* (London: Verso, 2010), 73.
43. Ibid., 73 *et passim*.
44. Or Raviv, 'Chasing the Dragon East: Exploring the Frontiers of Western European Finance', *Contemporary Politics* 14(3) (2008), 307.
45. Huang *et al.*, 'Financial Crisis, Economic Recovery, and Banking Development in Russia, Ukraine, and Other FSU Countries'.
46. Doroshenko, 'Global Financial Crisis and its Impact on Ukraine's Economic Development'.
47. Ibid.
48. Ibid.
49. Raviv, 'Chasing the Dragon East', 297.
50. Ibid.
51. S. Barisitz and M. Lahnsteiner, 'Investor Commitment Tested by Deep Crisis: Banking Development in Ukraine'. Oesterreichische Nationalbank, Financial Stability Report, 18 December 2009, 67.
52. Ibid.
53. Ukrstat, Ukrstat, Macroeconomic indicators (2017) at: https://ukrstat.org/en/operativ/oper_new_e.html; Barisitz and Lahnsteiner, 'Investor Commitment Tested by Deep Crisis', 67–68.
54. Doroshenko, 'Global Financial Crisis and its Impact on Ukraine's Economic Development'.
55. Ibid.
56. National Bank of Ukraine (NBU) (2010) Annual Report.
57. Ibid.
58. National Bank of Ukraine (NBU) (2008) Annual Report.
59. Ibid.
60. Becker and Jäger, 'Development Trajectories in the Crisis in Europe', 13.

61. National Bank of Ukraine (NBU) (2005) Annual Report, 85.
62. Ibid., 59.
63. Van der Pijl and Yurchenko, 'Neoliberal Entrenchment of North Atlantic Capital', 496–497.
64. For a discussion on the interconnection of the three forms of capital in each unit of capitalist production, that is, enterprise, see Henk Overbeek, 'Finance Capital and the Crisis in Britain', *Capital and Class* 4(2) (1980): 99–120.
65. Becker and Jäger, 'Development Trajectories in the Crisis in Europe', 6. See also R. Guttmann, 'A Primer on Finance-Led Capitalism and Its Crisis', *Revue de la regulation* 3(4) (2008), 1–19.
66. Swain and Mykhnenko, 'The Ukrainian Donbas in "Transition"'; A. Lyakh, 'The Evolution of the Industrial Structure in Donetsk Region', in Adam Swain (ed.), *Re-Constructing the Post-Soviet Industrial Region: The Donbas in Transition* (London: Routledge, 2007), 78–96.
67. Becker and Jäger, 'Development Trajectories in the Crisis in Europe', 6.
68. Ibid.
69. Ibid.
70. National Bank of Ukraine (NBU) (2009) Annual Report.
71. Ye Kraychak, 'Governing Ukraine's Foreign Debt in Conditions of Globalisation'. PhD thesis. National Academy of Ukraine, Institute for World Economy and International Relations, (2010), at: www.irbis-nbuv.gov.ua/cgi-bin/irbis_nbuv/cgiirbis_64.exe?C21COM=2&I21DBN=ARD&P21DBN=ARD&Z21ID=&Image_file_name=DOC/2010/10KEVVUG.zip&IMAGE_FILE_DOWNLOAD=1.
72. Roman Petrov, Guillaume Van der Loo and Peter Van Elsuwege, 'The EU–Ukraine Association Agreement: A New Legal Instrument of Integration Without Membership?', *Kyiv-Mohyla Law and Politics Journal* 1 (2015): 1 *et passim*. The EU–Ukraine Association Agreement: A New Legal Instrument of Integration Without Membership?', *Kyiv-Mohyla Law and Politics Journal* 1: 1–19.
73. Kravchuk, 'History of Ukraine's Debt Dependency Formation'.
74. Petrov, Van der Loo and Van Elsuwege, 'The EU–Ukraine Association Agreement', 2 *et passim*.
75. O. Onaran, 'From the Crisis of Distribution to the Distribution of the Costs of the Crisis: What Can We Learn from Previous Crises about the Effects of the Financial Crisis on Labor Share?'. PERI Massachusetts Working Paper, (2009), at: http://scholarworks.umass.edu/cgi/viewcontent.cgi?article=1164&context=peri_workingpapers.
76. Peter Havlik, 'Economic Consequences of the Ukraine Conflict', Wiener Institut für Internationale Wirtschaftsvergleiche, Policy Notes and Reports, November 2014, at: https://wiiw.ac.at/economic-consequences-of-the-ukraine-conflict-dlp-3427.pdf.
77. K. Mezentves, G. Pidhrushnyi and N. Mesentveva, 'Challenges of the Post-Soviet Development of Ukraine: Economic Transformations, Demographic Changes and Socio-Spatial Polarization', in T. Lang, S. Henn, K. Ehrlich and W. Sgibnev (eds), *Understanding Geographies of Polarization and Peripheralization Perspectives from Central and Eastern Europe and Beyond* (London: Palgrave Macmillan, 2015).
78. World Bank, Ukraine. Country Data, (2016), at: https://data.worldbank.org/country/ukraine; Ibid.

79. Focus, '100 самых богатых людей Украины: Полный список' ['100 Richest Ukrainians'], (2016), at: https://focus.ua/ratings/350253/.
80. Ivan Katchanovski, 'The Separatist Conflict in Donbas', 3.
81. Richard Sakwa, *Frontline Ukraine: Crisis in the Borderlands* (London: I.B. Tauris, 2015); Chris Kaspar de Ploeg, *Ukraine in the Crossfire* (Atlanta, GA: Clarity Press, 2017). See John Pilger's infamous contribution in *The Guardian*, 'In Ukraine, the US is Dragging Us Towards War with Russia', 13 May 2014, at: www.theguardian.com/commentisfree/2014/may/13/ukraine-us-war-russia-john-pilger.
82. For example, Pilger.
83. As example of an analysis, see De Ploeg, *Ukraine in the Crossfire*.
84. V. Likhachov, 'Report on Ukrainian Radical Right Presented in Tel-Aviv', *Euro Asian Jewish Congress*, 28 June 2013, at: www.eajc.org/page84/news39293.html, 'Na boj s nevidimym vragom: antisemitism, ekstremisty i Maidan' ['Fighting the Invisible Enemy: Anti-Semitism, Extremism and Maidan'], *Euro Asian Jewish Congress* (2014), at: http://eajc.org/page18/news45696.html, and 'The Far Right in the Conflict between Russia and Ukraine', *Notes de l'Ifri Russie Nei Visions* 95 (2016), www.ifri.org/sites/default/files/atoms/files/rnv95_uk_likhachev_far-right_radicals_final.pdf.
85. V. Ishchenko, 'Ukraine's Fractures', *New Left Review* 87 (May–June 2014). See also, Bereshkina and Khmelko, 'Майдан-2013: Кто Стоит и почему' ['Maidan-2013: Who is There and Why?']. Press Release on a survey. Kyiv International Institute of Sociology and Democratic Intitiatives Foundation, (2013), at: www.kiis.com.ua/?lang=rus&cat=reports&id=216.
86. V. Ishchenko, 'The Ukrainian Left During and After the Maidan Protests', a study for the DIE LINKE delegation in the GUE/NGL, (2016), at: http://cslr.org.ua/wp-content/uploads/2016/01/The_Ukrainian_Left_during_and_after_the.pdf.
87. CEC, The Central Electoral Commission [Центральна Виборча Комісія], Extraordinary Parlimentary Elections of 26 October 2014, at: www.cvk.gov.ua/pls/vnd2014/wp001e. It must be noted that: (a) the elections took place after the intensity of the armed conflict in the summer of 2014 that still has not tilted the voters to give stronger backing to the right wing parties; and (b) individual right-wing MPs have obtained parliamentary seats on a simple majority basis (under current legislation, half the parliament is elected on the basis of party lists, half on the simple majority basis to give representation to non-partisan politicians).
88. For a discussion on infowars, temnyky and manufacturing of protest, see Chapter 6.
89. For an analysis of the role of social media in the uprising, see T. Bohdanova, 'Unexpected Revolution: The Role of Social Media in Ukraine's Euromaidan Uprising', *European View* 13(1) (2014): 133–142; O. Onuch, 'Social Networks and Social Media in Ukrainian "Euromaidan" Protests', *The Washington Post*, 2 January 2014, at: www.washingtonpost.com/blogs/monkey-cage/wp/2014/01/02/social-networks-and-social-media-in-ukrainian-euromaidan-protests-2/; and G. Picchota and R. Rayzcyk 'The Role of Social Media During Protests on Maidan', *Communication Today* 6 (2) (2015): 86–97.
90. Hromadske.tv was organised by a group of 15 journalists upon ownership and potential censorship dispute with TVi channel owner; the platform was partly crowdfunded – 1,875,180₴ by the first quarter of 2014 (I, too, on a couple of

occasions, in early 2014, sent them small sums of money). Significant contributions during the same quarter came from the Fritt Ord Foundation (394,181₴), USA Embassy (287,898₴1, Canada Embassy (558,842₴). In 2013, support also came from the embassies of the Netherlands (793,089₴), USA (399,650₴), and the George Soros Foundation (247,860₴).

91. Picchota and Rayzcyk, 'The Role of Social Media During Protests on Maidan'.
92. E. Lucas and P. Pomeratzev, 'Winning the Information War Techniques and Counter-strategies to Russian Propaganda in Central and Eastern Europe'. CEPA Report (August 2016).
93. Bereshkina and Khmelko, 'Майдан-2013' ['Maidan-2013'].
94. Andrew Wilson, *Ukraine Crisis: What the West Needs to Know* (London: Yale University Press, 2014).
95. Ibid.
96. V. Ishchenko, 'Участь крайніх правих у протестах Майдану: спроба систематичної оцінки' ['Participation of the Far Right in Maidna Protests: Attempt at a Systemic Analysis'], *Commons* 9 (2015), at: http://commons.com.ua/ru/uchast-krainih-pravyh-u-protestah-maidanu/#return-note-19120-12.
97. Ishchenko, 'The Ukrainian Left During and After the Maidan Protests'.
98. Ibid.
99. Ishchenko, 'Участь крайніх правих у протестах Майдану' ['Participation of the Far Right in Maidna Protests'].
100. Plokhy, *The Gates of Europe*.
101. A. Zafesova, 'The Ultras' Role in the WAr', *EastWest*, 26 February 2015, at: http://eastwest.eu/en/east-58/the-ultras-role-in-the-war.
102. The name came from one mass media 'sensation', 'a "sporty guy" from Bila tserkva, a small town outside Kyiv' who 'managed to beat up two journalists' at a 'Rise Ukraine' rally in May 2013; Wilson, *Ukraine Crisis*, 78.
103. Historia Vivins quoted in Wilson, *Ukraine Crisis*, 87.
104. D. Arel, 'The Orange Revolution's Hidden Face: Ukraine and the Denial of its Regional Problem', *Revue Detudes Comparatives Est-Ouest* 37 (2006): 11–48.
105. Ivan Katchanovski, *Cleft Countries Regional Political Divisions and Cultures in Post-Soviet Ukraine and Moldova* (Stuttgart: Ibidem, 2006).
106. Katchanovski, 'The Separatist Conflict in Donbas'.
107. *The Washington Post*, 'Transcript: Vladimir Putin's April 17 Q&A', 17 April 2014. At: www.washingtonpost.com/world/transcript-vladimir-putins-april-17-qanda/2014/04/17/ff77b4a2-c635-11e3-8b9a-8e0977a24aeb_story.html?utm_term=.caaddf577a6c.
108. A. Barbashin and H. Thoburn, 'Putin's Brain: Alexander Dugin and the Philosophy Behind Putin's Invasion of Crimea', *Foreign Affairs*, 31 March 2014, at: www.foreignaffairs.com/articles/russia-fsu/2014-03-31/putins-brain.
109. Alexander Dugin, *Osnovy geopolitiki: Geopoliticheskoe budushchee Rossii. Myslit' prostranstvom* (Moscow: Arktogeiatsentr, 2000). See Sections 3.1–3.4 for the description of the inevitability and historical necessity of the 'Eurasian empire' led by Russia; and the rest of the book for more detail and 'context'.
110. M. Suslov, 'The Production of "Novorossiya": A Territorial Brand in Public Debates', *Europe-Asia Studies* 69(2) (2017): 202–221.
111. For details on how tradition gets constructed by means of a clipart approach to historical community experiences, see Eric J. Hobsbawm and Terence O. Ranger *The Invention of Tradition* (Cambridge: Cambridge University Press, 2012).

112. M. Suslov, 'The Production of "Novorossiya"', 214. See also M. Suslov and M. Bassin (eds), *Eurasia 2.0: Post-Soviet Geopolitics in the Age of New Media* (Lanham, MD: Lexington Books, 2016).

113. On constructedness of space and its politics, see H. Lefebvre, *State, Space, World: Selected Essays* (Minneapolis, MN, University of Minnesota Press, 2009), 170–171 *et passim*. For application of the approach to Russkiy Mir and Novorossiya, see Suslov, 'The Production of "Novorossiya"', and Suslov and Bassin, *Eurasia 2.0*, inter alia.

114. N. Popescu, *EU Foreign Policy and Post-Soviet Conflicts: Stealth Intervention* (New York: Routledge, 2010).

115. Suslov and Bassin, *Eurasia 2.0*.

116. S. Kudelia, 'Domestic Sources of the Donbas Insurgency', PONARS Eurasia Policy Memo, No. 351, (2014), at: www.ponarseurasia.org/memo/domestic-sources-donbas-insurgency.

117. Ibid., 2–3.

118. Espreso.tv, 'MIF detained ex-Slavyansk mayor Nelya Shtepa', (2014), at: http://espreso.tv/news/2014/07/11/mvs_zatrymalo_eks_mera_slovyanska_nelyu_shtepu.

119. Kudelia, 'Domestic Sources of the Donbas Insurgency', 2.

120. Ibid.

121. *The Guardian*, 'Ukraine's New Government is not Legitimate – Dmitry Medvedev', 24 February 2014, at: www.theguardian.com/world/2014/feb/24/ukraine-viktor-yanukovych-arrest-warrant.

122. K. Lally and W. Englund, 'Putin says he Reserves Right to Protect Russians in Ukraine', *The Washington Post*, 4 March 2014, at: www.washingtonpost.com/world/putin-reserves-the-right-to-use-force-in-ukraine/2014/03/04/92d4ca70-a389-11e3-a5fa-55f0c77bf39c_story.html?utm_term=.748e7e2ef064.

123. Kudelia, 'Domestic Sources of the Donbas Insurgency', 3–5; R. Petersen, *Understanding Ethnic Violence: Fear, Hatred, and Resentment in Twentieth-Century Eastern Europe* (Cambridge: Cambridge University Press, 2002), 22.

124. See mentions of Donbas identity construction and manufacturing throughout the text.

125. Ishchenko, 'The Ukrainian Left During and After the Maidan Protests', 4.

126. Ibid.

127. Y.M. Zhukov, 'Trading Hard Hats for Combat Helmets: The Economics of Rebellion in Eastern Ukraine', *Journal of Comparative Economics* 44(1) (2016), 1 *et passim*.

128. Euromaidan Press, 'Yanukovych's Secret Diaries', 12 March 2014, at: http://euromaidanpress.com/2014/03/12/yanukovychs-secret-diaries/#arvlbdat.

129. Wilson, *Ukraine Crisis*, 81.

130. R. Malko and T. Trehub, 'Volodymyr Vasylenko: When President Becomes a National Security Threat', *Tyzhden*, 30 January 2014, at: http://m.tyzhden.ua/publication/99894.

131. 'Ukraine Protests: Two Protesters Killed in Kiev Clashes', BBC, 22 January 2014, at: www.bbc.co.uk/news/world-europe-25838962.

132. Wilson, *Ukraine Crisis*, 86; www.theguardian.com/world/2014/jan/31/ukrainian-protester-kidnapped-tortured-kiev-bulatov.

133. It must be noted that some reports of individual cases of fabricated abuse by the security forces have transpired in the following years. This is not the place to investigate whether the initial stories or their 'dispelling' was fabricated.

134. Katchanovski, 'The Separatist Conflict in Donbas', 7.
135. Ibid.
136 Ibid.
137. Lally and Englund, 'Putin says he Reserves Right to Protect Russians in Ukraine'.
138. M. Elder, 'Ukrainians Protest Against Russian Language Law', *The Guardian*, 4 July 2012, at: www.theguardian.com/world/2012/jul/04/ukrainians-protest-russian-language-law.
139. Katchanovski, 'The Separatist Conflict in Donbas', 17.
140. Ibid.
141. KIIS (Kiev International Institute of Sociology), 'Attitude to the Unitary State and Separatism in Ukraine'. Report on the result of survey conducted in a period from 29 April to 11 May 2014, (2014), at: http://kiis.com.ua/?lang=eng&cat=reports&id=319.
142. Katchanovski, 'The Separatist Conflict in Donbas', 16–17.
143. R. Brubaker, 'National Minorities, Nationalizing States and External National Homelands in the New Europe', *Daedalus* 124(2) (1995): 107–132.
144. Ibid.
145. Wilson, *Ukraine Crisis*, 129.
146. Kudelia, 'Domestic Sources of the Donbas Insurgency', 6–7.
147. Ibid.
148. Ibid.
149. The storyline of Donbas being misunderstood in Kyiv and beyond has permeated the protest dynamic in the east since the 1990s, with slogans such as 'Hear Donbas' being a standard feature of protests, from miner strikes to paid protests.
150. K. Darden, 'How to Save Ukraine', *Foreign Affairs*, 14 April 2014, at: www.foreignaffairs.com/articles/russian-federation/2014-04-14/how-save-ukraine
151. Plokhy, *The Gates of Europe*.
152. Central Electoral Commission (May 2014).
153. On the forging of oligarchic grip over the economy, see Yurchenko, 'Black Holes in the Political Economy of Ukraine'. On retaining the power grip despite 20% drop in wealth, see V. Golstein, in 'Why Everything You've Read About Ukraine is Wrong', *Forbes*, 19 May 2014, at: www.forbes.com/sites/forbesleadershipforum/2014/05/19/why-everything-youve-read-about-ukraine-is-wrong/#3464bdd510e5; and S. Ayers, 'Ukraine's Oligarchs Remain Influential as Ever', *AlJazeera*, 21 June 2014, at: http://america.aljazeera.com/articles/2014/6/21/ukraine-oligarchsinfluence.html; and 'Рейтинг Forbes: 100 богатейших – 2016' ['Forbes Rating: 100 Richest 2016'], *Forbes* (2016) at: http://forbes.net.ua/ratings/4.
154. O. Shevel, 'The Parliamentary Elections in Ukraine, October 2014', *Electoral Studies* 39 (2015), 159.
155. Ibid., 162.
156. Ibid.; and Golstein, 'Why Everything You've Read About Ukraine is Wrong'.
157. Forbes, 'Рейтинг Forbes: 100 богатейших – 2016' ['Forbes Rating: 100 Richest 2016'].
158. G. Levy, 'Slave Labour in Lugansk: What War in Ukraine has "Achieved"', *People and Nature*, 4 October 2016, at: https://peopleandnature.wordpress.com/2016/10/04/slave-labour-in-lugansk-what-war-in-ukraine-has-achieved/.

159. 'Foreign-Born Ministers in Ukraine's New Cabinet', BBC, 5 December 2014, at: www.bbc.co.uk/news/world-europe-30348945.

8. GEOPOLITICS, THE ELUSIVE 'OTHER' AND THE NEBULOUS TELOS OF EUROPE

1. T. Berezovets, 'Анексія: Острів Крим. Хроніки «Гібридної Війни»' ['The Annexation: Crimea Island. "Hybrid War" Chronicle'] (Kyiv: Bright Books, 2015); V. Apryshchenko, 'Nationalism in Eastern Europe' [Debate]. (2014) at: http://richmedia.lse.ac.uk/lseideas/20140318_nationalistWarsInEurope.mp4, and 'Politics of Memory in Eastern Europe', BASEES, Cambridge University, March 2015; Taras Kuzio, *Putin's War Against Ukraine: Revolution, Nationalism, and Crime* (Amazon, 2017), *inter alia*.

2. BBC, 'Ukraine Crisis: Putin Signs Russia-Crimea Treaty', 18 March 2014, at: www.bbc.co.uk/news/world-europe-26630062.

3. BBC, 'Ukraine Crisis: Transcript of Leaked Nuland-Pyatt Call', 7 February 2014, at: www.bbc.co.uk/news/world-europe-26079957.

4. S. Kudelia, 'Domestic Sources of the Donbas Insurgency', PONARS Eurasia Policy Memo, No. 351, (2014), at: www.ponarseurasia.org/memo/domestic-sources-donbas-insurgency, 7.

5. See www.bbc.com/ukrainian/politics/2014/06/140619_ukraine_army_volunteers_hkю.

6. http://112.international/conflict-in-eastern-ukraine/40-thousand-volunteers-are-protecting-ukraine-today-poltorak-13495.html.

7. Andrew Wilson, *Ukraine Crisis: What the West Needs to Know* (London: Yale University Press, 2014; Sakwa, *Frontline Ukraine* (2015); Ivan Katchanovski, 'The Separatist Conflict in Donbas: A Violent Break-Up of Ukraine?', Canadian Institute of Ukrainian Studies Conference Paper, 2014, at: www.academia. edu/9092818/The_Separatist_Conflict_in_Donbas_A_Violent_Break-Up_of_Ukraine, 13.

8. Katchanovski (2014: 13).

9. Katchanovski, 'The Separatist Conflict in Donbas', 12.

10. A. Vasovic and M. Tsetvetkova, 'This Elusive Muscovite with 3 Names has Taken Control of Ukraine Rebels', *Business Insider*, 15 May 2014, at: www. businessinsider.com/r-elusive-muscovite-with-three-names-takes-control-of-ukraine-rebels-2014-15?IR=T.

11. From Chris Kaspar de Ploeg, *Ukraine in the Crossfire* (Atlanta, GA: Clarity Press, 2017).

12. Wilson, *Ukraine Crisis*, 140–141.

13. UN, 'Conflict in Ukraine Continues to take Civilian Toll – UN Human Rights Report', 8 December 2016, at: www.un.org/apps/news/story.asp?NewsID= 55750#.WYICm1FGnIU.

14. Ibid.

15. Ibid.

16. Ibid.

17. Human Rights Watch, 'Ukraine: Events 2016', (2016), at: www.hrw.org/world-report/2017/country-chapters/ukraine.

18. Ibid.

19. I. Webb, 'Billionaire Akhmetov denies claims that he finances separatism', *Kyiv Post*, 12 May 2014, at: www.kyivpost.com/article/content/war-against-ukraine/

donetsk-peoples-governor-claims-akhmetov-is-financing-separatism-347469. html.

20. http://fakty.ua/190041-lichnyj-samolet-ahmetova-bolshe-ne-zacshicshaet-zacshitnikov-doneckogo-aeroporta-foto-video.

21. Ibid.

22. BBC, 'Ukraine Governor Kolomoisky Sacked After Oil Firm Row', 25 March 2015, at: www.bbc.co.uk/news/world-europe-32045990.

23. OSCE was represented by Heidi Tagliavini, Ukraine was represented by former president Kuchma, Russia was represented by Russian ambassador to Ukraine Mikhail Zurabov, and the LNR and DNR were represented by Igor Plotnitsky and Alexander Zakharchenko, respectively.

24. For the full text, see BBC, 'Ukraine Ceasefire: The 12-Point Plan', 9 February 2015, at: www.bbc.co.uk/news/world-europe-29162903

25. See OSCE, at: www.osce.org/ru/home/123258?download=true

26. Taras Kuzio, 'Diplomatic Obfuscation Aside, 10 Reasons Why the Ceasefire in Ukraine is a Myth', *Financial Times*, 9 March 2015.

27. Ibid.

28. Kudelia, 'Domestic Sources of the Donbas Insurgency', 7.

29. Kataryna Wolczuk, 'Managing the Flows of Gas and Rules: Ukraine Between the EU and Russia', *Eurasian Geography and Economics* 57(1) (2016), 115.

30. Ibid.

31. www.youtube.com/watch?v=M1ApNW7r14Y

32. www.youtube.com/watch?v=wm244JXOU_0

33. https://golospravdy.com/valentina-semenyuk-samsonenko-u-moij-smerti-proshu-zvinuvachuvati/

34. http://pravda.if.ua/news-73210.html

35. Ibid.

36. V. Melkozerova and O. Goncharova, 'Poroshenko Convinces EU no Anti-Corruption Court Needed', *Kyiv Post*, 14 July 2017, at: www.kyivpost.com/ukraine-politics/poroshenko-convinces-eu-no-anti-corruption-court-needed. html. Accessed 15 July 2017.

37. Leshchenko quoted in Melkozerova and Goncharova, 'Poroshenko Convinces EU no Anti-Corruption Court Needed'.

38. Ibid.

39. Alec Luhn, 'Economic Minister's Resignation Plunges Ukraine into New Crisis', *The Guardian*, 3 February 2016, at: www.theguardian.com/world/2016/feb/04/economic-minister-resignation-ukraine-crisis-aivaras-abromavicius.

40. Natalia Zinets, 'After Praise and Death Threats, Ukraine's Central Bank Governor Quits', *Reuters*, 10 April 2017, at: www.reuters.com/article/us-ukraine-cenbank-resignation-idUSKBN17CoJ2.

41. Sergej Leschtschenko, 'Corruption Inc.', *Zeit Online*, 5 May 2017, at: www.zeit. de/politik/ausland/2017-04/ukraine-corruption-government-abatement-serhij-leschtschenko-politician.

42. R. Averchuk, 'Foreign Direct Investment in Ukraine: War and Peace', *VOX Ukraine*, 2 February 2017, at: https://voxukraine.org/2017/02/02/investments-in-ukraine-en/.

43. Ibid.

44. There has been poor progress in the privatisation processes of the last two years. Considering the high risks associated with investing in a country embroiled in an armed conflict, frozen or not, this dynamic is to be expected.

45. V. Movchan, 'First Year of EU-Ukraine FTA: Key Results', 112 UA, 29 December 2016, at: http://112.international/opinion/first-year-of-eu-ukraine-fta-key-results-12585.html.
46. Ukrstat, Macroeconomic indicators (2016), at: https://ukrstat.org/en/operativ/oper_new_e.html.
47. Movchan, 'First Year of EU-Ukraine FTA'.
48. Ibid.
49. Implemented by IER with financial support from the EU.
50. Movchan, 'First Year of EU-Ukraine FTA'.
51. Ibid.
52. Ukrstat, Macroeconomic indicators.
53. O. Kravchuk, 'History of Ukraine's Debt Dependency Formation', Commons, 30 April 2015, at: http://commons.com.ua/formuvannya-zalezhnosti/; and 'Changes in Ukrainian Economy after Maidan', Commons (Ukrainian; author's translation), 29 June 2016, at: http://commons.com.ua/zmini-v-ukrayinskij-ekonomitsi-pislya-majdanu/.
54. IMF, 'Ukraine: 2016 Article IV Consultation and third review under the Extended Arrangement, Requests for a Waiver of Non-Observance of a Performance Criterion, Waiver of Applicability, Rephasing of Access and Financing Assurances Review-Press Release; Staff Report; and Statement by the Executive Director for Ukraine', (2017 [2016]), at: www.imf.org/en/Publications/CR/Issues/2017/04/04/Ukraine-2016-Article-IV-Consultation-and-third-review-under-the-Extended-Arrangement-44798.
55. Ukrstat, Macroeconomic indicators (2017) at: https://ukrstat.org/en/operativ/oper_new_e.html.
56. Olearchyk and Buckley (2017).
57. N. Buckley and R. Olearchuk, 'Valeria Gontareva: Ukraine's Central Bank Reformer', Financial Times, 26 March 2017.
58. O. Raviv, 'Chasing the Dragon East: Exploring the Frontiers of Western European Finance', Contemporary Politics 14(3) (2008), 297.
59. Peter Gowan, 'Neoliberal Theory and Practice for Eastern Europe', New Left Review (1995) I(213): 3–60; Peter Gowan, 'The Crisis in the Heartland', in M. Konings (ed.), The Great Credit Crash (London: Verso, 2010), 47–72.
60. A. Kozyrska, 'Decommunisation of the Public Space in Post-Euromaidan Ukraine', Polish Political Science Yearbook 45 (2016): 130–144.
61. Ibid.
62. Ibid.
63. Amnesty International, 'Ukraine: Communist Party Ban Decisive Blow for Freedom of Speech in the Country', 17 December 2015, at: www.amnesty.org/en/latest/news/2015/12/ukraine-communist-party-ban-decisive-blow-for-freedom-of-speech-in-the-country/.
64. The Venice Commission is a body founded by the Council of Europe in 1990 to deal with the 'radical political change in Eastern Europe – through a resolution of the Committee of Ministers in order to provide "emergency constitutional aid" to states in transition'. The Venice Commission/Council of Europe 2017, at: www.europewatchdog.info/en/international-treaties/partial-agreements/venice-commission/.
65. The Venice Commission and OSCE/ODIHR, 'Draft Joint Opinion on the Law of Ukraine on the Condemnation of the Communist and National Socialist

(Nazi) Regimes, 4 December 2015, at: www.venice.coe.int/webforms/documents/default.aspx?pdffile=CDL(2015)050-e.

66. Verkhovna Rada (9 April 2015) Law #2558 'On Condemnation of Communist and National-Socialist (Nazi) Totalitarian Regimes in Ukraine and Ban of their Propaganda and Symbols'. Full text at: http://w1.c1.rada.gov.ua/pls/zweb2/webproc4_1?pf3511=54670.

67. www.unian.ua/incidents/1915058-na-lvivschini-zasudili-yunaka-za-propagandu-komunistichnoji-ideologiji.html.

68. www.unian.ua/society/1913473-v-odesi-politseyski-zatrimali-dvoh-osib-zanapis-sssr-na-futboltsi-i-rozpovsyudjennya-zaboronenih-listivok.html

69. Anthony D. Smith, *Theories of Nationalism* (New York: Holmes and Meier Publishers, 1988), 9–10.

70. Taras Kuzio and Andrew Wilson, *Ukraine: Perestroika to Independence* (Basingstoke: Macmillan, 1994), 1.

71. Anthony D. Smith, *Social Change: Social Theory and Historical Processes* (London: Longman, 1976), 1.

72. Ibid., 2.

73. Ibid., 3.

74. M. Molchanov, 'Russia as Ukraine's "Other": Identity and Geopolitics', in A. Pikulicka-Wilczewska and R. Sakwa (eds), *Ukraine and Russia: People, Politics, Propaganda and Perspectives* (Bristol: E-International Relations Publishing, 2015).

75. Serhii Plokhy, *The Gates of Europe* (Kindle Edition, 2015), 132.

76. Ibid., *et passim.*

77. S. Velychenko, 'Rival Grand Narratives of National History: Russian, Polish and Ukrainian Interpretations of Ukraine's Past', *Oesterreichische Osthefte* 3–4 (2000): 139–160, 140.

78. Anthony D. Smith, *National Identity* (Reno, NV: University of Nevada Press, 1991), viii.

79. Ibid.

80. Taras Kuzio, *Ukraine: Perestroika to Independence* (Basingstoke: Palgrave Macmillan, 1999), 16.

81. Ibid.

82. R. Brubaker, 'National Minorities, Nationalizing States and External National Homelands in the New Europe', *Daedalus* 124(2) (1995): 107–132.

83. Ibid.

84. V. Yevtukh, *Ethno-social Processes in Ukraine: Opportunities for Scientific Interpretations* [author's translation] (Kyiv: Stylos Publishing House, 2004), 220.

85. Ibid., 218–219.

86. Molchanov, 'Russia as Ukraine's "Other"', 207–210.

87. Ibid.

88. Yevtukh, Sakwa, Arel, Taras, Velychenko – to mention a few.

89. Vilen Gorsky, head of an institute of public opinion in Kiev, quoted in A. Lieven, *Ukraine and Russia: A Fraternal Rivalry* (Washington, DC: United States Institute of Peace Press, 1999), 138.

90. Neumann (1999: 103, 110) quoted in Molchanov, 'Russia as Ukraine's "Other"', 214.

91. Hubert Zimmermann and Andreas Dür, *Key Controversies in European Integration* (London: Palgrave Macmillan, 2016).

92. Richard Sakwa's talks about 'smaller Europe' upon the rejection of 'bigger Europe' concept in the late 1990s are relevant here, see Sakwa, *Frontline Ukraine*.

93. Bastiaan van Apeldoorn, *Transnational Capitalism and the Struggle over European Integration* (London: Routledge, 2003).

94. Laura Horn and Angela Wigger, 'Lobbying in the EU: How Much Power for Big Business?', in H. Zimmermann and A. Dür (eds), *Key Controversies in European Integration* (London: Palgrave Macmillan, 2016), 115–127.

95. Magnus Ryner and Alan Cafruny, *The European Union and Global Capitalism: Origins, Development, Crisis* (London: Palgrave Macmillan, 2016).

96. Ries Bode, 'De Nederlandse Bourgeoisie Tussen de twee Wereldoorlogen', *Cahiers voor de Politieke en Sociale Wetenschappen* 2 (1979): 9–50.

97. Ian Bruff, 'Authoritarian Neoliberalism, the Occupy Movements, and IPE'. *Journal of Critical Globalisation Studies* 1(5) (2012): 114–116; (2017).

98. S. Gill, 'New Constitutionalism, Democratisation and Global Political Economy', *Pacifica Review: Peace, Security & Global Change* 10(1) (1998): 23–38.

99. L. Oberndorfer, 'From New Constitutionalism to Authoritarian Constitutionalism: Economic Governance and the State of European Democracy', in Johannes Jäger and Elisabeth Springler (eds), *Asymmetric Crisis in Europe and Possible Futures: Critical Political Economy and Post-Keynesian Perspectives* (Abingdon: Routledge, 2015), 186–207.

100. Y. Yurchenko, 'Transnational Capital, Limits of the Possible, and the Vanishing Commons: TiSA, TTIP, and (Re)Production of Labour and Capital', Conference Paper. BISA IPEG (Liverpool, 2017).

101. B. Anderson, *Imagined Communities: Reflections on the Origin and Spread of Nationalism* (London: Verso, 1983).

102. A. Gramsci, *Selections from the Prison Notebooks*.

103. Here a reference is made to Slavoy Zizek and his series of interviews and newspaper contributions over the last few years in lieu with the Syrian refugee crisis. For example, see Slavoy Zizek, 'What Our Fear of Refugees says about Europe', *New Statesman*, 26 February 2016, at: www.newstatesman.com/politics/uk/2016/02/slavoj-zizek-what-our-fear-refugees-says-about-europe.

104. Copenhagen Criteria EC (1993).

105. The 35 Chapters are:

Chapter 1: Free movement of goods
Chapter 2: Freedom of movement for workers
Chapter 3: Right of establishment and freedom to provide services
Chapter 4: Free movement of capital
Chapter 5: Public procurement
Chapter 6: Company law
Chapter 7: Intellectual property law
Chapter 8: Competition policy
Chapter 9: Financial services
Chapter 10: Information society and media
Chapter 11: Agriculture and rural development
Chapter 12: Food safety, veterinary and phytosanitary policy
Chapter 13: Fisheries
Chapter 14: Transport policy
Chapter 15: Energy

Chapter 16: Taxation
Chapter 17: Economic and monetary policy
Chapter 18: Statistics
Chapter 19: Social policy and employment
Chapter 20: Enterprise and industrial policy
Chapter 21: Trans-European networks
Chapter 22: Regional policy and coordination of structural instruments
Chapter 23: Judiciary and fundamental rights
Chapter 24: Justice, freedom and security
Chapter 25: Science and research
Chapter 26: Education and culture
Chapter 27: Environment
Chapter 28: Consumer and health protection
Chapter 29: Customs union
Chapter 30: External relations
Chapter 31: Foreign, security and defence policy
Chapter 32: Financial control
Chapter 33: Financial and budgetary provisions
Chapter 34: Institutions
Chapter 35: Other issues

106. Y. Varoufakis, *And the Weak Suffer What They Must?: Europe's Crisis and America's Economic Future* (New York Nation Books, 2016).
107. Alberto Toscano, 'Notes on Late Fascism', (2017) [blog], at: www.historical materialism.org/blog/notes-late-fascism.
108. Ibid.
109. Ibid.
110. 'Rise of the Nationalists: A Guide to Europe's Far-Right Parties', *The New Statesman*, 8 March 2017, at: www.newstatesman.com/world/europe/2017/03/rise-nationalists-guide-europe-s-far-right-parties; 'In Europe, Right-Wing Parties Find Voice After Trump's Stunning Performance', *The Washington Post*, 24 November 2016, at: www.washingtontimes.com/news/2016/nov/24/right-wing-parties-loud-in-europe-after-trump-vict/.
111. David J. Bailey, Monica Clua-Losada, Nikolai Huke and Olatz Ribera-Almandoz, *Beyond Defeat and Austerity Disrupting (the Critical Political Economy of) Neoliberal Europe* (London: Routledge, 2018).
112. Ibid.
113. 'IMF says Ukraine Land Reform will be Key for Next Review', *Reuters*, 7 July 2017, at: www.reuters.com/article/us-ukraine-imf-reform/imf-says-ukraine-land-reform-will-be-key-for-next-review-idUSKBN19S1C5.
114. 'Медична реформа: За що доведеться платити українцям', *Espreso.tv*, June 2017, at: http://espreso.tv/article/2017/06/12/medreforma.
115. Radhika Desai, *Geopolitical Economy: After US Hegemony, Globalization and Empire (The Future of World Capitalism)* (London: Pluto Press, 2013).
116. Varoufakis, *And the Weak Suffer What They Must?.*
117. Oberndorfer, 'From New Constitutionalism to Authoritarian Constitutionalism'.
118. I borrow the term from John Berger and Jean Mohr's book, *A Seventh Man* (1975). The work is an exploration of material circumstances, exclusion and humiliation that are part of the experience of migrant workers.
119. R. Olearchuk and N. Buckley, 'Ukraine Nationalises its Largest Lender', *Financial Times*, 19 December 2015.

120. Ibid.
121. Karoly Attila Soos, *Politics and Policies in Post-Communist Transition Primary and Secondary Privatisation in Central Europe and the Former Soviet Union* (New York: Central European University Press, 2010); Andrew Wilson, *Virtual Politics: Faking Democracy in the Post-Soviet World*, 1st edn (New Haven, CT: Yale University Press, 2005).
122. IMF, 'Corruption: Costs and Mitigating Strategies', (2016), at: www.imf.org/external/pubs/ft/sdn/2016/sdn1605.pdf, 16, 20 *et passim.*
123. Transparency International, 'A Year after Maidan, Ukraine is still the Most Corrupt Country in Europe'. Press release, 3 December 2014, at: www. transparency.org/news/pressrelease/a_year_after_maidan_ukraine_is_still_ the_most_corrupt_country_in_europe.
124. D. Arel, 'Language Politics in Independent Ukraine: Towards One or Two State Languages?', *Nationalities Papers* 23(3) (1995): 597–662.
125. M. Søvik, *Support, Resistance and Pragmatism: An Examination of Motivation in Language Policy in Kharkiv, Ukraine* (Stockholm: Stockholm University, 2007).
126. D. Arel, 'Double Talk: Why Ukrainian Fight Over Language?', *Foreign Affairs*, 19 March 2014, at: www.foreignaffairs.com/articles/141042/dominique-arel/double-talk.
127. WFP, Ukraine – Food Security Update, June 2016. at: www.wfp.org/content/ukraine-food-security-update-june-2016.
128. Ibid.
129. Ibid.
130. V. Gienger, 'Ukraine's "Invisible Crisis": 1.5 Million Who Fled War With Russia', (2015), at: www.usip.org/publications/2015/11/ukraines-invisible-crisis-15-million-who-fled-war-russia.
131. IDMC, 'Displacement Figures in Ukraine Fail to Reflect a Complex Reality', (2015), at: www.internal-displacement.org/europe-the-caucasus-and-central-asia/ukraine/new-archive/displacement-figures-in-ukraine-fail-to-reflect-a-complex-reality. It must be mentioned that 'methodologies used to produce these two figures are different' (Ibid).
132. Ministry of Social Policy (28 August 2015).
133. Crimea State Emergency Service (2014), quoted in IDMC (2015).
134. Crimea Diaspora (3 August 2015), quoted in IDMC (2015).
135. Gienger, 'Ukraine's "Invisible Crisis"'.
136. Ibid.
137. V. Ishchenko, 'The Ukrainian Left During and After the Maidan Protests', a study for the DIE LINKE delegation in the GUE/NGL (2016), at: http://cslr.org.ua/wp-content/uploads/2016/01/The_Ukrainian_Left_during_and_after_the.pdf.
138. Ibid.

Bibliography

Acs, Z. and F. FitzRoy (1994) 'A Constitution for Privatizing Large Eastern Enterprises'. *Economics of Transition* 2(1): 83–94.

Aganbegyan, A. (1988) *The Challenge: Economics of Perestroika*. London: Hutchinson.

Aizenman, J. and P. Isard (1995) 'Production Bottlenecks and Resource Allocation during the Transition to a Market Economy'. *Economics of Transition* 3(3): 321–331.

Albritton, R. (2001) *Phases of Capitalist Development: Booms, Crises, and Globalizations*. New York: Palgrave.

Amnesty International. 'Annual Report. 2012. Ukraine'. At: www.amnesty.org/en/region/ukraine/report-2012.

Amnesty International (2015, 17 December) 'Ukraine: Communist Party Ban Decisive Blow for Freedom of Speech in the country'. At: www.amnesty.org/en/latest/news/2015/12/ukraine-communist-party-ban-decisive-blow-for-freedom-of-speech-in-the-country/.

Amsden, A., J. Kochanowicz and L. Taylor (1998) *The Market Meets its Match: Restructuring the Economies of Eastern Europe*. Cambridge, MA: Harvard University Press.

Anderson, B. (2006) *Imagined Communities: Reflections on the Origin and Spread of Nationalism*. London: Verso.

Anderson, P.J., G. Wiessala and Ch. Williams (2000) *New Europe in Transition*. London: Continuum.

Andrew, Ch. (1999) *The Sword and the Shield: The Mitrokhin Archive and the Secret History of the KGB*. 1st edn. New York: Basic Books.

Anievas, A. (2008) 'Theories of a Global State. A Critique'. *Historical Materialism* 16: 190–206.

Arel, D. (1995) 'Language Politics in Independent Ukraine: Towards One or Two State Languages?'. *Nationalities Papers* 23(3): 597–662.

Arel, D. (2006) 'The Orange Revolution's Hidden Face: Ukraine and the Denial of its Regional Problem'. *Revue Detudes Comparatives Est-Ouest* 37: 11–48.

Arel, D. (2014, 19 March) 'Double Talk: Why Ukrainians Fight over Language'. *Foreign Affairs*.

Arrighi, G. (2003) 'The Social and Political Economy of Global Turbulence'. *New Left Review* (March–April) 20.

Aris, B. (2006) 'Ukraine Rich List: Billionaires, Their Politics and Their Big Business Empires – Captains of Industry or Oligarchs?' *The Banker*, September.

Åslund, A. (2001) 'Ukraine's Return to Economic Growth'. *Post-Soviet Geography and Economics* 42(5): 313–28.

Åslund, A. (2002) *Building Capitalism: The Transformation of the Former Soviet Bloc*. New York: Cambridge University Press.

Åslund, A. (2005) 'Competitive Oligarchy: Russia, Ukraine and the United States'. CASE Network Studies and Analyses.

Åslund, A. (2006) *Revolution in Orange: The Origins of Ukraine's Democratic Breakthrough*. Washington DC: Carnegie Endowment for International Peace.

Åslund, A. (2007) *How Capitalism was Built: The Transformation of Central and Eastern Europe, Russia, and Central Asia*. New York: Cambridge University Press.

Åslund, A. (2009) *How Ukraine Became a Market Economy and Democracy*. Washington, DC: Peterson Institute for International Economics.

Averchuk, R. (2017, 2 February) 'Foreign Direct Investment in Ukraine: War and Peace'. *VOX Ukraine*. At: https://voxukraine.org/2017/02/02/investments-in-ukraine-en/.

Bailey, D.J., M. Clua-Losada, N. Huke and O. Ribera-Almandoz (2018) *Beyond Defeat and Austerity Disrupting (the Critical Political Economy of) Neoliberal Europe*. London: Routledge.

Balanyá, B., Ann Doherty, Olivier Hoedeman, Adam Ma'anit and Erik Wesselius (2003) *Europe Inc.: Regional and Global Restructuring and the Rise of Corporate Power*. London: Pluto Press.

Balmaceda, M. (2000) *On the Edge: Ukrainian – Central European – Russian Security Triangle*. Budapest: Akaprint.

Balmaceda, M. (2008) *Energy Dependency, Politics and Corruption in the Former Soviet Union, Russia's Power, Oligarchs' Profits and Ukraine's Missing Energy Policy, 1995–2006*. London: Routledge.

Barbashin, A. and H. Thoburn (2014) 'Putin's Brain: Alexander Dugin and the Philosophy Behind Putin's Invasion of Crimea'. *Foreign Affairs* 31 (March), www.foreignaffairs.com/articles/russia-fsu/2014-03-31/putins-brain.

Barisitz, S. and M. Lahnsteiner (18 December 2009). 'Investor Commitment Tested by Deep Crisis: Banking Development in Ukraine'. Oesterrieichische Nationalbank, Financial Stability Report.

Barisitz, S. and Z. Fungáčová (2015) 'Ukraine: Struggling Banking Sector and Substantial Political and Economic Uncertainty'. *BOFIT Policy Report #3*, at: https://helda.helsinki.fi/bof/bitstream/handle/123456789/13664/bpbo315%5B1%5D.pdf?sequence=1. Accessed 24 January 2017.

BBC World News (2004) 'Poll Dispute Sparks Ukraine Rally'. 22 November, at: http://news.bbc.co.uk/1/hi/world/europe/4031127.stm.

BBC World News (2006) 'The Case Against Pavlo Lazarenko'. 25 August, at: http://news.bbc.co.uk/1/hi/world/europe/4780743.stm.

BBC World News (2009) 'Ukraine Finds Reporter's Skull'. 28 July, at: http://news.bbc.co.uk/1/hi/world/europe/8173441.stm.

BBC World News (2014a) 'Ukraine Crisis: Putin Signs Russia-Crimea Treaty', 18 March, at: www.bbc.co.uk/news/world-europe-26630062.

BBC World News (2014b) 'Ukraine Crisis: Transcript of Leaked Nuland-Pyatt Call', 7 February, at: www.bbc.co.uk/news/world-europe-26079957.

BBC (2015) 'Ukraine Governor Kolomoisky Sacked After Oil Firm Row'. 25 March, at: www.bbc.co.uk/news/world-europe-32045990. Accessed 23 January 2017.

Becker, J. and J. Jäger (2010) 'Development Trajectories in the Crisis in Europe', *Debatte* 18(1).

Bideleux, R. and I. Jeffries (1998) *A History of Eastern Europe: Crisis and Change*. London: Routledge.

Bieler, A. and A. Morton (2006) *Images of Gramsci: Connections and Contentions in Political Theory and International Relations*. New York: Routledge.

Birch, Kean (2010) *The Rise and Fall of Neoliberalism: The Collapse of an Economic Order?* London: Zed Books.

Birch, K. and V. Mykhnenko (2009) 'Varieties of Neoliberalism?: Restructuring in Large Industrially Dependent Regions Across Western and Eastern Europe'. *Journal of Economic Geography* 9(3): 355–380

Birch, K. and V. Mykhnenko (eds) (2010) *The Rise and Fall of Neoliberalism: The Collapse of an Economic Order?*. London: Zed Books.

Blejer, M.I. and M. Škreb (1997) 'Stabilisation after Five Years of Reform: Issues and Experiences', in Mario I. Blejer, Marko Škreb (eds), *Macroeconomic Stabilization in Transition Economies*. New York: Cambridge University Press, 1–13.

Bode, R. (1979) 'De Nederlandse Bourgeoisie Tussen de twee Wereldoorlogen'. *Cahiers voor de Politieke en Sociale Wetenschappen* 2: 9–50.

Bogatov, O. (2007) 'The Donetsk Clan and the Demise of the Coal Industry', in Adam Swain (ed.), *Re-Constructing the Post-Soviet Industrial Region: The Donbas in Transition*. London: Routledge, 127–141.

Boguslavskiï, M. and P.S. Smirnov (1989) *The Reorganization of Soviet Foreign Trade: Legal Aspects*. Armonk, NY: M.E. Sharpe.

Bohdanova, T. (2014) 'Unexpected Revolution: The Role of Social Media in Ukraine's Euromaidan Uprising'. *European View* 13(1): 133–142.

Bojcun, M. (2001a) 'Where is Ukraine?: Civilization and Ukraine's Identity'. *Problems of Post-Communism* 48(5): 42–51.

Bojcun, M. (2001b) 'Russia, Ukraine and European Integration'. EUI Working Paper HEC No. 2001(4), at: http://diana-n.iue.it:8080/bitstream/handle/1814/56/heco1-04.pdf?sequence=1&isAllowed=y.

Bojcun, M. (2001c) 'Ukraine and Europe: A Difficult Reunion'. Dossier Series of the London European Research Centre, Kogan Page.

Borgatti, Stephen, Martin Everett and Lin Freeman (2002) *UCINET 6 for Windows Software for Social Network Analysis*. [Lexington, KY]: Analytic Technologies; University of Greenwich.

Borgatti, Stephen (2005) *NetDraw for Windows Software for Social Network Analysis*. Analytic Technologies; University of Greenwich.

Brenner, R. (1998) 'The Economics of Global Turbulence', Special Issue, *New Left Review*.

Brenner, R. (2006) *The Economics of Global Turbulence*. London: Verso Press.

Bromley, M. (2007) *United Nations Arms Embargoes: Their Impact on Arms Flows and Target. Behaviour Case Study: Former Yugoslavia, 1991–96*. Stockholm International Peace Research Institute.

Bruff, I. (2012) 'Authoritarian Neoliberalism, the Occupy Movements, and IPE'. *Journal of Critical Globalisation Studies* 1(5): 114–116.

Bruff, I. (2014) 'The Rise of Authoritarian Neoliberalism'. *Rethinking Marxism: A Journal of Economics, Culture & Society* 26(1): 113–129.

Buchanan, J.M. (1997) *Post-Socialist Political Economy*. Cheltenham: Edward Elgar.

Buckley, N. and R. Olearchuk (2017, 26 March) 'Valeria Gontareva: Ukraine's Central Bank Reformer'. *The Financial Times*.

Business Week (2004) 'Putin's Raw Power Grab'. 27 September, at: www.businessweek.com/magazine/content/04_39/b3901158_mz037.htm.

Cabinet of Ministers of Ukraine (2010) 'The Cabinet of Ministers of Ukraine Resolution N55 "On Normalization of Transliteration of the Ukrainian Alphabet by Means of the Latin Alphabet"'. 27 January, at: http://zakon.rada.gov.ua/cgi-bin/laws/main.cgi?nreg=55-2010-%EF.

Callinicos, A. (2001) 'Periodizing Capitalism and Analyzing Imperialism: Classical Marxism and Capitalist Evolution', in R. Albritton (ed.), *Phases of Capitalist Development: Booms, Crises, and Globalizations*. New York: Palgrave, 230–245.

Carroll, W.K. (2009) 'Transnationalists and National Networkers in the Global Corporate Elite'. *Global Networks* 9(3): 289–314.

Carroll, W.K. (2010) *The Making of a Transnational Capitalist Class: Corporate Power in the 21st Century*. London: Zed Books.

The Central Electoral Commission (1998) 'Parliamentary Elections Results, 1998', at: www.cvk.gov.ua/pls/vd2002/webprocov?kodvib=1&rejim=0

The Central Electoral Commission (2002) 'Parliamentary Elections Results, 2002', at: www.cvk.gov.ua/pls/vd2002/WEBPROCoV.

The Central Electoral Commission (2006) 'Parliamentary Elections Results, 2006', at: www.cvk.gov.ua/pls/vnd2006/w6p001.

The Central Electoral Commission (2007) 'Early Parliamentary Elections Results, 2007', at: www.cvk.gov.ua/pls/vnd2007/w6p001.

The Central Electoral Commission (1999) 'Presidential Election Results, 1999', at: www.cvk.gov.ua/pls/vp1999/WEBPROCo.

The Central Electoral Commission (2004) 'Presidential Election Results, 2004', at: www.cvk.gov.ua/pls/vp2004/wp0011.

The Central Electoral Commission (2010) 'Presidential Election Results, 2010', at: www.cvk.gov.ua/pls/vp2010/WP0011.

Cerny, Ph. (1991) 'The Limits of Deregulation: Transnational Interpenetration and Policy Change'. *European Journal of Political Research* 19(2–3): 173–196.

Clarke, S. (2002) 'Class Struggle and the Global Overaccumulaiton', in R. Albritton, M. Itoh, R. Westra and A. Zuege (eds), *Phases of Capitalist Development: Booms, Crises and Globalizations*. Basingstoke: Palgrave.

Comisso, E. (1991) 'Property Rights, Liberalism, and the Transition from the "Actually Existing" Socialism'. *East European Politics and Society* 5(1): 162–188.

Cox, R.W. (1981) 'Social Forces, States, and World Orders: Beyond IR Theory'. *Millennium: Journal of International Studies* 10(2): 126–155.

Cox, R.W. (1986) 'Social Forces, States and World Orders: Beyond International Relations Theory', in Robert O. Keohane (ed.), *Neorealism and Its Critics*. New York: Columbia University Press, 204–254.

Cox, R.W. (1987) *Production, Power and World Order: Social Forces in the Making of History*. New York: Columbia University Press.

Cox, R.W. and T.J. Sinclair (1996) *Approaches to World Order*. Cambridge: Cambridge University Press.

Crowley, S. (1997) 'Coal Miners and the Transformation of the USSR'. *Post-Soviet Affairs* 13(2): 167–195.

Crouch, D. (2000) 'Reinventing Allotments for the Twenty-First Century: The UK Experience'. *Acta Horticulturae* 523: 135–142.

Cutler, C.A. (2015) 'New Constitutionalism, Democracy and the Future of Global Governance', in S. Gill (ed.), *Critical Perspectives on the Crisis of Global Governance: Reimagining the Future*. London: Palgrave, 89–109.

Dahrendorf, R. (1990) *Reflections on the Revolution in Europe: In a Letter Intended to have been Sent to a Gentleman in Warsaw*, 1st edn. New York: Times Books.

D'Anieri, P.J. (2007) *Understanding Ukrainian Politics: Power, Politics, and Institutional Design*. London: M.E. Sharpe.

D'Anieri, P., R.S. Kravchuk and T. Kuzio (1999) *Politics and Society in Ukraine*. Boulder, CO: Westview Press.

Dejevsky, M. (2006) 'Boris Berezovsky: The First Oligarch'. *The Independent*, 25 November.

De Ploeg, C.K. (2017) *Ukraine in the Crossfire*. Atlanta, GA: Clarity Press.

Desai, P. (1989) *Perestroika in Perspective: The Design and Dilemmas of Soviet Reform*. Princeton, NJ: Princeton University Press.

Desai, R. (1994) 'Second-Hand Dealers in Ideas: Think-Tanks and Thatcherite Hegemony'. *New Left Review* I(203).

Desai, R. (2013) *Geopolitical Economy: After US Hegemony, Globalization and Empire (The Future of World Capitalism)*. London: Pluto Press.

Die Frankfurter Allgemeine Zeitung (2012) 'Das Prinzip Familie'. 27 August, at: www.faz.net/aktuell/politik/ausland/praesident-janukowitsch-das-prinzip-familie-11870003.html.

Dobrinsky, R. (2007) 'Capital Accumulation during the Transition from Plan to Market'. *The Economics of Transition* 15(4): 845–868.

Doroshenko, I. (2008) 'Global Financial Crisis and its Impact on Ukraine's Economic Development' (in Ukrainian). *Problems of a Systemic Approach to The Economy Enterprises* 3: 7.

Dreyfuss, B. (2014) 'Ukraine's Far Right Loses Big, but Europe's Russian-Backed Fascists Make Major Gains: The Crisis in Ukraine Winds Down in the Wake of Poroshenko's Chocolate-Covered Win'. *The Nation*, 30 May, at: www.thenation.com/article/ukraines-far-right-loses-big-europes-russian-backed-fascists-make-major-gains/.

Dubrovskiy, V., A. Paskhaver, L. Verkhovodova and B. Blaszczyk (2007) 'Conditions of Resuming and Completing Privatisation in Ukraine: Analytical report and recommendations for the State Privatization Program' [Report]. The Centre of Social and Economic Research, CASE Ukraine.

Dugin, A.G. (2000) *Osnovy geopolitiki: Geopoliticheskoe budushchee Rossii. Myslit' prostranstvom*. Moscow: Arktogeiatsentr.

Dugin, A.G. (2014) *Konflikte der Zukunft: Die Rückkehr der Geopolitik*. Kiel: Arndt-Verlag.

Dyczok, M. (2005) 'Breaking Through the Information Blockade: Elections and Revolution in Ukraine 2004'. *Canadian Slavonic Papers* 47(3–4): 241–264.

Dyczok, M. (2006) 'Was Kuchma's Censorship Effective? Mass Media in Ukraine before 2004'. *Europe-Asia Studies* 58(2): 215–238.

Dyczok, M. (2009) 'Do the Media Matter? Focus on Ukraine', in M. Dyczok and O. Gaman-Golutvina (eds), *Media, Democracy and Freedom: The Post-Communist Experience*. Bern: Peter Lang, 17–42.

Dyker, D.A. (1992) *Restructuring the Soviet Economy*. London: Routledge.

Dymski, G.A. (2010) 'From Financial Exploitation to Global Instability: Two Overlooked Roots of the Subprime Crisis', in Martijn Konings (ed.), *The Great Credit Crash*. London: Verso.

Easterly, W. (2006) *The White Man's Burden: Why the West's Efforts to Aid the Rest Have Done so Much Ill and so Little Good*. New York: Penguin Press.

EBRD (2010a) 'Our History', 8 April, at: www.ebrd.com/pages/about/history.shtml.

EBRD (2010b) 'Transition Report', at: www.ebrd.com/transitionreport.

Ellman, M., E. Gaidar and G. Kolodko (eds) (1993) *Economic Transition in Eastern Europe*. Oxford: Blackwell.

Eyal, G., I. Szelényi and E.R. Townsley (1998) *Making Capitalism without Capitalists: Class Formation and Elite Struggles in Post-Communist Central Europe*. London: Verso.

Fawkes, H. (2004) 'Battle Lines Drawn in Ukraine Vote'. *BBC World News*, 20 November, at: http://news.bbc.co.uk/1/hi/world/europe/4029347.stm.

Feldbrugge, F.J.M. (1984) 'Government and Shadow Economy in the Soviet Union'. *Soviet Studies* 36(4): 528–543.

Feldbrugge, F.J.M. (1989) 'The Soviet Second Economy in a Political and Legal Perspective', in E.L. Feige (ed.), *The Underground Economy: Tax Evasion and Information Distortion*. Cambridge: Cambridge University Press, 297–338.

Fennema, M. (1982) *International Networks of Banks and Industry*. The Hague: Martinus Nijhoff.

Foglesong, T.S. and P.H. Solomon, jnr (2001) *Crime, Criminal Justice and Criminology in Post-Soviet Ukraine*. Washington, DC: U.S. Dept. of Justice Office of Justice Programs National Institute of Justice.

ForUm (2007) 'Страшные подробности смерти Кравченко'. 23 April, at: http://for-ua.com/ukraine/2007/04/23/112635.html.

Freedom House (2012) 'Ukraine: Freedom of the Press 2011', at: www.freedomhouse.org/report/freedom-press/2011/ukraine.

Friedgut, Theodore and Lewis Siegelbaum, 'Perestroika from Below: The Soviet Miners' Strike and Its Aftermath'. *New Left Review* I(181): 5–32.

Fukuyama, F. (1989) 'The End Of History?'. *The National Interest* (Summer).

Fukuyama, F. (1992) *The End of History and the Last Man*. New York: Free Press.

Gill, S. (ed.) (1993) *Gramsci, Historical Materialism and International Relations*. Cambridge: Cambridge University Press.

Gill, S. (ed.) (2015) *Critical Perspectives on the Crisis of Global Governance: Reimagining the Future*. London: Palgrave.

Glenny, M. (2008) *McMafia: Crime Without Frontiers*. London: Bodley Head.

GlobalSecurity.org. 'Kolchuga Passive Early Warning Radar', at: www.globalsecurity.org/military/world/ukraine/kolchuga.htm.

Global Forest Watch (NA) (n.d.) 'Ukraine'. At: www.globalforestwatch.org/country/UKR. Accessed 23 January 2017.

Godson, R. (2003) *Menace to Society: Political-Criminal Collaboration around the World*. New Brunswick, NJ: Transaction Publishers.

Gorbachev, M. (1987) *Perestroika New Thinking for Our Country and the World* New York. Harper and Row.

Gowan, P. (1995) 'Neo-Liberal Theory and Practice for Eastern Europe'. *New Left Review* I(213): 3–60.

Gowan, P. (2010) 'The Crisis in the Heartland', in M. Konings (ed.), *The Great Credit Crash*. London: Verso, 47–72.

Gramsci, A. (1971) *Selections from the Prison Notebooks of Antonio Gramsci*. New York: International Publishers.

Grossman, G. (1977) 'The "Second Economy" of the USSR'. *Problems of Communism* 26(5): 25–40.

Glyn, A. (1990) 'Productivity and the Crisis of Fordism'. *International Review of Applied Economics* 4(1): 28–44.

Harrison, M. (1993) 'Soviet Economic Growth since 1928: The Alternative Statistics of G.I. Khanin'. *Europe-Asia Studies* 45(1): 141–167.

Harvey, D. (2003) *The New Imperialism*. Oxford: Oxford University Press.

Harvey, D. (2005) *A Brief History of Neoliberalism*. Oxford: Oxford University Press.

Havrylyshyn, O. (1997) 'Economic Reform in Ukraine', in Mario I. Blejer and Marko Škreb (eds), *Macroeconomic Stabilization in Transition Economies*. Cambridge: Cambridge University Press, 281–313.

Hayoz, Nicolas, and Andrej N. Lushnycky (2005) *Ukraine at a Crossroads*. Bern: P. Lang.

Hellman, J.S. (1998) 'Winners Take All: The Politics of Partial Reform in Post-Communist Transitions'. *World Politics* 50(2): 203–234.

Hesli, Vicki L. (2006) 'The Orange Revolution: 2004 Presidential Election(s) in Ukraine'. *Electoral Studies* 25(1): 168–177.

Holman, Otto (1992) *Restructuring the Ruling Class and European Unification*. Maarssen: CEPS.

Holman, Otto (1992) 'Transnational Class Strategy and the New Europe'. *International Journal of Political Economy* 22(1): 3–22.

Holman, Otto (1996) *Integrating Southern Europe: EC Expansion and the Transnationalisation of Spain*. London: Routledge.

Horn, L. and A. Wigger (2016) 'Lobbying in the EU: How Much Power for Big Business?', in H. Zimmermann and A. Dür (eds), *Key Controversies in European Integration*. London: Palgrave Macmillan, 115–127.

Huang, H. (2003) *Financial Crisis, Economic Recovery and Banking Development In Former Soviet Union Economies*. London: Centre for Economic Policy Research.

Huang, H., D. Marin and C. Hu (2004) 'Financial Crisis, Economic Recovery, and Banking Development in Russia, Ukraine, and Other FSU Countries'. *IMF Working Paper* WP/04/105, at: www.ckgsb.edu.cn/uploads/professor/201607/15/Huang-Marin-Xu_Russia%20WP04_105.pdf. Accessed 11 January 2017.

Hudson, M. and J. Sommers (2010) 'How Neoliberals Bankrupted "New Europe": Latvia in the Global Credit Crisis', in M. Konings (ed.), *The Great Credit Crash*. London: Verso, 244–264.

Human Rights Watch (2016) 'Ukraine: Events 2016', at: www.hrw.org/world-report/2017/country-chapters/ukraine.

IMF (n.d.) 'Ukraine. Ex Post-Evaluation of Exceptional Access under the 2014 Stand-by Arrangement'. *International Monetary Fund IMF Country Report* No.16/320, at: www.imf.org/external/pubs/ft/scr/2016/cr16320.pdf. Accessed 20 January 2017.

IMF (n.d.) 'Ukraine: Second Review under the Extended Fund Facility and Requests for Waivers of Non-Observance of Performance Criteria, Rephasing of Access and Financing Assurances Review – Press Release; Staff Report; and Statement by the Executive Director for Ukraine'. *International Monetary Fund IMF Country Report* No.16/319, at: www.imf.org/external/pubs/ft/scr/2016/cr16319.pdf. Accessed 20 January 2017.

Ingalis, Laura (2004) 'Ukraine: Media Under Increasing Threat Ahead of Elections'. Freedom House, 7 July, at: www.freedomhouse.org/template.cfm?page=70&release=32.

Institutional Investor (2005) 'Ukraine: Re-Privatization: Who Will Lose, Who Will Gain?'. *Institutional Investor*, 15 March, at: www.institutionalinvestor.com/Popups/PrintArticle.aspx?ArticleID=1024520.

InvestGazeta (2010) Рейтинг 100 крупнейших компаний Украины. 2 September, at: www.investgazeta.net/kompanii-i-rynki/top-100-159472/.

Ishchenko, V. (ed.) (2012) *Protesty, peremohy i represii v Ukrayini* [*Protests, Victories and Repressions in Ukraine*]. Kyiv: Center for Society Research.

Ishchenko, V. (2014) 'Ukraine's Fractures'. *New Left Review* 87 (May–June).

Ishchenko, V. (2015) 'Uchast' Krajnikh pravykh v protestakh majdany: sproba systematychnoji otsinky' ['Far Right Participation in Maidan Protests: An Attempt at Systematic Analysis']. Commons, at: http://commons.com.ua/en/uchast-krainih-pravyh-u-protestah-maidanu/

Ishchenko, V. (2016) 'Far Right Participation in the Ukrainian Maidan Protests: An Attempt of Systematic Estimation'. *European Politics and Society* 17(4): 453–472.

Iwasaki, I. and T. Suzuki (2007) 'Transition Strategy, Corporate Exploitation, and State Capture: An Empirical Analysis of the Former Soviet States'. *Communist And Post-Communist Studies* 40(4): 393–422.

iWatch (2002) 'Special Report: Kuchma Approved Sale of Weapons System to Iraq'. The Centre for Public Integrity: iWatch News, 15 April, at: www.iwatchnews. org/2002/04/15/3197/special-report-kuchma-approved-sale-weapons-system-iraq.

Jessop, B. (1983a) 'The Capitalist State and the Rule of Capital: Problems in the Analysis of Business Associations'. *West European Politics* 6(2): 139–162.

Jessop, B. (1983b) 'Accumulation Strategies, State Forms, and Hegemonic Projects'. *Kapitalistate* 10: 89–111.

Jessop, B. (1990) *State Theory: Putting the Capitalist State in Its Place*. University Park, PA: Pennsylvania State University Press.

Jessop, B. and N.-L. Sum (2017) 'Putting the 'Amsterdam School' in its Rightful Place: A Reply to Juan Ignacio Staricco's Critique of Cultural Political Economy'. *New Political Economy* 22(3): 342–354.

Johnson, S., H. Kroll, and S. Eder (1994) 'Strategy, Structure, and Spontaneous Privatisation in Russia and Ukraine' in Vedat Milor (ed.), *Changing Political Economies: Privatisation in Post-Communist and Reforming Communist States*. London: Lynne Rienner Publishers, 147–173.

Kalachova, H. and S. Abbasova (2016) 'How Much and Whom Ukraine Owes'. *Econominichna Pravda*, 30 March, at: www.epravda.com.ua/cdn/cd1/2016/03/ mvf/. Accessed 12 February 2017.

Karatnycky, A. (2001) 'Meltdown in Ukraine'. *Foreign Affairs* 80(3): 73.

Karatnycky, A. (2006) 'The Fall and Rise of Ukraine's Political Opposition: From Kuchmagate to the Orange Revolution', in Anders Åslund (ed.), *Revolution in Orange: The Origins of Ukraine's Democratic Breakthrough*. Washington DC: Carnegie Endowment for International Peace, 29–44.

Katsenlinboigen, A. (1977) 'Coloured Markets in the Soviet Markets'. *Soviet Studies* 29(1): 62–85.

Kautsky, K. (2007) *Ultra-Imperialism*. Marlborough: Adam Matthew Digital.

Keynes, J.M. (1970 [1936]). *The General Theory of Employment, Interest and Money*. London: Palgrave Macmillan.

Khanin, G.I. (1991) 'The Soviet Economy: From Crisis to Catastrophe'. Working Paper 33, Stockholm Institute of Soviet and East European Economics.

Klein, M. (2009) The Global Financial Crisis: Strategic Implications for Development Finance Institutions. Paper prepared for KfW Financial Sector Symposium, Berlin, 3–4 December 2009.

KMU (2005) 'Inaugural Address of the President of Ukraine Victor Yushchenko to the Ukrainian People on Independence Square', at: www.kmu.gov.ua/control/en/ publish/article?art_id=11100895.

Kolodko, G. (2000) *From Shock to Therapy: The Political Economy of Postsocialist Transformation*. Oxford: Oxford University Press.

Kolodiy, D. (2007) *The Orange Chronicles*. Maplewood, NJ: DK Productions.

Konings, M. (ed.) (2010) *The Great Credit Crash*. London: Verso.

Kononenko, V. and A. Moshes (eds) (2011) *Russia as a Network State: What Works in Russia When State Institutions Do Not?*. London: Palgrave Macmillan.

Kononchuk, S. and V. Pikhovshek (1997) *The Dnipropetrovs'k Family-2*, 2nd edn. Kyiv: Ukrainian Center for Independent Political Research.

Kornai, J. (1979) 'Resource-Constrained Versus Demand-Constrained Systems'. *Econometrica* 47(4): 801–819.

Kornai, J. (1980) *Economics of Shortage*. Amsterdam: North-Holland.

Kornai, J. (1992) *The Socialist System: The Political Economy of Communism*. Princeton, NJ: Princeton University Press.

Kornai, János (1992) *The Socialist System: The Political Economy of Communism*. Oxford: Oxford University Press.

Kornai, János (1995) 'Eliminating the Shortage Economy: A General Analysis and Examination of the Development in Hungary'. *Economics of Transition* 3(1): 13–37.

Korrespondent (2003) 'Top 100 most influential people of Ukraine. 2003', at: http://files.korrespondent.net/projects/top100/2003.

Korrespondent (2004) 'Top 100 most influential people of Ukraine. 2004', at: http://files.korrespondent.net/projects/top100/2004.

Korrespondent (2005) 'Top 100 most influential people of Ukraine. 2005', at: http://files.korrespondent.net/projects/top100/2005.

Korrespondent (2006) 'Top 100 most influential people of Ukraine. 2006', at: http://files.korrespondent.net/projects/top100/2006.

Korrespondent (2007) 'Top 100 most influential people of Ukraine. 2007', at: http://files.korrespondent.net/projects/top100/2007.

Korrespondent (2008) 'Top 100 most influential people of Ukraine. 2008', at: http://files.korrespondent.net/projects/top100/2008.

Korrespondent (2009) 'Top 100 most influential people of Ukraine. 2009', at: http://files.korrespondent.net/projects/top100/2009.

Korrespondent (2010) 'Top 100 most influential people of Ukraine. 2010', at: http://files.korrespondent.net/projects/top100/2010.

Korunets', Il'ko (2001) *Theory and Practice of Translation*. Kyiv: Vydavnychoho ob'yednannya 'Vyshcha shkola'.

Kotz, David (2001) 'The State, Globalisation and Phases of Capitalist Development', in Robert Albritton (ed.), *Phases of Capitalist Development: Booms, Crises, and Globalizations*. Houndmills: Palgrave, 93–109.

Kovaleva, Elena (2007) 'Regional Politics in Ukraine's Transition: The Donetsk Elite', in Adam Swain (ed.), *Re-Constructing the Post-Soviet Industrial Region: The Donbas in Transition*. London: Routledge, 62–77.

Kozyrska, A. (2016) 'Decommunisation of the Public Space in Post-Euromaidan Ukraine'. *Polish Political Science Yearbook* 45: 130–144.

Kramer, David, J. Nurick, Robert Wilson, Damon and Evan Alterman (2011). 'Sounding the Alarm: Protecting Democracy in Ukraine. A Freedom House Report on the State of Democracy and Human Rights in Ukraine'. Freedom House, at: www.freedomhouse.org/sites/default/files/inline_images/98.pdf.

Kravchuk, O. (2015) 'History of Ukraine's Debt Dependency Formation', *Commons*, 30 April, at: http://commons.com.ua/formuvannya-zalezhnosti/. Accessed 21 January 2017.

Kravchuk, O. (2016) 'Changes in Ukrainian Economy after Maidan', *Commons* (Ukrainian; own translation), 29 June, at: http://commons.com.ua/zmini-v-ukrayinskij-ekonomitsi-pislya-majdanu/. Accessed 20 January 2017.

Kravchuk, Robert (2002) *Ukrainian Political Economy: The First Ten Years*, 1st edn. New York: Palgrave Macmillan.

Kraychak, Ye (2010) 'Governing Ukraine's Foreign Debt in Conditions of Globalisation'. PhD thesis. National Academy of Ukraine, Institute for World Economy and International Relations, at: www.irbis-nbuv.gov.ua/cgi-bin/irbis_nbuv/cgiirbis_64.exe?C21COM=2&I21DBN=ARD&P21DBN=ARD&Z21ID=&Image_file_name=DOC/2010/10KEVVUG.zip&IMAGE_FILE_DOWNLOAD=1. Accessed 15 January 2017.

Kubicek, Paul (1999) 'Ukrainian Interest Groups, Corporatism, and Economic Reform', in Taras Kuzio (ed.), State and Institution Building in Ukraine. New York: St. Martin's Press, 57–81.

Kuromiya, H. (1998) Freedom and Terror in the Donbas. Cambridge: Cambridge University Press.

Kusznir, Julia and Heiko Pleines (2006) 'Informal Networks in Ukraine's Privatization Auctions', in Julia Kusznir (ed.), Informal Networks and Corruption in Post-Socialist Countries, KICES Working Paper #6, p. 43, at: www.kices.org/downloads/KICES_WP_06.pdf.

Kuzio, T. (1999) Ukraine: Perestroika to Independence, 2nd edn. Basingstoke: Palgrave Macmillan.

Kuzio, Taras (1999) State and Institution Building in Ukraine. New York: St. Martin's Press.

Kuzio, Taras (2002) '"Pro-ukrainian" or "Pro-Kuchma"?: Ukraine's Foreign Policy in Crisis'. RFE/RL Newsline 6(79), 26 April.

Kuzio, Taras (2005a) 'The Opposition's Road to Success'. Journal of Democracy 16(2): 117–130.

Kuzio, Taras (2005b) 'Regime Type and Politics in Ukraine under Kuchma'. Communist and Post-Communist Studies 38: 167–190.

Kuzio, Taras (2005c) 'Yushchenko Election Coalition Divided over Role for Lytvyn'. Eurasia Daily Monitor, 8 July.

Kuzio, Taras (2007) 'Oligarchs, Tapes and Oranges: "Kuchmagate" to the Orange Revolution'. Journal of Communist Studies and Transition Politics 23(1): 30–56.

Kuzio, Taras (2012) 'Five Minutes with Taras Kuzio: 'Ukraine is Sleepwalking into an Authoritarian State. We Are in a Dangerous Situation.' London School of Economics, Blogs. http://blogs.lse.ac.uk/europpblog/2012/05/11/five-minutes-with-taras-kuzio-ukraine.

Kuzio, Taras (2017) Putin's War Against Ukraine: Revolution, Nationalism, and Crime. Amazon.

Kuzio, T. and A. Wilson (1994) Ukraine: Perestroika to Independence. Basingstoke: Macmillan.

Kyiv Post (2001) 'Kroll Report Says Kuchma Not Involved in Gongadze Disappearance'. 27 September, at: www.kyivpost.com/news/nation/detail/9778/.

Kyiv Post (2002) 'Kuchma Under Siege'. 26 September, at: www.kyivpost.com/content/ukraine/kuchma-under-siege-11915.html.

Kyiv Post (2005) 'Jed Sunden Looks Back on 10 years with Kyiv Post and KP Publications', 19 October, at: www.kyivpost.com/content/business/jed-sunden-looks-back-on-10-years-with-kyiv-post-a-23376.html.

Kyiv Post (2010) 'Government to Direct Most of International Monetary Fund's Loan to Currency Reserves'. 12 May, at: www.kyivpost.com/article/content/politics/government-to-direct-most-of-international-monetar-66502.html.

Kyiv Post (2011) 'WikiLeaks: Gryshchenko Says Putin has Low Personal Regard for Yanukovych'. 8 March, at: www.kyivpost.com/content/ukraine/wikileaks-gryshchenko-says-putin-has-low-personal--99234.html.

Labriola, Antonio (1908) *Essays on the Materialistic Conception of History*. Chicago, IL: C.H. Kerr.

Lane, D. (1978) *Politics and Society in the USSR*, 2nd edn. London: M. Robertson.

Lane, D. (1988) *Elites and Political Power in the USSR*. Aldershot: Elgar.

Lane, D. (1990) *Soviet Society under Perestroika*. Boston, MA: Unwin Hyman.

Lane, D. (1992) *Soviet Society under Perestroika*. London: Routledge.

Lane, D. (2006) 'From State Socialism to Capitalism: The Role of Class and the World System'. *Communist and Post-Communist Studies* 39(2): 135–152.

Lane, D. (2007) *Varieties of Capitalism in Post-Communist Countries*. Basingstoke: Palgrave.

Lane, D. (2011) *Elites and Classes in the Transformation of State Socialism*. London: Transaction Publishers.

Lane, D. (2016) 'The International Context: Russia, Ukraine and the Drift to East-West Confrontation', *International Critical Thought* 6: 623–644. At: www.tandfonline.com/doi/abs/10.1080/21598282.2016.1242084

Lane, D. (2016) 'Is the Russian Federation a Threat to the International Order?'. *Valdi Discussion Club*. At: http://valdaiclub.com/a/highlights/is_the_russian_federation_a_threat_to_the_international_order/?sphrase_id=173665.

Lane, D. and C. Ross (1999) *The Transition from Communism to Capitalism: Ruling Elites from Gorbachev to Yeltsin*. London: Palgrave Macmillan.

Lapavitsas, C. (2009) 'Financialised Capitalism: Crisis and Financial Expropriation'. *Historical Materialism* 17(2): 114–148.

Ledeneva, Alena V. (1998) *Russia's Economy of Favours: Blat, Networking, and Informal Exchange*. Cambridge: Cambridge University Press.

Lenin, Vladimir (1939) *Imperialism, the Highest Stage of Capitalism: A Popular Outline*. New, rev. translation. New York: International Publishers.

Letki, Natalia (2002) 'Lustration and Democratisation in East-Central Europe'. Europe-Asia Studies 54(4): 529–552.

Levitsky, S. and L.A. Way (2002) 'Elections Without Democracy: The Rise of Competitive Authoritarianism'. *Journal of Democracy* 13(2): 51–66.

Levitsky, S. and L.A. Way (2010) *Competitive Authoritarianism: Hybrid Regimes after the Cold War*. Cambridge: Cambridge University Press.

Levy, G. (2016) 'Slave Labour in Lugansk: What War in Ukraine has "Achieved"'. People and Nature, at: https://peopleandnature.wordpress.com/2016/10/04/slave-labour-in-lugansk-what-war-in-ukraine-has-achieved/. Accessed 23 January 2017.

Łos, M. (1992) 'From Underground to Legitimacy: The Normative Dilemmas of Post-Communist Marketization', in Bruno Dallago, Gianmaria Ajani and Bruno Grancelli (eds), *Privatization and Entrepreneurship in Post-Socialist Countries: Economy, Law, and Society*. New York: St. Martin's Press.

Lucas, E. (2014) *The New Cold War: Putin's Threat to Russia and the West*. New York: St. Martin's Press.

Luxemburg, Rosa (2004) *The Accumulation of Capital*. London: Routledge.

Lyakh, A. (2007) 'The Evolution of the Industrial Structure in Donetsk Region', in Adam Swain (ed.), *Re-Constructing the Post-Soviet Industrial Region: The Donbas in Transition*. London: Routledge, 78–96.

Maksymiuk, Jan (2001) 'Forum for National Salvation is Established'. The Ukrainian Weekly, 18 February, at: www.ukrweekly.com/old/archive/2001/070108.shtml.

Marcus, Jonathan (2002) 'What Ukraine's Kolchuga Radar Does'. BBC World News, 14 October, at: http://news.bbc.co.uk/1/hi/world/europe/2326451.stm.

Marks and Sokolov Attorneys at Law (2009) 'Marks, Sokolov & Burd Offer Insight Into The Pavlo Lazarenko Trial'. 20 December, at: www.marks-sokolov.com/news_017.htm.

Marx, K. (1964 [1848]) The Communist Manifesto: Principles of Communism. New York: Monthly Review Press.

Marx, K. (1981) Capital: A Critique of Political Economy. Vol. I. London: Penguin Books in association with New Left Review.

Marx, K. (1993) Grundrisse: Foundations of the Critique of Political Economy. London: Penguin Books in association with New Left Review.

Marx, K. and F. Engels (1970) The German Ideology. Edited by C.J. Arthur. London: Lawrence and Wishart.

Mason, D.S. (1996) Revolution and Transition in East-Central Europe. Boulder, CO: Westview Press.

Matuszak, Slavomir (2012) 'The Oligarchic Democracy: The Influence of Business Groups on Ukrainian Politics'. OSW: Centre for Easter Studies 42.

Melkozerova, V. and O. Goncharova (2017) 'Poroshenko Convinces EU No Anti-Corruption Court Needed'. Kyiv Post, 14 July, at: www.kyivpost.com/ukraine-politics/poroshenko-convinces-eu-no-anti-corruption-court-needed.html. Accessed 15 July 2017.

Menon, R. and E.B. Rumer (2015) Conflict in Ukraine: The Unwinding of the Post-Cold War Order. Boston, MA: MIT Press.

Mezentves, K., G. Pidhrushnyi and N. Mesentveva (2015) 'Challenges of the Post-Soviet Development of Ukraine: Economic Transformations, Demographic Changes and Socio-Spatial Polarization', in T. Lang, S. Henn, K. Ehrlich and W. Sgibnev (eds), Understanding Geographies of Polarization and Peripheralization Perspectives from Central and Eastern Europe and Beyond. London: Palgrave Macmillan.

Miller, D. (2010) 'How Neoliberalism Got Where It Is: Elite Planning, Corporate Lobbying and the Release of the Free Market', in K. Birch and V. Mykhnenko (eds), The Rise and Fall of Neoliberalism: The Collapse of an Economic Order?. London: Zed Books, 24–41.

Milor, V. (1994) Changing Political Economies: Privatization in Post-Communist and Reforming Communist States. Boulder, CO: Lynne Rienner Publishers.

Minfin (2016) 'State Debt', at: www.minfin.gov.ua/news/borg/derzhavnij-borg. Accessed 25 February 2017.

Minfin (2017) 'Statistical Materials on state and state guaranteed debt of Ukraine', 2 February, at: www.minfin.gov.ua/news/view/statystychni-materialy-shchodo-derzhavnoho-ta-harantovanoho-derzhavoiu-borhu-ukrainy_2016?category=borg&subcategory=statistichna-informacija-schodo-borgu. Accessed 28 February 2017.

Ministry of Interior. State Penitentiary Service. At: www.kvs.gov.ua/punish/control/uk/index.

Molchanov, M.A. (2002) Political Culture and National Identity in Russian-Ukrainian Relations. College Station, TX: Texas A&M University Press.

Molchanov, M.A. (2015) 'Russia as Ukraine's "Other": Identity and Geopolitics', in A. Pikulicka-Wilczewska and R. Sakwa (eds), Ukraine and Russia: People, Politics, Propaganda and Perspectives. Bristol: E-International Relations Publishing.

Montgomerie, J. (2010) 'Neoliberalism and the Making of Subprime Borrowers', in M. Koning (ed.), The Great Credit Crash. London: Verso, 103–119.

Moore, P.V. (2018) The Quantified Self in Precarity: Work, Technology and What Counts. Abingdon: Routledge.

Moore, P. and A. Robinson (2016) 'The Quantified Self: What Counts in the Neoliberal Workplace'. *New Media & Society* 18(11): 2774–2792.

Morris, J. (1982) 'The Revenge of the Rentier or the Interest Rate Crisis in the United States'. *Monthly Review* 33(8): 28–34.

Motyl, Alexander, J. (2013) 'Ukraine's Orange Blues'. Weblog post at Foreign Affairs, 1 February, at: www.worldaffairsjournal.org/blog/alexander-j-motyl/ukraine's-'new-elite'. Accessed 15 February 2013.

Movchan, V. (2016) 'First year of EU-Ukraine FTA: key results'. *112 UA*, 29 December, at: http://112.international/opinion/first-year-of-eu-ukraine-fta-key-results-12585.html.

Munter, P. (2005) 'Ukraine to Unveil Target Companies: Privatisation Reversals'. *The Financial Times*, 16 March.

Myagkov, M., P.C. Ordeshook and D. Shakin (2009) *The Forensics of Election Fraud: Russia and Ukraine*. Cambridge: Cambridge University Press.

Mykhnenko, V. (2003) 'State, Society and Protest Under Post-Communism: Ukrainian Miners and their Defeat', in C. Mudde and P. Kopecký (eds), *Uncivil Society?: Contentious Politics in Eastern Europe*. London: Routledge, 93–113.

Mykhnenko, Vlad (2005a) Strengths and Weaknesses of 'Weak' Co-ordination Economic Institutions, Revealed Comparative Advantages, and Socio-Economic Performance of Mixed Market Economies in Poland and Ukraine. Glasgow: Centre for Public Policy for Regions, University of Glasgow.

Mykhnenko, V. (2005b) 'What Type of Capitalism in Eastern Europe? Institutional Structures, Revealed Comparative Advantages, and Performance of Poland and Ukraine'. Glasgow: Centre for Public Policy for Regions, University of Glasgow.

Mykhnenko, V. (2010) 'Ukraine's Diverging Space-Economy: The Orange Revolution, Post-Soviet Development Models and Regional Trajectories'. *European Urban and Regional Studies* 17(2): 141–165.

National Bank of Ukraine (NBU) (2007) 'Chronology of Issue of Hryvnia Banknotes'. National Bank of Ukraine. www.bank.gov.ua/Engl/Bank_coin/Banknoty/banknoty.htm.

National Bank of Ukraine (NBU) (2009) Annual Report.

Nesvetailova, A. (2004) 'Form "Transition" to Development: The New Periphery in Global Financial Capitalism', in N. Robinson (ed.), *Reforging the Weakest Link. Global Political Economy and Post-Soviet Change in Russia, Ukraine and Belarus*, Aldershot: Ashgate.

Nesvetailova, A. (2010) *Financial Alchemy in Crisis: The Great Liquidity Illusion*. London: Pluto Press.

Nesvetailova, A. and R. Palan (2010) 'A Very North Atlantic Credit Crunch: Geopolitical Implications of the Global Liquidity Crisis', in M. Konings (ed.), *The Great Credit Crash*. London: Verso. 198–222.

Norwegian Centre for Human Rights (2009) 'Contestants in the Parliamentary Elections 2002'. Norwegian Centre for Human Rights, 23 October, at: www.jus.uio.no/smr/english/about/programmes/nordem/publications/nordem-report/2002/06/nordem_report-Contesta.html.

Nuti, D.M. (1989) 'The New Soviet Cooperatives: Advances and Limitations'. *Economic and Industrial Democracy* 10(3): 311–327.

Nuti, D.M. (1992) 'The Role of New Cooperatives in the Soviet Economy', in B. Dallago, G. Ajaniand B. Grancelli (eds), *Privatization and Entrepreneurship in Post-*

Socialist Countries: Economy, Law and Society. New York: St. Martin's Press, 251–253.

OECD (2011) Development in Eastern Europe and the South Caucasus: Armenia, Azerbaijan, Georgia, Republic of Moldova and Ukraine, OECD Publishing, at: http://dx.doi.org/10.1787/9789264113039-en.

Olearchyk, Roman (2000) 'Ukraine Without Kuchma Leader Yury Lutsenko'. *Kyiv Post*, 21 December.

Olearchyk, Roman (2011) 'Ex-Leader Focus of Ukraine Scandal'. *The Financial Times*, 1 April.

Olearchyk, Roman and Wagstyl, Stefan (2010) 'Ukraine Election Divides Oligarchs'. *The Financial Times*, 15 January.

Onaran, O. (2009) 'From the Crisis of Distribution to the Distribution of the Costs of the Crisis: What Can We Learn from Previous Crises about the Effects of the Financial Crisis on Labor Share?'. PERI Massachusetts Working Paper, at: http://scholarworks.umass.edu/cgi/viewcontent.cgi?article=1164&context=peri_workingpapers. Accessed 20 February 2017.

Onuch, O. (2014) 'Social Networks and Social Media in Ukrainian "Euromaidan" Protests'. *The Washington Post*, 2 January, at: www.washingtonpost.com/blogs/monkey-cage/wp/2014/01/02/social-networks-and-social-media-in-ukrainian-euromaidan-protests-2/.

Oosterbaan, G. (1997) 'Clan Based Politics in Ukraine and Implications for Democratisation', in J.S. Micgiel (ed.), *Perspectives on Political and Economic Transitions after Communism.* New York: Columbia University Press.

Overbeek, Henk (1980) 'Finance Capital and the Crisis in Britain'. *Capital and Class* 4(2): 99–120.

Overbeek, Henk (2002) 'Transnational Historical Materialism: Theories of Transnational Class Formation and World Order', in Mark Rupert (ed.), *Historical Materialism and Globalization.* London: Routledge, 168–183.

Overbeek, Henk (2004) 'Transnational Class Formation and Concepts of Control: Towards a Genealogy of the Amsterdam Project in International Political Economy'. *Journal of International Relations and Development* 7(2): 113–141.

Overbeek, Henk (2007) *The Transnational Politics of Corporate Governance Regulation.* London: Routledge.

Overbeek, Henk and Kees van Der Pijl (1993) 'Restructuring Capital and Restructuring Hegemony: Neo-liberalism and the Unmaking of the Post-War Order', in Henk Overbeek (ed.), *Restructuring Hegemony in the Global Political Economy: The Rise of Transnational Neo-Liberalism in the 1980s.* London: Routledge, 1–28.

Palan, Ronen (2003) *The Offshore World: Sovereign Markets, Virtual Places, and Nomad Millionaires.* Ithaca, NY: Cornell University Press.

Peet, R. (2007) *Geography of Power: the Making of Global Economic Policy.* London: Zed Books.

Perotti, E.C. (1994) A Taxonomy of Post-Socialist Financial Systems: Decentralized Enforcement and the Creation of Inside Money'. *Economic of Transition* 2(1): 71–81.

Picchota, G. and R. Rayzcyk (2015) 'The Role of Social Media During Protests on Maidan'. *Communication Today* 6(2): 86–97.

Pilger, John (2014) 'Nato's Action Plan in Ukraine is Right out of Dr Strangelove'. *The Guardian*, 17 April, at: www.theguardian.com/commentisfree/2014/apr/17/nato-ukraine-dr-strangelove-china-us.

Pilger, John (2015) 'Why the Rise of Fascism is Again the Issue'. *JohnPilger.com*, 26 February, at: http://johnpilger.com/articles/why-the-rise-of-fascism-is-again-the-issue.

Pickles, John and Adrian Smith (eds) (1998) *Theorising Transition: The Political Economy of Post-Communist Transformations*. London: Routledge.

Pivovarsky, Alexander (2003) 'Ownership Concentration and Performance in Ukraine's Privatized Enterprises'. *IMF Staff Papers* 50(1).

Plokhy, S.M. (1995) 'The History of a "Non-Historical" Nation: Notes on the Nature and Current Problems of Ukrainian Historiography'. *Slavic Review* 54(3) (Autumn): 709–716.

Plokhy, S. (2014) *The Last Empire: The Last Days of the Soviet Union*. New York: Basic Books.

Plokhy, S. (2015) *The Gates of Europe*. London: Penguin.

Pohlyad (2014) *Не отримавши необхідних імпульсів, Євромайдан очікує розкол, – Карасьов* [*Without Necessary Impulses Euromaidan Will Split – Karasiov*]. 11 January, at: www.pohlyad.com/news/n/34499.

Pond, E. (2002) *The Rebirth of Europe*. Washington, DC: Brookings Institution Press.

Popescu, N. (2010) *EU Foreign Policy and Post-Soviet Conflicts: Stealth Intervention*. New York: Routledge.

Poulantzas, N. (1975a) *Classes in Contemporary Capitalism*. London: New Left Books.

Poulantzas, N. (1975b) *Political Power and Social Classes*. London: New Left Books; Sheed and Ward.

Poulantzas, N. (1978) *State, Power, Socialism*. London: New Left Books.

Poulantzas, N. (2008) *The Poulantzas Reader: Marxism, Law, and the State*. London: Verso.

Poznanski, K. (1997) *Poland's Protracted Transition: Institutional Change and Economic Growth, 1970–1994*. Cambridge: Cambridge University Press.

Poznanski, K. (2001) 'Building Capitalism with the Communist Tools: Defective Transition in Eastern Europe'. *East European Politics and Societies* 15(2): 317–352.

Pradella, L. (2015) 'The Working Poor in Western Europe: Labour, Poverty and Global Capitalism'. *Comparative European Politics* 13(5): 596–613.

Przeworski, A. (1991) *Democracy and the Market: Political and Economic Reforms in Eastern Europe and Latin America*. Cambridge: Cambridge University Press.

Rachkevych, M. (2010) 'U.S. Official: Austrian Bank's Ties to RosUkrEnergo Suspicious'. *Kyiv Post*. 3 December.

Radice, H. (1995) 'The Role of Foreign Direct Investment in the Transformation of Eastern Europe', in H-J Chang and P. Nolan (eds), *The Transformation of the Communist Economies: Against the Mainstream*. New York: St. Martins Press.

Radio Svoboda (2005) 'Transcript: What Do Melnychenko's Tapes Say About Gongadze Case?', 3 March, at: www.rferl.org/content/article/1057789.html.

Randall, L. (2001) *Reluctant Capitalists: Russia's Journey through Market Transition*. New York: Routledge.

Raviv, O. (2008) 'Chasing the Dragon East: Exploring the Frontiers of Western European Finance'. *Contemporary Politics* 14(3): 297–314.

Reporters without Borders (2012) 'Setbacks to Media Freedom in Run-up to Elections', 22 July, at: http://en.rsf.org/ukraine-setbacks-to-media-freedom-in-run-23-07-2012,43079.html.

Roberts, A. and Soederberg, S. (2014) 'Politicizing Debt and Denaturalizing the "New Normal"'. *Critical Sociology* 40(5): 657–668.

Robinson, N. (ed.) (2004) *Reforging the Weakest Link. Global Political Economy and Post-Soviet Change in Russia, Ukraine and Belarus*. Aldershot: Ashgate.

Robinson, W.I. (2001) 'Social Theory and Globalization: The Rise of a Transnational State'. *Theory and Society* 30(2): 157–200.

Robinson, W.I. (2002) 'Global Capitalism and Nation-State Centric Thinking: What We Don't See When We Do See Nation-States. Response to Arrighi, Mann, Moore, van der Pijl, and Went'. *Science & Society* 65(4): 500–508.

Robinson, W.I. (2004) *Theory of Global Capitalism: Production, Class and State in a Transnational World*. Baltimore, MD: Johns Hopkins University Press.

Robinson, W.I (2005a) 'Global Capitalism: The New Transnationalism and the Folly of Conventional Thinking'. *Science & Society* 69(3): 316–328.

Robinson, W.I. (2005b) 'Gramsci and Globalisation: From Nation-State to Transnational Hegemony'. *Critical Review of International Social and Political Philosophy* 8(4): 559–574.

Robinson, W.I. (2006) 'Reification and Theoreticism in the Study of Globalisation, Imperialism and Hegemony: Response to Kiely, Pozo-Martin and Valladão'. *Cambridge Review of International Affairs* 19(3): 529–533.

Robinson, W.I. and J. Harris (2000) 'Toward a Global Ruling Class: Globalization and the Transnational Capitalist Class'. *Science & Society* 64(1): 11–54.

Roland, G. (1994) 'The Role of Political Constraints in Transition Strategies'. *Economic of Transition* 2(1): 27–41.

Ruggie, J.G. (2000) 'International Regimes, Transactions, and Change: Embedded Liberalism in the Postwar Economic Order'. *International Organisation* 36(2): 379–415.

Rugman, A. (2008) 'A New Perspective on the Regional and Global Strategies of Multinational Services Firms'. *MIR: Management International Review* 48(4): 397–411.

Rugman, A. and A. Verbeke (2004) 'Regional Transnationals and Triad Strategy'. *Transnational Corporations* 13(3): 1–20.

Rutland, P. (1993) *The Politics of Economic Stagnation in the Soviet Union: The Role of Local Party Organs in Economic Management*. Cambridge: Cambridge University Press.

Ryner, M. and A. Cafruny (2016) *The European Union and Global Capitalism: Origins, Development, Crisis*. London: Palgrave Macmillan.

Sachs, J. (1993) *Poland's Jump to the Market Economy*. Cambridge, MA: MIT Press.

Jeffrey Sachs, J. (1994) *Understanding 'Shock Therapy'*. London: Social Market Foundation.

Sakwa, R. (2015) *Frontline Ukraine: Crisis in the Borderlands*. I.B. Tauris: London.

Salamaniuk, T. (2013) 'Самоорганізація Майдану вражає. Та активісти більше зайняті облаштуванням місця протесту, ніж досягненням перемоги' ['Self-Organisation of Maidan is Impressive. However, Activists are Busier Improving their Protest Site Than Achieving Victory']. *Texty*, 16 December, at: http://texty. org.ua/pg/article/editorial/read/50461/Samoorganisacija_Majdanu_vrazhaje_Ta_ aktyvisty_bilshe_zajnati.

Sassen, S. (2007a) *Deciphering the Global: Its Scales, Spaces and Subjects*. New York: Routledge.

Sassen, S. (2007b) *Sociology of Globalization*, 1st edn. New York: W.W. Norton.

Sassen, S. (2014) *Expulsions: Brutality and Complexity in the Global Economy*. Cambridge, MA: Harvard University Press.

Savitsky, V. (1992) 'What Kind of Court and Procuracy?', in Donald Barry (ed.), *Toward the "Rule of Law" in Russia?: Political and Legal Reform in the Transition Period*. Armonk, NY: M.E. Sharpe.

Schneider, Friedrich G., Andreas Buehn and Claudio E. Montenegro (2010) 'Shadow Economies All over the World: New Estimates for 162 Countries from 1999 to 2007'. *Policy Research Working Paper* 532007, Washington, DC: World Bank.

ScienceDaily (2009) 'Dioxin Decomposition in The Yushchenko Case: Elimination Rate Faster Than Expected', 6 August, at: www.sciencedaily.com/releases/2009/08/090805075638.htm.

SCM (n.d.) System Capital Management, at: www.scm.com.ua/.

Shekhovtsov, A. 'Alexander Dugin and the West European New Right, 1989–1994' in … (2014–2015) 'The Ukrainian Far Right and the Ukrainian Revolution', in N.E.C. Black Sea Link Programme Yearbook, 215–237.

Shekhovtsov, A. (2015) 'Aleksandr Dugin's neo-Eurasianism and the Russian-Ukrainian war', in…

Shekhovtsov, A. (2016) 'The No Longer Silent Counter-Revolution'. *Illiberal Tendencies* 9(10): 9–10.

Shelley, Louise (1984) *Lawyers in Soviet Work Life*. New Brunswick, NJ: Rutgers University Press.

Shelley, Louise I. (1999) 'Transnational Organized Crime: The New Authoritarianism', in H.R. Friman and P. Andreas (eds), *The Illicit Global Economy and State Power*. New York: Rowman and Littlefield.

Shelley, Louise (2003) 'Russia and Ukraine: Transition or Tragedy?', in Roy Godson (ed.), *Menace to Society: Political–Criminal Collaboration around the World*. New Brunswick, NJ: Transaction Publishers.

Siegelbaum, L.H. (1997) 'Freedom of Prices and the Price of Freedom: The Miners' Dilemma in the Soviet Union and Its Successor States'. *Journal of Communist Studies* 13(4): 1–27.

Siegelbaum, L.H. and D.J. Walkowitz (eds) (1995) *Workers of the Donbass Speak: Survival and Identity in the New Ukraine, 1989–1992*. Albany, NY: State University of New York Press.

Sklair, L. (2000) 'The Transnational Capitalist Class and the Discourse of Globalisation'. *Cambridge Review of International Affairs* 14(1): 67–85.

Sklair, L. (2001) *The Transnational Capitalist Class*. Oxford: Wiley-Blackwell.

Sklair, L. (2002a) *Globalization: Capitalism and its Alternatives*. Oxford: Oxford University Press.

Sklair, L. (2002b) 'The Transnational Capitalist Class and Global Politics: Deconstructing the Corporate-State Connection'. *International Political Science Review* 23(2): 159–174.

Slavyanks City Council (n.d.) 'Slavyansk Town Council Portal', at: www.slavrada.gov.ua/.

Smallbone, David, Friederike Welter, Nina Isakova and Anton Slonimski (2001) 'The Contribution of Small and Medium Enterprises to Economic Development in Ukraine and Belarus: Some Policy Perspectives'. *Most: Economic Policy in Transition Economies* 11(3): 253–273.

Smith, Adrian and Adam Swain (1998) 'Regulating and Institutionalising Capitalisms: The Microfoundations of Transformation in Eastern and Central Europe', in John Pickles (ed.), *Theorising Transition: The Political Economy of Post-Communist Transformations*. London: Routledge, 25–53.

Smith, G. and A. Wilson (1997) 'Rethinking Russia's Post-Soviet Diaspora: The Potential for Political Mobilisation in Eastern Ukraine and North-East Estonia'. *Europe-Asia Studies* 49(5): 854–864.

Solomon, D.P. (2006) 'A Tsar is Born: The Consolidation of Power in Putin's Russia'. The Centre for Security Policy, August.

Solomon, P. (2011) 'Yanukovych's Judicial Reform: Power and Justice'. *Ukraine Watch*, 2 March, at: https://ukrainewatch.wordpress.com/2011/03/02/yanukovychs-judicial-reform-power-policy/.

Solomon, P.H. and T.S. Foglesong (2000) 'The Two Faces of Crime in Post-Soviet Ukraine'. *East European Constitutional Review* (Summer): 70:75.

Soos, Karoly Attila (2010) *Politics and Policies in Post-Communist Transition Primary and Secondary Privatisation in Central Europe and the Former Soviet Union.* New York: Central European University Press.

The State Property Fund of Ukraine. At: www.spfu.gov.ua/ukr/.

Suslov, M. (2014). '"Crimea Is Ours!": Russian Popular Geopolitics in the New Media Age'. *Eurasian Geography and Economics* 55(6): 588–609.

Suslov, M. (2017) 'The Production of "Novorossiya": A Territorial Brand in Public Debates'. *Europe-Asia Studies* 69(2): 202–221.

Swain, Adam (2004) 'Yanukovich Hits the Campaign Trail Early Ukraine Election'. *The Financial Times*, 10 December.

Swain, Adam (2006) 'Disputed Links to an Alleged Crime Boss'. *The Financial Times*, 14 July.

Swain, Adam (ed.) (2007) *Re-Constructing the Post-Soviet Industrial Region: The Donbas in Transition.* London: Routledge.

Swain, Adam and Vlad Mykhnenko (2007) 'The Ukrainian Donbas in "Transition"', in Adam Swain (ed.), *Re-Constructing the Post-Soviet Industrial Region: The Donbas in Transition.* London: Routledge, 7–46.

Swain, A., V. Mykhnenko and S. French (2010) 'The Corruption Industry and Transition: Neoliberalising Post-Soviet Space?', in K. Birch and V. Mykhnenko (eds), *The Rise and Fall of Neoliberalism: The Collapse of an Economic Order?.* London: Zed Books.

Terazi, E. and S. Senel (2011) 'The Effects of the Global Financial Crisis on the Central and Eastern European Union Countries'. *International Journal of Business and Social Science* 2(17): 186–192.

The Trade Union Federation of Ukraine (2012) 'Протягом останнього року рівень абсолютної бідності в Україні скоротився на 3,3%'. Report based on data from the UN Development Programme and Ptukha Institute for Demographic and Social Research, 3 August.

Transparency International (2011) 'Annual Report 2000', at: www.transparency.org/news_room/in_focus/2011/ukraine_nis_2011.

Transparency International (2014) 'A Year after Maidan, Ukraine is Still the Most Corrupt Country in Europe'. Press release, 3 December, at: www.transparency.org/news/pressrelease/a_year_after_maidan_ukraine_is_still_the_most_corrupt_country_in_europe.

Tymoshenko, Yulia (n.d.) 'About Yulia Tymoshenko' Official site. www.tymoshenko.ua.

Ukrainian Radio (2006) 'Ukrainian Parliament Amended List of State Assets not Subject to Privatization to Include Nikopol Ferro-Alloy Plant', 10 February, at: www.nrcu.gov.ua/index.php?id=148&listid=24845.

Ukrrudprom (2007) 'Геннадий Васильев, Ринат Ахметов и другие: Вячеслав Синенко сдал донецкую мафию', 13 February, at: www.ukrrudprom.com/news/nghdsfjjj130207.html.

Umansky, Serhiy (2005) "The Price for the Nikopol Ferroalloy Plant'. *Zerkalo Nedeli*, 16 July.

UN (2016) 'Conflict in Ukraine Continues to Take Civilian Toll – UN human Rights Report', 8 December, at: www.un.org/apps/news/story.asp?NewsID=55750#.WYICm1FGnIU.

Uvalic, Milica and Daniel Vaughan-Whitehead (eds) (1997) *Privatization Surprises in Transition Economies Employee-Ownership in Central and Eastern Europe*. Cheltenham: Edward Elgar.

Van Apeldoorn, B. (2000) 'Transnational Class Agency and European Governance: The Case of the European Round Table of Industrialists'. *New Political Economy* 5(2): 157–181.

Van Apeldoorn, B. (2003) *Transnational Capitalism and the Struggle over European Integration*. London: Routledge.

Van der Hoeven, M. (2012) 'Energy Policies Beyond IEA Countries: Ukraine 2012, Review'. OECD Report.

Van Der Pijl, K. (1984a) *Atlanticism & the European Ruling Class*. Pub By Ve.

Van Der Pijl, K. (1984b) *The Making of an Atlantic Ruling Class*. London: Verso.

Van Der Pijl, K. (1993) 'Soviet Socialism and Passive Revolution', in Stephen Gill (ed.), *Gramsci, Historical Materialism and International Relations*. Cambridge: Cambridge University Press, 237–258.

Van Der Pijl, K. (1998) *Transnational Classes and International Relations*. London: Routledge.

Van der Pijl, K. (2001) 'International Relations and Capitalist Discipline', in Robert Albritton (ed.), *Phases of Capitalist Development: Booms, Crises, and Globalizations*. Houndmills: Palgrave.

Van der Pijl, K. (2004) 'Two Faces of the Transnational Cadre Under Neo-Liberalism'. *Journal of International Relations and Development*, suppl. Special Issue: *Transnational Historical Materialism* 7(2): 177–207.

Van der Pijl, K. (2006) *Global Rivalries: From the Cold War to Iraq*. London: Pluto Press.

Van der Pijl, K. (2009) 'A Survey of Global Political Economy', at: www.sussex.ac.uk/ir/research/gpe/gpesurvey.

Van der Pijl, K. (2010a) 'Historicising the International: Modes of Foreign Relations and Political Economy'. *Historical Materialism* 18(2): 3–34.

Van der Pijl, K. (2010b) 'The Resurgence of German Capital in Europe: EU Integration and the Restructuring of Atlantic Networks of Interlocking Directorates after 1991'. *Review of International Political Economy* 1(25).

Van der Pijl, K. (2011) *The Making of Atlantic Ruling Class*. London: Pluto Press.

van der Pijl, K., O. Holman and O. Raviv (2011) 'The Resurgence of German Capital in Europe: EU Integration and the Restructuring of Atlantic Networks of Interlocking Directorates after 1991', *Review of International Political Economy* 18(3): 384–408.

van der Pijl, K. and Y. Yurchenko (2015) 'Neoliberal Entrenchment of North Atlantic Capital: From Corporate Self-Regulation to State Capture'. *New Political Economy* 20(4): 495–517.

van Niekerk, P. and A. Verlöy (2002) *Kuchma Approved Sale of Weapons System to Iraq*. Washington, DC: Public Integrity project, 15 April, at: http://projects. publicintegrity.org/report.aspx?aid=209.

Van Selm, B. (1997) *The Economics of Soviet Break-Up*. London: Routledge.

van Zon, H. (1998) *Social and Economic Change in Eastern Ukraine: The Example of Zaporizhzhia*. Aldershot: Ashgate.

van Zon, H. (2007) 'The Rise of Conglomerates in Ukraine: The Donetsk Case', in A. Fernández Jilberto (ed.), *Big Business and Economic Development Conglomerates and Economic Groups in Developing Countries and Transition Economies under Globalisation*. London: Routledge, 378–397.

Varfolomeev, O. (1998) 'Ukraine: Regional Clans Attempts the Transition to Party Politics'. *Prism* 4(5), 6 March, at: www.jamestown.org/single/?no_cache=1&tx_ ttnews%5Btt_news%5D=27804&tx_ttnews%5BbackPid%5D=220>.

Vasovic, A. and M. Tsetvetkova (2014) 'This Elusive Muscovite with 3 Names Has Taken Control Of Ukraine Rebels', 15 May, at: www.businessinsider. com/r-elusive-muscovite-with-three-names-takes-control-of-ukraine-rebels-2014- 15?IR=T.

Vaughan-Whitehead, Daniel (1998) *Paying the Price: The Wage Crisis in Central and Eastern Europe*. New York: St. Martin's Press.

Veblen, Thorstein (1934) *The Theory of the Leisure Class: An Economic Study of Institutions*. New York: Modern library.

Velychenko, S. (2000) 'Rival Grand Narratives of National History: Russian, Polish and Ukrainian Interpretations of Ukraine's Past'. *Oesterreichische Osthefte* 3–4: 139–160, 140.

Velychenko, S. (ed.) (2007) *Ukraine, The EU and Russia: History, Culture and International Relations*. Basingstoke Palgrave Macmillan.

Verkhovna Rada of Ukraine (1996) 'The Constitution of Ukraine. Chapter 5'. *Verkhovna Rada Ukrayiny*, at :http://gska2.rada.gov.ua/site/const_eng/ constitution_eng.htm#c5.

Verkhovna Rada of Ukraine (2015) Law #2558 'On Condemnation of Communist and National-Socialist (Nazi) Totalitarian Regimes in Ukraine and Ban of their Propaganda and Symbols'. 9 April, full text, at: http://w1.c1.rada.gov.ua/pls/zweb2/ webproc4_1?pf3511=54670.

Vlasiuk, A. (2011) 'The World Financial Crisis and Principles of Anticrisis Regulation in Ukraine'. *Problems of Economic Transition* 53(2): 35–59.

Volodarsky, Boris (2010) *The KGB's Poison Factory: From Lenin to Litvinenko*. Minneapolis, MN: Zenith Press.

VPG. 'Monitoring Overview of Violations of Human Rights in Penitentiary Facilities in the Particular Districts of Donetsk and Luhansk oblasts (PDDLo).

Wagstyl, S. and T. Warner (2004) 'Ukraine has been Transformed by the Political Turmoil of Recent Months'. *The Financial Times*, 21 December.

Warner, Tom (2006) 'RosUkrEnergo Hits at Critics by Naming Owners'. *The Financial Times*, 27 April, at: www.ft.com/cms/s/0/bc326650-d58a-11da-93bc-000077 9e2340.html#axzz1YlE6Hpkx.

Weber, Max (1930) *Protestant Ethic and the Spirit of Capitalism*. London: Unwin Hyman. At: www.marxists.org/reference/archive/weber/protestant-ethic/index. htm.

Went, Robert (2002) 'Globalization in the Perspective of Imperialism'. *Science & Society* 66(4): 473–497.

Williams, Colin (2008) 'The Illusion of Capitalism in Post-Soviet Ukraine'. *Debatte* 16(3): 331–345.

Williams, C.C. and J. Round (2008) 'The Illusion of Capitalism in Post-Soviet Ukraine'. *Debatte* 16(3).

Wilson, A. (1997) *Ukrainian Nationalism in the 1990s: A Minority Faith*. Cambridge: Cambridge University Press.

Wilson, A. (2002a) 'Elements of a Theory of Ukrainian Ethno-National Identities'. *Nations and Nationalism* 8(1): 31–54.

Wilson, A. (2002b) *The Ukrainians: Unexpected Nation*. New Haven, CT: Yale Nota Bene.

Wilson, A. (2005a) *Ukraine's Orange Revolution*. New Haven, CT: Yale University Press.

Wilson, A. (2005b) *Virtual Politics: Faking Democracy in the Post-Soviet World*, 1st edn. New Haven, CT: Yale University Press.

Wilson, Andrew (2010) *Dealing with Yanukovych's Ukraine*. London: European Council on Foreign Relations (ECFR).

Wilson, A. (2014) *Ukraine Crisis: What the West Needs to Know*. London: Yale University Press.

Wolchik, S.L. and J.L. Curry (2011) *Central and East European Politics: From Communism to Democracy*. Lanham, MD: Rowman & Littlefield.

Wood, Ellen (1999) *The Origin of Capitalism*. New York: Monthly Review Press.

Wood, Ellen (2002) 'Global Capital, National States', in Mark Rupert and Hazel Smith (eds), *Historical Materialism and Globalization*. London: Routledge.

World Bank Group (2010) BEEPS At-A-Glance 2008: Ukraine.

Woronowycz, Roman (2001) 'American Detective Agency Says Kuchma not Involved in Gongadze's Disappearance'. *The Ukrainian Weekly*, 30 September, at: www.ukrweekly.com/old/archive/2001/390112.shtml.

Yalta European Strategy. 'YES at a Glance'. *Yalta European Strategy*. At: http://yes-ukraine.org/en/about/yes-history.

YES. 'Yalta Economic Strategy'. *YES*. At: http://yes-ukraine.org/en/about.

Yevtyh, V. (2004) Ethno-Social Processes in Ukraine: Opportunities for Scientific Interpretations, Publishing House 'Stylos': Kyiv (my translation).

Yevtyh, V. 'Yulia Tymoshenko Bloc. Batkivshchyna'. *BYuT*. At: http://byut.com.ua/.

Yurchenko, Y. (2008) 'The Role and Locus of Mass Media in the Orange Revolution in Ukraine', Conference paper. Newcastle University EU Postgraduate Conference.

Yurchenko, Y. (2013) 'Black Holes in the Political Economy of Ukraine: The Neoliberalisation of Europe's "Wild East"'. *Debatte* April.

Yushchenko, Viktor (2005) 'Inaugural Address of the President of Ukraine Victor Yushchenko to the Ukrainian People on Independence Square'. 24 January. At: www.kmu.gov.ua/control/publish/article?art_id=11100895.

Zaslavskaya, Tatyana (1990) *The Second Socialist Revolution: An Alternative Soviet Strategy*. London: I.B. Tauris.

Zaslavskaya, Tatyana (1992) 'A Voice of Reform'. *Studies in Comparative Communism* 25(1): 79.

Zelinksa, O. (2017) 'Ukrainian Euromaidan Protest: Dynamics, Causes, and Aftermath Authors'. *Sociology Compass* 11(9).

Zhukov, Y.M. (2016) 'Trading Hard Hats for Combat Helmets: The Economics of Rebellion in Eastern Ukraine'. *Journal of Comparative Economics* 44(1): 1–15.

Zhurzhenko, T. (2014) *Borderlands into Bordered Lands: Geopolitics of Identity in Post-Soviet Ukraine*. Stuttgart: Ibidem.

ZIK (Zakhidna Information Corporation) (2011) 'NCRTVB Decries Violations by 5 Kanal'. *ZIK Information Agency*, 25 January. At: http://zik.ua/en/news/2011/01/25/268669.

Zimmer, K. (2007) 'Trapped in Past Glory: Self-Identification and Self-Symbolisation in the Donbass', in Adam Swain (ed.), *Re-Constructing the Post-Soviet Industrial Region: The Donbas in Transition*. Abingdon: Routledge.

Zimmer, K. and C. Sabić (2004) 'Ukraine: The Genesis of a Captured State', in Melanie Tatur (ed.), *The Making of Regions in Post-Socialist Europe: The Impact of Culture, Economic Structure and Institutions: Case Studies from Poland, Hungary, Romania and Ukraine*, 1st edn. Wiesbaden: VS Verlag für Sozialwissenschaften.

Zimmermann, H. and A. Dür (eds) (2016) *Key Controversies in European Integration*. Palgrave Macmillan: London.

SOURCES IN UKRAINIAN AND RUSSIAN

[Aryev, Vladimir] Арьев, Владимир (2007) Донецкая мафия: Перезагрузка. Documentary/journalistic investigation. At: http://video.i.ua/user/2689167/30891/164471/.

[Bleak, Lyudmila] Блик, Людмила (2010) 'Юлія Тимошенко оголошує війну олігархам при владі'. Укрінформ.

[Boyko, Alexander] Бойко, Александр (2007) Криминальная оккупация: История Партии Регионов [*Criminal Occupation: History of the Party of Regions*]. Documentary/journalistic investigation. At: http://video.i.ua/user/613823/8535/252016/.

[Bondarenko, Konstanin] Бондаренко, Константин (2009) Леонид Кучма. Харьков: Фолио.

[Verkhovna Rada of Ukraine] Верховна Рада України (1999) 'Про спеціальні економічні зони та спеціальний режим інвестиційної діяльності в Донецькій області: N356-XIV'. Відомості Верховної Ради України, at: http://zakon.rada.gov.ua/cgi-bin/laws/main.cgi?nreg=356-14.

[Verkhovna Rada of Ukraine] Верховна Рада України (2004) 'Про внесення змін до Конституції України'. Верховна Рада. At: http://zakon1.rada.gov.ua/cgi-bin/laws/main.cgi?nreg=2222%2D15.

[Verkhovna Rada of Ukraine] Верховна Рада України (2005) 'Закон України. Про внесення змін до Закону України "Про Державний бюджет України на 2005 рік" та деяких інших законодавчих актів України N2505-IV'. *Verkhovna Rada Ukrayiny*, 25 June, at: http://zakon.rada.gov.ua/cgi-bin/laws/main.cgi?nreg=2505-15.

[Verkhovna Rada of Ukraine] Верховна Рада України (2011) 'Закон України № 3319-VI. Про деякі питання заборгованості за спожитий природний газ та електричну енергію'. Верховна Рада. At: http://zakon.rada.gov.ua/cgi-bin/laws/main.cgi?nreg=3319-17.

[Yvgen Dobogriz] Добогриз, Євген (2005) 'Скарби нації'. Галицькі контракти. At: http://archive.kontrakty.ua/gc/2005/3/31-sokrovishha-nacii.html.

[Kiselev, Sergey] Киселев, Сергей (2006) '30½ тижнів'. Українська правда. At: www.pravda.com.ua/rus/articles/2006/02/6/4396601/.

[Kolomiets, Victor] Коломиец, Виктор (2010) 'Мельниченко передаст в Генпрокуратуру записи о гибели Вячеслава Чорновила'. Газета 24, 18 December. At: http://gazeta.24.ua/news/show/id/23582.htm.

[Kravchenko, M.B] Кравченко, М.В. (2011) 'Особливості державної політики щодо подолання бідності в Україні'. Демографія та соціальна економіка. National Academy of Sciences. Institute for Demographic and Social Research. 15(1): 135–140.

[Kudryachenko, Andrew] Кудряченко, Андрій (2006) Політична історія України XX століття. Київ: МАУП.

[Lanovyk, Boris] Лановик, Борис (2006) З. Матисякевич, and Роман Матейко. Економічна історія України і світу. Київ: Вікар.

[Laziba, Maxim] Лациба, Максим (2006) Становлення бізнес-асоціацій як суб'єктів публічної політики в регіонах України, 2004–2006. Український незалежний центр політичних досліджень. At: www.ucipr.kiev.ua/modules. php?op=modload&name=News&file=article&sid=5749&mode=thread& order=0&thold=0.

[Leshchenko, Sergii] Лещенко, Сергій (2009) 'Юлія Тимошенко зарила "сокиру війни" з Віктором Пінчуком'. Українська правда. At: www.pravda.com.ua/arti-cles/4b1aa85922e52/.

[Losev, Anton] Лосев, Антон (2010) 'Реанімація СЕЗ – перше випробування "донецьких" на монолітність …'. Information Agency. UNIAN, 26 March. At: http://economics.unian.net/ukr/detail/41490.

Makohon, Yuriy (2005) '"Нові форми організації територій з особливим податковим режимом (СЕЗ і ТПР)'. Аналітична записка." National Institute of Strategic Studies, at: www.niss.gov.ua/articles/271/.

[Melnichenko, Mykola] Мельниченко, Микола (2011) 'Пукач заявив, що Кравченко при ньому дзвонив Президенту Кучмі, доповідаючи про вбивство Гонгадзе'. Personal website. Микола Мельниченко, 1 September. At: http://melnychenko.com.ua/2011/09/01/pukach_zajaviv_shho_kravchenko_pri_nomu_dzvoniv_prezidentu_kuchm_dopovdajuchi_pro_vbivstvo_gongadze.html.

[Mendeleev, Dimitriy] Менделеев, Дмитрий (2011) 'Украина: «Именем «РосУкрЭнерго»…»'. Зеркало недели. At: http://zn.ua/articles/74825.

[Mishchenko, Masha] Міщенко, Маша (2010) 'Чи вправі конституційний суд зробити Януковича Кучмою?' Уніан Право, 6 September. At: http://rights.unian. net/ukr/detail/4823.

[Nemtsov, Boris and Vladimir Milov] Немцов, Борис and Владимир Милов (2008) Путин и Газпром. Москва.

NewsRu (2005) 'Тимошенко поручила срочно начать процесс повторной приватизации "Криворожстали"'. NewsRu.com, at: www.newsru.com/finance/ 06jun2005/steel.html.

[Paskhaver, O.Y., L.T. Verkhovodova and K.M. Aheyeva] Пасхавер, О.Й., Л.Т. Верховодова and К.М. Агеєва (2006) Приватизація та реприватизація в Україні після 'помаранчевої'v революції. Центр економічного розвитку; 'Міленіум'.

[Penchuk, Brois and Sergey Kuzin] Пенчук, Борис and Сергей Кузин (2006) Донецкая мафия. Фонд 'Антикоррупция'. At: http://dony07.narod.ru/dm. html#a2.

[Pekhnyk, Andriy] Пехник, Андрій (2007) Іноземні інвестиції в економіку України: навчальний посібник. Київ: Знання.

[Pynzenyk, B] Пинзеник, В. (2002) 'Оцінка тенденцій економічної динаміки у 2002 році'. Економічні есе: Інститут реформ 1, no. 12: 5–13.

[Pirozhuk, Marina] Пирожук, Марина (2010) 'Кому «послужить» Конституційний Суд – верховенству права чи Януковичу?' Radio website.

Radio Svoboda, 23 March. At: www.radiosvoboda.org/content/article/1991910.html.

[Pihovshek] Піховшек, В'ячеслав (1998) Корупція в Україні. Походження, джерела, сучасна ситуація. Київ: Агенство Україна.

[Popov, Dimitry and Ilya Milstein] Попов, Дмитрий and Илья Мильштейн (2006) Оранжевая принцесса: загадка Юлии Тимошенко. Издательство Ольги Морозовой.

[Ukraine is Young] Україна молода (2011) '2001: перший арешт Юлії Тимошенко'. Українська правда. At: www.istpravda.com.ua/videos/2011/08/8/50163/.

[Ukraine Pravda] Українська Правда (2003) 'Верховна Рада змінила голову ФДМ'. Українська правда. At: www.pravda.com.ua/news/2003/04/3/2993434/.

[Ukraine Pravda] Українська Правда (2004) 'Ответ вашингтонского пиарщика Януковича'. Українська правда, 16 November. At: www.pravda.com.ua/rus/articles/2004/11/16/4382871/.

[Ukraine Pravda] Українська Правда (2005) 'Тимошенко заработает еще 12 миллиардов на приватизации'. Українська правда. At: www.pravda.com.ua/rus/news/2005/08/30/4391409/.

[Ukraine Pravda] Українська Правда (2009) 'Янукович наобіцяв газ і спеціальні зони'. Українська правда, 29 September. At: www.pravda.com.ua/news/2009/09/29/4213269/.

[Ukraine Pravda] Українська Правда (2011) '9 березня 2001 року: спогади активіста'. Історична правда, 3 March. At: www.istpravda.com.ua/blogs/2011/03/9/30359/.

[Ukraine Pravda] Українська Правда (2011) ' Януковичу дозволили знищувати суди'. Українська правда, 23 June. At: www.pravda.com.ua/news/2011/06/23/6323766/.

[Foundation 'Democratic iniciaTIVi'] Фонд "Демократичні ініціативи". (2004) Фонд 'Демократичні ініціативи', 27 November. At: http://dif.org.ua/ua/archive.

[Chivokunya] Чивокуня, Віктор (2006) 'РосУкрЕнерго – матрьошки Фірташа-Фурсіна'. Українська правда, 2006. At: www.pravda.com.ua/articles/2006/04/27/3100046/.

ZIK (Zakhidna Information Corporation) (2005) 'Голова Яворівської райради Іван Карпа: Ющенко визнав помилкою закриття 24 вільних економічних зон: СЕЗ «Яворів» чекає на її негайне виправлення'. *ZIK* Lviv. Ukraine, 14 November. At: http://zik.ua/ua/news/2005/11/14/24477.

Index

Printed and bound by CPI Group (UK) Ltd, Croydon, CR0 4YY

21/01/2025

14629901-0002